Questions & Answers

Land Law

Questions & Answers

Land Law

EIGHTH EDITION

Margaret Wilkie

formerly Visiting Lecturer in Law, University of Sheffield

Peter Luxton

Solicitor
Professor of Law, Cardiff University

Rosalind Malcolm

Barrister
Professor of Law, University of Surrey

2011 and 2012

OXFORD
UNIVERSITY PRESS

OXFORD
UNIVERSITY PRESS

Great Clarendon Street, Oxford OX2 6DP

Oxford University Press is a department of the University of Oxford.
It furthers the University's objective of excellence in research, scholarship,
and education by publishing worldwide in

Oxford New York

Auckland Cape Town Dar es Salaam Hong Kong Karachi
Kuala Lumpur Madrid Melbourne Mexico City Nairobi
New Delhi Shanghai Taipei Toronto

With offices in

Argentina Austria Brazil Chile Czech Republic France Greece
Guatemala Hungary Italy Japan South Korea Poland Portugal
Singapore Switzerland Thailand Turkey Ukraine Vietnam

Oxford is a registered trade mark of Oxford University Press
in the UK and in certain other countries

Published in the United States
by Oxford University Press Inc., New York

Fifth edition 2005
Sixth edition 2007
Seventh edition 2009

British Library Cataloguing in Publication Data
Data available

Library of Congress Cataloging in Publication Data
Data available

Typeset by Laserwords Private Limited, Chennai, India
Printed in Great Britain
on acid-free paper by
Ashford Colour Press Limited, Gosport, Hampshire

ISBN 978-0-19-959990-5

1 3 5 7 9 10 8 6 4 2

Contents

The Q&A Series

Key features

The Q&A series provides full coverage of key subjects in a clear and logical way.

The book contains the following features:

- Questions
- Commentaries
- Bullet-pointed answer plans
- Diagrams
- Tables
- Suggested answers
- Further reading sections

online resource centre

www.oxfordtextbooks.co.uk/orc/qanda/

Every book in the Q&A series is accompanied by an Online Resource Centre, hosted at the URL above, which is open access and free to use.

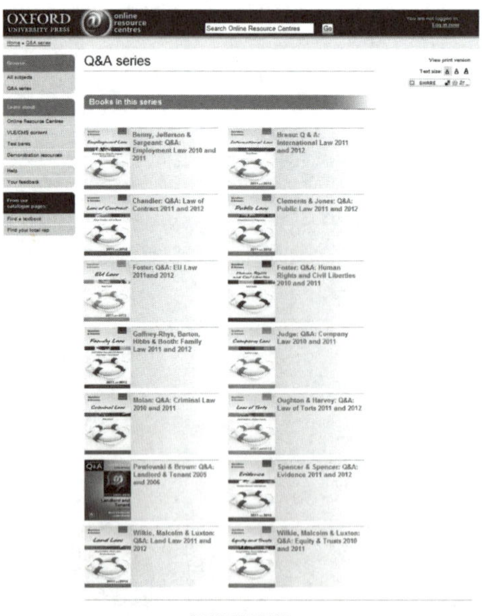

The Online Resource Centre for this book contains revision and exam advice, a glossary of land law terms, and links to websites useful for the study of land law.

Preface

Examination technique is an important skill for the law student to learn. After months of hard work studying the law, to be let down in the examination, not by lack of knowledge or understanding of the law, but by technique in answering the questions set, is indeed a sad thing. It is not, however, at all uncommon. As tutors and examiners, we have seen many students fail to achieve their potential in examinations because they have not mastered the method of answering questions.

Law students necessarily spend much of their time reading cases in the reports, articles in law journals, and textbooks; but the style in which these are written is rarely the same style that is needed for an answer to an examination question. Much valuable guidance on examination technique, of course, will be given to the student in the form of tutorial discussion, and comments on essays written during the course. In our experience, however, only a minority of law teachers meet the issue head-on by providing students with suggested answers designed to show the student how a question might be tackled.

In our view, one of the best ways of learning is by example, and it is examples that this book provides. It is to be treated as a learning tool or aid. The answers are 'suggested' rather than 'model', to indicate that they are not the only way in which a question can be answered. Together, they are designed to help the student see how questions in general, rather than any particular question, can be tackled. We would advise readers that the rote learning of model answers will prove quite unprofitable.

The student can use the book in several ways. First, as another means of learning the law itself, through seeing the law applied to specific questions or problems. The relevant chapter could be studied in tutorial preparation. Many of the commentaries provide additional comments to help with this. Secondly, through the study of the answers to the questions, the student can learn how answers (whether to an examination question or a piece of assessed work) should be structured. In this regard, it can be useful for one student, or for a small group, to look at a question on an area studied, and then attempt an outline structure of an answer before comparing it with that suggested in this book. Thirdly, the book can be used to help the student prepare for the examination itself; there are suggestions on a variety of matters, including e.g. time management and the use of diagrams. The feedback we have had from other lecturers suggests that they consider a book of this nature a good revision tool.

Since the last edition, there have been important legal developments in land law in both judicial decisions and in statute. Key decisions of the House of Lords (which were amongst the last before its appellate jurisdiction was removed from 1 October 2009) include *Thorner v Major* (2009), on estoppel, which clarifies and effectively restricts the potential impact of its earlier decision in *Yeoman's Row Management v Cobbe* (2008); and *Ofulue v Bossert* (2009), on adverse possession. Crucial decisions of the Supreme Court (established on 1 October 2009) are *Manchester City Council v Pinnock* (2010), on the impact of the European Convention on Human Rights on local authorities tenancies with limited security of tenure, and *Star Energy Weald Basin Ltd v Bocardo SA* (2010), on whether ownership of land includes ownership of what lies thousands of feet beneath the surface. Notable decisions of the Court of Appeal are: *Jones v Kernott* (2010), applying the decision of the House of Lords in *Stack v Dowden*, and *Link Lending Ltd v Bustard* (2010) on the meaning of 'actual occupation' in the Land Registration Act 2002. High Court decisions include *Thompson v Foy* (2009) on actual occupation; *Hapeshi v Allnatt* (2010) on common intention constructive trusts; *Close Invoice Finance Ltd v Abaowa* (2010) on the presumptions of advancement and resulting trust; *Horsham Properties Group v Clark* (2009), on the impact of the European Convention on Human Rights on the right of a purchaser from a mortgagee to obtain a possession order against the mortgagor; *Baxter v Mannion* (2010), on adverse possession and rectification of the register; and *Good Harvest Partnership LLP v Centaur Services Ltd* (2010), on the liability of guarantors under post-1995 leases. Also worthy of note is *Henry v Henry* (2010), where the Privy Council considered the doctrine of proprietary estoppel.

Since the last edition, there have been several developments in statute law. The Coroners and Justice Act 2009 makes some changes to the law relating to treasure. Section 199 of the Equality Act 2010 abolishes the presumption of advancement; but, at the time of going to press, this section had not yet been brought into force. The Mortgage Repossessions (Protection of Tenants) Act 2010, in force since 1 October 2010, does what its short title suggests. The Perpetuities and Accumulations Act 2009, which came into force on 6 April 2010, introduces a new and simplified regime for perpetuities and accumulations.

Finally, we thank everyone at Oxford University Press for their excellent work on the publishing side, and for the speed with which they have been able to produce the finished volume which you are now holding. We hope you enjoy reading it as much as we enjoyed writing it.

Margaret Wilkie
Rosalind Malcolm
Peter Luxton
November 2010

Table of Cases

Table of Legislation

Statutes

Statutory Instruments

Other

1

Introduction

One of the difficulties that all three authors of this book have encountered is that students new to the study of land law often approach it with trepidation. Horror tales about its complexity abound and are frequently promoted by former students. Yet the subject must be covered at least by those undertaking a qualifying law degree and by all those who must pass the 'core subjects' for professional purposes. Land law is also the gateway to other subjects such as conveyancing and the law of landlord and tenant. Students on professional property courses such as surveying and estate management will find that land law is unavoidable. These are perhaps not the best reasons for embarking on the study of any subject and there are better reasons than these for tackling land law.

These reasons lie in the very nature of the subject itself. Although it is undoubtedly the case that land law is complex, it is a subject which is stimulating and challenging. Sometimes it is like following a detective story with different clues emerging until a composite picture of 'whodunit' eventually emerges. This analogy is important, for just as it is critical not to miss one episode in the detective story, so is it important not to miss one chapter in the study of land law. Land law does not consist of a number of discrete subjects. The subjects interlock and the earliest topics form the basis of an understanding of the whole area of land law. For example, initial lectures usually deal with such concepts as the distinction between real and personal property, proprietary and personal rights and legal and equitable interests. An understanding of these concepts is essential for an understanding of the transfer of title and the differences between registered and unregistered land and incumbrances.

This imperative of having to deal at the outset with concepts which seem to have no footing in 'the real world' causes many of the difficulties in the study of land law. Many students can get lost in the wilderness in their first few weeks and, once lost, it is very hard to find the way again. The moral is to get in there at the outset and stay there until the end! Here also lies the way to a true appreciation of the joys of the subject. If you can give yourself up to study at the beginning of a purely intellectual subject, then you will acquire a familiarity with the concepts which will make further study a pleasure. The concepts are like building blocks which form the foundation and like all foundations they must be carefully laid.

Answering examination questions requires the same rigorous approach. A question which is exclusively on easements may depend on an understanding of the distinction between legal and equitable easements, the equitable doctrine of notice, the difference between a registered and an unregistered title—all topics which will have been dealt with in the first part of the course. Of course, such information will not have to be spelt out in every question. In fact, it is unlikely that you will ever come across an exam question which requires you simply to state the difference between a legal and an equitable interest. The question will assume this knowledge and will require you to apply it in specified circumstances. When you have laid all the building blocks to make the wall you are not expected to dismantle it to explain its construction. At the end of the course you will be expected to be able to handle the concepts with ease. Herein lies the fascination of the subject. Once you have grasped the essentials, then it suddenly comes down to earth and is applicable in all the circumstances of daily life. We all have to live somewhere so we buy a freehold property or rent a flat. We may acquire rights over someone else's land in the process. We may give someone else rights over our land (very often a mortgagee!). We might buy property jointly with a spouse, partner or friend. Relationships sometimes break up and the property rights need to be disentangled. Families may come to blows over ownership of property. All these situations which make up our social activities require a knowledge and application of land law. It is an essential element of the organisation of our lives. Very often, exam questions will read like problems out of a soap opera and then you can perceive how that early understanding of airy concepts has a firm practical application.

Success in the examination requires a disciplined approach and attention to exactitude. Land law is the last subject in which vagueness will do. Answers must be clear and organised like a military encounter. Precision in language is essential. As with all subjects, a thorough knowledge of the cases is vital. In addition, you must be conversant with the Law of Property Act 1925 and its attendant legislation. Look at the original statutory material from day one. With a little perseverance, it is often easier to understand the meaning of a section directly than to understand someone else's explanation. At least, look at the section as well as reading the textbook. It is particularly important to know your way around your statute book if you are allowed to take it into the exam. Find this out at the outset. Do not leave it until the examination itself to look at the original statutes. In the exam you should know exactly where to look up a particular section rather than waste time hunting for it. Familiarity with the statute book will also give you confidence (like taking a comfort blanket with you).

Similarly with cases: while we would never suggest that you should read every case (and some of the very old ones are virtually incomprehensible except perhaps to the legal historian), reading more than only the occasional judgment on a difficult topic will be very helpful. When you read about a case in a textbook, you are, after all, reading only the writer's interpretation of what the judge said. To read for yourself the full judgment, as expressed in the judge's own words, may be more enlightening.

Robert Walker LJ's judgments in ***Yaxley v Gotts* [2000] Ch 162** and in ***Jennings v Rice* [2003] 1 P & CR 100** are examples of excellent and clear expositions of the law. Dissenting judgments can also be enlightening: a notable instance is Lord Neuberger's powerful dissenting speech in ***Stack v Dowden* [2007] AC 432**.

Land law does require commitment but if you give it that you will be repaid with success in your exam performance.

2

Definition of land

Introduction

One of the earlier parts of most land law courses deals with the definition of land. Immediately, the unsuspecting student is confronted with the mysteries of law in the form of unfamiliar and seldom used words. Land does not simply mean something physical. The word 'hereditament', to which the student will be introduced, implies the nature of the right involved in the ownership of land. It is a clue as to what the study of land law is all about—not the land (the soil, the grass, the trees, the buildings), but the rights that people may have in land. Thus, land is to be reclassified as including corporeal and incorporeal hereditaments. Ownership of land may equally include ownership of a house and ownership of a right of way over someone else's house (an incorporeal hereditament).

This classification has given rise to some jurisprudential debate as to the nature of corporeal and incorporeal rights and some courses may address this topic from that perspective (see, for example, Austin, *Jurisprudence*, 5th edn, London: Murray, 1885, vol. 1, p. 362). Other courses may, however, concentrate on the distinction between fixtures and chattels since this develops and applies the distinction between real and personal property which may have formed a part of an early lecture. The difficulty with the distinction between fixtures and chattels is that it rests on a factual basis and, although basic principles have been established and can be applied, there are numerous cases which have been decided on their own individual facts. Thus, in one case, a seat can be a fixture, in another, a chattel.

There are also some Latin maxims on the loose here despite attempts to modernise the law. *Cuius est solum eius est usque ad coelum et ad inferos* (the owner of the land owns everything up to the sky and down to the centre of the earth) and *quicquid plantatur solo, solo cedit* (whatever is attached to the land becomes part of the land) are regulars. Some discussion of these maxims and their application to practical problems may be anticipated, especially as the scope of the first of these maxims was considered recently by the Supreme Court in *Star Energy Weald Basin Ltd v Bocardo SA* (2010). A good starting point is the Law of Property Act 1925, s. 205(1)(ix) which gives the statutory definition of land.

Apart from the *Star Energy* case, there is little new in this topic; the modern case law is mostly an application of established principles. From this point of view, the topic is a safe one to prepare.

Question 1

***Cuius est solum, eius est usque ad coelum et ad inferos* (the owner of the land owns everything up to the sky and down to the centre of the earth).**

Discuss.

Commentary

This question is either a dream or a nightmare. There is a vast amount of material to be covered and it is unlikely that you can deal with it all. You may be guided by what you have covered in lectures. Treasure trove, for example, has been topical (with the growth in the use of metal detectors) and modern law has now significantly extended the meaning and ambit of 'treasure'.

The usual advice not to regurgitate all you know holds good. Discuss the maxim critically: what are its limitations? Don't just dismiss it—consider to what extent it holds true.

Answer plan

- Limitations on fee simple owner's rights:
  - Airspace;
  - Water;
  - Boundaries—presumptions.
- Land—minerals.
- Chattels—fixtures or not? **Treasure Act 1996**.
- Wild animals.
- Social legislation—planning, housing.

Suggested answer

This maxim, which was coined by Accursius, a professor at the University of Bologna, in the thirteenth century, relates to the extent of the ownership enjoyed by the fee simple owner. There are, in fact, a number of limitations on the ownership of the fee simple owner. Some are statutory, others are founded in the common law.

The first aspect to be considered is the extent of the fee simple owner's rights in the airspace above the property. The owner's rights extend to such a height as is reasonably necessary for the ordinary use and enjoyment of the land. In ***Baron Bernstein of Leigh v Skyviews and General Ltd*** **[1978] QB 479**, Griffith J stated that it was necessary to balance the rights of an owner to enjoy the land against the rights of the general public to take advantage of all that 'science now offers in the use of airspace'. Thus, the rights of the owner were limited to such a height as is necessary for the ordinary use and enjoyment of the land and above that height the fee simple owner has no greater rights than any other member of the public.

Where there is an interference with the legitimate rights of the fee simple owner then these rights may be maintained by an action for nuisance or trespass. In ***Kelsen v Imperial Tobacco Co (of Great Britain and Ireland) Ltd*** **[1957] 2 QB 334**, the action of the defendant in allowing an advertisement to overhang the plaintiff's premises amounted to a trespass as was the action of the defendant in ***Woollerton and Wilson Ltd v Richard Costain Ltd*** **[1970] 1 WLR 411**, in allowing the jib of a crane to swing over the plaintiff's property.

Under the **Civil Aviation Act 1982**, it is a defence to an action in trespass or nuisance for aircraft to fly at such a height which is reasonable under the circumstances.

The rights of the fee simple owner in water on the land are, in part, derived from statute. The right to abstract water is controlled by the **Water Resources Act 1991** and depends on the grant of a licence from the Environment Agency.

Where water flows in a defined channel across the land, then there is a distinction between water which is tidal and that which is non-tidal. The water itself is not capable of ownership, but there are rights in the bed and the right to take the fish to be considered. Where the water is tidal, the bed belongs to the Crown and the public have a right of navigation and a right to fish up to the point where the water ceases to be subject to the ebb and flow of tides. In many rivers this point is determined by the presence of a lock-gate. Where the water is non-tidal, then the bed belongs to the riparian owner. If the water forms the boundary between two plots of land, then subject to any contrary agreement or evidence, the riparian owners own up to the midway point in the river or stream. They are also entitled to take the fish, a valuable property right on many country estates. A riparian owner does not own the water itself, but may use it for ordinary purposes connected with the riparian tenement, regardless of the amount he uses. If he uses it for any extraordinary purpose, such as manufacturing, then he must restore it in approximately the same quantity and quality.

Water percolating underneath the land and not contained in a defined channel, is not capable of ownership until such moment as it is appropriated, when it becomes the property of the person appropriating it (***Ballard v Tomlinson*** **(1885) 29 ChD 115**).

Where water, such as lakes and ponds, lies on the land, it is the property of the landowner, subject to the **Water Resources Act 1991**.

If the land verges on the seashore, the fee simple owner owns that part of the land down to a point reached by an ordinary high tide.

Where the land is bordered by a hedge and ditch the rebuttable presumption is that the boundary lies at the furthest edge of the ditch (*Vowles v Miller* (1810) 3 Taunt 137; *Alan Wibberley Building Ltd v Insley* [1999] 2 All ER 897).

The maxim also states that the landowner owns everything down to the centre of the earth. While it is true that at common law all minerals are owned by the landowner, ownership is in fact vested by various statutes in the Crown or other public bodies. For example, petroleum in its natural state is vested in the Crown by virtue of the Petroleum Act 1998 and coal is vested in the Coal Authority by the Coal Industry Act 1994.

In *Star Energy Weald Basin Ltd v Bocardo SA* [2010] UKSC 35, Star Energy, which had a licence under statute to search for and extract petroleum, had drilled wells that went directly under Bocardo's land at a minimum depth of 800 feet, and which reached depths of up to 2,900 feet in order to reach the natural reservoir of petroleum and gas. The drilling under Bocardo's land was done without its consent, and (for many years) without its knowledge. Bocardo claimed damages for trespass from Star Energy; in order to succeed it needed to show that it had title to the subterranean land at the depths at which the drilling took place. Lord Hope (with whose judgment the other members of the Supreme Court agreed) concluded that, in relation to what lies below the surface, the maxim is still good law. He admitted that at great depths, where there is enormous pressure and molten rock, it is impractical to seek to apply the maxim; but that was not the case here. Although the drilling was at such depths that it did not interfere with Bocardo's own use of its land, the fact that the petroleum could be reached by human activity raised the question of who owned the strata in which it was found. Although the Crown owned the petroleum, it did not own the surrounding strata; the only possible owner was therefore Bocardo, and the drilling was held to be an actionable trespass and Bocardo was awarded damages. No injunction was claimed in the case, and it seems unlikely that an injunction would be awarded in these sorts of circumstances, where the trespass is technical and does not cause the claimant any loss or inconvenience.

The fee simple owner is *prima facie* entitled to all chattels found in or on the land, in the absence of a legitimate claim from the owner of the chattel, unless (where the object is found on the land) the finder acquires a prior right. Treasure (as defined in the Treasure Act 1996) is an exception to this: it vests in the Crown, subject to prior rights and interests.

Wild animals are not subject to ownership (*The Case of Swans* (1592) 7 Co Rep 156), but may be hunted by the fee simple owner on whose land they run. There are, however, a number of limitations to this right in respect of protected species (Wildlife and Countryside Act 1981 (as amended) and the Protection of Badgers Act 1992, for example).

Land is defined in the Law of Property Act 1925, s. 205(1)(ix) as including 'the surface, buildings or parts of buildings' and whatever is attached to the land becomes part of the land under another Latin maxim, *quicquid plantatur solo, solo cedit*. This raises, in practice, an important problem relating to ownership of those items which, but for the fact that they are attached to the land, would constitute chattels. The distinction needs to be drawn between those items which are fixtures, and therefore part of the realty, and those which are not, and therefore remain personalty.

There are two tests for determining whether an object is a fixture or a chattel. The first test relates to the degree of annexation. If the object is annexed to the land then it is, *prima facie*, a fixture. So, in *Holland v Hodgson* (1872) LR 7 CP 328, spinning looms bolted to the floor of a factory were attached other than by their own weight and were fixtures. In *Hulme v Brigham* [1943] KB 152, however, heavy printing presses which stood on the floor without any attachment other than the force of gravity, were chattels. In *Chelsea Yacht & Boat Co v Pope* [2000] 1 WLR 1941, a houseboat which was moored to the bank and which moved up and down with the tide, was held to be a chattel.

The paramount test, however, was foreshadowed by Blackburn J in *Holland v Hodgson* and relates to the purpose of annexation. Under this test, the question to be asked is whether the chattel has been affixed to the land for the better enjoyment of the object as a chattel, or for the more convenient use of the land. This leads to the result that the same object may constitute a fixture in one case, but a chattel in another. For example, in *Leigh v Taylor* [1902] AC 157, tapestries nailed to a wall were held not to be fixtures, but in *Re Whaley* [1908] 1 Ch 615, similar objects were held to be fixtures because the object of their annexation was to enhance the room. Lord Halsbury LC in *Leigh v Taylor* confirmed that the key test was the purpose of annexation, and this was confirmed in *Hamp v Bygrave* (1982) 266 EG 720 where garden ornaments that formed part of a landscape display were held to be fixtures despite the fact they rested on the ground simply by their own weight.

In *Elitestone Ltd v Morris* [1997] 1 WLR 687, the House of Lords held that what is of primary importance is the intention involved. It was indicated that this is an objective test to determine whether the object was intended for the use or enjoyment of the land, or for the more convenient use of the object itself. Clearly, the courts are prepared to apply a common-sense approach to this issue (*Botham v TSB Bank plc* (1997) 73 P & CR D1).

There are some exceptional cases where there is a right to remove fixtures. A tenant may remove trade fixtures that have been attached to the land for the purpose of carrying out his trade; ornamental and domestic fixtures provided their removal will cause no substantial damage to the property; agricultural fixtures in accordance with the procedure set out in the Agricultural Holdings Act 1986.

There are also a number of limitations on the right of the fee simple owner to enjoy the land in the form of the Town and Country Planning Act 1991 and related legislation, which controls developments on land, and the Housing Acts and Rent Acts, which control the standard for houses for human habitation and the security of tenure of certain tenants.

Question 2

Abel has entered into a contract to sell his house to Baal. He consults you as to whether the following items (which were not mentioned in the contract of sale) are to be included in the sale:

(a) a replica of the 'Three Graces' which is standing in the garden;

(b) a stained glass lampshade, attached to the ceiling by a chain, which was given to him by friends when he got married;

(c) the fitted kitchen which Abel installed himself (he wants to dismantle it and adapt it for his new house);

(d) adjustable bookshelves which slot into strips of metal screwed into the wall; and

(e) an ornamental fireplace which is on hire-purchase from Quickfire Ltd.

Commentary

Unusual in a land law examination, this question concentrates on one aspect of a subject—that of the distinction between fixtures and chattels. There is an abundance of well-known case law in this area and the principles are well established. The judgment of Scarman LJ in ***Berkley v Poulet* (1976) 242 EG 39** lays out the principles clearly and concisely, and the area was considered by the House of Lords in ***Elitestone Ltd v Morris* [1997] 1 WLR 687**. For the effect of hire-purchase agreements see Guest and Lever (1963) *Conv* (NS) 30; McCormack [1990] *Conv* 275.

Many of the cases vary according to their facts so it is important to distinguish principles of law in this area from issues of fact.

Land and chattels are treated differently at law; freehold land is real property and chattels are personal property. A contract to sell land will not include chattels unless they are expressly included. Sometimes an item that was once a chattel may become part of the land and there are, on occasions, difficulties in naming the distinction between fixtures (which form part of the land) and chattels (which remain items of personal property). Under the **Law of Property Act 1925, s. 62**, fixtures are included in a conveyance of land. This question deals with this fundamental distinction.

Answer plan

- Purpose of distinguishing between fixtures and chattels.
- Tests to distinguish between fixtures and chattels.
- Discussion of development of tests through case law.
- Initial test—degree of annexation.
- Discussion of case law in relation to each scenario in (a), (b), (c), (d), and (e).

Suggested answer

(a) There are two tests to determine whether an item has become part of the freehold:

(i) the method and degree of annexation;

(ii) the object and purpose of the annexation.

The earlier law emphasised the first test, while later cases introduced the second test to alleviate the injustice where limited owners had affixed items of value to the land. The second test is now dominant, so if the item is physically annexed to the land this does not necessarily resolve the matter any more. Nevertheless the degree of annexation remains a relevant question. According to Scarman LJ in ***Berkley v Poulet* (1976) 242 EG 39**, if there is such a degree of physical annexation that an object cannot be removed without serious damage to, or some destruction of, the realty, then there is a strong case for the item to be classified as a fixture. In ***Chelsea Yacht & Boat Co v Pope* [2000] 1 WLR 1941**, a houseboat which was moored by ropes, chain, and an anchor was held to be a chattel.

Thus, the determination of the question whether the 'Three Graces' is a fixture will depend on an application of the two tests. It is not clear whether the statue is physically fixed to the land, although it would seem from the question that it is merely 'standing' on the land. If that is the case, then, *prima facie*, the statue is not a fixture. In the case of ***Berkley v Poulet*** itself, a white marble statue of a Greek athlete weighing half a ton and standing on a plinth, was considered not to be a fixture. Similarly, a printing machine secured by its own weight and weighing several tons was held not to be a fixture (***Hulme v Brigham* [1943] KB 152**). However, the general rule can be displaced where the object of annexation is that the chattels should become part of the land. Thus, a drystone wall which was constructed of blocks of stone placed one on top of another was held to have been intended to become part of the realty (***Holland v Hodgson* (1872) LR 7 CP 328**). Intention refers to the purpose which the object serves, not to the purpose of the person who put the object in place: ***Elitestone Ltd v Morris* [1997] 1 WLR 687 (HL)**.

The fact that the 'Three Graces' is an ornamental object may not be a conclusive indication that it is not intended to become part of the land. In ***Lord Chesterfield's Settled Estates* [1911] 1 Ch 237**, Grinling Gibbons carvings were held to be fixtures; and in ***Re Whaley* [1908] 1 Ch 615**, chattels, which were placed in the room in order to create a beautiful room as a whole, were held to be capable of being fixtures. In ***D'Eyncourt v Gregory* (1866) LR 3 Eq 382**, statues which were part of the architectural design of a property were held to be fixtures.

However, in this problem, regardless of the question whether the 'Three Graces' are in fact physically affixed to the ground, it would seem probable that the statue remains a chattel unless, as in ***Hamp v Bygrave* (1982) 266 EG 720**, it can be objectively viewed as a feature of, and part and parcel of, the garden, or, as in ***D'Eyncourt v Gregory***, as a part of the architectural design of the house.

(b) The stained glass lampshade would not seem to pose the same difficulties. It is an object that is essentially a chattel and it is unlikely that any evidence could be adduced to change its character into a fixture. If the first test were to be applied alone, then there is a degree of physical annexation which might suggest that the lampshade was a fixture. This test is no longer decisive. In *Leigh v Taylor* [1902] AC 157, tapestries were fixed to the wall. The House of Lords held that the purpose of their annexation to the realty was for their better enjoyment as tapestries. Annexation on its own was not enough to make them fixtures. This decision was followed in the case of *Spyer v Phillipson* [1931] 2 Ch 183, where oak and pine panelling and a chimney-piece had been erected, and, in *Berkley v Poulet* (1976) 242 EG 39, in relation to pictures which were hung in recesses in a panelled room. Thus, it is likely that the lampshade will be a chattel.

(c) The fitted kitchen poses a different problem. In the first place it is clearly annexed so it raises the general rule that it constitutes a fixture. Secondly, it would seem to be unarguable that the object of its annexation was for any other purpose than to create a room which could be used as a kitchen. While the fitted furniture may have been aesthetically pleasing, its primary purpose was for use as a kitchen. In *Re Whaley* [1908] 1 Ch 615 the design of a beautiful room, 'an Elizabethan Room', by the installation of chattels of beauty, meant that those chattels became part of the room—they were fixtures. The unity of design of the room meant that the objects were part of the realty. The result in *Lord Chesterfield's Settled Estates* (above) was similar. In *Botham v TSB Bank plc* (1997) 73 P & CR D1 the Court of Appeal decided that bathroom and kitchen units were fixtures whereas kitchen white goods, such as refrigerators, were still chattels.

(d) Similar arguments might prevail in respect of the bookshelves. They are annexed although they could be easily removed with little damage. The object of their annexation is to make the room useful as a library (*Re Whaley*). In fact, there would seem to be no question as to their intrinsic merit as chattels. The bookshelves have been installed for the more convenient use of the property, not for their use as chattels. In *Vaudeville Electric Cinema Ltd v Muriset* [1923] 2 Ch 74, seats secured to the floor of a cinema hall were fixtures. Normally, free-standing seats would be considered chattels. Here, however, they were affixed to make the hall more convenient as a cinema and were held to be fixtures. On these grounds, therefore, it is arguable that the shelves become fixtures.

(e) Here the fireplace is annexed to the room. It is described as ornamental and might, therefore, fall into the category of the tapestries in *Leigh v Taylor* which, although affixed, were deemed to be chattels because the object of their annexation was for their better enjoyment as such.

However, there is a further complication in that the fireplace is being purchased as part of a hire-purchase scheme. If the fireplace has been annexed to the land of the hirer, then it becomes annexed to the realty and the original owner (Quickfire Ltd) loses its title. It will be necessary to consider the contract of hire-purchase to see whether

Quickfire Ltd has reserved to itself the right to remove the fireplace in the event of default in the payment of the hire-purchase instalments. If there is such a right of removal, then this confers on Quickfire Ltd an equitable interest in the land which is a right of entry (*Re Morrison, Jones & Taylor* [1914] 1 Ch 50).

Whether this right of entry is binding on Baal will depend on whether the land is registered or unregistered. If unregistered, then the equitable doctrine of notice prevails and Baal will be bound unless he is a *bona fide* purchaser of a legal estate for value without notice (*Poster v Slough Estates Ltd* [1969] 1 Ch 495). If the land is registered, then strangely enough, the right of entry will not bind a purchaser since it is not an overriding interest and may not be registrable as a minor interest.

Further reading

Austin, J., *Jurisprudence*, 5th edn, Murray, 1885, vol. 1, p. 362.

Burn, E. H., and Cartwright, J., *Cheshire and Burn's Modern Law of Real Property*, 17th edn, Oxford, 2006.

Guest, A., and Lever, J. (1963) *Conv* (NS) 30.

McCormack, G. [1990] *Conv* 275.

3

Finders' titles

Introduction

The law of finders' titles is often dealt with near the beginning of property courses. One of the main advantages of studying this topic is that it illustrates the basic nature of property rights at common law. A study of finders' titles brings home to the student, perhaps more than any other topic, an appreciation of the principle that titles to chattels are not absolute, but may vary in quality. The cases indeed reveal four significant points.

First, they illustrate that at common law all titles depend ultimately upon possession. For this reason, the finder of a chattel on someone else's land may acquire a title to the chattel if he takes it into his possession. It should be noted, however, that although title to unregistered land, like title to chattels, also depends ultimately upon possession, the Land Registration Act 2002 effectively severs the link between this principle and registered land. Under the 2002 Act, title to registered land depends solely on registration.

Secondly, they reveal that title at common law is itself a relative concept. The finder of a chattel acquires a title weaker than that of the true owner, but (depending on the circumstances), perhaps a stronger title than that of anyone else.

Thirdly, they indicate that at common law the relative strength of property rights in a chattel depends largely upon the time at which they are acquired—titles acquired earlier in time generally have priority over those acquired later. Thus, if the owner of land is held to have a better title to an object found than the person who discovered it, this will be on the basis that the owner of the land had a prior title to it—and such a prior title may be found to exist even though the owner of the land did not know that the object was there. The courts are particularly willing to find that the owner of land has a prior possession of a chattel where the finder is a trespasser or dishonest (as in *Hibbert v McKiernan* [1948] 2 KB 142, where the golf club as occupier of the land was found to have a title to lost balls good against dishonest finders). Even a dishonest finder, however, will have a better title than someone who cannot establish prior possession (*Costello v Derbyshire Chief Constable* [2001] 1 WLR 1437).

Fourthly, they demonstrate that the claimant wins merely by showing that he has a title better than that of the defendant. Thus the defendant cannot plead that someone else has a better right to the chattel than the claimant. The chimney sweep's boy in *Armory v Delamirie* (1722) 5 Stra. 505 succeeded in his claim against the jeweller; but he could not have resisted a claim brought by the true owner, and the case did not decide whether the boy could have successfully defended a claim brought by his master, or by the owner of the house in which the jewel had been found.

A question on finders' titles will, therefore, inevitably be a test of the student's understanding of these fundamental principles. These are not, however, difficult to grasp, and the case law is itself interesting, involving matters as diverse as the finding of prehistoric boats, Roman coins, and bracelets in airport lounges.

Question 1

Lord Blandish, the freehold owner of Brandy Towers, decided two years ago to open his home and its grounds to the public. In order to make the premises ready, he hired the firm of Dogget & Co to construct a Visitors' Centre. One morning, Noggs, an employee of the firm, had just entered the main driveway of Brandy Towers while on his way to work, when he found a bag containing £500 in notes lying next to the driveway. All attempts to trace the owner of the bag and contents failed.

Shortly after this, Brandy Towers threw its gates open to the public. Victor, a member of the public, while visiting the grounds with his dog, Columbus, found Columbus digging in one of the flower beds. When Victor went to investigate, he found that Columbus had unearthed a bronze bracelet. Victor handed the bracelet to the receptionist at the Brandy Hall Visitors' Centre; but, despite the efforts of the staff, the owner of the bracelet (which was discovered to have been made in 1932) could not be found.

Lord Blandish had purchased Brandy Towers from Viscount Willow in 1980, who had himself purchased it in 1930. Expert evidence suggests that the bracelet had lain in the ground for at least 30 years.

Consider the relative strengths of the claims that may be made to the bag of notes and to the bracelet.

Commentary

The student should note carefully what is asked: to consider the relative strengths of the claims to the bag of notes and to the bracelet. This means that the student needs to identify who may have a claim to these items, and then to discuss the strengths of the claims relative to each other. It is not meaningful to attempt to state definitely who will be entitled to the items found, since this will depend upon who puts in a claim.

As in every problem question, the student should apply the law to the facts from the outset. The suggested answer, it will be seen, begins merely by setting out the basic principle in one short sentence, and then immediately seeks to apply such principle to the given facts. There then follows a discussion of the relative position of possible claimants to the bag: Lord

Blandish, Noggs and Dogget & Co. Lord Blandish's claim is discussed first: this is logical, because his claim depends upon his having a title to the bag and its contents before they were found, in which case his title, being prior in time, would be better than those of the other potential claimants (with the exception, of course, of the true owner).

Students sometimes ask what became of the prehistoric boat in ***Elwes v Brigg Gas Co.* (1886) 33 ChD 562**, and whether they can go and see it: alas no! After the decision in that case, the lord of the manor exhibited the boat in a special building near Brigg Railway Station until 1909, when he donated it to a public museum in Hull. Unfortunately, it was destroyed in an air raid on the museum in 1943: see Michael L. Nash, 'Are Finders Keepers? One Hundred Years since *Elwes* v *Brigg Gas Co.*' (1987) 137 *NLJ* 118, 119.

Answer plan

- Better title by prior possession.

The bag of notes

- Object lying *on* the land.
- Relative claims of:
  - Lord Blandish (present owner of the land);
  - Dogget & Co (finder's employers);
  - Noggs (finder).

The bronze bracelet

- Object found *in* the land.
- Possible claim of Crown (treasure).
- Relative claims of:
  - Victor (finder, but as trespasser);
  - Lord Blandish (present owner of the land);
  - Viscount Willow (previous owner of the land).

Suggested answer

Possible claimants to the bag of notes are Noggs, as the finder; Dogget & Co, as his employer; and Lord Blandish, as the owner of the land upon which it was found.

In English law, the person who can establish a prior possession to a chattel has a better claim than another whose possession is later in time: *Armory v Delamirie* (1722) 5 Stra. 505 and *Costello v Derbyshire Chief Constable* [2001] 1 WLR 1437. In this problem, the issue is whether Lord Blandish, the owner of the land on which the bag was found, can be considered to have possession of it before it was found. If he can, he has a right to it better than everyone other than the true owner. It is possible for Lord

Blandish to have possession of a chattel lying upon his land, even without his knowing it is there, but only if he can show that he manifested an intention to exercise control over the land and the things upon it, i.e. an *animus possidendi*. This may be difficult to establish if the land upon which the chattel is found is open to the public. Thus in ***Bridges v Hawkesworth*** **(1851) 21 LJQB 75** a travelling salesman who found a bag of money lying on the customer side of a shop was held to have a better title to it than the owner of the shop. More recently, in ***Parker v British Airways Board*** **[1982] 1 QB 1004**, the Court of Appeal held that an air passenger who found a gold bracelet in the international executive lounge of an airport had a better claim to it than the occupiers, the British Airways Board, because it was found that the Board did not have a policy of searching for lost articles.

If the bag had been found inside Brandy Towers itself, the requisite intention to possess would have been readily inferred: see Donaldson LJ in ***Parker v British Airways Board*** at p. 1020. Such intention might, however, be more difficult to establish in respect of the grounds. On the other hand, at the time the bag was found, the grounds were not open to the public. The answer will depend, therefore, upon an analysis of all the facts, including evidence as to the range of persons who commonly used the driveway, the frequency of its use, and whether it was barred by a gate.

If Lord Blandish was in possession of the bag of money when it was found, he will have a better title to it than the finder. Even if he was not in possession of it at that time, however, he may still have a better claim than the finder. Where an item is found by an employee in the course of his employment, his employer has a better right to it than the employee: see *dicta* in ***City of London Corporation v Appleyard*** **[1963] 2 All ER 834** at p. 839; and ***South Staffs Water Co v Sharman*** **[1896] 2 QB 44**, as explained by D. R. Harris, 'Concept of Possession in English Law', in *Oxford Essays in Jurisprudence* (A. G. Guest, ed.), 1961. This principle extends (as in the ***Appleyard*** case itself), to independent contractors. As Dogget & Co were hired by Lord Blandish, anything that they or their own employees find on the land while constructing the Visitors' Centre, they find on Lord Blandish's behalf. The finder would therefore have merely custody of the bag and its contents, legal possession of which would pass to Lord Blandish. On either of these grounds, therefore, Lord Blandish is likely to have a better title than that of either Dogget & Co or Noggs.

It might be difficult for Noggs to assert a better title than either Lord Blandish or Dogget & Co, since, even in the absence of a claim by Lord Blandish, Noggs's find might be treated as made on behalf of his employer, Dogget & Co Noggs might argue that he did not find the bag in the course of his employment, since it is arguable that his employment did not start until he reached that part of the grounds where the Visitors' Centre was being built. Against this, there is a stronger counter-argument that he was lawfully on the grounds only as an employee of Dogget & Co, which was there only as an independent contractor hired by Lord Blandish. It is therefore only in the unlikely event that neither Lord Blandish nor Dogget & Co claims, that Noggs could assert a claim as finder.

As the bracelet is modern and made of bronze, it cannot be treasure within the Treasure Act 1996, so ownership would not vest in the Crown. Possible claimants to the bracelet might therefore include Victor, as the finder; Lord Blandish, as the present owner of the grounds; and, possibly, Viscount Willow, as the owner of the land at the time when the bracelet was deposited in it.

Where, as here, the chattel is attached to the land, the freehold owner of the land can generally establish possession to it prior to that of the finder. Where the chattel is affixed to or buried in the land, the freehold owner's *animus possidendi* is presumed, so he will have rights to the chattel superior to those of the finder: ***Parker v British Airways Board*** at pp. 1017–18. Thus in ***Elwes v Brigg Gas Co.*** **(1886) 33 ChD 562**, the life tenant was held to have a better title to the prehistoric boat contained in the soil than the finder, who was also a lessee. Lord Blandish's claim is even stronger in the present case because, unlike the finder of the prehistoric boat, Victor has no interest in the land.

Furthermore, although Victor is a lawful visitor to the grounds, his licence will almost certainly not extend to digging in the land: ***Waverley Borough Council v Fletcher*** **[1995] 4 All ER 756 (CA)**. Since he finds the bracelet only by the excavations of his dog, he finds it as a trespasser. Whilst a trespasser may have some limited rights of possession, the court is even more likely in such circumstances to hold that Lord Blandish has a prior claim to possession (***Hibbert v McKiernan*** **[1948] 2 KB 142**).

The final issue is therefore the relative strengths of the claims of Lord Blandish and his predecessor in title to the land, Viscount Willow. If Willow (or his estate) could establish that he was the true owner of the bracelet, and that he had lost (and not abandoned) it, he (or his estate) would have the prior claim (***Moffatt v Kazana*** **[1968] 3 All ER 271**). Apart from this, his claim to it would be merely as predecessor in title to the land. Fixtures, being part of the freehold, would have passed to Lord Blandish when Brandy Towers was conveyed to him; but the bracelet, even though it was apparently buried in the earth before the conveyance, is unlikely to be treated as a fixture (***Elwes v Brigg Gas Co.*** **(1886) 33 ChD 562**). Furthermore, it seems that the **Law of Property Act 1925, s. 62**, will not operate to pass title to the bracelet on the conveyance (***Moffatt v Kazana*** at p. 275).

None of the reported cases has decided the rights of a previous freehold owner. The Viscount's claim might, however, be based upon two lines of argument. First, an analogy might be drawn with the law relating to items concealed in goods after they have been sold. In ***Merry v Green*** **(1841) 7 M & W 623**, a sum of money was found in a secret compartment of a bureau after it had been sold at auction. It was held that the seller of the bureau, even though not the true owner of the money, had a better title to it than the current owner of the bureau who had discovered the money. Secondly, it might be contended that the rights of a previous freehold owner were akin to the rights of the life tenant in ***Elwes v Brigg Gas Co.*** In that case, the life tenant was held to have a prior claim to the boat, even though it was discovered by lessees in possession under a 99-year lease.

However, whilst a lessor ceases to occupy the land upon the commencement of the term, he retains a reversionary interest in the land, unlike a vendor who conveys the freehold. The second argument is therefore a weaker one. Furthermore, it has been pointed out that there could be, in theory at least, 'an indefinite chain of claims from previous occupiers or their personal representatives' (Hoath [1990] *Conv* 348, at p. 352). There is no fear of this in the problem, since the bracelet was deposited in the ground no earlier than 1932. Nevertheless, the courts might prefer to adopt the principle that the rights to the bracelet would have passed to Lord Blandish 'as an ordinary common law incident of land ownership' (Hoath [1990] *Conv* 348, at p. 350).

In the case of both the bag of money and the bracelet, the true owner of the item in question will have six years from the time of the find before his rights are barred (**Limitation Act 1980, ss. 2, 4, and 32**). Time does not, however, run against a dishonest finder, i.e. one who does not attempt to trace the true owner. It has also been argued that time does not in any event run against a true owner until he makes a demand (Marshall (1949) 2 *CLP* 68, referring to ***Spackman v Foster* (1883) 11 QBD 99**).

Question 2

Julian and Julia were joint tenants both at law and in equity of a plot of land in Sevenoaks in Kent, which comprises a dwelling-house and an area of woodland. In 1985 they leased the plot to Noel for a term of 99 years. Julian died in 1987, leaving all his personal property to charity. Julia died in 1988, leaving her entire estate to their daughter, Dorothy, who is now the owner of the freehold reversion on the lease.

A number of trees in the wood fell in the Great Storm of 1987; but Noel, a keen environmentalist, decided to leave them as they were, and he began using the trunk of one of them, an ancient oak, as a seat. Three months ago, however, while Noel was attempting to sit on the trunk, it gave way. Noel discovered inside it a clay pot, which contained a solid gold locket, and some coins. Noel contacted his local museum, which identified the locket and coins as dating from the early sixteenth century. The latter were found to be made of an alloy of silver and base metal. The silver content of some of the coins was 20 per cent; of others, only 5 per cent.

Crafty read about the find in a report in the local newspaper the following week and entered the wood at the dead of night with a metal detector. By this means, he uncovered, beneath the roots of a birch tree, a silver ashtray that had been made in 1900. Crafty took the ashtray home and hid it in a cupboard. His nocturnal activities have now come to light.

Last week, Noel found an old deed box under the floorboards of the attic. It contained £20,000 in bank notes. Evidence has revealed that the deed box and its contents belonged either to Julian or to Julia, or to both of them; but more precise evidence of ownership is lacking.

Consider who is entitled to the items found.

Commentary

The mere length of a question deters many candidates from answering it. The length of a question on the examination paper, however, is no guide to its difficulty. This problem, though relatively long, is not particularly difficult; indeed, some of the information given is used to create an atmosphere rather than to convey facts of legal significance.

In the context of treasure, objects may qualify as treasure if they are at least 200 years old when found and belong to a class designated by the Secretary of State as being of outstanding historical, archaeological or cultural importance: **Treasure Act 1996, s. 2(1)**. As the answer indicates, however, the only designation order made to date applies only to metal objects from the Iron Age. The reason for the making of this Order is explained in the Code of Practice. It is apparently to deal primarily with Bronze Age gold-covered perannulur rings whose surface is gold over a base-metal core. The main aim is to remove the need for invasive and possibly harmful scientific analysis of such rings that would be necessary to determine the percentage of precious metal. See *The Treasure Act* 1996 *Code of Practice (Revised) England and Wales* (2002 edn), at p. 10 (para. 12).

Although not divided into sections by letters or numbers, the question naturally divides into several parts. The question-setter has been fairly kind, because each part is broadly contained in a separate paragraph. The candidate should take care, however, because one possibly vital piece of information relating to the money in the deed box is contained in the opening paragraph.

Answer plan

Possible claims to gold locket, coins and clay pot

- Crown (if items are treasure):
  - **Treasure Act 1996**;
  - payment and division of reward?
- Noel (finder, lessee and occupier).
- Dorothy (freehold owner).

Possible claims to ashtray

- Crown (if item is treasure).
- Crafty (finder, but trespasser and dishonest).
- Noel (lessee and occupier of the land; terms of lease?).
- Dorothy (prior title as freehold owner?).

Possible claims to deed box and contents

- Dorothy (as successor to Julia):
  - (presumption from ownership of the land containing the chattel).

Suggested answer

Since the items found by Noel and Crafty were found very recently, they may belong to the Crown as treasure under the Treasure Act 1996, subject to prior interests and rights: s. 4(1). Prior interests and rights include any (or those which derive from any) which were held when the treasure was left where it was found: s. 4(2). The successor in title to the owner of the property at the time it was left or deposited in the ground would have a prior interest and right, but if the clay pot and its contents have been in the earth for hundreds of years it is highly unlikely that there will be any person able to make such a claim to them. There may be a slightly better chance of a claim by the successor in title to the true owner of the ashtray.

Subject to this, the Crown's claim depends upon the items comprising treasure, which is defined in s. 1. An object which is at least 300 years old when found and which is not a coin ranks as treasure if it has a metallic content of at least 10 per cent by weight of precious metal (which means gold or silver: s. 3(3)). The solid gold locket therefore qualifies as treasure. Since the coins are at least 300 years old, they will all rank as treasure, whatever their metal content, if there are at least ten of them in the same find; if there are fewer than ten, each will rank as treasure (under para. (a) of s. 1(1)) only if it has a precious metal content of at least 10 per cent by weight. If, therefore, there are only four coins, the two at 20 per cent qualify under this criterion, but not those of merely 5 per cent. Each of the latter may still qualify as treasure under para. (d), however, as being an object which, when found, was part of the same find as an object which was treasure (i.e. the locket and the 20 per cent silver coins). Objects which are found together are part of the same find: s. 3(4)(a). The clay pot may also qualify on this basis. An object may also qualify as treasure if (being an object at least 200 years old when found) it belongs to a class designated by the Secretary of State as being of outstanding historical, archaeological or cultural importance: s. 2(1). The only order made to date under this paragraph, however, is the Treasure (Designation) Order 2002, SI 2002/2666, which designates only *metal* objects (whether of gold or silver or a base metal) that date from the Iron Age or earlier (and excluding coins). Even if (which seems unlikely on the facts) the pot were to date from the Iron Age, it falls outside the designation since it is made, not of metal, but of clay.

A person who finds an object, or who acquires property in an object, which he believes or has reasonable grounds for believing is treasure must notify the Coroner for Treasure (established under the Coroners and Justice Act 2009). The notification must be within 14 days of the day after the find (in the case of a finder) or of the day after the object is acquired (in the case of an acquirer). In each case, however, the 14 days will not start to run until the finder or acquirer first believes and has reason to believe that the object is treasure. Failure to report in time is a criminal offence punishable by imprisonment or a fine, or both: Treasure Act 1996, ss 8, 8A.

The Coroner for Treasure must investigate whether the object is treasure, and may hold an inquest: Coroners and Justice Act 2009, ss 26, 27. Before conducting an investigation, the Coroner for Treasure must notify the appropriate national museum (which in the case of an object found in England is the British Museum) and must take reasonable steps to notify the finder and the occupier of the land where the object was found: Treasure Act 1996, s 9.

If treasure has vested in the Crown and is to be transferred to a museum, the Secretary of State must determine whether a reward is to be paid by the museum before the transfer and (if it is) the amount of the reward (which must not exceed the treasure's market value) and to whom it should be paid. If it is payable to more than one person, he must also determine how much each is to receive. The reward may be payable to the finder or later acquirer, to the occupier of the land at the time of the find and to any person who had an interest in the land at that time, or who has had such an interest at any time since: s. 10. The determination of the Secretary of State must be in accordance with a code of practice which he is required to prepare (s. 11), the latest being the Code of Practice 2002. Any reward is likely to be divided between Noel (assuming that he has reported the find in time), as both finder and leaseholder, and Dorothy, as owner of the freehold reversion.

Assuming that the ashtray found by Crafty is not itself part of the same find as an object which is treasure, it is unlikely to be treasure. Whatever its silver content, it was made too recently to satisfy any of the above mentioned criteria. The Treasure Act does, however, provide that any object which would have been treasure trove had it been found before the Act came into force is treasure within the meaning of the Act. Under the law of treasure trove, even a relatively modern object can comprise treasure trove provided it is substantially of gold or silver (which appears to mean at least 50 per cent: *A-G for the Duchy of Lancaster v G. E. Overton (Farms) Ltd* [1982] Ch 277). It must also be impossible to identify the true owner, and the object must not have been lost or abandoned; rather it must have been hidden by the true owner with the intention of retrieving it at some later date. The court may draw an inference from surrounding circumstances: *Overton (Farms)* case. The unusual location of the ashtray may suggest that it was hidden with a view to being retrieved. The Crown's title to treasure may, however, be disclaimed at any time, in which case the treasure may be delivered to any person in accordance with the Code of Practice: s. 6. Even if the ashtray ranks as treasure trove at common law, and therefore as treasure under the new Act, as it is a modern object the Crown's title to it is likely to be disclaimed. Since Crafty was both a trespasser and a dishonest finder, it is unlikely that the ashtray, following a disclaimer, would be delivered to him.

Assuming that the ashtray is not treasure, the next issue is to identify who has the best title to it. Crafty was a trespasser on the land and, since he took no steps to trace the true owner, was also dishonest. He will not therefore be able to assert a prior title: *Hibbert v McKiernan* [1948] 2 KB 142. Indeed, he may be subject to a criminal prosecution for theft. Noel will have a claim to the ashtray as lessee and occupier of the land on which it was found.

Dorothy may argue that she has a prior title as freehold owner. In ***Elwes v Brigg Gas Co.* (1886) 33 ChD 562**, the tenant for life was held to have a prior title to the prehistoric boat found by his lessees. The boat had been in the land before the lease had been granted; the property granted by the lease did not extend to the boat; and the lease itself was for a particular purpose only, namely, for the exploration and extraction of gas.

By contrast, in ***City of London Corporation v Appleyard* [1963] 2 All ER 834**, contractors, hired by lessees in possession to demolish a building, found a wall safe containing a large sum of money in bank notes. The court held that the lessors were not in possession of the notes before they were found; however, on the facts, they were able to assert, as against the lessees, at least a (superior) equitable title because of an express clause in the lease which reserved articles of value to the lessors. But for this clause, the lessees, as the persons in possession of the premises, and so in *de facto* possession of the notes, would have had the better claim. In regard to the general principle, ***Appleyard*** might be distinguished from ***Elwes*** either on the timing of the deposition (which, in ***Appleyard***, must have occurred during the lease) or on the degree of annexation (on the principle that an object buried in the ground is more deeply embedded than one merely lodged in a safe).

Noel's lease will need to be scrutinised for restrictions or reservations such as were contained in the leases in ***Elwes*** or ***Appleyard***. In the absence of any clear term or of any evidence as to the date of the ashtray's deposition, it will be difficult to ascertain which of Noel or Dorothy has the better right to it.

In the absence of any further evidence as to the ownership of the deed box and its contents, the court will apply the presumption that the ownership of land carries with it ownership of the chattels it contains. This principle was applied (to somewhat similar facts) in ***Re Cohen* [1953] Ch 88**, where Vaisey J said (at p. 94) that the principle was 'a straw to be grasped at by the swimmer in this sea of ambiguity'. Since, by virtue of the right of survivorship, Julia acquired the sole legal title to the reversion on Julian's death, she will also be treated as the sole owner of the deed box and its contents. Therefore, upon her death, the box and the money it contains will pass under her will to Dorothy. The charity will receive nothing.

Further reading

Battersby, G. (2002) 65 *MLR* 603 (comment on ***Costello v Derbyshire Chief Constable***).

Harris, D. R., 'The Concept of Possession in English Law', in A. Guest (ed.), *Oxford Essays in Jurisprudence* (First Series), 1961.

Hoath, D., 'Some Conveyancing Implications of "Finding" Disputes' [1990] *Conv* 348.

Smith, R., *Property Law*, 5th edn, Longman Law Series, Pearson Education, 2006, pp. 53–60.

4

Adverse possession

Introduction

The Land Registration Act 2002 has considerably reduced the significance of the doctrine of adverse possession in the system of registered titles; and as that system is rapidly replacing the unregistered system, the importance of adverse possession will diminish rapidly. Although the 2002 Act came into force on 13 October 2003, there are savings provisions for the rights of squatters that had already accrued by that date: LRA 2002, Schedule 12, para. 18(1). However, if your course covers adverse possession, it is likely that, in the context of registered land, you will be expected to know the position under the 2002 Act only. If appropriate, any problem question on your examination paper may expressly state that candidates are to assume that the Land Registration Act 2002 has been in force at all relevant times.

Proof of title under the unregistered system depends on an examination of the title deeds, as well as on the making of various searches and an inspection of the land. There is a much greater risk with an unregistered title that it might be found to be subject to rights which cannot be discovered by any of these means. Title to unregistered land is relative (as it is in relation to finders' titles to chattels). In this context, the system of limitation of actions for the possession of land operates to safeguard such titles. It may be, for instance, that the title derives from somebody in the past who was in adverse possession of the land, and this fact may not even be discoverable if the act of adverse possession lies behind the root of title. In practice, it is likely that any title claimed by the previously dispossessed paper owner will have become statute-barred. In the unregistered system, the barring of titles by limitation therefore acts as a sort of guarantee of title to a person who has been (or who acquires title from someone who has been) in possession for a long period. One of the merits of this system is that it protects long user and defeats claims that have become stale. In some ways, adverse possession might be considered the cornerstone of the unregistered system.

In the registered system, by contrast, title is obtained, not by possession, but by registration, and such registered title is backed by a state guarantee. There is therefore less need for the doctrine of adverse possession in registered titles. Nevertheless, before the coming into force of the relevant parts of the Land Registration Act 2002, the registered land system contained in the Land Registration Act 1925 broadly reflected the position in unregistered titles, which implicitly recognises that there are other merits in the doctrine (notably the barring of stale claims) that justified its retention in registered titles.

For quite a number of years, however, there had been concern at the way the doctrine had operated, and there was particular concern following several cases in which squatters managed to bar the titles of local authorities to valuable properties, with a consequent loss of public assets (*Ellis v Lambeth LBC* (1999) The Times 28 September 1999; *Lambeth LBC v Blackburn* (2001) 82 P & CR 494). Some considered this to be effectively legalised theft, and there was pressure to change the law of adverse possession. Reform proposals were put forward by the Law Commission in its report, *Land Registration for the Twenty-First Century: a Conveyancing Revolution*, Law Com. No. 271 (2001), and were enacted in the Land Registration Act 2002.

The 2002 Act effectively draws the teeth on the doctrine of adverse possession in registered titles by permitting the squatter to apply for an initial registration after ten years, which application will (unless the registered owner fails to serve a counter-notice) succeed only if one of three conditions is met. In essence, the three conditions (set out in para. 5 of Schedule 6 to the Land Registration Act 2002) are:

(1) where the squatter has an equity by estoppel so that it would be unconscionable of the registered proprietor to dispossess the squatter, and in the circumstances the squatter ought to be registered;

(2) where the squatter is for some other reason entitled to be registered as the proprietor; or

(3) where the squatter owns the land adjacent to the disputed land, and reasonably believed during the period of adverse possession that the land belonged to him.

Although the precise scope of these circumstances must await judicial interpretation, they seem to be narrowly drawn. Most applications are therefore likely to be refused. In the event of a refusal, the squatter then has to wait a further two years before being able to apply for registration of title as of right. The hammer-blow to adverse possession lies in the fact that, on the squatter's first application for registration, the Land Registry will notify the registered owner and anyone else affected; the result is to wake up the registered owner to the need to act to prevent the squatter gaining title by adverse possession, and the registered owner has two years in which to do so.

Question 1

In 1989, Len leased a plot of land in Lancaster called Greenacre (the title to which is unregistered) to Tim for a term of 39 years at a premium of £50,000. The lease contains (*inter alia*) covenants by Tim as follows:

(a) to pay an annual ground rent of £20;

(b) not to part with possession of Greenacre; and

(c) not to build any dwelling house on Greenacre.

In 1994, Adrian entered into adverse possession of Greenacre. He was, however, dispossessed in 2004, by Sue, who has remained in possession of Greenacre since that date. Tim continued to pay the ground rent under the lease until last year, but the rent is presently £20 in arrears. Sue intends to build a house on Greenacre, and has already obtained planning permission for this purpose.

Len wishes, if possible, to regain possession of Greenacre in order to grant a fresh lease of it to Tim. If he cannot achieve that, he wishes at least to prevent Sue from building the dwelling house. Adrian cannot, at present, be traced.

(a) Advise Len.

(b) How (if at all) would your advice differ if the leasehold title to Greenacre were registered? You should assume that the relevant provisions of the **Land Registration Act 2002** have been in force at all relevant times.

Commentary

This question involves an analysis of the legal position where an adverse possessor is squatting upon land subject to a lease, both where the title is unregistered and where it is registered. Whilst this may appear to be a somewhat narrow point, it does in fact involve a discussion of fundamental principles of property law. The central case to be discussed in part **(a)** is ***Fairweather v St Marylebone Property Co Ltd*** **[1963] AC 510**.

It is to be noted that, although the question is one on adverse possession, it also demands some knowledge of other areas: a basic knowledge of leases, some particular knowledge of restrictive covenants, and an understanding of the application of the principles of registered land. All these topics throw additional light on the problem. It will therefore be clear that, if you miss out a topic which you have been taught, you reduce your basic understanding of land law as a whole, and this could reduce (even if only slightly) your ability to produce a good answer to a question on a topic which you have revised.

It should be remembered that a restrictive covenant in a lease is not registrable as a land charge under the **Land Charges Act 1972**. The doctrine of the *bona fide* purchaser therefore applies; and a squatter (such as Sue) will be bound by such a covenant since a squatter acquires title not by purchase (in the technical legal sense) but by operation of law. Similarly, an adverse possessor of *freehold* land, not being a 'purchaser' within the **Land Charges Act 1972, s. 4(6)**, will take subject to a restrictive covenant even if it is not protected by registration.

Part **(b)** calls for a comparison with the position in registered land. Before the **2002 Act** came into force, upon the completion of the period of adverse possession against him, the registered owner held the estate in trust for the squatter until the latter was registered (by having the title transferred into his name). This meant that if the tenant in the meantime surrendered the lease to the landlord, the landlord would itself merely hold the registered leasehold estate in trust for the squatter. The **2002 Act** has abolished the mechanism of the trust in this context. It therefore seems that the landlord and tenant can now collusively defeat the squatter by the tenant's surrendering the lease before the squatter has secured registration. In this respect, the **2002 Act** produces a result similar to that which was held to apply to unregistered titles in the ***Fairweather*** case.

Answer plan

(a) Unregistered title

- Adding together Adrian and Sue's adverse possession.
- Only Tim's title is barred, not Len's.
- Len's right to forfeit for breach of covenant.
- Sue has no right to relief from forfeiture (***Tickner v Buzzacott***).
- Effect of a surrender by Tim (***Fairweather***).
- Restrictive covenant binds Sue.

(b) Registered title

- Sue may apply for registration after ten years.
- Sue's application likely to be refused.
- Tim receives notice of application.
- Sue cannot make final application for further two years.
- In that period, Tim can regain possession or surrender lease.
- Adrian's title barred by 12 years' adverse possession by Sue.

Suggested answer

(a) Where, as in this problem, land which is adversely possessed is subject to a lease, the Limitation Act 1980, s. 15(1), operates, at the end of 12 years, to bar the title of the tenant. It would appear that the leasehold estate in Greenacre has been adversely possessed for such a period, because in unregistered titles an adverse possessor is permitted to add the period of adverse possession of the person whom he dispossesses (*Willis v Earl Howe* [1893] 2 Ch 545). Thus, the period of adverse possession, which was begun by Adrian in 1994, was continued by Sue, so that Tim's title was barred in 2006. If Adrian were to be traced, he would be able to bring an action for possession against Sue, since, although his period of adverse possession was merely ten years, his possession was prior in time to hers (*Asher v Whitlock* (1865) LR 1 QB 1). This would not, however, avail Tim, since his title, once barred in 2006, cannot be subsequently revived. Any action by Adrian would itself be barred 12 years after his dispossession by Sue, i.e. in 2016.

The title of the landlord, Len, is not barred, however, unless the adverse possession continues for 12 years after the expiration of the lease (**Limitation Act 1980, Schedule 1, para. 4**), which has not yet occurred. By the same token, however, until Tim's lease comes to an end, Len is not entitled to bring an action for possession against Sue. This is because the statute bars the tenant's title only as regards the adverse possessor; *vis-à-vis* the landlord, the tenant's lease continues.

Thus it would seem that Sue has acquired, through 12 years' adverse possession, a legal freehold estate in Greenacre, despite the possibility of its being brought to an end by Len's exercise of any right of re-entry contained in Tim's lease (**Law of Property Act 1925, s. 7**). If, therefore, Len is to gain possession of Greenacre immediately, he must seek to terminate the lease. If (as will usually be the case) the lease contains a right of re-entry for breach of covenant, Len may be able to forfeit the lease for existing breaches. He will not, however, be able to effect a forfeiture for the breach of the covenant against parting with possession for two reasons: first, by accepting rent from Tim after Adrian went into adverse possession, he has waived the right to forfeit for that breach; secondly, since the breach occurred more than 12 years ago, the statute has itself barred any right of action based on that breach (**Limitation Act 1980, s. 15(1)**, and **Schedule 1, Pt I, para. 7(1)**).

Len may, however, bring an action for forfeiture against Tim for breach of the covenant to pay rent. Since Tim's title has already been barred by Sue, there is no reason for him to defend the action: on the contrary, the termination of the lease will be to his advantage in ending his own continuing liability under it. Although there seems to be no reason why the adverse possessor should not be entitled to pay the rent on the tenant's behalf (see Wade (1962) 78 *LQR* 541), the rent in the problem is already in arrears. Len may therefore be able to forfeit on this ground. It has been held, moreover, that an adverse possessor of a leasehold title, lacking privity of estate with the landlord, is not entitled to claim relief from forfeiture (***Tickner v Buzzacott* [1965] Ch 426**). Thus, relief is not available to a squatter under the **Common Law Procedure Act 1852, ss. 210–212**, since the squatter cannot claim under the lease.

If, however, the lease in the question contains no such proviso for re-entry, Len may still be able to terminate the lease by accepting a surrender from Tim. The House of Lords has held that a surrender by the tenant gives the landlord the right to immediate possession, thereby accelerating his right of action against the adverse possessor (***Fairweather v St Marylebone Property Co Ltd* [1963] AC 510** (criticised, however, by Wade, above, on the ground that it offends the maxim, *nemo dat quod non habet*)). An alternative possibility would be for Tim to purchase Len's reversion, and thereby bring the lease to an end through the doctrine of merger.

If Len cannot use any of these methods to terminate the lease, he will be unable to gain possession of Greenacre from Sue. Furthermore, since the statute does not transfer Tim's title to Sue, who has her own independent title to Greenacre, there is no privity of estate between Len and Sue. Therefore, Len cannot bring an action against Sue for the rent. Len can, however, sue Tim, who remains liable to pay the rent and to observe and perform the leasehold covenants even after his title is barred in 2006.

Sue will, however, be subject to the leasehold covenant against building. Such a covenant, being restrictive in nature, is enforceable in equity against anyone coming to the land other than a *bona fide* purchaser of the legal estate without notice. Sue cannot establish this defence since an adverse possessor does not take by purchase (***Re Nisbet and Potts' Contract*** **[1905] 1 Ch 391**). Len can, therefore, obtain injunctive relief to restrain Sue from building.

(b) If the title to the land were registered, the position would be different. The period of limitation under the **Limitation Act 1980, s. 15**, does not run against a person in respect of an estate in land the title to which is registered: **LRA 2002, s. 96(1)**. At the end of ten years' adverse possession, Sue may apply to be registered as proprietor of Tim's lease: **LRA 2002, Schedule 6, para. 1(1)**. The registrar must give notice of such application to both Tim and (if the freehold title is also registered) Len: ibid., **para. 2**. Unless Tim and Len fail to serve a counter-notice, Sue's application must satisfy any of the conditions set out in **para. 5**. The first condition applies only where there is an estoppel, and the third only where there is a boundary dispute, neither of which is relevant to Sue. It is also difficult to see how Sue could rely on the second condition, namely that she is 'for some other reason entitled to be registered'. Assuming that none of these conditions is satisfied, Sue's application will be rejected.

If Sue remains in adverse possession, she will be entitled to make a further application two years after such rejection (**para. 6(1)**). In practice, however, it is likely that Tim, having been notified by the Land Registry of Sue's initial application, will bring an action for possession before Sue can remain in adverse possession for the additional two-year period.

If Sue remains in adverse possession for a further two years after the rejection of her initial application, she becomes entitled to be registered as proprietor on making such further application (**para. 7**). The onus is on Sue to apply for registration. If Tim brings an action for possession against her before she has applied for registration, she cannot make such application during the proceedings (ibid., **para. 6(2)(a)**). Alternatively, there would be nothing to stop Tim from surrendering his lease to Len before Sue makes such application, thereby enabling Len to bring an action for possession.

The foregoing presupposes, however, that Sue can establish an initial period of ten years' adverse possession in order to make a first application. The **Land Registration Act 2002** enables a squatter who is a successor in title to add her predecessor's period of adverse possession to her own for this purpose (ibid., **para. 11(2)(a)**). This does not, however, enable Sue to add the prior period of adverse possession of Adrian, since she is not his successor in title, but rather is in adverse possession against his title. This is different from the position in unregistered titles (***Willis v Earl Howe***). Sue's ten-year period against Tim therefore runs only from 2004, not from 1994. Sue cannot therefore make her first application for registration until 2014. Moreover, even if Sue were to apply in 2014, her application would probably be rejected, so Tim would still be able to obtain possession against her for the following two years (or even during any longer period if she has not by then made a further application for registration).

Since Adrian does not have a registered title, Sue will bar Adrian's title after twelve years' adverse possession against Adrian (i.e. in 2016).

Question 2

In November 1991, Squirrel, whose garden adjoined a plot of waste land, decided to make use of it for his own benefit. By the end of that year, he had levelled the plot, made a path across it, constructed flower beds, laid a lawn, and put up a child's swing. From that time, Squirrel and his family used the plot as part of their own garden. In 1993, Squirrel fenced the plot off from the surrounding land on all sides, except where it adjoined his garden.

The fee simple owner of the plot, the title to which was unregistered, was Nutkin Ltd (Nutkin). The company soon became aware of Squirrel's use of the plot, but took no steps to remove him, because it intended to develop the plot in due course as a housing estate, when the requisite planning permission could be obtained, and it therefore had no use for the plot at the time. In 2002, Nutkin wrote to Squirrel indicating that it was treating Squirrel as a licensee of the plot, and inviting him to enter into a licence agreement. Squirrel did not reply. Last year, Nutkin, who had just obtained planning permission to build, again wrote to Squirrel stating that it was terminating the licence agreement. Squirrel wrote back saying: 'Tough luck—I'm claiming squatter's rights.' Following receipt of this letter, Nutkin brought proceedings against Squirrel for possession of the plot.

(a) Advise Squirrel.

(b) How would your advice differ if the title to the plot had been registered?

Commentary

When the court is determining whether a title has been barred by adverse possession, it is generally engaged in an application of the legal principles to a complex set of facts. A range of different acts may have been performed on the land, and whether they amount to acts of adverse possession depends on their combined impact. Since law and fact are here intertwined, it is probable that your lectures on this topic will go through the facts of some of the cases in a fair amount of detail. The student must however appreciate that the cases turn on their own particular facts, and that a holding that a specified act in a given set of circumstances comprises an act of adverse possession does not mean that such an act will inevitably be held to have the same effect in a later case.

At each stage of the answer, the law is related to the facts of the problem. There is a tentative conclusion based on an application of the law to the totality of the facts supplied. No definite answer is, however, possible, since too much turns on the interpretation of the facts and the inferences which may be drawn from them. The examiner will expect a clear statement of the relevant law and an application of the law to the facts given. It is, however, quite likely that the facts of an examination problem on adverse possession will be capable of more than one interpretation. If this is so, you should point this out, and not try to suggest that there is only one possible answer. To do so may indicate a failure to appreciate a basic principle—the difference between law and fact.

In ***J.A. Pye (Oxford) Ltd v UK* (2008) 46 EHRR 45**, the Grand Chamber of the European Court of Human Rights (ECtHR) was asked to determine whether the English law of adverse possession under the **Land Registration Act 1925** breached Article 1 of the First Protocol to the European Convention on Human Rights (ECHR). As Lord Neuberger recently explained in the House of Lords in ***Ofulue v Bossert* (2009)** (at para. 68), the Grand Chamber decided that, whilst Article 1 was engaged, the statute fell within the margin of appreciation afforded to the UK government. The decision of the House of Lords in ***J.A. Pye (Oxford) Ltd v Graham* [2003] 1 AC 419** on the meaning of adverse possession is therefore good law, and was applied by the House of Lords in the ***Ofulue*** case. Although ***Pye*** involved adverse possession under the **Land Registration Act 1925**, there is no reason why the meaning of adverse possession laid down by the House of Lords in that case should not apply also to claims brought under the **Land Registration Act 2002**.

If, in part **(b)** of the problem, Squirrel had completed 12 years' adverse possession before 13 October 2003, this being the date that the **LRA 2002** came into force, he might have been able to claim under the **LRA 1925**, which provides that, at the end of the period of adverse possession, the registered proprietor holds the title in trust for the squatter. On the facts, however, because 12 years' adverse possession had not been completed before that date, the applicable statute is the **LRA 2002**. The new regime is so tough for squatters that few cases falling outside the three special circumstances set out in **para. 5 to Sch. 6** are likely to succeed. In practice, most well-advised squatters will prefer to sit tight, rather than risk eviction by serving an initial application for registration. What this means is that there will be cases in the future where adverse possessors will have been on land for decades without having acquired the title against which they are squatting. It might become increasingly difficult for courts to resist the conclusion that an action by the registered proprietor against such persons infringes **Article 8 of the ECHR**. Alternatively, future courts might extend the doctrine of proprietary estoppel to these sorts of circumstances, although it is clear that the present requirements for an estoppel would not be met by long use alone.

Answer plan

(a) Unregistered title

- Act of adverse possession:
  - status of ***Leigh v Jack***;
  - impact of **Article 1 to First Protocol ECHR**: ***Beaulane***.

- Intention to possess (*animus*).
- Unilateral express licence:
  - impact of **Article 1 to First Protocol ECHR**: ***Pye v UK***.
- Possible impact of **Article 8 ECHR**: ***Connor v UK***; ***Leeds CC v Price***.

(b) Registered title

- Regime under **LRA 2002**.
- Possible impact of **Article 8** (as in (a)).

Suggested answer

(a) Squirrel will be unable to resist Nutkin's action for possession unless he can establish that he has acquired a title by adverse possession and that Nutkin's right to possession has been barred by the Limitation Act 1980. The period of limitation cannot, in any event, begin to run unless and until Nutkin was either dispossessed or discontinued possession of the plot, and Squirrel took adverse possession of it. For possession to be adverse, two elements must be present: first, Squirrel must have taken exclusive possession of the plot without Nutkin's consent; secondly, Squirrel must establish that he had the necessary *animus possidendi* (intention to possess).

The acts that are sufficient for adverse possession vary with the circumstances of each case. In the House of Lords, in *J.A. Pye (Oxford) Ltd v Graham* [2003] 1 P & CR 10, 140, Lord Browne-Wilkinson approved a statement of Slade J in *Powell v Macfarlane* (1977) 38 P & CR 452, at pp. 470–1, that what has to be shown as constituting factual possession 'is that the alleged possessor has been dealing with the land in question as an occupying owner might have been expected to deal with it and that no-one else has done so'. What acts constitute adverse possession depend (*inter alia*) on the character and value of the property and the uses to which it can be put (*Lord Advocate v Lord Lovat* (1880) 5 App Cas 273). Thus, in *Red House Farms (Thorndon) Ltd v Catchpole* (1976) 244 Estates Gazette 295, the mere act of shooting rabbits on marshy land (which could be used for little else) was held enough. By contrast, in *Tecbild v Chamberlain* (1969) 20 P & CR 633, the playing of children and the tethering of ponies were held, in the circumstances, too trivial to amount to acts of adverse possession. Similarly, in *Boosey v Davis* (1987) 55 P & CR 83, the grazing of goats on land that could (subject to planning permission) be developed, was held insufficient: the quality and quantity of such acts were minimal. The growing of vegetables on the land and the erection of sheds for breeding greyhounds were held to be inadequate in *Williams v Raftery* [1958] 1 QB 159. Acts that change the nature or potential use of the land, however, are likely to suffice (*Treloar v Nute* [1976] 1 WLR 1295–infilling of a gully).

Since the land in the question is capable of being developed, it is unlikely that the placing of the swing (which can presumably be easily removed), the planting of flowers, or the laying of a lawn, can be considered anything more than trivial acts. The levelling of the plot, however, indicates some change in the nature of the land and this act may be more significant, depending on how extensive such alterations were. Fencing off the land is generally considered the strongest act of adverse possession (***George Wimpey & Co Ltd v Sohn* [1967] Ch 487; *Williams v Usherwood* (1983) 45 P & CR 235**).

The next issue is whether the fact that Nutkin had a future intention to develop the plot and had no use for it at the time prevents Squirrel's possession from being adverse. In ***Beaulane Properties Ltd v Palmer* [2006] Ch 79**, the judge interpreted the expression 'adverse possession' in the statute narrowly so as to revive the doctrine of ***Leigh v Jack* (1879) 5 Ex D 264**: namely, that there can be no dispossession of the paper owner unless the squatter's acts are inconsistent with the purpose for which the paper owner intends to use the land. That doctrine had been condemned as wrong by the House of Lords in the ***Pye*** case (above); but when the ***Pye*** case was considered by the Lower Chamber of the ECtHR, it was held that the English law of adverse possession under the **Land Registration Act 1925** was incompatible with **Article 1 to the First Protocol: (2006) 43 EHRR 3**. In the light of this, the judge in the ***Beaulane*** case considered it appropriate to adopt (in accordance with **s 3, Human Rights Act 1998**) an ECHR-compatible interpretation of the statute by reviving ***Leigh v Jack***. Shortly after ***Beaulane***, however, the Grand Chamber of the ECtHR reversed the lower Chamber in ***Pye***, and held that the English law of adverse possession in the case did not breach the Convention: **(2008) 46 EHRR 45**. This swept away the rationale for the interpretation of 'adverse possession' in ***Beaulane***. As the English law of adverse possession is in this respect Convention-compliant, there is no reason for a court to apply ***Beaulane*** in future. It is therefore highly unlikely that ***Beaulane*** will be followed; indeed it was recently disapproved of by the Court of Appeal in ***Ofulue v Bossert* [2009] Ch 1**, and no argument based on it was raised when ***Ofulue*** went on appeal to the House of Lords: [2009] UKHL 16. Nutkin's future intention to develop cannot therefore prevent Squirrel's possession from being adverse.

The *animus* required of an adverse possessor is merely an intention to possess. In the ***Pye*** case, the House of Lords rejected the notion that the intention to possess must be to the exclusion of all others including the true owner (which had been laid down in ***Littledale v Liverpool College* [1900] 1 Ch 19**). The court will require clear evidence that the trespasser had not merely an intention to possess, but made such intention clear to the whole world: ***Powell v Macfarlane*** (above). In most instances, the intention of the occupier will need to be inferred from his acts. In the problem, the act of fencing is probably sufficient to indicate the requisite *animus*.

Nutkin might argue that there was no adverse possession at any time on the basis that it should be assumed, from the fact that it had a future intended use for the land and that Squirrel's occupation was not inconsistent with such intended use, that Squirrel was in occupation with its permission. Such doctrine of implied licence emerged in ***Wallis's Cayton Bay Holiday Camp Ltd v Shell-Mex & BP Ltd* [1975] QB 94**, but the effect of the decision itself was reversed by para. 8(4) of Sch. 1 of the Limitation Act 1980, which provides that an implied licence is not to be assumed by implication of law from such circumstances alone. This leaves open the possibility that Nutkin could argue that permission is to be inferred from other evidence in the case. In the problem, even if the possession were initially adverse, such other evidence might be that Nutkin wrote to Squirrel in 2002 stating that it was treating him as a licensee.

Nutkin's writing to Squirrel looks, however, more like an attempt to create an express licence. Had Squirrel accepted the offer of a licence, any adverse possession would have stopped immediately—but he did not do so. The issue is therefore whether Nutkin can unilaterally turn Squirrel into a licensee. This point was considered for the first time in *BP Properties Ltd v Buckler* (1987) 55 P & CR 337, where the Court of Appeal held that a unilateral licence communicated to the erstwhile adverse possessor had this effect, whether the recipient liked it or not. The court expressed the view that the result might have been different if the adverse possessor had written back contesting the licence. Although the principle in the *Buckler* case has been subject to academic criticism (see Wallace [1994] *Conv* 196), it was treated as sound after a detailed analysis in the implied licence case of *Colin Dawson Windows Ltd v King's Lynn, West Norfolk BC* [2005] 2 P & CR 19 (CA), and Hart J was happy to rely on it for additional support in *Clowes Developments (UK) Ltd v Walters* [2006] 1 P & CR 1.

If Squirrel were to fail to establish that he had barred Nutkin's title under the Limitation Act, he might still argue that, by enabling Nutkin to evict him without just cause after he has been in occupation (whether adverse or under a licence) for so many years, English domestic law breaches the right to respect for his home and family life under Article 8 of the ECHR.

In *Connor v UK* (2004) 40 EHRR 189, Connor and his family had lived as licensees on a local authority gypsy site for 16 years when, following allegations that their behaviour had breached the terms of the licence, they were given notice to quit. The local authority dropped the complaints of misbehaviour, but nevertheless brought proceedings for possession, and, after the order was made, forcibly evicted Connor and his family from the site. Although the claim for possession had no defence under English law, the ECtHR held that the rights of Connor under Article 8 had been breached. Although it was agreed in the case that the interference had a legitimate aim, the court took account of the fact that no misbehaviour had been relied upon and that gypsies were a vulnerable minority. In *Leeds City Council v Price* [2006] UKHL 10, the House of Lords was able to distinguish *Connor* on the ground that the gypsies in the case before them had entered the land as trespassers and had been there only a few weeks before the local authority evicted them.

The decision in *Doherty v Birmingham City Council* [2008] UKHL 57 was also a case concerning the right of gypsies to remain on land they had occupied as their home. In *Doherty*, the gypsies had occupied the land under a licence for 17 years when the council served notice to recover possession in order to carry out essential improvement works. The House of Lords considered that the statutory framework was defective in that it did not provide safeguards for the travellers and Doherty was granted leave to apply for judicial review. In *Manchester City Council v Pinnock* [2010] UKSC 45, the Supreme Court held that this test was too narrow and that if the claimant raises Article 8, the court must consider proportionality.

Squirrel's position in the problem seems to fall between that of the applicants in *Connor* and in *Price*. Squirrel initially entered onto the plot as a trespasser, but the registered proprietor purported to grant him a licence, and he has been occupying the plot for many years. Nevertheless, it seems unlikely that Squirrel would succeed under Article 8. First, it is doubtful whether the plot amounts to a 'home', because it has merely been an addition to Squirrel's garden. Secondly, Article 8(2) prohibits interference by a public authority with the exercise of the right, and it has been said that the aim of Article 8 is to protect a person against the arbitrary acts of a public authority: *Kroon v Netherlands* (1994) 9 ECHR 263. In seeking to evict Squirrel from its land, Nutkin is not acting as a public authority, so Article 8 would not appear to be engaged. On the other hand, the court is a public authority, and so the judge hearing the case is obliged to abide by Convention rights. If this means that the courts must apply Article 8 in cases where the person bringing the possession action is not a public authority, the Article would have horizontal effect. Surprisingly, it is still unclear under Strasbourg jurisprudence whether Convention rights can operate in this way. Thirdly, unlike the gypsies in *Connor* and *Doherty*, Squirrel's status as occupier of the plot is not that of a member of a minority in need of special protection. An argument based on Article 8 on the facts of the problem is therefore probably one of last resort.

(b) If the title to the plot of waste ground had been registered, Squirrel's position would be much weaker. Even if the acts of adverse possession began at the earliest date, November 1991, Squirrel (assuming he has the necessary *animus possidendi*) cannot establish 12 years' adverse possession before 13 October 2003, being the date on which the relevant provisions of the LRA 2002 came into force. Any claim he has to adverse possession cannot, therefore, be based on the regime in the LRA 1925, but only under the (for him) harsher regime of the LRA 2002. Under the 2002 Act, an adverse possessor cannot bar the title of the registered owner unless he complies with the procedure that the Act specifies: LRA 2002, ss. 96–8 and Sch. 6. If Squirrel has completed ten years' adverse possession, he can apply to the Land Registry for registration. As he does not fall within one of the three exceptional circumstances set out in para. 5 to Sch. 6, he will not obtain immediate registration. Instead, the Land Registry will inform the registered proprietor of the application, who will no doubt, in the vast majority of cases, object. If exceptionally the registered proprietor does not object within the requisite period (approximately three months), the applicant will be registered in its place; in which event, in order to regain its legal estate, the former registered proprietor will have to establish a ground for rectification, as in *Baxter v Mannion* [2010] EWHC 573 (Ch). Assuming, however, it objects within that period, the registered proprietor will not lose its title at this stage; rather it has a further two years in which to evict the squatter. If the squatter has not been evicted within such additional period, he may apply a second time to be registered as proprietor, and this time the registered owner's title will be transferred to the squatter. However, as Squirrel has not made even an initial application to the Land Registry to set the final two-year period rolling, he will be unable to rely on adverse possession to resist Nutkin's action for possession. Furthermore, as was considered in part **(a)**, a defence based on Article 8 is unlikely to succeed.

Further reading

Mackenzie, J. A., and Phillips, M., *Textbook on Land Law*, 12th edn, Oxford University Press, 2008, chapter 6.

Wade, H. W. R., 'Landlord, Tenant and Squatter' (1962) 78 *LQR* 541.

5

Transfer of title and third party rights

Introduction

The property legislation of 1925 laid the foundation of our present system of land law. It comprised six statutes. The four most concerned with land law were the Law of Property Act, the Settled Land Act, the Land Charges Act and the Land Registration Act (LRA). The Land Charges Act 1925 was replaced by the Land Charges Act 1972; the Act applies only to unregistered title and so has an ever-diminishing application as the title to most land is now registered. After the Trusts of Land and Appointment of Trustees Act 1996 (TLATA) came into effect on 1 January 1997, no new settlements can be made under the Settled Land Act, although it will continue to apply to existing pre-1997 settlements. The Act also abolished trusts for sale under the Law of Property Act 1925 and all such trusts became trusts of land under TLATA from 1 January 1997.

The reforms effected by the legislation were sweeping; it envisaged the registration of title to all land and an entirely new system of conveyancing. This all took much longer than originally planned and registration of title only became compulsory for all areas of England and Wales in 1990. Third party interests over the land, and rights enjoyed for the benefit of the land, were to be entered on the register as far as possible so that a purchaser would know about them, and these registrable interests were extended by the Land Registration Act 2002. The Land Registration Act 1925 provided however that certain interests (overriding interests) should be binding on a purchaser of the land in any event. These were listed in s. 70(1) LRA 1925 and much of the litigation arising on registered titles has been on the interpretation and application of these interests. The LRA 2002 extends registrable estates and interests considerably and reduces correspondingly the number and nature of overriding interests (now set out in Schedule 3, para. 2 of the LRA 2002). It also provides for electronic conveyancing eventually, and certain types of application to change the register can already be lodged electronically. Information can be found in Practice Guide 71 (March 2010) on the Land Registry website. The list includes at the moment changes of name on marriage and changes of address, the entry and removal of restrictions, notice and cancellation of home rights and an application to enter someone on the register who requires notice of any application for a title by adverse possession. All this will of course speed up the transfer of title. However, it is not the transfer of title to land which is the main cause of delay in conveyancing transactions. Before committing themselves to a purchase, a purchaser will want to know about planning consents and local land charges, they will probably require a mortgage to finance the purchase, and the purchase may be dependent upon a sale of their existing property and any or all of these matters may cause a delay.

Many of the overriding interests (originally contained in s. 70 LRA 1925) are now binding on a purchaser only if they are protected by the relevant entry on the register, and the new list of overriding interests in Schedule 3, para. 2, LRA 2002 is very much depleted. Where an interest is capable of entry on the register however, its registration is essential if it is to bind a purchaser of the land, and it will only be binding if it is so registered unless it can be brought within one of the overriding interests listed in Schedule 3, para. 2.

Electronic transfer of title will entail simultaneous completion and registration of a transaction (thus avoiding the 'registration gap') and it will be possible to view the progress of all connected transactions in a chain. The LRA 2002 therefore makes changes which bring registered title nearer to its ultimate goal of the register being a 'mirror' of the title which contains all that a purchaser needs to know. The substantive registration of leases is extended to leases of over seven years (and will eventually extend to all leases exceeding three years); legal easements expressly created or reserved in a transfer of land are 'registrable dispositions' and must be entered on the register, and the Limitation Act no longer applies. The overriding interests contained in s. 70(1) LRA 1925 are therefore much diminished or removed in Schedule 3, para. 2, LRA 2002 and many of them must be entered on the register in order to bind a purchaser. Although electronic conveyancing will not be introduced for some time yet, the sections dealing with the other matters came into force in October 2003. All the questions in this chapter therefore consider the position in registered title under the 2002 Act.

Question 1 in this chapter takes an overall view of the main simplifications effected by the 1925 legislation. Question 2 considers the extent to which the old equitable doctrine of notice has, in practice, been eradicated in the new system. Although there can be little doubt that it was the intention of the legislature to expunge this equitable doctrine in the context of registered land (with one notable exception), the doctrine's influence can be detected in many difficult decisions, including an important one in the House of Lords. The attraction of the doctrine is its basic fairness, which a system based entirely on registration may lack.

Question 3 is a question which looks more generally at property legislation, and in particular at the formality requirements for the transfer of land; it contrasts these with the case law and the influence and developments of equity.

Questions 4 and 5 show how, in practice, encumbrances may, or may not, bind a purchaser of land. Both questions deal with this in registered and unregistered title a common form of examination instruction although presumably now most courses will give more emphasis to registered title.

Question 6 considers the requirements for a valid and enforceable contract to sell land under the **Law of Property (Miscellaneous Provisions) Act 1989**, and some of the cases in which the courts have had to interpret the statute.

The legislation underpinning property law is an important area which, if you are to understand and enjoy the intellectual challenges of land law, you must get to grips with at a fairly early stage of your studies. Together with basic common law concepts such as the doctrine of estates and possession, it is the foundation and structure upon which the whole edifice of land law is built. Once this has been conquered, however, the rest of the edifice will slot into place like pieces in a jigsaw puzzle, so you should have no further very serious problems with the subject. Failure to understand the basic structure of the legislation, though, could leave you with pieces of the puzzle fitting badly, or perhaps never at all.

Question 1

The object of all property legislation is to ensure that a purchaser of land obtains a good title easily and cheaply, whilst at the same time providing protection for third party rights in the land. Consider how property legislation has sought to achieve this, and how successful it has been.

Commentary

This question looks at the statutory structure of our property and conveyancing system, the foundation of which was the 1925 legislation. There have been statutory amendments and judicial modifications, the most fundamental being the **Trusts of Land and Appointment of Trustees Act 1996** (**TLATA**) and the **Land Registration Act 2002**, but the structure remains basically the same. For a proper understanding of land law, you need to understand the underlying objectives of the legislation. The **LRA 2002** brings the system of registered title nearer to the ultimate goal of the **LRA 1925** that the register should be a mirror of the title which contains all that a purchaser needs to know.

To answer the question well, you will need to have a very brief knowledge of certain aspects of property law before the legislation. However, most land law courses and textbooks will include some reference to these, which assist in understanding our present day system.

The question can be considered very much in conjunction with Question 2 in this chapter, as equitable notice was a central problem which the 1925 legislation had to address. Many of the social factors mentioned in the introduction to Question 2 are also relevant to the second part of this question how successful has the legislation been? Its inadequacy in some areas is due to the very changed social background in which we now live.

The **Land Charges Act 1925** was replaced by the **Land Charges Act 1972**, which is itself rapidly becoming redundant as land throughout the whole country is now subject to compulsory registration (speeded up by the **Land Registration Acts 1997 and 2002**).

The **TLATA 1996** provides that equitable beneficial interests in land shall in future take effect behind a trust of land. It has repealed and amended those sections of the **Law of Property Act 1925** which deal with trusts for sale, and prohibits the creation of any new settlements under the **Settled Land Act 1925**.

Answer plan

- The 1925 legislation established a structure to make land more freely alienable whilst also protecting any interests of third persons in the land.
- **Section 1, LPA 1925** reduced estates and interests 'capable of subsisting' at law (although they may also be equitable), necessarily making all other estates and interests equitable. Equitable 'estates' take effect behind a trust of land and are overreached on a disposition by two trustees. They are therefore off the legal title to the land. A purchaser of the land is protected if he gets a receipt for the purchase money from two trustees.
- Equitable interests in unregistered land which attach to the land itself are registrable under the **Land Charges Act 1925** (now **1972**), and registration where applicable replaces the doctrine of notice (**s. 198, LPA**).
- Residual category of equitable interests neither overreachable nor registrable whose binding effect on a purchaser still depends upon the doctrine of notice.
- Simplification of legal title in co-ownership fragmentation of title only in equity.
- Problems with registration of charges under the **Land Charges Act** a 'names' register and cases where search made against the wrong name, reduction in period of title in **LPA 1969** meant a special provision relating to 'actual' notice had to be made (**s. 24, LPA 1969**), and Act has given rise to some fraudulent cases.
- System of registration of title under the **Land Registration Act 1925** everything a purchaser needs to know is on the register. But this principle is distorted by overriding interests and rectification. The extension of registration and reduction in the overriding interests in the **Land Registration Act 2002** should assist in making the register more a 'mirror' of the title.

Suggested answer

The 1925 legislation established a system that has lasted for many years. Its main purpose was to make land more freely alienable and to avoid the necessity for a purchaser to investigate title every time the land changed hands, whilst at the same time affording protection to the owners of equitable interests in the land. The problem in land law is to achieve a balance between the interests of a purchaser (in the broad definition of the Law of Property Act 1925 and including a lessee and a mortgagee) on the one hand, and those of the owner of an equitable interest in the land on the other hand.

In unregistered land, a purchaser was always bound by *legal* estates and interests in the land (rights '*in rem*'), but was not bound by equitable ones if he was a *bona fide* purchaser for value without notice of them (equity's darling).

Because of the reduction in the number of estates which *may* subsist at law to two (Law of Property Act 1925, s. 1(1)), and the number of interests which *may* subsist at law to five (s. 1(2)), there was a drastic reduction in the number of legal estates and interests by which a purchaser would be bound.

The effect of s. 1, Law of Property Act 1925, was inevitably to increase the number of estates and interests which became equitable. The reason for this was to remove these as far as possible from the title to the legal estate which the purchaser is buying. The legal estate is vested in an estate owner, who conveys it to a purchaser, leaving this unencumbered. Certain types of equitable interests which arose under a settlement or a trust for sale (now a trust of land) are overreached by a sale by two trustees. This means that they attach to the proceeds of sale of the land instead of to the land itself. Where this is not possible because the equitable interests are of the type which attach to the land itself (generally commercial interests), they are registrable and a purchaser can discover them by searching the register set up under the Land Charges Act 1925 (now 1972). After 1925, therefore, most equitable interests in land became either overreachable or registrable.

Overreachable interests are the old estates which, because of the Law of Property Act 1925, s. 1(1), became necessarily equitable. These include life estates, fee tails (largely extinct now!), and fee simples which are not absolute, such as conditional and determinable fees, or are not in possession, such as fee simple remainders and reversions. They all have the common feature that they give a right, at some time, to beneficial ownership and occupation of the land. After 1925, such interests could only take effect behind either a trust or a settlement. The Law of Property Act 1925, s. 2(1), provides that they are overreached on a sale of the land, which means that they no longer attach to the land itself, but attach instead to the proceeds of sale of the land. They are protected by the overreaching machinery of the trust of land and the settlement, namely, that a purchaser will not get a good title to the land unless he gets a good receipt for the purchase money from two trustees. This same machinery protects the purchaser also, because if the purchaser complies with the requirement for a receipt from two trustees, he gets a good title to the legal estate, freed from the equitable interests.

The trust of land and settlement allow considerable flexibility of ownership in land, but not at the expense of complicating the title to the legal estate. Wherever land is held on limited forms of ownership (for any estate less than a fee simple absolute in possession), then these now have to take effect behind a trust of land under TLATA 1996. They are off the legal title and are of no concern to a purchaser provided he gets a good receipt from two trustees. The TLATA 1996 (which came into force on 1 January 1997) prohibited the creation of any future settlements under the Settled Land Act 1925 (although the few which do exist continue) and converted all existing trusts for sale under the Law of Property Act 1925 into trusts of land. The basic protection of interests under a trust of land and a settlement, and the protection given to a purchaser, remain, however, the overreaching provisions of s. 2(1), Law of Property Act 1925.

The simplification of title to land is illustrated also by the 1925 provisions for co-ownership. After 1925, only a joint tenancy may subsist at law (s. 34(2), Law of Property Act 1925); and as the right of survivorship applies to this, there can be no fragmentation of the legal title. A purchaser therefore knows that he can take a conveyance of the legal title from the surviving joint tenants. Wherever there is co-ownership of land there is a trust of land and the *equitable* interests of the co-owners may be either a joint tenancy or a tenancy in common, and so may either pass to the surviving co-owners (if a joint tenancy) or to their estates (if a tenancy in common). There were possible hazards for a purchaser in taking a conveyance from only one surviving joint tenant, however, as there could have been a hidden severance of the equitable joint tenancy before the death of the predeceasing joint tenant. The Law of Property (Joint Tenants) Act 1964 therefore provides that a purchaser will get a good title from a single surviving joint tenant if the conveyance specifically states that the vendor is a beneficial owner, and there is no endorsement of a severance on the conveyance to the joint tenants. If the title to the land is registered, a restriction can be entered on the register to warn a purchaser that there is a tenancy in common in equity. The provision of a trust and the overreaching mechanism simplified the legal title to land as far as fragmentation of ownership was concerned, but did not solve the problem for a purchaser of interests in the land which a third party might have. These interests were necessarily equitable after 1925, with the exception of easements and profits and charges over land which may be legal if they comply with the requirements of s.1(2), Law of Property Act 1925, but may also be equitable. Whether an equitable interest was binding on a purchaser or not depended upon the equitable doctrine of notice, which could be hazardous for a purchaser. The Land Charges Act 1925 (now Land Charges Act 1972) made these equitable interests registrable. They include restrictive covenants, equitable easements, estate contracts, options to purchase and general equitable charges. They are protected, in unregistered title, by registration under the Land Charges Act, and a purchaser may search the register to discover these. Registration, where applicable, replaces the old doctrine of notice (s. 198, LPA 1925). Constructive notice was particularly hazardous for a purchaser, as he might find himself bound by an equitable interest which the court decided that he *should have* discovered, even though he had no actual knowledge of it at all. After 1925, the purchaser will be bound only by those registrable interests which are registered irrespective of notice (*Midland Bank Trust Co. v Green* [1981] AC 513).

Even in 1925, the legislation affecting unregistered titles did not cater for all equitable interests, and there was a residual class of equitable interests to which the old doctrine of notice still applied. It was obviously felt to be too onerous a task to register all the old restrictive covenants affecting land, and so the Land Charges Act 1925 provided for registration of only those restrictive covenants and equitable easements created after the legislation came into force on 1 January 1926. Those interests created before that date still depend upon the old doctrine of notice for their validity against a purchaser.

Moreover, a bare trust (where there is a schism of the legal and equitable ownership in land, arising, for example, from a resulting trust) is not protected by the overreaching machinery, which requires two trustees, and its binding effect on a purchaser is again determined by notice in unregistered title.

Since 1925, the equitable doctrine of estoppel has developed considerably, and now the courts recognise proprietary interests created by estoppel. These interests are not registrable as land charges however (see Lord Denning MR in ***E. R. Ives Investment Ltd v High*** **[1967] 2 QB 379**), and so must depend for their validity against a purchaser of unregistered land upon the doctrine of notice. In registered land, the **Land Registration Act 2002, s 116**, states that 'for the avoidance of doubt ... an equity by estoppel ... has effect from the time the equity arises as an interest capable of binding successors in title'. The wording is, however, unclear, and it remains uncertain precisely when an equity by estoppel arises.

The main 'breach' of the 1925 scheme has arisen in hidden co-ownership. Due to changing social circumstances, working wives and cohabitees frequently contribute to the high price of a home. The courts have recognised that such persons may acquire a beneficial equitable interest in the home under a resulting or constructive trust, or both, even though their names do not appear on the legal title. The Law Commission's Report on the implications of ***Williams & Glyn's Bank Ltd v Boland*** **(Law Com. No. 115 (1982))** recommended that co-ownership interests should be made registrable, but this has not been implemented, and it is difficult to see how it could be when such interests are acquired informally, and may often be disputed by the owner of the legal title. However, the decision of the House of Lords in ***Williams & Glyn's Bank Ltd v Boland*** **[1981] AC 487** that such interests were overriding under **s. 70(1)(g) of the Land Registration Act 1925** (now capable of being overriding under **Schedule 3, para. 2 of LRA 2002** provided they satisfy the requirements of the section) has caused conveyancers of registered land to enquire avidly about the 'occupiers' of property they are buying. The underlying rationale for these sections is that occupation is usually notice of an interest in the land. The effect of this type of notice in registered land has influenced notice in the unregistered system and evidence of occupation was a relevant factor in ***Kingsnorth Finance Co. v Tizard*** **[1986] 1 WLR 783**, so that the increased caution of conveyancers has reduced the potential hazards in this area for a purchaser.

It is important to realise, however, that if there is a sale (or mortgage or other dealing) by two co-owners and trustees of land, then any hidden beneficial interests in the land are overreached and attach instead to the proceeds of sale. They can then no longer be 'rights' or 'interests' in the *land* and so cannot be overriding and binding on the purchaser (***City of London Building Society v Flegg*** **[1988] AC 54**). Moreover, **s. 26, Land Registration Act 2002** provides that an owner's powers in respect of registered land are to be taken to be free of any limitation (such as a limitation under **s. 8, TLATA** that the trustees shall not make any disposition of the land without the consent of certain persons) unless such limitation is protected by a restriction on the register.

One of the difficulties of the registration of land charges in unregistered title is that they are registrable against the name of the estate owner at the time of their creation. For such a system to work, however, it is necessary to have the full and correct name of the estate owner. In ***Diligent Finance Ltd v Alleyne* (1972) 23 P & CR 346**, a wife registered a Class F land charge against her husband in the name of Erskine Alleyne, whereas his full name on the conveyance of the property was Erskine Owen Alleyne. The wife's registration was held to be void against a mortgagee who obtained a clear search against his full name. In ***Oak Co-operative Building Society v Blackburn* [1968] Ch 730** an estate contract was registered against the name of an estate agent as Frank (not Francis) David Blackburn. A subsequent mortgagee obtained a clear search against the name of Francis Davis Blackburn. It was held that where there is an error in the search as well as in the name against which the charge is registered, the charge will be good against the subsequent purchaser.

In theory, a purchaser needs to search against all estate owners since 1 January 1926 when the **Land Charges Act 1925** came into force. A purchaser was given only 30 years' title however, and so, from 1956 onwards, could not know the names of all the persons against whom he had to search. The situation was further aggravated when the **Law of Property Act 1969** reduced the period of title to 15 years (**s. 23**). The Act therefore made some allowances for this difficulty, and **s. 24** provides that as regards a *purchaser* a land charge shall be binding only if he actually knows of it. It also provides for compensation to a purchaser adversely affected by not having a root of title sufficiently old to disclose registered land charges (**s. 25**). In practice, land charges searches are carefully kept by solicitors with the deeds, so that there is often a complete chain of them going back for many years, and very few claims for compensation have been made.

Another criticism which may be made of the **Land Charges Act** system is that, because registration is the sole criterion of whether an interest is binding or not, it may operate unfairly. Its provisions may be used deliberately to evade interests of which a purchaser has actual knowledge. In ***Midland Bank Trust Co. v Green* [1981] AC 513**, a collusive sale, not for value, was held to defeat an option to purchase which had not been registered. In ***Hollington Bros v Rhodes* (1951) 2 TLR 691**, a purchaser who bought the freehold reversion on an equitable lease was held not to be bound by it because it had not been registered, notwithstanding that he paid a discounted price because of the equitable lease. Given the development of constructive trusts and the courts' willingness to apply the equitable maxim that 'equity will not allow a statute to be used as an engine of fraud' (see the concluding paragraphs of the suggested Answer to Question 3 in this chapter), it is possible that these cases might be differently decided today.

It should of course be borne in mind that the **Land Charges Act 1925** was only ever intended to be a stopgap measure. The **Land Registration Act 1925** extended the system of registered title to land, and when the title to land becomes registrable, the **Land Charges Act 1972** (formerly **1925**) no longer applies. All those interests which, prior to registration of title, were registrable in the Land Charges Registry at Plymouth (under the **Acts of 1925 or 1972**) are then registrable in the local Land Registry. In 1925, it was envisaged that the title to all land in the country would be registered very much more quickly than in fact happened, so that the problems arising because of the length of title were not foreseen.

The Land Registration Act 2002 (replacing the Land Registration Act 1925) provides for the title to land to be registered at the local Land Registry. There are three registers the property register, the proprietorship register and the charges register. The register is intended to be a 'mirror' of the title, and title is deduced by furnishing a purchaser's solicitor with office copy entries on the register. This avoids the necessity (in unregistered title) for a vendor to deduce 15 years' title to a purchaser each time the land is sold. The title information document, issued by the Land Registry, contains a copy of the register entries and the date when it was last compared with the register, and this is the evidence of title to registered land. A purchaser takes subject to any minor interests which are noted on the register, and subject in any event to any overriding interests. Many of the overriding interests (although not all) are the same as the legal interests in unregistered title, and many of the minor interests are equitable interests in unregistered land.

Some of the flaws in the system of registered titles contained in the Land Registration Act 1925 were dealt with by the Land Registration Act 2002, which came into force on 1 October 2003. This made substantial changes to land law with the same underlying objective of making conveyancing easier and safer for a purchaser. It includes significant measures towards the ultimate goal of registration that the register should be a mirror of the title. More estates and interests are now registrable, and the overriding interests, which are binding on a purchaser in any event, are much reduced. (Chapter 7 deals with this, particularly Question 2.) There are new requirements for a person claiming title as an adverse possessor to first serve a notice on the registered proprietor, and this seems likely to reduce considerably claims to titles by adverse possession except for a few cases such as boundary disputes. The changes made to adverse possession are discussed in Chapter 4, particularly in the Introduction to the chapter.

Most conveyancers would agree that the system of registered titles is an easier system of conveyancing than unregistered, and it was finally introduced for the last area in the country in 1990. The system is not perfect, and J. T. Farrand made scathing attacks on it (*Contract & Conveyance*, 4th edn, London: Oyez Longman, 1983). He commented on the claim that the register is a 'mirror of the title' (Ruoff, *The Torrens System*), and that 'The view may be taken by conveyancers that [overriding interests and rectification of the register] render the mirror image seriously and unacceptably incomplete . . .'. (It is possible, in certain circumstances, to rectify the register against a registered proprietor. For a question on this see Chapter 7, Question 3.) Although the system may be cheaper in some saving of solicitors' time in investigating title, this is probably offset by the Land Registry's fees!

Given the enormous social changes since 1925, which have caused problems for the scheme set up by the 1925 legislation, it is remarkable that much of the basic structure remains intact, and that the courts have largely been able to adapt it to our modern requirements. Conveyancing practice has similarly adapted to an awareness of the overriding interests by which a purchaser will be bound, and conveyancers now make exhaustive enquiries of anyone in 'actual occupation' who might thereby have an overriding interest formerly under s. 70(1)(g) of the Land Registration Act 1925 and now under Schedule 3, para. 2, LRA 2002.

Question 2

'In my opinion therefore, the law as to notice as it may affect purchasers of unregistered land, whether contained in decided cases, or in a statute . . . has no application even by analogy to registered land.' (Lord Wilberforce in *Williams & Glyn's Bank Ltd v Boland* [1981] AC 487.)

Explain and discuss this statement.

Commentary

This question again addresses the central issue of any system of land law and conveyancing, namely, the balance to be achieved between the desire of a purchaser for a clear title to land, and the protection of a possible third party's rights and interests in the land.

It is a problem dealt with differently in the unregistered and registered systems of conveyancing. However, the principles of the unregistered system were not entirely abandoned in the **Land Registration Act 1925**, and recent cases suggest that the old doctrine of notice is gaining favour again with the judiciary as a fair and just way to solve this central problem (see the speech of Lord Browne-Wilkinson in ***Barclays Bank plc v O'Brien* [1994] 1 AC 180**).

The problem has been further aggravated by the continually changing social patterns of the last 40 years or so. Although at one time unusual, it is now quite normal for a wife to contribute to the purchase price of a matrimonial home, and her resulting property rights have been recognised. Cohabitation, comparatively rare some forty years ago, is recognised and accepted today. This includes lesbian (***Tinsley v Milligan* [1993] 3 WLR 126**) and male homosexual (***Wayling v Jones* [1993] EGCS 153**) relationships. The **Civil Partnership Act 2004** provides that a civil partnership, when registered, gives the partners the same status and rights as spouses, including statutory property and occupation rights. It is recognised that partners in such relationships may acquire property rights in a shared home. A person who acquires such rights informally may be unaware of them, or unable to obtain recognition of them without a court order, so that registration of them is not an appropriate means of protection. Although the Law Commission's Report in the wake of ***Williams & Glyn's Bank v Boland* [1981] AC 487 (Law Com. No. 115 (1982))** suggested that such rights should be registered, this recommendation was (probably rightly) never implemented, and their binding effect in unregistered land depends upon the doctrine of notice. In registered title they are minor interests which may be protected by an entry on the register, but could also become overriding under **s. 70(1)(g), Land Registration Act 1925** if the person was in actual occupation. Many of these rights will still be overriding under the 'slimmed down' version of **s. 70(1)(g)** contained in **Schedule 3, para. 2, Land Registration Act 2002**.

For a fuller discussion of this subject (although not up to date) see R. H. Maudsley, 'Bona fide purchasers of registered land' (1973) 30 *MLR* 25.

Answer plan

- The aim of the 1925 legislation was to simplify conveyancing by removing equitable interests from the legal title. This was achieved by the overreaching machinery in **s. 2(1) LPA 1925** and registration of land charges under the **Land Charges Act s 1925** and **1972**. These two measures largely eliminated the doctrine of notice, which was hazardous for a purchaser, particularly constructive notice.
- There is, however, a residual class of equitable interests for which registration would not be appropriate (pre-1926 restrictive covenants and equitable easements, co-ownership interests arising informally, and estoppel interests). In unregistered land, the old doctrine of notice still applies to determine whether they are binding on a purchaser or not.
- In registered title, minor interests will only bind a purchaser if they are protected by an entry on the register, but overriding interests are binding in any event. Although these are largely the same as legal interests in unregistered land (which bind a purchaser in any event), the rights of a person in actual occupation even though equitable were overriding under **s. 70(1)(g), Land Registration Act 1925**, and many will still be overriding under **para. 2, Schedule 3, Land Registration Act 2002**.
- The rationale for this is that in most cases (but not in all) occupation will give notice of a person's possible interest. It is similar to the rule in ***Hunt v Luck* [1902] 1 Ch 428**, which applied to unregistered land before 1926, but wider than ***Hunt v Luck***, which did not apply if a person's occupation was consistent with their rights, which were therefore not discoverable by a purchaser. Thus the wife's occupation in ***Boland***, even though consistent with her rights, was held to be binding on the bank because (*per* Lord Wilberforce) occupation was what mattered for the section and not notice. Improved conveyancing practice has avoided many previous problems with the section.
- As to failure to protect minor interests on the register, the courts have been prepared to uphold them by imposing a constructive trust in appropriate cases. In ***Barclays Bank v O'Brien* [1994] 1 AC 180** (followed in a number of subsequent cases), the House of Lords said that notice of a mortgagor's undue influence over a co-mortgagor or guarantor should determine whether a mortgagee was bound by the co-mortgagor's interest or not.
- Both **TLATA 1996** and **LRA 2002** refer to 'actual knowledge' in the context of determining whether rights are binding or not. It remains to be seen how the courts will interpret these words in the cases.

Suggested answer

The quotation expresses what may come to be seen as the high-water mark of the rejection of the doctrine of notice in registered land. As will be discussed in this answer, the trend more recently has been tacitly to recognise that the doctrine has a limited role to play.

The main aim of the 1925 legislation was to simplify conveyancing for a purchaser (see Question 1). To this end, it provides that the legal fee simple estate shall be vested in an estate owner, who, on sale, deduces title and conveys it to a purchaser. If the title is registered, the estate owner(s) is(are) the registered proprietor and can transfer the title to a purchaser. Any equitable interests are 'off the title'. On sale, those which take effect behind a trust are overreached and attach to the proceeds of sale of the land; if not overreachable, many are registrable under the Land Charges Act 1972 (formerly the Land Charges Act 1925) or on the register of title at the Land Registry, and so are discoverable by a purchaser who can search the register.

The overreaching provisions of the Law of Property Act apply to both unregistered and registered title (*City of London Building Society v Flegg* [1988] AC 54). In registered land, the trustee estate owners are the registered proprietors and a restriction in the proprietorship register alerts a purchaser to the existence of a trust and of the necessity to obtain a receipt for purchase money from two trustees. Those equitable interests registrable in unregistered land under the Land Charges Act 1972 become registrable as minor interests in the register of the local Land Registry (usually in the charges register).

One of the problems of pre-1926 conveyancing, which the 1925 legislation sought to solve, was the hazard to a purchaser of the doctrine of notice. In particular, it was recognised that constructive notice (the notice which a purchaser should have had if the proper enquiries had been made) was a haphazard affair which could expose a purchaser to considerable risks. To avoid this, those equitable interests which attach to the land itself, and are not capable of satisfaction out of the proceeds of sale of the land, were made registrable (in unregistered titles) under the Land Charges Act 1925 (now 1972). Moreover, s. 4, Land Charges Act 1972 provides that registrable land charges which are not registered are void against certain classes of purchaser. This means that, where applicable, registration is the sole determinant of whether a registrable interest will bind a purchaser of the land or not.

The overall decisiveness of registration under the Land Charges Act 1972, even at the expense of justice, is demonstrated by the case of *Midland Bank Trust Co. v Green* [1981] AC 513. In that case, an unregistered option to purchase was void for want of registration even against someone who *actually* knew of it, had not given value, and was most certainly not *bona fide*. The case might be treated as an example of the adage that hard cases make good law. Lord Wilberforce recognised this, but said 'The Act is clear and definite . . . it should not be read down or glossed; to do so would destroy the usefulness of the Act'. The decision is nevertheless open to criticism in that it permitted the destruction of an equitable interest by a fraudulent conveyance. Lord Denning MR, in the Court of Appeal in the same case, gave a dissenting judgment in which he said 'No court in this land will allow a person to keep an advantage which he has obtained by fraud. . . . Fraud unravels everything'.

Even in 1925, however, it was conceded that the legislation could not cover all equitable interests. It was obviously too mammoth a task for the Land Charges

Registrar to register all the old restrictive covenants on unregistered titles (many over a century old), and the binding effect of these, and equitable easements, was left dependent upon the old doctrine of notice. Since 1926 the doctrine has also been applied to beneficial interests arising under a resulting or constructive trust and estoppel interests. All these interests arise from informal arrangements, and this in itself presents a difficulty in registering them.

In registered title, interests are either overriding (binding in any event on the registered proprietor or a transferee from him) or minor and binding only if protected by an entry on the register. It is a curious paradox, therefore, that at the same time as registration alone could make an interest binding in unregistered titles, the Land Registration Act 1925, s. 70(1)(g) introduced into registered titles what can only have been intended to be a limited and particular form of notice. This section made overriding 'the rights of every person in actual occupation of the land... save where enquiry is made of such person and the rights are not disclosed'. It is re-enacted in a modified and restricted form in Schedule 3, para. 2, LRA 2002.

The section roughly corresponds with the old rule in *Hunt v Luck* [1901] 1 Ch 45, which was of general application to unregistered land before 1926, but which was largely superseded by the Land Charges Act 1925. The rule fixes a purchaser with notice of rights which he should have discovered by reason of persons in occupation of the land. The rule did not operate however to fix a person with notice of rights which were consistent with, and therefore not discoverable by reason of, the occupation (*Barnhart v Greenshields* (1853) 9 Moo PCC 18).

This rationale was applied in *Caunce v Caunce* [1969] 1 WLR 286, a case involving unregistered title, where it was held that a wife's occupation of the matrimonial home with her husband did not give a mortgagee notice of the fact that she had a beneficial interest in the home. Stamp J said 'She was there, ostensibly, because she was the wife, and her presence there was wholly consistent with the title offered by the husband to the bank'. This case was regarded as wrong in *Boland*, and in 1981 it would probably have been decided differently, as co-ownership by wives was by then much more common. It was, however, decided very much according to the application of the rule in *Hunt v Luck*.

The notice imposed by the rule in *Hunt v Luck* did not apply where an occupier had concealed his rights, and, in registered land, the saving in the Land Registration Act 1925, s. 70(1)(g), reflected this. Where a purchaser had enquired of *the person in actual occupation* (not merely of the vendor's solicitor or agent), he had a clean bill of health and took free from any interests which *that person* had failed to disclose. In *Lloyds Bank plc v Rosset* [1989] Ch 350 (CA) (reversed on other grounds by the House of Lords [1991] 1 AC 107), Mustill LJ said '[E]ven if constructive notice no longer applies in this field, the old law still gives a flavour to the new words of [s. 70(1)(g)]'. Otherwise, he said, s. 70(1)(g) would produce an unacceptable contrast with the workmanlike solution in *Caunce v Caunce*. The new para. 2, Schedule 3, Land Registration Act 2002 also provides that a person of whom enquiry is made who fails to disclose their interest will not be protected, but there is an additional requirement that such a person 'could reasonably have been expected' to disclose the interest. Presumably therefore an enquiry made of a person who is senile, or an infant of tender years (who could have an interest under a trust) would not allow a purchaser to take free of their interests. Conversely, if the criterion of competence of a person of whom enquiry should be made is that they can be expected to respond to the enquiry, then the paragraph may well reverse the decision in *Hypo-Mortgage Services Ltd v Robinson* [1997] 2 FLR 71 for a minor who has reached years of discretion. There are no decisions on this amended wording as yet.

Regarding occupation as the sole determinant of whether a right is binding upon a purchaser or not has caused problems in the registered system of conveyancing, as it is not always apparent that an occupier has *rights*. The mortgagee in *Boland* did not expect the wife to have rights in the property, and the purchaser in *Hodgson v Marks* [1971] Ch 892 assumed that the lady he saw at the house was the housekeeper and not the beneficial owner of the property. These cases, where the inference that occupiers had rights could not necessarily be drawn, therefore involved an extension of the rule in *Hunt v Luck*.

Although in most cases occupation will give notice to a purchaser, it will not necessarily do so, as the rule in *Hunt v Luck* recognised. In *Williams & Glyn's Bank v Boland* the House of Lords refused to limit the section by reference to the old rule of notice and Lord Wilberforce said 'In the case of registered land, it is the fact of occupation that matters'. The new paragraph 2 however appears to bring the 'occupation' section back close to the notice rule as it exempts from its protection an interest of a person whose occupation would not have been apparent on a reasonably careful inspection, and of whose rights the purchaser did not have any actual knowledge.

Happily, these problems have been largely overcome by improved conveyancing practice. The very whisper of an occupier, other than the vendor, sends shivers down the spine of any experienced conveyancer, and will produce a barrage of questions as to his status and rights. Such questions are now included in all forms of conveyancers' pre-contract enquiries. A purchaser or mortgagee will require a person in occupation other than the vendor to sign a waiver of any rights they may have and to undertake to vacate the property on completion. Mortgagees require applicants to sign declarations as to who will occupy the mortgaged property, thereby seeking to obtain an admission that only the mortgagor has rights in the property. There is much to be said for this improved practice which takes account of para. 2, Schedule 3.

Moreover, there has been some cross-fertilisation from the registered to the unregistered system. In *Kingsnorth Finance Co. v Tizard* [1986] 1 WLR 783, the standards of enquiry as to occupation in registered land were applied to unregistered title. A mortgagee was found to have constructive notice of the rights of a wife whose occupation, although intermittent, should have been apparent, and whose existence was evident from the mortgage application form.

As regards the requirement for a minor interest to be protected by a notice on the register, the courts have been prepared to use a constructive trust in order to give effect to interests which were void for want of registration, but which would have been binding under the old equitable doctrine of notice. In *Lyus v Prowsa Developments Ltd* [1982] 1 WLR 1044, an estate contract which had not been registered as a minor interest in registered land, and was not overriding, was held to be binding on a subsequent purchaser who took expressly subject to it. The rationale for this was that 'equity will not allow a statute to be used as an instrument of fraud'. The case contrasts starkly however with the earlier decision in unregistered title of *Hollington Bros v Rhodes* [1951] 2 TLR 691. There, a purchaser who paid less than the market price for property because of an equitable lease affecting it, nevertheless took free from the lease as it was not registered. In *Peffer v Rigg* [1977] 1 WLR 285, Graham J was prepared to find a constructive trust to protect a beneficial minor interest in registered land which had not been registered (although he also reached the same conclusion by ascribing requirements of good faith to the Land Registration Act 1925, s. 59(6), and the decision has been strongly criticised). For the imposition of a constructive trust there must be some element of unconscionability and unjust enrichment, which is of course more than mere notice.

In *Barclays Bank plc v O'Brien* [1994] 1 AC 180, the House of Lords applied notice as the criterion to determine whether a lender should be bound by any undue influence which a borrower might have over a surety or a co-borrower. It is not clear whether this case concerned registered or unregistered title, but presumably the principle is intended to apply to both. (This was queried by Professor Mark Thompson in his note on the case in [1994] *Conv* 140.) In *Barclays Bank plc v Boulter* [1997] 2 All ER 1002, Mummery LJ in the Court of Appeal said that in cases like *O'Brien* it was irrelevant whether the land was registered or unregistered title.

The reality, then, is that the courts appear to be ready, in some circumstances, to recognise the unjustness of a system depending entirely upon registration. They are prepared to resort to the old doctrine of notice as offering a fair and just solution to the problem of whether a purchaser should be bound or not by an interest in the land. And in appropriate circumstances, they are prepared to impose a constructive trust to give effect to some of these interests.

Although clearly not countenancing constructive notice, recent statutes have referred to 'actual knowledge' as relevant in determining a person's rights. Section 16, TLATA, which applies only to unregistered land, provides that a conveyance by trustees contrary to a limitation on their powers of disposition will not invalidate it as regards a purchaser unless he has 'actual knowledge' of the limitation. As mentioned above, Schedule 3, para. 2, Land Registration Act 2002 refers to a purchaser's 'actual knowledge' of a person's interest, and it seems that the legislation is prepared to recognise the significance of notice in some circumstances.

It remains to be seen how the courts will interpret 'actual knowledge' in these contexts!

Question 3

'The property statutes generally prescribe a very high degree of formality for transactions relating to land. It is a curious paradox therefore that wide-ranging exceptions to these general rules have been recognised'.

Explain and discuss this statement.

Commentary

This question is a very general one requiring a considerable overall knowledge of land law both the statutes and the case law. It is one which is more likely to be set for course work rather than in an examination as it requires wide reading and reflective thought! It is an interesting question, the answer to which demonstrates how the judges have applied principles of equity to prevent injustice from the strict application of statutory requirements.

For further reading on the topic of comparing constructive trusts and estoppel, see articles by David Hayton at [1990] *Conv* 370 and (1993) 109 *LQR* 485, and the judgment of Robert Walker LJ in ***Yaxley v Gotts* [2000] 1 All ER 711 at 713**.

Answer plan

- Explanation of why formalities are required in transactions concerning land.
- Brief overview of principal legislative requirements in land transactions.
- Statutory exceptions where no formalities are required and reasons for them.
- Case law exceptions arising from the application of equitable principles such as resulting and constructive trusts and estoppel.

Suggested answer

Land was always of great importance in a feudal society and was transferred publicly by handing over the title document in a ceremony known as 'livery with feoffment of seisin'. In our modern society, a house is likely to be the most expensive and important purchase which anyone makes. Most people live in their house for a number of years, so that their proof of ownership needs to be enduring. Often they will need a mortgage to assist them in their purchase, and the building society or bank will require proof of ownership and notice of their charge to appear on the title to the property. There may be third party rights, such as easements or restrictive covenants, which the property enjoys, or which are enjoyed over it, and these need to be properly created and recorded. There may be a fragmentation of ownership, as with co-owners or successive owners, and this also needs to be recorded in some way. The formalities for transactions with land are to ensure that all these matters are correctly created and recorded, and that third party rights are protected by the appropriate registration.

In order to create or to transfer a legal estate or a legal interest in land, s. 52, LPA 1925 requires a deed to be executed. (The exception to this is s. 54(2), LPA 1925 which allows a lease not exceeding three years to be created by word of mouth.) The requirements for a document to constitute a deed are contained in s. 1, Law of Property (Miscellaneous Provisions) Act 1989. A deed no longer has to be sealed, but must be signed as a deed and delivered. Where the title is registered (as most titles are nowadays) there is a transfer of the title by deed but the legal title is not completed until the purchaser registers the transfer (s. 27(1), LRA 2002) and the purchaser's name then appears in the proprietorship register instead of the vendor's. The Land Registration Act 2002 envisages electronic deeds with electronic signatures eventually, although this provision in the Act will not be introduced for some years yet.

A trust of land must be evidenced in writing and signed by the person declaring it (s. 53(1)(b), LPA 1925), and a disposition of a beneficial interest under a trust (of any property) has to be in writing and signed by the transferor or his agent (s. 53(1)(c), LPA 1925). The Wills Act 1837, s. 9 (as amended by the Administration of Justice Act 1982), prescribes the formalities required for leaving any property (including land) by will. The will must be signed by the testator, whose signature must be attested by two witnesses, and, broadly speaking, all three must be present and sign at the same time.

Because of the enquiries which have to be made and the documentation required for the purchase of land, a conveyancing transaction is usually effected in two stages a contract to sell and the actual transfer of the legal estate. The formalities for a contract for the sale are prescribed by s. 2(1), Law of Property (Miscellaneous Provisions) Act 1989; they are that the contract must be in writing and signed by both parties, or in two parts, one part signed by each party, and the two parts exchanged. This is the usual procedure followed by solicitors in a conveyancing transaction.

In addition to the formality provisions for the actual transactions, the Land Charges Act 1972 provides for the registration of certain interests in unregistered land in order to give notice of them to a purchaser and to protect them, and LRA 2002 provides for the registration of many interests created. The Land Registration Act 2002 extends the registration of interests created in land with registered title and correspondingly reduces the number of overriding interests that are binding on a purchaser without registration.

There are some statutory exceptions to the general requirement of formality. The statutory exception contained in s. 54(2), LPA 1925 provides that a lease taking effect in possession for a term not exceeding three years at the best rent reasonably obtainable without taking a fine (i.e. a capital sum) can be created informally without a deed. This exception is one of pure convenience and a recognition that many people create periodic tenancies of a flat or a room quite informally. Registration of such leases is not necessary to give notice of them to a third party. Another statutory exception to the rule was the Limitation Act 1980, under which, for the same rationale of convenience, the law was prepared to recognise that a person who adversely possessed land extinguished the title of the true owner after 12 years and acquired a possessory title. Lord St. Leonards described the purpose of the Limitation Acts as 'the prevention of the rearing up of claims at great distances of time when evidences are lost' (*Dundee Harbour Trustees v Dougal* (1852) 1 Macq. 317). It was undesirable that the true paper owner should be allowed to 'sleep' on his rights and the policy of land law has always been to keep property freely alienable. Some unfortunate cases involving local authorities (see, for example, *Ellis v Lambeth LBC* [1999] *The Times*, 28th September 1999) received public condemnation, however, and the Land Registration Act 2002 severely limits the application of the Limitation Acts to registered title. They are regarded as inconsistent with a system of registered title, and the Act introduces a new procedure involving the service of notices for extinguishing a paper title.

The main exceptions to the requirements for formalities, however, are to be found in the applications by the courts of the principles of equity. Implied, resulting, and constructive trusts are specifically exempted by s. 53(2), LPA 1925 from the formality requirements for the creation of a trust in s. 53(1), LPA 1925, and these trusts are recognised by s. 1(2)(a), TLATA 1996 as trusts of land. Where property is purchased by one person but conveyed into the name of another, without any intention of gift or presumption of advancement, equity will infer a resulting trust of the beneficial equitable interest for the person who has provided the purchase price (see *Hodgson v Marks* [1971] Ch 892, where the freeholder owner of a house conveyed the legal title to someone else). Where someone provides part only of the purchase price, such as a one third contribution, then their equitable interest under a resulting trust will be one third of the beneficial ownership (*Bull v Bull* [1955] 1 QB 234). A constructive trust is one imposed by the court on the owner of the legal title to the property requiring such person to hold the whole or part of the beneficial equitable interest for someone else. The courts have imposed constructive trusts in a variety of circumstances, but basically to divest a person of their beneficial ownership when they have obtained an unjust enrichment by unconscionable dealing. Thus in *Bannister v Bannister* [1948] 2 All ER 133 the defendant had purchased two freehold cottages from his sister-in-law at below the market price on the oral understanding that she should be allowed to live in one of them for the rest of her life. The court gave effect to this arrangement by imposing on the defendant a constructive trust. Constructive trusts have been applied also to commercial transactions such as the case of *Lyus v Prowsa Developments Ltd* [1982] 1 WLR 1044. The principles of constructive trusts are still developing in recent case law to determine the extent of beneficial co-ownership between cohabitees (see *Stack v Dowden* [2007] 2 AC 432 where Lady Hale expressed the view that a wide variety of social circumstances could also be relevant in establishing a constructive trust).

The courts have also been prepared to recognise proprietary interests arising from an estoppel, where a person acts to their detriment in reliance upon a statement made by someone as to their rights in property. The doctrine of proprietary estoppel, like constructive trusts, has been applied to a variety of widely differing circumstances. It was said in *Crabb v Arun District Council* [1976] Ch 179 that the court should satisfy the estoppel by 'the minimum equity to do justice to the plaintiff' (*per* Scarman LJ), and a variety of interests have been awarded on the finding of an estoppel. In *Crabb v Arun DC*, the estoppel interest was one in the nature of an easement, in *Inwards v Baker* [1965] 2 QB 29 and *Matharu v Matharu* [1994] 2 FLR 597 a licence, in *Griffiths v Williams* (1977) 248 EG 947 a long lease, and in *Pascoe v Turner* [1979] 1 WLR 431 a conveyance of the fee simple absolute. In *Gillett v Holt* [2001] Ch 210, the Court of Appeal allowed an estoppel to limit the principle of testamentary freedom. An issue of continuing uncertainty is how the court should satisfy the estoppel. The maximum equity is the claimant's expectation, as in *Pascoe v Turner*. In other cases, the courts have regarded the equity as already satisfied (as by some countervailing benefit, for example, *Sledmore v Dalby* (1996) 72 P & CR 196). It was suggested in *Jennings v Rice* [2002] EWCA Civ 159 that where the extent of the expectation is uncertain, the court should lean towards merely compensating for the detriment. In *Thorner v Major* [2009] 1 WLR 776, by contrast, the expectation was certain, as there had been a mutual understanding that the claimant would inherit a farm that he had worked on unpaid for nearly 30 years; the House of Lords restored the decision of the trial judge, who had held that the minimum equity to do justice was to award the claimant the farm.

One of the time-honoured maxims of equity is that 'equity will not allow a statute to be used as an instrument of fraud'. This is a very general maxim with potential for a very wide application. It was the basis of the old doctrine of part performance which provided an exception to the formality requirements of s. 40, Law of Property Act 1925, and underpins the enforcement of secret trusts contrary to the formality requirements of the Wills Act 1837. A case such as *Midland Bank Trust Co v Green* [1981] AC 513 demonstrates very clearly that an inflexible requirement of statutory compliance can be a fertile ground for fraud, and that a modification of the requirement with an application of equitable principles may be highly desirable. The applications of resulting and constructive trusts and estoppel show that the courts are ready to apply equitable principles to create exceptions to the formality requirements of the statutes where they believe that justice requires it. In *Lyus v Prowsa Developments Ltd* [1982] 1 WLR 1044, Dillon J refused to allow an express agreement to be rendered void by a failure to comply with the registration requirements of the Land Registration Act 1925. In *Yaxley v Gotts* [2000] Ch 162, referring to the Law of Property (Miscellaneous Provisions) Act 1989, Robert Walker LJ said 'the doctrine of estoppel may operate to modify (and sometimes perhaps even counteract) the effect of s. 2 of the 1989 Act', and 'any general assertion of s. 2 as a no-go area for estoppel would be unsustainable'. He pointed out that s. 2(5) expressly exempts the operation of resulting, implied, or constructive trusts from the section, and considered the analogies drawn in various cases between constructive trusts and estoppel.

Whilst formality in land transactions is desirable therefore, there must necessarily be some temperance of the requirement to allow for circumstances where there are sound reasons for enforcing informal arrangements and undertakings between parties which do not comply with the statutory formalities.

Question 4

Peter is considering purchasing a freehold house from Vincent. The title is unregistered and Peter has discovered the following matters:

(a) Two sets of restrictive covenants, one made in 1922 and one made in 1945.

(b) The next door neighbour uses a track across the bottom of the garden as access to his garage, which he cannot reach in any other way. Vincent has told Peter that this is an informal arrangement which he made with the neighbour some years ago, before the garage was built.

(c) Although Vincent appears to be living alone in the property, there is a Class F land charge registered against his name at the Land Charges Registry.

Advise Peter how these matters may affect his title to the property.

How would your answer differ if the title to the house were registered?

Commentary

This is a very common type of examination question. Even if the subject-matter is not addressed as directly as it is here, it may feature in a more disguised form in other questions!

You need to consider the nature of the interests created (unless, as with the restrictive covenants, you have actually been told about them) and then to decide whether or not they will bind a purchaser of the legal estate in the land.

It is usual to ask the question for both unregistered and registered titles, and the answers may be different! For an amusing and lightly written comparison of the binding effect of certain interests in the two systems, see the article by J. G. Ridall, 'Unwin Avenue and Reginald Road' (1977) *Conv* 405, but remember that it was written before the LRA 2002 came into force!

Answer plan

(a)

- The restrictive covenants made in 1922 are not registrable and whether they bind a purchaser such as Peter depends upon whether he has notice of them or not. If, however, there has been a *bona fide* purchaser for value of the land without notice of the covenants at any time, then this will permanently destroy their binding effect (***Wilkes v Spooner* [1911] 2 KB 473**).
- The 1945 covenants were registrable under the **Land Charges Act 1925**, and if they have been registered they are binding. If not registered, they are not binding. **Section 25, LPA 1969** allows Peter to claim compensation for a pre-root of title land charge of which he did not have actual knowledge (**s. 24**).
- In registered title, restrictive covenants are minor interests binding only if protected by a notice on the register.

(b)
- An informal arrangement cannot create a legal easement within **s. 1(2) LPA 1925** for which a deed is necessary, nor an equitable easement for which a document in writing complying with **s. 2, Law of Property (Miscellaneous Provisions) Act 1989** would be required.
- Enjoyment of the right for 20 years 'next before action' would give the neighbour the right to an easement by prescription which would be a legal easement. Legal easements are binding in unregistered land. In registered land, an easement acquired by prescription may be overriding under **para. 3, Schedule 3, Land Registration Act 2002** if it complies with the requirements of that paragraph.
- If the easement is supported by an estoppel, it will be equitable. In unregistered land, estoppel interests are not registrable, and whether they bind a purchaser depends upon the doctrine of notice. In registered title only legal easements can be overriding. **Section 116 of the Act** specifically states, however, that interests arising by estoppel are capable of binding successors in title.

(c)
- A Class F land charge protects a spouse's right of occupation of the matrimonial home under the **Family Law Act 1996**, even if she is not in occupation at the time. The **Civil Partnership Act 2004** extends this right to a registered civil partner. Registration will give notice that there is a wife or registered civil partner around and, as such a person may have an equitable interest in the home nowadays, Peter should make enquiries. A beneficial interest as such is not registrable under the **Land Charges Act** and its validity against a purchaser depends upon the doctrine of notice.
- In registered title, a spouse's rights of occupation under the Act are minor interests only and cannot be overriding, even if the spouse is in actual occupation.

Suggested answer

(a) Restrictive covenants entered into before 1926 are not registrable under the Land Charges Act 1972 (formerly the Land Charges Act 1925). Their binding validity against a purchaser of the land therefore depends upon the doctrine of notice. If Peter were a *bona fide* purchaser for value of the land without notice of the covenants, he would take free from them. His investigation of the title appears to have revealed the covenants however, so that he will take subject to them as he has actual notice of them. The only exception to this would be if, although Peter himself knew of the restrictive covenants, there were a purchaser in the chain of title who was a *bona fide* purchaser for value without notice of them for some reason (see *Wilkes v Spooner* [1911] 2 KB 473).

The 1945 restrictive covenants were registrable under the Land Charges Act 1925 (now the Land Charges Act 1972), and if registered, will be binding on Peter. They will be registered against the name of the estate owner in 1945, which Peter is unlikely to have on his title as the period of title deduced to a purchaser was reduced to 15 years, starting with a good root, by the Law of Property Act 1969. However, there may well be an old search with the deeds showing the covenants and s. 24, LPA 1969 provides that *actual* notice of a pre-root land charge determines its validity against a purchaser so that s. 198 LPA 1925, which provides that registration constitutes notice, shall not apply. If Peter enters into the contract without *actual* knowledge of the covenants, the Law of Property Act 1969, s. 25 provides for compensation for a purchaser affected by the land charge.

If the title to the land were registered, the restrictive covenants would be registered in the charges register as minor interests. They are binding if so registered, but not binding if not registered. In practice, many old pre-1926 restrictive covenants are registered in the charges register of a registered title. They are evident from the title as each subsequent conveyance of the land is made expressly subject to them, and the Registrar enters them on first registration.

(b) The neighbour is enjoying a right of access which is similar to an easement, and Peter needs to investigate this situation. It cannot be a legal or equitable easement expressly granted for which a deed or contract in writing would be necessary.

If the neighbour has used the track for 20 years, then he may have a *prima facie* right to a claim to an easement under the Prescription Act 1832, or possibly under the doctrine of lost modern grant. The right may be negatived (in either case) by permission having been granted to him, as one of the essentials of all forms of prescription is that the user upon which they are based must be as of right. It is possible that the 'informal arrangement' may amount to an oral permission at the start of the 20-year period and it may be sufficient to defeat it if it refers to the continued user throughout the period. If the neighbour has acquired an easement by prescription, then it will be a legal one, which will be binding upon Peter.

If the right of access was informally granted before the garage was built, then it may be possible for the neighbour to claim a right of access supported by estoppel. In *E.R. Ives Investment Ltd v High* [1967] 2 QB 379, the facts were similar to this and a neighbour, relying upon an agreement for access, built a garage. The successor in title to the person who had agreed to the access was estopped from denying the right. There were, however, other considerations, as the doctrine of *Halsall v Brizell* [1957] Ch 169 also applied. Nevertheless, the court also recognised a right of access supported by an estoppel in *Crabb v Arun District Council* [1976] Ch 179.

If the neighbour is therefore able to say that he built the garage in reliance upon the agreement for access, and so acted to his detriment, then it may well be binding on Vincent. As an unregistrable equitable interest, it would be binding upon Peter unless he was a *bona fide* purchaser for value without notice of it. As he clearly has notice, he would not appear to fall into that category.

In registered title, a legal easement acquired by prescription may be an overriding interest under Schedule 3, para. 3, LRA 2002 if exercised within one year of Peter's purchase, or if Peter actually knows of it (which he appears to do), or it would have been discoverable on a reasonably careful inspection of the land.

An equitable easement is not an overriding interest under Schedule 3, para 3, Land Registration Act 2002 and so will only bind a purchaser if protected by a notice on the register. Section 116 states, however, that estoppel interests are capable of binding successors in title of registered land. This means that the estoppel will bind Peter if, assuming that it has not been protected by entry of a notice on the register of title, the neighbour is in actual occupation of the track (which seems unlikely to be established merely by walking along the track). If, however, Peter were to obtain registered title to the house, and the neighbour were later to establish that he had an estoppel protected as an overriding interest through actual occupation of the track, the neighbour might be able to obtain rectification of the register by the entry of an equitable easement against the registered title (assuming the equity was satisfied by the award of an equitable easement).

(c) A Class F land charge indicates that Vincent's wife (or registered civil partner under the Civil Partnership Act 2004) is claiming a right of occupation of the matrimonial home under the Family Law Act 1996, Pt. IV. (The Civil Partnership Act 2004 extends such rights of occupation to a civil partner where that partnership has been registered.) It is irrelevant that she has actually left the home. It was held in *Watts v Waller* [1973] QB 153 that a wife not in occupation of the matrimonial home still had a conditional right of occupation capable of registration as a land charge under the forerunner of the 1996 Act. Peter will have to insist that this charge is cleared off the title before he completes the purchase of the property.

As Peter is aware of the existence of such a person, he should also make enquiries as to whether they have any beneficial interest in the matrimonial or shared home. It is sufficiently usual nowadays for a wife to have contributed to the purchase of a matrimonial home so that a purchaser who is put on notice that there is a wife should make enquiries as to any beneficial interest she may have (*Kingsnorth Finance Co. v Tizard* [1986] 1 WLR 783). So although the Class F land charge will not protect any such beneficial interest and only protects a wife's right of occupation, it might well be held to give a purchaser notice that there is a wife who might have a beneficial interest.

In registered title, the statutory right of occupation of a spouse or registered civil partner under the Family Law Act 1996 is registrable as a minor interest, and would be binding on Peter if so registered. Section 31(10)(b) of the Act provides that it will not become an overriding interest, even if they were in actual occupation within the meaning of the Land Registration Act 2002, Schedule 3, para. 2. Any beneficial interest, which would be a minor interest, would be binding on Peter if protected by a restriction on the register. It could not be an overriding interest under para. 2 as the person is not in actual occupation. Under the Land Registration Act 2002, rights under the Family Law Act remain minor interests.

Question 5

Petra has entered into a contract to purchase the freehold title in a bungalow, which was registered in 1960. An investigation of the property and its title has revealed the following transactions.

(a) in 1980 Vera's predecessor in title granted to a neighbour, Nell, a right of way across the back garden; and

(b) in 2000 Vera leased a garage at the side of the bungalow to her friend, Freda; and

(c) earlier this year Vera made a declaration of trust in relation to the property in favour of her son Ben who is aged 16.

Advise Petra whether she will take the land free from, or subject to, the interests of Nell, Ben, and Freda.

What difference would it make to your answer if the land were still unregistered?

Commentary

This is another question which adapts well to the instruction to consider the situation in both registered and unregistered land. To make the question clearer to follow, we have put in sub-headings to indicate 'registered land' and 'unregistered land' in each part of the answer.

Very often examination questions deal with the application or not of overreaching, as does part (c) of this question. You need to know the principles which apply in both registered and unregistered title and the relevant cases which establish these.

Answer plan

(a) Right of way

- If granted by deed and it complies with **s. 1(2)(a), LPA 1925**, this will be capable of being a legal easement. In order to 'operate at law' however, it must be completed by registration against the title of the burdened land.
- If an equitable easement, it can only be a minor interest and will be binding if protected by a notice on the register.
- In unregistered land, a legal easement (granted by deed and complying with **s. 1(2)(a), LPA**) is a right *in rem* binding on everyone. An equitable easement is a Class D land charge and only binding if entered on the register, even if (as here) the purchaser Petra actually knows of it.

(b) Lease

- A legal lease exceeding seven years is registrable substantively; leases not exceeding seven years (including periodic tenancies) are overriding interests under **Schedule 3, para. 1**. An equitable lease is a minor interest capable of protection on the register. It may also be overriding under **Schedule 3, para. 2, LRA 2002** as Petra, who has been told of it, has 'actual knowledge' of it.
- In unregistered land, a legal lease is a right *in rem* and binding on everyone. An equitable lease is an estate contract and binding if registered as a class C(iv) land charge under the **Land Charges Act 1972**, but not binding if not registered.

(c) Declaration of trust

- Assuming that the declaration of trust complies with the formality requirements of **s. 53(1)(b), LPA 1925**, then it is an equitable interest, but is not overreachable as there is only one trustee. It is a minor interest and may be protected by an entry on the register. If not so protected, if Ben is of mature years and may be expected to respond to enquiries, then his interest may be overriding under **Schedule 3, para. 2(b), LRA 2002**.
- In unregistered title, Ben's equitable interest is neither overreachable nor registrable under the **Land Charges Act 1972**. Its binding effect therefore depends upon notice, which presumably Petra has.

Suggested answer

(a) Right of way

Nell has a right of way across Vera's garden. To be a legal easement this must comply with the definition contained in the Law of Property Act 1925, s. 1(2)(a). Thus, it must be for a period equivalent to a fee simple or a term of years. The use of the word 'granted' implies that it was created by deed as required by the Law of Property Act, s. 52. If it was created by deed which complies with s. 1(2)(a) Law of Property (Miscellaneous Provisions) Act 1989, then it will be a legal interest. If it was not created by deed then it may be possible to argue that provided the right of way has been exercised openly and without permission or the use of force and has been used without interruption since 1980, a legal easement has been created by prescription, although the 'grant' may prevent this.

If the easement is not legal, it may still be enforceable in equity. It will be necessary to show that there is an enforceable contract in respect of which equity would grant specific performance. Since such a contract would have been entered into in 1980, it will be necessary to show that it complied with the rules in the Law of Property Act 1925, s. 40 (now repealed and replaced by the Law of Property (Miscellaneous Provisions) Act 1989, s. 2). This requires that there must be some written evidence of the contract signed by the party to be charged or an agent. If there is no such written evidence then it may be possible to rely on the equitable doctrine of part performance (Law of Property Act 1925, s. 40(2)). Thus if there is an oral agreement between Vera's predecessor in title and Nell as to the right of way and Nell has exercised the right in reliance on the agreement to the knowledge of the other party, this may be enforceable in equity (*Morritt v Wonham* (1994) NPC 2).

As an equitable easement, it can be protected in registered land as a minor interest by a notice on the register.

Under the Land Registration Act 2002, a legal easement expressly granted is a registrable disposition under s. 27(2)(d) and will not operate at law until registered (s. 27(1)). It will not be an overriding interest under Schedule 3, para. 3. A legal easement acquired by prescription may be an overriding interest under the paragraph however if it was exercised within one year of the sale to Petra, or Petra actually knew about it, or its existence was discoverable on a reasonably careful inspection of the land.

Equitable easements are minor interests and not binding on a purchaser unless they are protected by an entry on the register.

If the title to the bungalow is unregistered, then if the easement is legal, it binds Petra since legal interests bind the whole world. The issue as to whether it is legal or equitable depends on the same arguments as in the first part of the answer.

If the right of way is equitable, then, as it was created after 1925, it must be registered as a Class D(iii) land charge under the Land Charges Act 1972, s. 2(5). If it is not registered as such it is unenforceable against Petra as the purchaser for money or money's worth of a legal estate. There is no equivalent category in unregistered land to the overriding interest, so, if the equitable interest is not registered it is unenforceable by Nell, regardless of the state of knowledge of the purchaser, Petra.

(b) Lease

The lease, if a legal lease for more than seven years, is an estate which must be registered substantively with its own title number. Where the lease is a legal lease (created by deed or within the Law of Property Act 1925, s. 54(2) see below) for a period not exceeding seven years it will be an overriding interest under the Land Registration Act 2002, Schedule 3, para. 1 and so binding on Petra. This would apply also to a periodic tenancy which is legal under s. 54(2), Law of Property Act 1925, even if created by word of mouth. In *City Permanent Building Society v Miller* [1952] Ch 840, it was held that the words 'leases granted' in s. 70(1)(k), Land Registration Act 1925 (the forerunner to Schedule 3, para. 1) could mean only legal leases and not equitable leases, and similarly the word 'grant' in para. 1 would not include equitable leases. If the lease is an equitable lease, it will be a minor interest and binding if noted on the register. However, if Freda could be said to be in actual occupation of the garage, then it may be possible for her to bring her lease, even if only equitable, within the protection of the Land Registration Act 2002, Schedule 3, para. 2. It has been held that the intermittent use of a garage can amount to actual occupation (*Kling v Keston Properties Ltd* (1983) 49 P & CR 212). Since the lease relates to a garage which can clearly be subject to physical occupation, it would seem that Freda's lease could be protected even where it is equitable as an overriding interest. However, Schedule 3, para. 2 is not as wide as the former s. 70(1)(g), Land Registration Act 1925, and para. 2(c) excludes the interest of a person whose occupation would not have been obvious on a reasonably careful inspection of the land if the purchaser does not have actual knowledge of it. It is quite likely that a reasonable inspection would not have discovered Freda's occupation, but Petra does seem to have 'actual knowledge' of the lease, so that it will still be overriding even if only equitable.

In unregistered land, if the lease is legal, it will bind the whole world. To be legal, the lease must be for a term certain and must be created by deed in accordance with the Law of Property Act 1925, s. 52, except where s. 54(2) applies. This subsection provides that leases taking effect in possession for a term not exceeding three years at the best rent which can reasonably be obtained without taking a fine can be created by parol. The section includes all periodic tenancies.

A valid contract complying with the requirements of the Law of Property (Miscellaneous Provisions) Act 1989, s. 2 will create an equitable lease which is registrable as an estate contract under Class C(iv) of the Land Charges Act 1972, s. 2(4). For the same reasons that prevailed in respect of an equitable easement, if it is not registered, it is unenforceable against Petra.

(c) Declaration of trust

A preliminary point raised by this question, which applies to both registered and unregistered titles, is whether the declaration of trust of land has complied with the formality requirements of the Law of Property Act 1925, s.53(1)(b). This requires a declaration of a trust of land to be evidenced in writing and signed by the person declaring it (Vera), and if this has not been done, then the trust is unenforceable by Ben, although not void. In *Hypo-Mortgage Services Ltd v Robinson* [1997] 2 FLR 71 it was argued that the creation of a trust for children by a co-owner would amount to a transfer of that co-owner's beneficial equitable interest which would be caught by s. 53(1)(c) rather than s. 53(1)(b) and so require to be actually in writing and signed by the transferor or their agent, and whilst not actually deciding the point, Nourse LJ expressed the opinion that this might well be right.

As Vera is a sole trustee the overreaching provisions of the Law of Property Act 1925, s. 2(1) will not apply as Petra will not obtain a receipt for the purchase moneys from two trustees.

If the title were registered, then Ben's interest would be a minor interest and could be protected by a restriction on the register. It would then be binding upon Petra. If not so protected, had Ben been 18 years of age and in actual occupation of the bungalow, then he would have had an overriding interest under the Land Registration Act 2002, Schedule 3, para. 2 which would also have been binding upon Petra (*Williams & Glyn's Bank Ltd v Boland* [1981] AC 487).

Hypo-Mortgage Services Ltd v Robinson [1997] 2 FLR 71, which was a case on the now repealed s. 70(1)(g), Land Registration Act 1925, held that a minor's interest cannot be overriding by reason of their occupation, which is merely as a shadow of their parents. There was some criticism of this decision (see Note by Kenny (1997) *Conv* 84) and Roger Smith felt that a better rationale for the decision would have been that a minor might well not be able to respond to enquiries from a purchaser (Roger J. Smith, *Property Law*, 5th edn, Longman, 2006).

These criticisms have been taken into account in the wording of Schedule 3, para. 2, where para. 2(b) exempts from overriding status the interest of a person of whom enquiry was made who did not disclose their right when he could reasonably have been expected to do so. Ben, aged 16, might be such a person, so that he might have an overriding interest if no enquiry is made of him.

In unregistered title, Ben's interest would be a family-type beneficial equitable interest which is not registrable. Its binding effect on a purchaser therefore depends upon notice, and if Petra were a *bona fide* purchaser for value without notice of Ben's interest, then she would take free from it. Notice may be actual, imputed or constructive (as in *Kingsnorth Finance Co. v Tizard* [1986] 2 All ER 54), but as Vera has actually told Petra, then she may well have actual notice.

Question 6

Alan is the registered proprietor of a row of three cottages Nos. 2, 4, and 6 Cowslip Lane. His friend, Betty, telephones him to ask if she can rent No. 2 while she is looking for somewhere to buy. Alan agrees and she moves in and starts paying rent on a monthly basis from 1 January.

Alan decides to put No. 4 on the market and he receives two offers from Carl and Damien. Carl makes the higher offer but wishes to defer completion of the contract until he returns from six months' employment abroad. Carl suggests to Alan's estate agent that the property should not be sold to Damien, that Carl will better any offer from Damien by £5,000 and will exchange contracts within a month, but with completion to be deferred until his (Carl's) return from abroad. The estate agent telephones Alan, who agrees to this proposal. The next day, however, Alan receives a draft contract from Damien and Alan and Damien exchange contracts by the end of that week.

Alan is short of money and he approaches his bank for a loan. The bank agrees to lend him £10,000 but suggests that it should hold the land certificate of No. 6 (which is in a safety deposit box at the bank) as security for the loan. Alan agrees.

Alan has now decided to emigrate and he agrees to sell Nos. 2 and 6 to Edith. Edith moves into No. 2, but is surprised when Betty, who has been away on holiday, lets herself into the cottage. Edith then receives a letter from the bank threatening to foreclose on the mortgage on No. 6. Damien receives a letter from Carl, saying that he has an agreement with Alan which takes precedence over Damien's agreement.

Advise Edith and Damien whether Betty, the bank and Carl have contracts which are enforceable against them.

Commentary

The question concerns the judicial interpretations of the **Law of Property (Miscellaneous Provisions) Act 1989, s. 2**. As usual, the advice is to separate out the issues and to deal with each in turn. If the precedents are conflicting, then say so, but grasp the nettle and suggest what, in your view, would be the likely outcome. For a recent case on a 'joint venture' agreement between a property owner and a developer, where both parties anticipated that there would eventually be a written contract drawn up once planning permission for the project was obtained and that the oral agreement which they reached was binding in honour only, see ***Yeoman's Row Management Ltd v Cobbe* [2008] UKHL 55**. In this case, the House of Lords refused to follow Etherton J or the Court of Appeal in finding a constructive trust or an estoppel. The speeches in the House of Lords review a number of cases on estoppel which they said was only appropriate to a proprietary claim, which this was not.

The part of the question dealing with leases is straightforward. The status of collateral agreements, which do not comply with the formality requirements of the section, and 'lock-out' agreements has featured in a number of cases, some of which have received comment in Case Notes in *The Conveyancer* (see for example ***Pitt v PHH Asset Management***, Thompson [1994] *Conv* 58 and ***Record v Bell***, Harwood [1991] *Conv* 471).

Since the **Land Registration Act 2002** came into force it is no longer possible to create a mortgage by depositing a land certificate.

Answer plan

- Exception for leases not exceeding 3 years (**s. 2(5), Law of Property (Miscellaneous Provisions) Act 1989**; **s. 54(2), Law of Property Act 1925**).
- Overriding interests: **Schedule 3, para. 1, Land Registration Act 2002**.
- Creation of mortgage by deposit of title deeds.
- Effect of ***United Bank of Kuwait plc v Sahib* (1997)**
- Determination of whether contract to exchange contracts or 'lock-out' agreement.
- Discussion of case law.

Suggested answer

There are three issues to be addressed in this problem: (a) whether Edith is bound by the agreement between Alan and Betty; (b) whether Edith is bound by the agreement between Alan and the bank; and (c) the effect of the agreement between Alan and Carl on Damien.

Betty

Betty is occupying No. 2 and is paying rent. Under the Law of Property (Miscellaneous Provisions) Act 1989, s. 2(1) a contract in writing is required for the sale or other disposition of an interest in land. There is no suggestion of writing in Betty's case; the agreement appears to have been concluded over the telephone. However, there is an exception in s. 2(5) in respect of contracts to grant a lease for a term not exceeding three years to which the Law of Property Act 1925, s. 54(2) applies. Section 54(2) applies to leases taking effect in possession for a term not exceeding three years at the best rent which can be reasonably obtained without taking a fine. The 'best rent' in the sub-section means the 'market rent': *Fitzkriston LLP v Panayi* [2008] EWCA Civ 283; and see *Looe Fuels Ltd v Looe Harbour Commissioners* [2008] EWCA Civ 414.

If the lease is a monthly periodic tenancy (which from the agreement it would appear to be) and satisfies the other statutory requirements, then it falls within s. 54(2) and, therefore, within the exception contained in s. 2(5). This means that there would be a valid contract, and, once Betty has taken possession, a legal lease is in existence. A legal lease not exceeding seven years is an overriding interest within the Land Registration Act 2002, Schedule 3, para. 1 and so is binding on Edith. Edith would have to give Betty one month's notice to quit.

The bank

The bank can only enforce its loan against No. 6 if it has a property right binding on Edith. Alan did not grant the bank a legal mortgage, and the issue is therefore whether the bank has an equitable mortgage. It was established in *Russel v Russel* (1783) Bro CC 269 that the deposit of title deeds as security for a loan creates an equitable charge over the land to which the deeds relate. The deeds had to be deposited for the purpose of securing the loan: *Thames Guaranty Ltd v Campbell* [1985] 1 QB 210. In registered land, the equivalent principle used to be the creation of an equitable lien over the land by the deposit of the land certificate with the lender as security, and this was expressly provided for by the Land Registration Act 1925, s. 66. Although the mere deposit with such purpose did not comply with the evidential requirements for a contract to create an interest in land laid down in the Law of Property Act 1925, s. 40(1), the principle in *Russel v Russel* was based on the doctrine of part performance, which was expressly preserved by the Law of Property Act 1925, s. 40(2). However, s 40 was repealed and replaced by the formality requirements of s. 2 of the Law of Property (Miscellaneous Provisions) Act 1989, under which there is now no valid contract unless there is compliance with s. 2. The mere deposit of title deeds can no longer be treated as creating an equitable mortgage by virtue of part performance because, as there is now no contract, it cannot be partly performed. In *United Bank of Kuwait plc v Sahib* [1997] Ch 107, it was argued that the principle in *Russel v Russel* survived s. 2 on the basis that the creation of a mortgage by deposit of title deeds is *sui generis* and independent of contract; but the Court of Appeal rejected that argument. After the decision in *Sahib*, there was no reason to preserve that method of creating equitable mortgages in registered land, so it was abandoned in the Land Registration Act 2002.

Therefore, in the absence of a written contract complying with s. 2, the bank will not have an equitable mortgage, and can have no property right binding on Edith; it has merely personal remedies against Alan. If there was a written contract satisfying s. 2, the bank should have protected such contract by entry of a notice on the charges register; if it has not done so, its equitable mortgage will not be binding on Edith if she has taken a transfer of the legal estate.

Carl

The validity of Carl's agreement with Alan depends on whether it may be said to amount to a contract to exchange contracts or a 'lock-out' agreement. If it can be construed so as to impose an obligation on Alan to exchange contracts with Carl, then it needs to be in writing in accordance with the requirements of the Law of Property (Miscellaneous Provisions) Act 1989, s. 2(1). If it is a negative agreement simply preventing Alan from negotiating with anyone else, then it does not require formality.

In *Walford v Miles* [1992] 2 WLR 174, there was an agreement that, in consideration for the plaintiffs' agreeing not to withdraw from negotiations, the plaintiffs would terminate negotiations with any third party. This was held to be simply an agreement to negotiate and was not actionable (other than as a misrepresentation). Other types of agreement occurring at the point of exchange of contracts are sometimes classifiable as collateral contracts. In *Record v Bell* [1991] 1 WLR 853, an oral warranty as to the state of the title was given as an inducement to exchange contracts. Again, it was held that such a warranty was outside the requirements of s. 2(1). Similarly, in *Pitt v PHH Asset Management Ltd* [1994] 1 WLR 327, an agreement whereby the vendor's agent agreed not to consider any further offers for the property on the basis that the plaintiff would exchange contracts within two weeks of the receipt of the draft contract, constituted a lock-out agreement outside the ambit of s. 2(1). In *Grossman v Hooper* (2001) 27 EG 135, the Court of Appeal considered that it was inappropriate to describe separate agreements as 'collateral contracts'. They were either part of the contract for the transfer of the land or they were separate from it.

The agreement between Carl and Alan that Alan will not sell to Damien amounts to a lock-out agreement in that it prevents any further negotiations with Damien. In that respect, it is outside the ambit of s. 2(1) (*Pitt v PHH Management*). However, the agreement also commits Carl to exchanging contracts within a month. It is arguable that such an agreement concerns an interest in land and requires formalities for it to be valid (*Dallia v Four Millbank Nominees* [1978] Ch 231). But, it may instead fall into the category of collateral contracts as in *Record v Bell*. Clearly, it is difficult to reconcile the authorities. However, on the basis of *Pitt v PHH Asset Management*, where the agreement did include an obligation to exchange within a month, and *Record v Bell*, where the warranty related to the title of the property, it would seem more likely that the courts would construe Carl's agreement not to sell to Damien as not subject to the requirements of s. 2(1). In that event, the agreement not to sell to Damien would be enforceable as a separate agreement between Carl and Alan.

If, therefore, pursuant to his contract with Damien, Alan conveys No. 4 to Damien, Alan will be liable in damages to Carl for breach of the lock-out agreement. If, on the other hand, Alan were to convey No. 4 to Carl (with whom he has no valid contract of sale), he would be liable in damages to Damien for breach of contract; but Damien's contract will be binding upon Carl only if Damien had protected it by registration as a minor interest.

6

Acquisition of title on death

Introduction

Some land law courses consider the three basic ways in which an estate in land can be acquired: by a disposition *inter vivos*, by adverse possession, and by will. The last method will usually involve a study of the formal requirements for a valid will a topic sometimes studied separately in a course on succession.

If your land law or property course does involve a study of the formal requirements for wills, do not imagine that every question that states that someone has made a will demands that you explain what the formal requirements are. Where a will is mentioned in a question, you are entitled to assume, in the absence of any specified indications to the contrary, that it was validly made, and you should not even mention the requirements of the Wills Act 1837 (as amended).

A discussion of the formal requirements for a will is, however, needed if the question itself suggests that such requirements might not have been complied with—as is evidently the case with both the questions in this chapter.

Question 1

In 1997, Croesus decided to make a codicil to his will. He drew a box at the top of a sheet of paper and made an inked impression of his right thumb inside it. He then wrote underneath that he gave Goldacre, of which he was the fee simple owner, to Delilah and Edwina jointly. Later the same day, he asked Delilah, together with Ajax and Sampson, to act as witnesses. Croesus showed them his right thumb and placed it over the inky print of it made earlier. Ajax then left the room to fetch more wine. During his absence, Delilah and Sampson (in the presence of Croesus) signed their names as witnesses at the bottom of the sheet. None of them noticed that the sheet was not dated.

Croesus's mobile telephone then rang, summoning him to an urgent meeting. Making his apologies, he immediately went to his car. The chauffeur accidentally put the engine into

reverse, so that the car drew up opposite the window of the room to which Ajax had just returned, and in which, at that moment, Ajax began to sign as a witness. Ajax managed to write only the first three letters of his name, however, before suffering an asthmatic attack. He did not complete his signature.

Six months ago, Sampson married Edwina. Two months after the wedding, Croesus died. The validity of the 1997 document as a codicil and of the devise of Goldacre are now being challenged by Maud, who is the sole beneficiary of Croesus's entire estate under the will, which had been made in 1970.

Advise Delilah.

Commentary

This is a typical sort of examination question on the formal requirements for a will. As in other areas, you should keep a look out for important recent cases, as examination questions may well be drafted so as to demand a knowledge of them.

Answer plan

Validity of codicil (**Wills Act 1837, s. 9**)

- Date?
- Signed by testator:
  - thumb print?
  - signed at top of document?
- Mark made *before* dispositive words (same occasion)?
- Acknowledgement in presence of two witnesses?
- Attestation or acknowledgement by witnesses:
  - in presence of testator (clear line of sight)?
  - partial signature by Ajax (did all he could)?

Forfeiture of gifts to witnesses or spouses? (**Wills Act 1837, s. 15**)

- Delilah:
  - forfeit unless there are two other valid witnesses (**Wills Act 1968, s. 1**);
  - so was Ajax's signature sufficient?
- Sampson:
  - no forfeiture, since marries beneficiary only after codicil's execution.
- Effect of any forfeiture on devolution of Goldacre:
  - does Edwina take whole, or does she share it equally with Maud?

Suggested answer

Delilah and Edwina will be entitled to Goldacre only if the codicil was validly executed and if the witnessing of the codicil does not cause either of them to forfeit the devise.

A will (including a codicil) does not need to be dated (*Corbett v Newey* [1996] 2 All ER 914); but it must (*inter alia*) be 'signed by the testator' (Wills Act 1837, s. 9(a)). The ink print of an illiterate testator is a valid signature for this purpose (*Re Finn* (1935) 105 LJP 36). Presumably the same applies to a testator who is physically incapable of holding a pen; but it is not clear whether the ink print of a literate and physically capable testator would also be valid. We need to know whether Croesus is literate and physically capable of signing. In any event, assuming that the print comprises a signature, it does not matter that it appears at the top of the document, as the necessity for the signature to be at the foot or end was abolished for wills made after 1982 (Administration of Justice Act 1982, ss. 17, 73(6)). It is now enough that the testator 'intended by his signature to give effect to the will' (Wills Act 1837, s. 9(b)). In *Re Hornby* [1946] P 171, the placing of the signature in a box near the end of the document met the requirements of the Wills Act 1837, s. 9, in its original form, and would now probably meet the current requirements of the substituted section.

The additional problem here, however, is that, unlike the testator in *Re Hornby*, Croesus made his mark before, rather than after, the writing of the dispositive words. In *Wood v Smith* [1993] Ch 90, the Court of Appeal held that, provided the document was signed and executed on one occasion, the testator's signature which preceded in time the writing of the dispositive words could still 'give effect to' them. The Court of Appeal left open the question of whether the same result would ensue if the events occurred on different occasions; but Scott LJ doubted whether it would. More evidence is needed in the problem as to the timing of the events, in order to ascertain whether they can be considered to have occurred on a single occasion.

Assuming that they did, the signature must still be 'made or acknowledged in the presence of two or more witnesses present at the same time' (Wills Act 1837, s. 9(c)). Although the drawing of a dry pen over a previously written signature is not, for this purpose, a signing (*Re Maddock* (1847) LR 3 P&D 169), it may be effective as an acknowledgement. Croesus's actions in relation to the thumb-print may similarly comprise an acknowledgement, which was evidently properly witnessed, as Delilah, Ajax and Sampson were present at the same time.

A further requirement is that each witness must either attest and sign the will, or acknowledge his signature (which was not possible in the case of the pre-1983 requirements: *Re Colling* [1972] 3 All ER 729), in each case in the presence of the testator (Wills Act 1837, s. 9(d)). This requirement is clearly met in the case of Delilah and Sampson; and, as only two witnesses are needed, the codicil will not be void on this ground. A witness's attestation and signature can also be considered to be made 'in the presence of' the testator, even if the testator has left the room, provided he could have seen the witness sign had he chosen to look (*Casson v Dade* (1781) 1

Bro CC 99, approved in *Couser v Couser* [1996] 3 All ER 256). A clear line of sight leads to a presumption that the attestation was good (*Winchilsea v Wauchope* (1827) 3 Russ 441). If, therefore, like the testatrix who retired to her carriage in *Casson v Dade*, Croesus could have seen Ajax signing had he looked, Ajax's signature would have been made in the presence of Croesus as the section requires.

Did Ajax, however, sign the will? In *Re Chalcraft* [1948] P 222, a testatrix close to death managed to complete only the first part of her signature. This was held to be a valid signature as she did all that she could. By analogy, this principle might be extended to signatures by witnesses, in which case Ajax might also be treated as having done enough.

Assuming that the codicil is valid, Delilah has the problem that the Wills Act 1837, s. 15, provides that a gift to a witness is void. Since Delilah, a beneficiary under the codicil, also witnessed the codicil, this section would result in her forfeiting the devise. The Wills Act 1968, s. 1, however, provides that the witnessing of a beneficiary under the will is disregarded if the will is duly executed 'without his attestation and without that of any other such person'. Sampson might appear to be another 'such person', because he married another beneficiary, Edwina, before Croesus died. This is not, however, the case, because it has been held that the Wills Act 1837, s. 15, does not invalidate a gift to a witness's spouse if the marriage took place only after the will was executed (*Thorpe v Beswick* (1881) 6 QBD 311).

If Ajax's signature is not valid, s. 15 will bite and Delilah will forfeit her share. The issue is then whether Edwina would take Goldacre absolutely, or whether s. 15 would sever the devise by operation of law, so that Edwina takes only a half share in Goldacre, the other half passing to Maud under the will of 1970. There is no case law on this; but the former result appears to be more in line with the intended effect of the section and the nature of a joint tenancy.

If, however, Ajax's signature is valid, Delilah does not forfeit her share as joint tenant. On this basis, assuming that the codicil is itself valid, the devise of Goldacre will be excepted from the gift to Maud under the will made in 1970 (which is, to this extent, revoked), and Goldacre will pass instead to Delilah and Edwina as joint tenants.

Question 2

(a) Potts, a 19-year-old cook in the British army, was sent to the Republic of Rubovia in 2010 as part of the British contingent of a peace-keeping force. The aeroplane that took him to Rubovia left from a military air-base in the south of England. Just before boarding the plane, Potts told his friend and fellow-cook, Pans, 'If anything happens to me, everything goes to Daisy'. Daisy was Potts' sister. Shortly after his arrival in Rubovia, Potts told Pans, 'I've been thinking. If I don't make it, I want Sally to have the lot'. Sally was Potts' girlfriend. A few months ago, Potts completed his period of service in Rubovia and

returned to England. While on a few weeks' home leave, he accidentally strayed over the cliffs at his home near Hastings, and was killed.

Advise Potts' elderly widowed mother, who would be entitled to his estate (which includes the fee simple of Heavyacre) under the intestacy rules.

(b) By his will, Quark gave the lease of a third floor flat in Boson Villas, Hammersmith, to Higgs (who was one year his junior), and the residue of his estate to Charm. Last year, the flat was completely destroyed in a massive gas explosion. Quark and Higgs, who were in the flat at the time, were both killed instantly. At the time, the lease on the flat had two years to run, and there is no possibility of Boson Villas' being rebuilt before its expiration. Quark had taken out insurance on the flat with the Strange Insurance Co Ltd, and under the policy, the sum of £15,000 has become payable to Quark's executors.

Advise Quark's executors whether they should pay this money to the executors of Higgs's estate, or whether they should hold it for Charm as part of Quark's residuary estate.

Commentary

Part **(a)** is a fairly standard type of problem on privileged wills. Part **(b)** is different: it is a somewhat eclectic fantasy, involving the doctrines of lapse and ademption mixed up with the termination of a lease by analogy with ***National Carriers Ltd v Panalpina (Northern) Ltd* [1981] AC 675**. The examiner probably had great fun setting part **(b)**, and is more likely than not to be well disposed to anyone who has a reasonable stab at it.

Answer plan

(a) Privileged will

- **Wills Act 1837, s. 11**:
  - includes realty (Heavyacre) (**Wills (Soldiers and Sailors) Act 1918, s. 3**).
- Can a cook be a soldier?
  - Yes if in armed forces (***Re Wingham***).
  - But what if civilian employee (cf. ***Re White's Application***)?
- In actual military service (***Re Wingham, Re Jones, Re Stable***)?
- Words on boarding:
  - testamentary intent (***Re Stable***);
  - or mere statement of belief (***Re Knibbs' Estate***)?
- Words after arrival:
  - later privileged will can revoke earlier (even if formal) (***Re Gossage's Estate***).
- Manner of Potts' death irrelevant.

(b) (i) Doctrine of lapse

- Did H predecease Q?
- No lapse if H was Q's child or issue and himself left issue:
  - **Wills Act 1837, s. 33** (but no evidence given).
- Otherwise apply **Law of Property Act 1925, s. 184** (***Hickman v Peacey***).

(ii) Doctrine of ademption

- Frustration of lease on destruction of flat (***National Carriers Ltd v Panalpina***)?
- If yes, was it before or after Q's death?
  - If no evidence, Q presumed to survive a chattel, so ademption (***Re Mercer***);
  - but same for lease?

(iii) Insurance moneys

- If H survives the lease and the lease survives Q, H's estate entitled (***Re Hunter***).
- Otherwise held for C.

Suggested answer

(a) Potts' mother will be entitled to his estate only if Potts died intestate. At first sight this may appear to be the case, since he died without having made a will complying with the formalities of the Wills Act 1837, s. 9. The section does not, however, apply if it can be established that Potts was entitled to make, and did make, a privileged will that remained unrevoked at his death.

Under the Wills Act 1837, s. 11, 'any soldier being in actual military service' may dispose of his personal estate as he may have done before the passing of that Act. This means that even a nuncupative (i.e. oral) will made by such a person is valid. Under the Wills (Soldiers and Sailors) Act 1918, s. 3, this privilege was extended to wills of realty. Thus, Heavyacre is also capable of being the subject of a gift under a privileged will.

A member of the armed forces (which Potts would appear to be) ranks as a soldier even if he is allocated a non-combative role, such as that of a doctor or a chaplain (*Re Wingham* [1949] P 187) or (as in the problem) that of a cook. If, however, Potts was a civilian employee, the position is less clear. In *Re White's Application* [1975] 2 NSWLR 125, an Australian court held that a British subject employed by the United States Army as a civilian engineer was doing the job of a soldier and was therefore entitled to the privilege. It remains to be seen if an English court would adopt a similarly wide interpretation.

Assuming Potts was a soldier, the next issue is whether he was 'in actual military service'. It is doubtful whether a soldier about to be sent as part of a peace-keeping force merely to a disturbed area can be said to be in actual military service (*Re Wingham*, Denning LJ). Potts might nevertheless have been in actual military service even if Britain was not at war with Rubovia. Thus in *Re Jones* [1981] 1 All ER 1, a corporal in the Parachute Regiment was shot whilst on patrol. It was held that, in aiding a civil power to put down an insurrection, he was in actual military service, and so entitled to make a privileged will. If a war was raging between various factions in Rubovia at the time when Potts was sent there, he is also likely to be held to have been in actual military service. Moreover it is not necessary for Potts to be in the war zone at the time of making the privileged will. Thus in *Re Stable* [1919] P 7, the privilege applied to a nuncupative will made in England by a soldier under orders to go to the front.

Potts was therefore capable of making a privileged will just before boarding the aeroplane: but did he in fact do so? It is not necessary that the deceased should be aware that he is making his will; it is enough if he intends that his estate should be disposed of in accordance with his statement (*Re Stable*). It is not sufficient, however, if the words are a mere statement of how the deceased believes his property will devolve in the absence of a will (*Re Knibbs' Estate* [1962] 2 All ER 829). It is therefore a matter of evidence whether Potts' words to Pans on boarding the aeroplane were meant to be testamentary or indicated merely a misunderstanding of the intestacy laws.

Even if the former construction were found to be the correct one, however, what is the effect of Potts' further words to Pans made after their arrival? A fresh privileged will can be made provided the deceased was in actual military service at the relevant time—as Potts evidently was here. Furthermore, even though the Wills Act 1837, s. 20, requires the same formalities for the revocation of a will as for its creation, it has been held that a later privileged will revokes an earlier will (even an earlier formal will (*Re Gossage's Estate* [1921] P 194)) to the extent that it is inconsistent with it, even though the later will does not comply with the Wills Act 1837, s. 9. Potts' later words to Pans therefore appear to revoke his earlier privileged will in favour of Daisy, and to create a fresh privileged will in favour of Sally.

A privileged will does not cease to be valid merely because its maker ceases to be in actual military service, as Potts was while on leave at home. Furthermore, the manner of Potts' death is also irrelevant.

It would therefore appear that Sally is entitled to Potts' estate, and that Potts' mother (unless she can make a claim under the Inheritance (Provision for Family and Dependants) Act 1975) will receive nothing.

(b) Quark's executors must pay the insurance money to the executors of Higgs's estate if Higgs died with a vested interest in the lease. This will not be the case if Higgs predeceased Quark, since the general rule is that a gift by will lapses if the beneficiary predeceases the testator. This rule does not apply if Higgs was Quark's child or remoter issue and himself left issue living at Quark's death (see Wills Act 1837, s. 33) but there is no possibility of that in the problem. Thus, in the absence of evidence indicating which of Quark or Higgs died first, the presumption in the Law of Property Act 1925, s. 184, applies. This provides (*inter alia*) that if two persons have died in circumstances rendering it uncertain which died first, for the purpose of determining title to property the younger is deemed to survive. If the section applies, the person treated as dying first is Quark. Even where it is considered likely that the deaths were simultaneous, in the absence of proof of this, the presumption applies (*Hickman v Peacey* [1945] AC 304).

For Higgs's estate to take, however, it is not enough that Higgs dies after Quark; the property which Higgs is to take under the will must also be in existence at the time of Quark's death. Land is generally regarded as indestructible and, strictly, so is the legal estate of an airspace, since the right to the space survives the destruction of the part of the building which encloses it. Nevertheless, the destruction of a building ends the tenant's capacity to make use of it, and it appears that the law is coming to recognise that such destruction can terminate (and thus, in effect, destroy) the lease itself. Thus, in *National Carriers Ltd v Panalpina (Northern) Ltd* [1981] AC 675, the House of Lords considered that the doctrine of frustration might apply to a lease if, owing to circumstances beyond the control of either of the parties to it, the tenant was unable to use the premises for the purposes contemplated. Since the lease of the third floor of Boson Villas will expire before the property can be reinstated, it is possible that the court, applying the reasoning of *Panalpina*, would hold that the destruction of the building terminated the lease.

If this is held to have occurred, the next issue is whether the destruction occurred before or after the death of Quark. If it was before, the gift adeems: if after, the lease vests in Higgs. In the absence of evidence on this point, the court will need to apply a presumption. If the testator dies in the same calamity which destroys one of his assets and it is uncertain which perished first, the asset is deemed to have been destroyed before the testator, so that the gift adeems (*Re Mercer* [1944] 1 All ER 759). This presumption was, however, developed in the context of chattels, the existence of which might be considered more precarious than that of a leasehold estate. It is therefore uncertain whether the court would apply that presumption in the problem, or, indeed, whether, in respect of leasehold property, the presumption might be reversed.

If the court were to apply the reverse presumption in the case of a leasehold estate, the combined effect of such presumption and the Law of Property Act 1925, s. 184, would be that Higgs would be treated as having acquired a vested interest in the lease on Quark's death. In these circumstances, the interest of Higgs (or, after his death, the interest of his estate) would be transferred to the rights under the insurance policy when the lease terminates on the destruction of the building (*Re Hunter* (1975) 58 DLR 175 (Ontario)).

If any of the foregoing requirements is not satisfied, Quark's executors should hold the insurance money for Charm as residuary beneficiary under Quark's will.

Further reading

Harpum, C., *Megarry & Wade: The Law of Real Property*, 7th edn, Sweet & Maxwell, 2008.

7

Registered land

Introduction

Originally introduced in the nineteenth century, the system of registration of titles to land has gradually been extended to different areas throughout England and Wales, and on 1 December 1990 all remaining areas became areas of compulsory registration. The system of registration is now therefore overwhelmingly dominant. A key change in this area was the repeal and replacement of the **Land Registration Act 1925** by the **Land Registration Act 2002**.

The purchaser's title under all conveyances of freehold land, grants of leases for more than seven years, and assignments of leases with more than seven years unexpired, must be registered substantively (i.e. with their own separate title) at HM Land Registry on completion of the transaction. The **LRA 2002** also extended the list of estates which may be registered substantively to include franchises, profits à prendre in gross, and rent charges. The **Land Registration Act 1997** had earlier extended the transactions requiring registration of title to include dispositions by way of gift, dispositions by personal representatives, and dispositions in pursuance of a court order.

Where any such transactions are effected with regard to land where the title is not yet registered, the transaction is effected in the normal way for unregistered land. At the conclusion of the transaction, however, the transferee must register his legal title within two months (or within such longer period as the registrar, on application, may allow). Failure to do so in respect of the purported transfer of the legal estate results in his being divested of the legal title which the vendor (or other transferor) holds on trust for him (**Land Registration Act 2002, s. 7(1)(a)**). In the case of a grant or creation of a mortgage the effect of failure to register is to treat the grant or creation as a contract made for valuable consideration (**LRA 2002, s. 7(1)(b)**).

Registration of title to all land was the ultimate aim of the 1925 legislation. Registration under the **Land Registration Act 1925** furnished a title guaranteed by the State and the underlying principle was that the register at HM Land Registry should, so far as possible, reflect the title to the land. The **Land Registration Act 2002** further extended this 'mirror' principle in ways which will be pointed out in the answers to the questions in this chapter. The Act also includes sections which provide for the gradual introduction of electronic conveyancing.

Under the old law, the title document to registered land was the land certificate issued by HM Land Registry to the registered proprietor. This contained the entries recorded on the register on the date on which it was last compared with it. If the registered proprietor granted a legal mortgage of the land, the Land Registry issued a charge certificate to the mortgagee. Land and charge certificates are now abolished. The LRA 2002 also makes provision for the issue of a form of land certificates known as title information documents, but these do not constitute conclusive evidence of title. A contemporary official copy of the register of title supplied by the Land Registry will provide good evidence (s. 67, LRA 2002, and Land Registration Rules 2003, r. 134. See also the 'Report on responses to Land Registration Rules 2003 a Land Registry Consultation' (2003) p. 11, paras. 2.2, 2.18). On a transfer of land with registered title, the legal title passes only when the transfer is registered at HM Land Registry.

The system of registration of title also recognises two categories of interests which, unlike the legal estates mentioned above, are not registrable substantively. The first of these are registrable interests which can be protected by the entry of a notice on the register (s. 32(1), LRA 2002). Under the old law these interests were known as minor interests and some commentators continue to adopt this nomenclature for ease of reference.

The second of these are interests which override the register (usually referred to as overriding interests) which are set out in LRA 2002, Schedule 1 (unregistered interests that override first registration), and Schedule 3 (unregistered interests which override registered dispositions). Overriding interests are interests which, although not entered on the register, are nevertheless interests subject to which registered dispositions of the land take effect (s. 11(4)(b) and s. 30(2)(ii), LRA 2002). The overriding interests which are set out in Schedule 3 to the Act are much reduced and modified, as part of the general policy of the Act to make the register a mirror of the title and so avoid the presence of any binding interests which do not appear on it. The existence of overriding interests is an important qualification to the basic principle that the register is an accurate reflection of the title to the land.

Under the old law, the most litigated paragraph of s. 70(1), LRA 1925, was para (g), which made overriding 'the rights of every person in actual occupation of the land or in receipt of the rents and profits thereof, save where enquiry is made of such person and the rights are not disclosed'.

This proved to be a very wide section which made overriding, and therefore binding, all sorts of rights which would not have been binding in unregistered title, where their binding effect would have depended upon registration under the Land Charges Act 1972 or notice. The section caused the widest divergence from the principles of unregistered title, and was therefore a favourite for examination questions such as 'how would your answer differ if the title to the land were unregistered...?'

Schedule 3, para. 2 contains a modified version of s. 70(1)(g), LRA 1925, protecting the interests of persons in actual occupation. It is therefore the case that much of the case law under s. 70(1)(g), LRA 1925 will remain relevant for the time being.

The LRA 2002 also has transitional provisions and, in particular, it should be noted that Schedule 1 lists unregistered interests which override first registration. In answering any exam question, therefore, you should consider carefully whether you are being asked to deal with a disposition of unregistered land when Schedule 1 applies or a registered disposition when Schedule 3 applies. In general, we have focused on registered dispositions and Schedule 3 in this book.

In this chapter, Question 1 concentrates on the overriding interests of persons in actual occupation of the land under Schedule 3, para. 2, Land Registration Act 2002. Question 2 is broader and calls for a critique of the concept of overriding interests and the balance which property law strives to achieve between the purchaser of land and the owners of interests in that land. Question 3 considers the application of the remedy of rectification.

Question 1

Hector is the registered proprietor of a large Victorian house that he bought in the spring of 2009 with the aid of a loan of £50,000 from the Troy Building Society, which registered its legal charge a month later. His mother provided half the deposit and agreed to pay half the mortgage instalments. As she was recently widowed, Hector invited her to set up home with him. The house required some extensive redecoration and rewiring before it was habitable, and the vendor allowed Hector to have access for these purposes before completion. After completion, Hector's mother took a fortnight's holiday, and Hector had the work finished during this time. She moved in with her furniture and possessions on her return.

In the autumn of 2009, Hector converted the house into three flats. He now occupies the ground floor himself with his mother and he let the flat on the first floor to Ajax on a monthly tenancy in December 2009. Early in 2010, Hector's brother, Paris, took possession of the flat on the second floor under a seven-year lease at a rent of £3,000 per year. Paris had a friend, Helen, who had recently become unemployed, so he allowed her to share the flat free of charge. In September 2010, Paris accepted an offer of a two-year contract abroad. He decided to keep the flat on, however, and has continued to pay Hector the rent. Paris had told Helen she can remain there as long as she wants provided she pays the electricity bills.

At the rear of the house, there is a large car-parking area. Hector entered into an agreement in October 2010 with his neighbour Odysseus that Odysseus could park his caravan there when not travelling abroad with it.

Hector, unbeknown to his mother, took out a second mortgage from the Sparta Bank in November 2010 to prop up his failing business. As he has not been making any repayments recently to either the Troy Building Society or the Sparta Bank, they are both seeking to recover their loans. Hector has now fled the country and his business is insolvent.

Discuss.

Commentary

This is a question that mixes different issues relating to overriding interests. The major area of difficulty is without question that of **Schedule 3 para. 2, LRA 2002** and the effect of the case law under the former provisions in the **Land Registration Act 1925, s. 70(1)(g)**. So, a knowledge of the case law on **s. 70(1)(g)** is indispensable. Whilst many interests may become overriding under **Schedule 3**, such as the interest of Hector's mother, they may well be minor interests in their own right and you should not omit to say that, as such, they may be protected by an entry on the register. The question also includes some of the other interests which may override the register and those which require to be completed by registration.

Answer plan

- Consider what interest Hector's mother has and whether it is minor or overriding. Then decide if it is binding on (i) the Troy Building Society and (ii) the Sparta Bank.
- What interest has Ajax? Is it a minor or overriding interest? Is it binding on the Building Society and the Bank?
- What interest has Paris? Is it a legal or equitable lease? (As the Question does not specifically indicate, you should consider both.) In both cases, is it a minor or an overriding interest, and is it binding on the Building Society or the Bank?
- What is the nature of Helen's occupation? Is this capable of being a minor or an overriding interest? Is it binding on the Building Society or the Bank?
- What sort of interest may have been created by Hector's agreement with Odysseus? Would such an interest be a minor or an overriding interest and therefore binding or not?

Suggested answer

Hector's mother

Hector's mother has an equitable interest behind a resulting trust in the house by virtue of her contribution to the purchase price. The question arises as to whether her interest can override the interest of the legal mortgagees. A beneficial equitable interest under a trust is not specifically included in the list of overriding interests in **Schedule 3, Land Registration Act 2002**. It is, however, a proprietary interest and is therefore a minor interest which Hector's mother could have protected by an entry of a restriction in the proprietorship register of the title to which it relates (**LRA 2002, ss. 40, 43**). The restriction would have prohibited a dealing with the registered estate unless the purchaser or mortgagee obtained a receipt from two trustees. This would not have given her protection against the Troy Building Society (for the same reasons given below as to why her overriding interest would be postponed to them) but would have prevented Hector from mortgaging to Sparta Bank without appointing a second trustee.

Even though Hector's mother did not enter a restriction, under the Land Registration Act 2002, Schedule 3, para. 2, an interest belonging to a person in actual occupation of land at the time of the disposition is protected as an overriding interest. The effect of LRA 2002, s. 29(1) and Schedule 3, para. 2 is to make it clear that such an interest must be of a proprietary, not a personal, nature. Two issues arise here: what is actual occupation and when must such occupation occur?

In answering this question, the case law decided under the old law contained in s. 70(1)(g), Land Registration Act 1925 will continue to be relevant. A person claiming such an overriding interest must establish actual occupation at the time of the completion of the disposition, that is, in this case, the two mortgages. This is also now clear from the wording of Schedule 3, para. 2 and confirms the position established under the old law in *Abbey National Building Society v Cann* [1991] 1 AC 56. Such claim to an overriding interest is enforceable provided that the rights remain subsisting at the date of registration. Thus Hector's mother's claim to an overriding interest will depend upon her establishing that she was in actual occupation at the date of the completion in the spring of 2009.

Actual occupation naturally includes the physical presence of the person claiming the interest (*Hodgson v Marks* [1971] Ch 892). In *Williams & Glyn's Bank Ltd v Boland* [1981] AC 487, actual occupation was said to be a matter of fact to be construed in ordinary words of plain English. However, later cases found shades of meaning within this apparently literal interpretation of the section. In *Abbey National Building Society v Cann*, it was thought that occupation by a caretaker or company representative could satisfy the section. In *Lloyd v Dugdale* [2002] 2 P & CR 13, it was held that actual occupation could not be claimed by a company's managing director since he was there as an agent of the company and not on his own account. In *Lloyds Bank v Rosset* [1991] 1 AC 107, the presence of builders in occupation of the site of a semi-derelict farmhouse was held to be capable of satisfying the requirements of the section, but in *Cann* it was doubted whether acts in preparation for a future occupation, such as laying carpets and moving in furniture, were sufficient. Thus, the physical presence of the mother may not be necessary if it can be shown that the decorators were present in the property as her agents. They were, in fact, hired by Hector not his mother, so there may be an argument that they were not acting as her agents for these purposes. It is a controversial question whether someone who is not physically present on the premises, but who is employing a builder who is on the site, can claim to be in actual occupation. Someone whose presence is merely fleeting such as a prospective purchaser who enters to measure the premises for curtains is not to be considered to be in actual occupation (*Abbey National Building Society v Cann*). Nor is a builder who enters to carry out repairs and renovations, himself in actual occupation (*Canadian Imperial Bank of Commerce v Bello* (1992) 64 P & CR 48). A temporary absence may not destroy the absentee's continuing to be in actual occupation. In *Chhokar v Chhokar* [1984] FLR 313, a wife was held to remain in actual occupation during the period she was in hospital having a baby. In *Link Lending Ltd v Bustard* [2010] EWCA Civ 424, the Court of Appeal held that a mental patient who had been staying (as she was obliged to do) in a residential care home for over a year was nevertheless still in actual occupation of the house where she had previously been living; key factors were: it was her only furnished home, she made weekly supervised visits there to collect the post, and she intended to reside there again when she could. By contrast, in *Thompson v Foy* [2009] EWHC 1076 (Ch), Mrs Thompson left the property with no intention to return, and this was crucial in the court's holding that she thereupon ceased to be in actual occupation, despite the fact that most of her furniture and bedding had not yet been removed. In the problem, Hector's mother does not begin actual occupation until a fortnight after the completion of the transaction. This would seem to be distinguishable from a case where the continuity of occupation has been broken by a temporary absence. Thus, it would be necessary for the mother to establish vicarious occupation through the decorators a task which may prove too difficult.

A further requirement in Schedule 3, para. 2(c)(i) is that the occupation would have been obvious on a reasonably careful inspection of the land at the time of the disposition. Given that neither Hector's mother nor her possessions were present until a fortnight later she clearly will not fulfil this requirement. However, Schedule 3, para. 2(c)(ii) sets out the additional requirement that the person to whom the disposition was made must have been unaware of the interest. Although this point is not made clear in the question it is quite possible that the Troy Building Society did know of her interest since she provided part of the deposit and is paying half of the mortgage repayments. If this is the case then the Troy Building Society would not be able to rely on this exception.

It might be argued, however, that Hector's mother has waived her right as against the Troy Building Society as she must have known of its charge over the property and must have impliedly consented to its taking priority over her interest (*Paddington Building Society v Mendelsohn* (1985) 50 P & CR 244). Indeed, she had agreed to pay half the mortgage instalments. In any event, as the charge in favour of the Troy Building Society was contemporaneous with the purchase, her trust was engrafted on an already encumbered title (*Abbey National Building Society v Cann*).

These arguments will not prevail against the Sparta Bank. By the time the mortgage with the Sparta Bank had been entered into, Hector's mother was in occupation and it is likely that such occupation would have been obvious on a reasonably careful inspection of the land (Schedule 3, para. 2(c)(i)). Not only is she, therefore, clearly in actual occupation at the time of the creation and registration of its charge, but she is unaware of it and, therefore, cannot be taken to have waived her priority. Her beneficial interest will be, under Schedule 3, para. 2, an overriding interest and binding on the Bank.

In neither case will her interest have been overreached, since there is only one trustee Hector (*Williams & Glyn's Bank Ltd v Boland* [1979] Ch 312; s. 27, Law of Property Act 1925).

Ajax

Ajax occupies a flat in the house under a monthly tenancy, which is presumably a legal periodic tenancy within the Law of Property Act 1925, s. 54(2). It is protected as an overriding interest under the LRA 2002, Schedule 3, para. 1, as a legal lease granted for a term not exceeding seven years. Leases for more than seven years are registrable substantively under the LRA 2002. Ajax's lease, being a proprietary interest, is also protected under Schedule 3, para. 2, provided Ajax is in actual occupation. Overriding interests must be in existence before the date of the disposition and at the date of registration of the purchaser's interest. Thus, Ajax's interest will be enforceable against the Sparta Bank by virtue of its protection under Schedule 3, para. 1, but not against the Troy Building Society, whose legal charge was created and registered before the lease was created.

Paris and Helen

Paris's lease is not registrable substantively as it is not for more than seven years and as it was not created until after the acquisition of the property and the creation and registration of the charge in favour of the Troy Building Society, his interest will not be binding on that Building Society.

Paris is in occupation of the second-floor flat under a seven-year lease. If this is a legal lease then it is protected under the Land Registration Act, Schedule 3, para. 1 and would be binding on the Sparta Bank. If it is equitable that paragraph does not apply and he would have to rely on Schedule 3, para. 2 unless it was protected by an entry of a notice on the charges register. However, he is no longer in actual occupation himself although Helen is occupying the property in his absence, so his occupation would not be discoverable on a reasonable inspection so as to satisfy Schedule 3, para. 2(c)(i). Helen is occupying the flat under an informal arrangement and her occupancy would constitute no more than a personal right to occupy as a bare licensee. As such she does not satisfy the requirement of Schedule 3, para. 2 (*Strand Securities Ltd v Caswell* [1965] Ch 958). At the time of the second mortgage, Paris is no longer in occupation himself. Neither he, therefore, nor Helen, has any protection under Schedule 3, para. 2 against the Sparta Bank.

Odysseus

Odysseus has an agreement which has been created expressly to park his caravan on the car park. If this constitutes an easement then, in order to be legal it should have been both granted by deed (ss. 52 and 1(2), Law of Property Act 1925) and registered.

Section 27(2)(d) Land Registration Act 2002 provides that an expressly created easement is only legal and binding if it is registered against the title of the burdened land (Hector's land). If that has been done, then it will be binding upon the Sparta Bank, but not otherwise. If the easement is equitable, then it will be a minor interest only and may be protected by an entry of a notice on the register. If it is not so protected, it will not be overriding under Schedule 3, para. 3 as only legal easements which are not caught by the registration requirements of s. 27 fall within that paragraph.

It remains to be considered whether, if Odysseus's easement is equitable it falls to be protected under Schedule 3, para. 2, since Odysseus has an interest of a proprietary nature and it might be arguable that he is in actual occupation. In *Epps v Esso Petroleum Co Ltd* [1973] 1 WLR 1071, a case decided under the old law in s. 70(1)(g), LRA 1925, the parking of a car on a strip of land did not suffice to establish actual occupation. However, in *Kling v Keston Properties Ltd* (1983) 49 P & CR 212, the parking of a car in a garage by agreement was held to constitute sufficient occupation to satisfy the section as regards a right of pre-emption of the garage. Indeed, it was suggested in that case, that had the car not actually been parked at the time, its intermittent presence in the garage would have sufficed.

In the problem, the caravan is not parked in any defined area such as a garage. It may be possible, therefore, to distinguish *Kling v Keston Properties Ltd*. In addition, the requirement contained in Schedule 3, para. 2(c)(i) prescribes that the interest must have been obvious on a reasonably careful inspection of the land at the time of the disposition. The intermittent presence of the caravan may be unlikely to satisfy that requirement. In any case, the overriding interest would only be exercisable against the second mortgagee on the same grounds as before.

Question 2

'. . . the traditional view of overriding interests is now being questioned. If the system of registered title is to be wholly effective, the register should be an accurate reflection of the state of the title, and the range of enquiries beyond the register should be kept to a minimum.' (Megarry, R. and Wade, W., *The Law of Real Property*, 7th edn, Charles Harpum (ed.), London: Sweet & Maxwell, 2007.)

(a) Discuss with regard to the overriding interests protected under Schedule 3 of the Land Registration Act 2002, indicating how these differ from the overriding interests formerly contained in s. 70(1) of the Land Registration Act 1925.

(b) How has the Land Registration Act 2002 lessened the impact of overriding interests?

Commentary

This question requires, in the first instance, an account of the system of registered title in general, and overriding interests in particular. But it will not be sufficient simply to list the different types of interests without more. What is required is a critical analysis of the problems to be encountered in the system of registered conveyancing brought about by a group of interests which, despite their non-appearance on the register, still bind the purchaser. There are two Law Commission Reports which provide some useful background analysis of these issues: 'Third Report on Land Registration', Law Com. No. 158 (1989) (HC 269) and 'Land Registration for the Twenty-first Century' Law Com. No. 254 (1998).

As mentioned in the Introduction to this chapter, the **Land Registration Act 2002** represents a considerable shift towards the mirror principle, and as part of this, the overriding interests in **s. 70(1) Land Registration Act 1925** have been greatly modified and reduced; they are now 'interests which override' in **Schedule 3 to the 2002 Act**. Various changes and modifications have been pointed out in the answer to part **(a)** of this question, and part **(b)** is a general overall view of the changes.

Answer plan

(a)
- Mirror principle of the register.
- Overriding interests represent a serious flaw in this, but the justification for them is that they are the interests of persons unable to protect them, or even unaware of them.
- Relevant date for overriding interests to exist to be binding on a purchaser.
- **Section 70(1)(g), LRA 1925** and its replacement by **Schedule 3, para. 2, LRA 2002**.
- Case law on the nature of 'actual occupation' for the purposes of the section, indicating any changes under the **LRA 2002**.

(b)
- Interests overriding on a first registration of title and on a registered disposition (**Schedules 1 and 3, LRA 2002**).
- **Section 70(1)(a), LRA 1925** and provision for legal easements under the **LRA 2002**.
- Equitable easements under the **LRA 1925** and changes under the **LRA 2002**.
- **Section 70(1)(f), LRA 1925** makes overriding rights acquired (or being acquired) under the Limitation Acts but these are not applicable to registered land under the **LRA 2002**.
- **Section 70(1)(g), LRA 1925** and judicial interpretations of it in the cases. The new **para. 2, Schedule 3, LRA 2002** is narrower and would reverse some of these decisions.
- How legal leases are dealt with under the **LRA 2002**.

Suggested answer

(a) The fundamental principle of registered conveyancing is that the purchaser is bound by everything on the register which provides a mirror of the title and all the interests affecting the land. As part of the 1925 legislation, the Land Registration Act 1925 was concerned to simplify conveyancing and provide certainty for the purchaser. The LRA 1925 has now been repealed and replaced by the LRA 2002.

Under the system of registration before the LRA 2002, legal freeholds and leases of more than 21 years were registrable substantively with their own title number and land certificate. (So also were legal rentcharges, but these are now virtually extinct as the Rentcharges Act 1977 provided for them to cease after sixty years and a procedure for their redemption before then in certain cases.) Certain interests are now registrable dispositions (such as the express grant or reservation of a legal easement within s. 1(2), LPA 1925 and the grant of a legal charge) which must be completed by registration in order to be legal and binding. Other interests can be protected as minor interests by means of a notice or restriction under the LRA 2002. Thus many interests affecting the land are to be found on the register of title.

But 'the register of title is not a perfect mirror of the title to a registered property. It is not possible to rely on entries on the register as the complete record of everything that affects the title' (*per* Peter Gibson LJ, *Overseas Investments Ltd v Simcobuild Construction Ltd* (1995) 70 P & CR 322 at 327). This limitation to the mirror principle is primarily to be found in the category of overriding interests. These are interests which, although not registered or protected on the register, bind a registered proprietor regardless of his state of knowledge as to their existence (LRA 2002, Schedule 3).

The list of overriding interests is contained in Schedule 3 of the LRA 2002. It includes a range of interests such as certain rights of way, rights under local land charges, property rights of a person in actual occupation, and legal leases for seven years or less.

Under the former law, the class of overriding interests which caused the most litigation was contained in s. 70(1)(g), Land Registration Act 1925. This subsection protected the rights of persons in actual occupation of the land or in receipt of rent save where enquiry had been made of them and their interest had not been disclosed.

The justification for having a category of interests which exists outside the register is that they will be discoverable on inspection. The balance between the interest of the purchaser and the objective of the 1925 legislation, and the interest of the person who for some social or technical reason requires the additional protection of an overriding interest, should therefore be struck. The purchaser, simply by carrying out an inspection of the property, as might be expected during the process of the conveyance of a legal title, can discover the interest. The person with the interest is not vulnerable because of any failure to have the interest protected on the register.

The difficulty with this theory is that it presupposes that overriding interests are all discoverable by inspection. Before the LRA 2002, this was not necessarily the case. For example, the rights of an adverse possessor were protected under s. 70(1)(f), Land Registration Act 1925, but there was no requirement that he should be in actual occupation. His rights might not, therefore, have been discoverable on inspection; indeed, they might not even have been known to the vendor, as in *Red House Farms (Thorndon) Ltd v Catchpole* [1977] 2 EGLR 125 where the owner was unaware that the defendant was shooting fowl on its land, and *Prudential Assurance Co Ltd v Waterloo Real Estate Inc.* [1998] EGCS 51, where a neighbour took over a party wall without the owner's knowledge.

Furthermore, there was a question as to the date when an overriding interest took effect. A purchaser will have inspected the property before the completion of the disposition to him, but in registered land, the disposition does not itself transfer the legal estate to him. This only happens when the disposition is subsequently registered at HM Land Registry. The LRA 2002 will ultimately avoid the problem of the 'registration gap' when electronic conveyancing is introduced, as completion and registration of a disposition will then be simultaneous. Should overriding interests be allowed to arise during the time between completion and registration? The majority of the House of Lords in *Abbey National Building Society v Cann* [1991] 1 AC 56, decided that the critical time was the date of registration except for interests arising under s. 70(1)(g), LRA 1925 which were a special case. Their Lordships decided that the date when actual occupation should be relevant is the date of the completion of the disposition. That paragraph has been replaced by Schedule 3, para. 2, which refers to 'An interest belonging at the time of the disposition to a person in actual occupation'. In *Thompson v Foy* [2009] EWHC 1076 (Ch), Lewison J thought that this wording suggested that it was the interest that had to belong at the time of the disposition; so that actual occupation would have to exist both at that time (to affect the estate immediately before the disposition), and at the date of registration (for that interest to be protected). He decided, however, to leave the point open. In any event, all other overriding interests can be created, unbeknown to the purchaser, between completion and registration. A purchaser could, for instance, be bound by an easement or a short lease created after completion. It was for this reason that Lord Bridge in the *Abbey National* case dissented on this point, preferring the date of disposition as the relevant date for all overriding interests (except for local land charges).

The concept of overriding interests within the system of registered conveyancing contrasts remarkably with the effect of the Land Charges Act 1972 in unregistered conveyancing. Any registrable interest left unprotected under that Act is void against specified categories of purchasers (*Midland Bank Trust Co. v Green* [1981] AC 513). This applies regardless of the state of knowledge of the purchaser, and was considered by the court in *Midland Bank Trust Co. v Green* to reflect the intention of the legislature in keeping the process of conveyancing simple and in protecting the purchaser.

The most difficult overriding interests have been those protected under s.70(1)(g) of the LRA 1925. The impact of this was noted in the case of *Williams & Glyn's Bank v Boland* [1981] AC 487 where the equitable interest of Mrs Boland was held to prevail as an overriding interest against the legal mortgagee. This case reflects the social policy of the legislature in protecting this type of interest. There was, in fact, nothing to prevent Mrs Boland protecting her interest as a minor interest on the register. The fact that she did not is symptomatic of the nature of these interests which arise unbeknown to the individuals concerned who are likely to be unaware of the need for, or manner of, their protection. For this reason the legislature deemed that they should be protected regardless of their appearance on the register. Although s. 70(1)(g) placed a heavy duty of inquiry on a purchaser, it nevertheless operated more fairly than the 'all or nothing' of registration of an interest under the Land Charges Act 1972 in unregistered title. Conveyancers have adapted to the system and, since *Boland*, make exhaustive enquiries as to occupiers of land. Paragraph 2, Schedule 3 of the LRA 2002 requires that enquiries are made of the occupier himself and not of his solicitor or the vendor's solicitor, and an occupier other than the vendor will often be asked to sign a disclaimer or waiver of their rights before the purchaser or mortgagee can safely be advised to proceed with the transaction. In *Woolwich Building Society v Dickman & Todd* (1996) 72 P & CR 470 a waiver signed by tenants protected under the Rent Acts was held ineffective as regards a mortgagee of the property and the Court of Appeal indicated that such a waiver would only be valid if noted on the register. It is possible to distinguish the case as one invalidating a waiver of statutory rights, but in any event it has been much criticised and is dubious authority. Such waivers of rights are commonly used by institutional lenders and have not been questioned since.

The paternalistic attitude of protecting overriding interests as the rights of persons who cannot, or do not, protect them by an entry on the register is to be found in s.116, LRA 2002, which specifically states that estoppel interests and mere equities are capable of binding successors in title of registered land. Such interests arise informally from a course of conduct, so that a person who has such a right may not realise this, or may have difficulty in proving it without a court order.

For purchasers or mortgagees in the position of the bank in *Boland*, this involves a heavy burden of inspection and enquiry prior to the completion of the transaction. It is not sufficient for the purchaser to make enquiries of the vendor; para. 2, Sch. 3 is specific in requiring enquiries to be made of the person benefiting from the overriding interest (*Hodgson v Marks* [1971] Ch 892).

The concept of actual occupation is not further defined in Schedule 3 of the LRA 2002. The case law decided on the meaning of 'actual occupation' under s. 70(1)(g), LRA 1925 is likely, therefore, to remain relevant. This former case law gave the term a wide meaning. It could include, for example, occupation through an agent as in *Lloyd's Bank plc v Rosset* [1991] 1 AC 107, where it was said *obiter* that builders employed by Mrs Rosset who were occupying the property at the relevant date could be in actual occupation as her representatives.

Although the occupation must in general be continuous, a temporary absence from the property will not cause the interest to be lost, as in *Chhokar v Chhokar* [1984] FLR 313, where Mrs Chhokar was absent from the property while giving birth to a child. However, preparatory acts such as laying carpets in readiness for occupation will not be sufficient to establish actual occupation under s. 70(1)(g) (*Abbey National Building Society v Cann* [1991] 1 AC 56 and *Canadian Imperial Bank of Commerce v Bello* (1992) 64 P & CR 48). It was held under s. 70(1)(g) of the LRA 1925 that children living with their parents are not in actual occupation and so do not put a purchaser under a duty of enquiry (*Hypo-Mortgage Services Ltd v Robinson* [1997] 2 FLR 71). The rationale for this was that the saving for a purchaser who makes enquiries of an occupier who does not disclose their rights would clearly be absurd and inapplicable for a child of tender years. The case has been criticised (see Kenny, 'Children are Spare Ribs' [1997] *Conv* 84) as children of more mature years ought to be able to reply to enquiries made of them. The LRA 2002 allows for this in Schedule 3, para. 2(b) where it refers to an enquiry made of a person who fails to disclose the right 'when he could reasonably have been expected to do so'. As well as exempting a purchaser from making enquiries of young children, this would presumably also exempt him from enquiring of someone who was obviously insane or senile.

In *City of London Building Society v Flegg* [1988] AC 54 the House of Lords rejected an attempt to extend the principle of *Boland* to a situation where a mortgage was created by two trustees instead of just one, thereby complying with the overreaching principle of s. 2, Law of Property Act 1925. It was held that once overreaching has taken place by a conveyance (or mortgage in the particular case), the interests of the beneficiaries are no longer interests in land but are instead interests in the proceeds of sale of the land. They could not therefore be proprietary interests binding on the purchaser (or mortgagee) for the purpose of s. 70(1)(g), LRA 1925. An ingenious argument that the effect of the Trusts of Land and Appointment of Trustees Act 1996 was to reverse the decision in *Flegg* in circumstances where there is a limitation on the trustees' power of sale under the Act (see Ferris and Battersby [1998] *Conv* 168) now appears to have been dealt with by s. 26(1), Land Registration Act 2002 which says that an owner's powers to deal with a registered title are presumed to be free of any limitation except for one appearing on the register. Moreover, even a charge to secure future indebtedness where no capital monies are handed over will overreach the interest of the beneficiaries so that they may no longer subsist as proprietary interests in the land (*State Bank of India v Sood* [1997] Ch 276).

A further problem with s. 70(1)(g), Land Registration Act 1925 was thrown up by the case of *Ferrishurst Ltd v Wallcite Ltd* [1999] 1 All ER 977 where it was held that a person who is in occupation of part only of property over which he has rights may assert those rights as regards the remainder of the property in the title of which he is not in occupation. The case concerned a lease under which the lessee was given an option to purchase the remainder. The option was held to be protected under s. 70(1)(g) even though the lessee was occupying only part of the leased property. This case has been reversed by the wording of Schedule 3, para. 2, LRA 2002, which makes it clear that the interest of the occupier can only be overriding 'so far as relating to land of which he is in actual occupation'.

It must be accepted that overriding interests in general represent a considerable resiling from the fundamental principle that the register is a mirror of the title. The LRA 2002 has reduced them in number by providing protection on the register for some of them and by modifying s. 70(1)(g). The Act is yet a further step towards the ultimate goal of the register being a mirror of the title.

(b) Overriding interests are a blemish upon the mirror of the title to which the system of registration ultimately aspires. The LRA 2002 has therefore modified and reduced these interests in various ways.

It should be noticed that interests which override on a first registration of title are contained in Schedule 1 to the LRA 2002, whilst interests which override on a registered disposition are contained in Schedule 3. They are largely the same, except for the rights of a squatter, but Schedule 1 is slightly wider in scope. For example, the 'occupation' paragraph in Schedule 1 is not quite so specific and restricted as para. 3 of Schedule 3, presumably to allow for the doctrine of notice which applies in unregistered conveyancing. Also, there is no restriction on the types of legal easements which will be overriding as there is in Schedule 3. Section 11(4)(c) LRA 2002 provides that a first registered proprietor takes subject to interests acquired under the Limitation Act 1980 of which he has notice, whereas the rights of a squatter are no longer overriding under the new Act and there is no equivalent of s. 70(1)(f), LRA 1925 in Schedule 3. The Law Commission did not see rights of adverse possession as consistent with a system of registered title. Various other old rights, such as customary rights, public rights and franchises, are to be found in both Schedules, as are local land charges.

Section 70(1)(a), LRA 1925 made overriding certain specific rights in the nature of easements, profits à prendre and other easements not being equitable easements. By a liberal interpretation of r. 268 of the Land Registration Rules, in *Celsteel Ltd v Alton House Holdings Ltd* [1985] 2 All ER 562 (and confirmed in *Thatcher v Douglas* (1996) 146 *NLJ* 282) an equitable easement which was openly exercised and enjoyed was held also to be an overriding interest. Under the LRA 2002, an express easement cannot become a legal easement until it is registered against the title of the servient tenement; merely meeting the formality of a deed is not enough. This recognises that most easements are created on the transfer of part of a plot of land. Provision is made in Schedule 3, para. 3 for legal easements or profits created by implied grant and by prescription, of which the purchaser knows or which could have been discovered on a reasonably careful inspection of the land, or which have been exercised within one year of the purchase. The paragraph does not include equitable easements (thereby reversing the decision in *Celsteel*), which become minor interests binding on a purchaser only if they are protected by a notice on the register.

The Act makes a profound change to the law of adverse possession. Rights acquired or being acquired under the Limitation Acts were overriding interests under s. 70(1)(f), Land Registration Act 1925. Rights under the Limitation Acts are viewed as incompatible with the concept of registration of title however, and Part 9 and Schedule 6 of the Act provide that the Limitation Acts do not apply to a registered title. There is provision for a person who has adversely possessed land for ten years to apply to the Registry for registration as proprietor, but the Registry must then serve notice on the present registered proprietor. If the registered proprietor serves a counter-notice objecting within the prescribed period (some three months), the adverse possessor will only obtain registration if he can show that one of three grounds set out in para. 5 of Schedule 6 applies. If he is unable to do so, then the registered proprietor has two years in which to recover possession of the land. If the registered proprietor takes no action, then the adverse possessor may apply again for registration after the two years have expired. These changes should assist local authorities and other large landowners and prevent cases such as *Ellis v Lambeth LBC* (1999) *The Times*, 28 September 1999, which caused much public indignation.

Section 70(1)(g), LRA 1925, the overriding interest which has caused most litigation, is to be found in a very much more specific and restricted form in para. 2, Schedule 3 to the 2002 Act. Paragraph 2 seems to indicate that the time of the disposition is the relevant time for actual occupation, thus endorsing the decision in *Abbey National v Cann*; but the point was left open in *Thompson v Foy* [2009] EWHC 1076 (Ch). When electronic conveyancing has been introduced there will be no 'registration gap' at all as the disposition and registration of it will be simultaneous.

The interest is only overriding as regards land of which a person is in actual occupation (so reversing the decision in *Ferrishust Ltd v Wallcite Ltd* [1999] 1 All ER 977).

As before, enquiry and non-disclosure of an interest will mean that a purchaser takes free of it, but only when 'such person' with the right could reasonably have been expected to disclose it. This recognises the criticism of *Hypo-Mortgage Services Ltd v Robinson* [1997] 2 FLR 71 (see Kenny, 'Children are Spare Ribs' [1997] *Conv* 84), but would also include persons in occupation who are senile or of unsound mind.

Paragraph 2(c)(i) would appear to be capable of a wide interpretation which might exclude interests which have been held to be overriding under s. 70(1)(g). It exempts a purchaser from the rights of an occupier whose occupation would not have been obvious on 'a reasonably careful inspection of the land' and of which occupation the purchaser does not have actual knowledge. It remains to be seen how the courts will apply it. Paragraph 2(d) excludes a reversionary lease which is not to take effect for more than three months after its grant. This, no doubt, is to encourage a person with a lease who is not in occupation to register it substantively, or to protect it by an entry on the register if it is not capable of being registered substantively. The previous alternative to actual occupation in s. 70(1)(g), LRA 1925 that a person is in receipt of the rents and profits of the land has disappeared altogether.

There is no further definition in the section of 'actual occupation' so that the case law on s. 70(1)(g) will still apply. The legislature have obviously heeded Lord Oliver's warning in *Abbey National v Cann* that 'it is, perhaps, dangerous to suggest any test for what is essentially a question of fact, for occupation is a concept which may have different connotations according to the nature and purpose of the property which is claimed to be occupied'. Paragraph 2, Sch. 3 refers to an 'interest' rather than a 'right' and this would seem to emphasise that it must be an interest of a proprietary nature as for s. 70(1)(g). The paragraph can be seen as an attempt to 'plug the hole' made by some of the decisions which have given a liberal interpretation to s. 70(1)(g).

The final significant change to the overriding interests is the way in which the LRA 2002 deals with legal leases. Whereas under the LRA 1925 legal leases not exceeding 21 years were overriding interests under s. 70(1)(k) and legal leases of over 21 years were registrable substantively with their own title, the LRA 2002 extends the substantive registration of legal leases to those exceeding seven years (with the expressed ultimate aim of further reducing this period to leases exceeding three years). Schedule 3, para. 1 therefore makes overriding legal leases not exceeding seven years. There are three exceptions to this (a reversionary lease to take effect in possession more than three months after it is granted and certain leases arising under the Housing Act 1985).

It is apparent that the intention of the LRA 2002 is greatly to reduce the categories of overriding interests that formerly applied under s. 70(1), LRA 1925. It achieves this by making some of these interests registrable (leases of over seven years and express easements), and by restrictions on the 'actual occupation' provision. Rights of adverse possession under the Limitation Acts have disappeared altogether as overriding interests, and an entirely new regime has been introduced for adverse possession.

Question 3

Until last year, Walter, an elderly retired farmer, was the registered proprietor of Sheepdale Farm. He lived in Bluebell Cottage on part of the farm. His daughter Delia and son-in-law Steve ran the farm and lived with their two children, Bill aged 17 and Ben aged 6, in the farmhouse.

Last year, Steve exercised undue influence over Walter to persuade him to transfer Sheepdale Farm to Tick and Tack to hold upon trust for himself (Steve) and Delia for life, with remainder to Bill and Ben absolutely. As a result of a foot and mouth epidemic, the farm stock was destroyed, and Steve and Delia decided to take the opportunity to make a prolonged visit to Australia for three months to investigate the possibilities for sheep-farming there. Steve's brother and his wife Joan went to live in the farmhouse while they were away to look after Bill and Ben and to ensure that Walter was properly cared for.

Jasper, a neighbouring farmer, has been in adverse possession of Pony Field on the farm for over 10 years.

Delia and Steve returned recently to discover that Tick and Tack, who were the registered proprietors of the farm, had charged it to the Abbey Bank plc for £60,000 and absconded with the mortgage monies.

(a) Advise Walter, Delia and Steve whether they could obtain alteration of the register against Tick and Tack and the Abbey Bank plc, and if so, advise whether any indemnity might be payable to anyone.

(b) Advise Jasper if he is likely to obtain alteration of the register to reflect his adverse possession, and whether this could give rise to a claim for indemnity in any circumstances.

Commentary

There have been comparatively few orders for rectification of the register and it is not an area of law which has given rise to much litigation. There are therefore not many decisions on the interpretation of the former provisions contained in the **LRA 1925**.

As yet a further step towards the register being a mirror of the title, the meaning and availability of rectification of the register have been considerably narrowed by the **LRA 2002**, although there are a number of grounds for administrative alterations to the register set out in **Schedule 4** to the Act. The law relating to indemnity was amended by the **LRA 1997** and is largely unaffected by the **LRA 2002**, although there does seem to be an omission in **Schedule 8 to the 2002 Act**, to which attention is drawn in the suggested answer to the Question.

Answer plan

(a)
- Alteration of register to restore Walter as registered proprietor.
- Walter's right to avoid transfer for undue influence takes effect as an equitable interest capable of binding successors in title:
  - Tick and Tock take subject to that right to avoid as transfer to them was not for valuable consideration.
  - So Walter should be able to have the register altered to restore his name as registered proprietor.
  - Alteration of register would not be 'rectification' (since not a mistake and not prejudice title of Tick and Tock—they took subject to Walter's equity)—so no indemnity would be payable to the trust.
- Undue influence binds the bank because, although bank's registrered charge was for valuable consideration, Walter was in actual occupation and so his equity to avoid gained protection as an overriding interest:
  - So Walter should be able to have the register altered to remove the bank's charge.
  - The alteration would not be a 'rectification' because the bank's charge was subject to Walter's overriding interest.
  - So no indemnity would be payable to the bank.
- If in either case no alteration is ordered, Walter cannot obtain an indemnity, so he can have only a personal action against Steve, Tick and Tock.

(b)
- Jasper may have an overriding interest as a person in actual occupation under **Schedule 3, para. 2**.
- He may apply for registration after ten years, but the application will usually be unsuccessful. Furthermore, the registered proprietor must be given notice of the application and (assuming it is unsuccessful) has a further two years to bring an action for possession before the squatter can re-apply.

Suggested answer

(a) There are two issues in this part of the question. The first is whether the register of title of Sheepdale Farm will be altered to restore Walter as the registered proprietor and, if so, whether any indemnity is payable to the trust (and so will benefit the beneficiaries). The second is whether the register will be altered to remove the registered charge, and, if so, whether any indemnity is payable to the bank.

The grounds for obtaining alteration of the register are set out in the LRA 2002, s. 65 and Schedule 4. These provisions replace those contained in the LRA 1925, s. 82(1)(a)-(h). Any change made to the register is now called an 'alteration', and the term 'rectification' is reserved for alterations that involve correction of a mistake and that prejudicially affect the title of a registered proprietor: LRA 2002, Sch. 4, para. 1.

As the transfer by Walter to Tick and Tock was a result of the undue influence exercised by Steve, the transfer is voidable in equity. Such right to avoid is a mere equity which has effect from the time the equity arises as an interest capable of binding successors in title: LRA 2002, s. 116. Walter's equity therefore has priority over the transfer to Tick and Tock as, although the disposition to them was completed by registration, it does not appear to have been for valuable consideration: LRA 2002, s. 28. Walter should therefore be able to obtain an alteration of the register to restore his name as the registered proprietor.

As Tick and Tock took the transfer subject to Walter's equity, an alteration to the register to restore Walter as the registered proprietor would be giving effect to a 'right or interest' excepted from the effect of registration: LRA 2002, Schedule 4, paras 2(1)(c) (court), 5(c) (registrar). It seems, however, that the alteration would not rank as a 'rectification', both because the registration was not a mistake and because the title of the registered proprietors would not be prejudicially affected by the alteration. The registration would not be a 'mistake' because a mistake seems to refer to a mistake in the process of obtaining registration from the Land Registry. An analogy may be drawn with an earlier provision: under the LRA 1925, s. 82(1)(d) rectification was allowed where any entry on the register had been obtained by fraud; but in *Norwich and Peterborough Building Society v Steed* [1993] Ch 116, the Court of Appeal construed that provision narrowly to mean fraud in obtaining registration rather than to a fraudulent transaction subsequently registered correctly. The fraud had to be practised on the Land Registry: ibid. p. 134. In contrast, there had been a 'mistake' in *Baxter v Mannion* [2010] EWHC 573 (Ch), where the register was rectified against a registered proprietor because he had obtained registration by swearing in a statutory declaration that he had been in adverse possession for ten years when he had not: the mistake was his supply of inaccurate information to the Land Registry. The registration of Tick and Tock, however, is not a mistake. The significance of the alteration's not being a rectification is that no indemnity would be payable to the trust as a result of the alteration.

The next issue is whether the register may be altered to remove the Abbey Bank plc's registered charge. As the registered charge was made for valuable consideration,

Abbey will take free of Walter's equity to avoid the transfer for undue influence unless it was protected either as a notice on the charges register or as an overriding interest through actual occupation: LRA 2002, s. 30. Walter clearly did not protect such right by notice, but as he appears to have been in living in Bluebell Cottage throughout, he was probably in actual occupation of Sheepdale Farm when Tick and Tock charged the farm to Abbey: LRA 2002, Schedule 3, para. 2. As Abbey did not evidently ask Walter if he had any rights, it will have taken its registered charge subject to his overriding interest. The registrar may alter, or the court may order the registrar to alter, the register to give effect 'to any estate, right or interest excepted from the effect of registration': LRA 2002, Schedule 4, paras 5(c) (registrar), 2(1)(c) (court). Walter should therefore be able to obtain an alteration of the register to remove Abbey's charge.

As an overriding interest is excepted from the effect of registration, neither of the alterations (namely the removal of the bank's charge from the title of the farm, and the closure of the bank's registered charge) ranks as a rectification because the alterations merely gives effect to the overriding interest to which Abbey's registration was subject. The significance of this is that, whilst an indemnity is payable when a 'rectification' is ordered against a registered proprietor (unless he contributed to the registration through his own fraud or lack of proper care), no indemnity is paid where the register is altered to give effect to an overriding interest. The rationale is that the registered proprietor suffers no 'loss' when the register is altered in this way, as the alteration merely gives effect on the face of the register to an interest to which the registered proprietor was already subject. This is the same principle as under the former law, as seen in *Re Chowood's Registered Land* [1933] Ch 574, 582, and *Malory Enterprises Ltd v Cheshire Homes (UK) Ltd* [2002] Ch 216 (CA). The bank would therefore obtain no indemnity.

If the court or the registrar were to refuse to alter the register to restore Walter as the registered proprietor or to remove the bank's registered charge (or both), Walter would obtain no indemnity as, unlike the earlier provision in the LRA 1925, s. 83(2), nothing in the LRA 2002, Schedule 8, enables an indemnity to be paid where loss is suffered when the register is not altered. In the event of Walter's failing to obtain alteration of the register, he would be left to pursue his personal remedies for compensation against Steve, Tick and Tock.

(b) Rights acquired or being acquired under the Limitation Act, which were overriding rights under s. 70(1)(f), LRA 1925 are no longer overriding under Schedule 3, LRA 2002. Furthermore, a squatter is not regarded as being in possession of land so as to satisfy the requirements of s. 131(1), LRA 2002 (s. 133(3)). A squatter does, however, have an overriding interest if he is in actual occupation within LRA 2002, Schedule 3, para. 2. Jasper will not be regarded as in adverse possession while the estate is subject to a trust, unless the interest of each of the beneficiaries is an estate in possession: LRA 2002, Schedule 7, para. 12. This is clearly not the case in relation to the trust for Steve, Delia, and their two sons. Furthermore, under the 2002 Act, a squatter cannot acquire the title of the registered proprietor unless the squatter first applies for registration after having been in adverse possession for 10 years, and (unless he then satisfies specified conditions) he then remains in adverse possession for a further two years and applies for registration a second time. As the registrar will notify the registered proprietor when the first application for registration is made, the registered proprietor is likely to take action to evict Jasper before he has time to make a second application. However, if Jasper were able to satisfy all these requirements, then on his second application for registration, the register would be altered to substitute his name as registered proprietor. The former registered proprietor would have no claim for an indemnity as his registered estate would have been subject to Jasper's overriding interest in any event.

Further reading

Dixon, M. 'HM Adjudicator to the Land Registry and Questions of Rectification' [2010] *Conv 207*.

8

Successive interests and trusts of land

Introduction

This is an area of land law that has been simplified! The Trusts of Land and Appointment of Trustees Act 1996 (TLATA), which came into effect on 1 January 1997, provides that any trust which includes land shall (with a few exceptions) after that date be a trust of land under the Act.

Because the only freehold estate which may subsist at law after 1925 is the fee simple absolute in possession, all successive interests (such as life interests and fee simple remainders) must necessarily be equitable and take effect behind a trust. They are removed from the legal title to the land. Under the 1925 legislation, there were two kinds of trusts of land—a settlement under the Settled Land Act 1925 (SLA) and a trust for sale under the Law of Property Act 1925 (LPA). Land held under settlements, which had been used since the thirteenth century as a means of keeping large estates within a family, was made more easily saleable by the SLA. However, as large estates were sold off (often to raise money to pay taxes on the death of a life tenant) settlements became less common. Moreover, the legal machinery of the SLA was much more cumbersome than that of a trust for sale, so that even where successive interests in a fairly modest suburban house were created (for example, under the will of a husband who left the house to his wife for life and then to their children equally) a trust for sale would be the usual means of achieving this. There are probably very few settlements surviving therefore, and the vast majority of conveyancers are unlikely ever to encounter one during their working lives! The TLATA 1996 provides that no new settlements under the SLA may be created, but those in existence will continue until they come to an end. The SLA has been omitted from many land law courses for some time now, and we do not therefore propose to deal with it in this chapter other than by references to where it would have applied before TLATA.

In addition to settlements expressly created, settlements under the SLA have been used by the courts to give effect to informal family arrangements supported by an estoppel or a constructive trust. An example of the courts' use of a settlement for these purposes is *Costello v Costello* (1995) 27 HLR 12. For a discussion of the application of a settlement in this way in *Costello* and other cases, see M. P. Thompson [1994] *Conv* 391. This type of arrangement will presumably now take effect under a trust of land and Question 4 considers the type of circumstances which might give rise to this.

Trusts for sale under the LPA had also given rise to certain problems, particularly as the equitable doctrine of conversion applied to them. The equitable maxim that 'equity looks on that as done which ought to be done' meant that there was a notional sale in the eyes of equity, so that land subject to a trust for sale was regarded, for some purposes, as money and personalty. This gave rise to some very strained decisions and the courts were inconsistent in their application of the doctrine. On 1 January 1997 all trusts for sale became trusts of land and the doctrine of conversion as regards trusts for sale was abolished. You should note however that there are two provisions for trusts of land which have to be expressly adopted by deed in order to apply to a pre-1997 trust for sale. These are the requirement for the trustees to consult the beneficiaries under s. 11(1), and the appointment and retirement of trustees under s. 21(6).

Although settlements and trusts for sale, which are both replaced by trusts of land under TLATA, are now almost legal history, trusts for sale (and very occasionally settlements under the SLA) will of course remain relevant for investigations of title in unregistered land for a few years yet. (As mentioned above, settlements are now comparatively rare and have been so for some time.)

TLATA has achieved a simplified and more coherent form of a trust of land. Many of the sections of TLATA are similar in effect to sections relating to trusts for sale in the LPA, and others, such as s. 16, have a distinct resemblance to sections in the SLA. These similarities have been referred to in the answers both in this chapter and in Chapter 9 on Co-ownership. The large body of case law on s. 30, LPA (applications for sale of land held under a trust for sale) has been codified in s. 15(1), TLATA, but there are conflicting decisions at first instance as to how s. 15(1) should be interpreted. One of these treated s. 15(1) as a codification of the previous case law (*TSB Bank plc v Marshall* [1998] 3 EGLR 100), but in another case the court held itself to be unfettered by the previous authorities on s. 30 LPA in its jurisdiction to order a sale of property under TLATA (*The Mortgage Corporation v Shaire* [2000] 1 FLR 973, considered critically by Pascoe [2000] *Conv* 315). This case may represent a trend towards a more sympathetic attitude by the courts towards family circumstances (see, for instance, *Judd v Brown* [1998] 2 FLR 360 and *Edwards v Lloyds TSB Bank* [2005] 1 FLR 139, mentioned in the suggested answer to Question 1). However, the wider interpretation of s. 15(1) was not applied by the Court of Appeal in *Bank of Ireland Home Mortgages v Bell* [2001] 2 FLR 809.

Question 1 is a straightforward consideration of the rights of beneficiaries under TLATA, and this often applies to trusts arising from co-ownership as well as to successive interests. Question 2 looks at the application of TLATA to certain situations. Question 3 applies the provisions of the Act, and especially those relating to the duties of trustees, to a problem situation and Question 4 deals with the situations mentioned above where the courts have hitherto used a settlement under the

SLA to give effect to an informal arrangement. Question 5 considers the effect of creating determinable fees and fees subject to defeasance by reason of a condition subsequent—fairly unusual types of disposition which may not be included in many land law courses.

Question 1

What rights have the beneficiaries under a trust of land?

Commentary

A trust of land may be expressly created by deed or by will or may arise from a situation, such as co-ownership, where statute imposes a trust of land. The definition of a trust of land in **s. 1, TLATA 1996** also includes a bare trust and implied, resulting and constructive trusts, which arise by operation of law or under equitable principles. Before **TLATA** came into force on 1 January 1997, there were two ways in which land might be held on trust—a settlement under the **SLA 1925** or a trust for sale under the **LPA 1925**. For various reasons, there were very few settlements still in existence in 1996 and **TLATA** provides that those that were are to continue as settlements under the **SLA** until they come to an end, but trusts for sale under the **LPA** became trusts of land under **TLATA** on 1 January 1997. The question considers the rights of beneficiaries under a trust of land however the trust arises.

Answer plan

- Beneficiaries under a trust of land have an interest in the land itself, unlike beneficiaries under a trust for sale whose interest was sometimes treated as personalty (the proceeds of sale) because of the doctrine of conversion.
- All co-owners have a right of possession and no one co-owner can exclude another. **Section 12, TLATA** gives beneficiaries entitled in possession a right to occupy the land in certain circumstances, and **s. 13** gives the trustees guidance on how to manage this right.
- Beneficiaries may manage the trust property under the trustees' power to delegate their management functions to them (**s. 9**).
- Beneficiaries have a right to be consulted by trustees about the exercise of their powers, but this applies only to pre-1997 trusts if expressly adopted.
- Beneficiaries of full age and absolutely entitled may require the trustees to partition the land between them (**s. 7**).
- In an expressly created trust of land, the settlor may require the trustees to obtain the consent of certain persons before exercising certain powers.

- Beneficiaries may apply to the court under **s. 14** for an order concerning a wide range of matters, including sale of the land. The court is directed to have regard to the matters set out in **s. 15** in deciding whether or not to order a sale. **Section 335A, Insolvency Act 1986** applies to an insolvency rather than **s. 15**.

Suggested answer

The rights of the beneficiaries under TLATA are the same however the trust arises, but the Act makes a distinction between beneficiaries who are of full age and beneficially entitled in possession, and those who have a future interest. There are some rights given to the beneficiaries under TLATA, however, which only apply to a pre-1997 trust for sale converted into a trust of land if they are expressly adopted by deed. If the trust arises from a will or disposition, then the beneficiaries may be given additional powers to those under TLATA, or certain TLATA powers may be restricted.

Although the legal estate in land held on trust is vested in the trustees, who are given all the powers of an absolute owner (s. 6(1)), the beneficiaries under the trust have an interest in land. The equitable doctrine of conversion applied to trusts for sale created before 1 January 1997 so that the beneficiaries had an interest in the proceeds of sale of the land, which was sometimes regarded by the courts as personalty. The doctrine was abolished by s. 3, TLATA, however, and the beneficiaries' interests are now in land and are therefore realty. (There is an exception made for testators who died before 1 January 1997 leaving 'realty' to one person and 'personalty' to another, but this can only be relevant now in tracing title to unregistered land and such wills were, in any event, unusual because a testator will usually refer specifically to property in a will.) In *Bull v Bull* [1955] 1 QB 234, Lord Denning MR decided that all co-owners of property have a right of possession and so cannot be excluded from occupation by any other co-owner. Section 12, TLATA provides that a beneficiary of full age with an interest in possession has a right of occupation of the land provided that this is contemplated by the trust, or the trustees so decide, having regard to the intentions of the settlor, the purposes for which the land is held and the circumstances and wishes of any other beneficiaries who also have a right of occupation. The right does not apply if the land is unavailable or unsuitable for occupation by the beneficiary. In addition to co-owners of full age, any persons entitled to a life interest under a trust under which there are successive interests in land will also be persons with an interest in possession and have a right to occupy the land under s. 12. Under a trust for sale, because co-owners all had rights of possession, one co-owner could not charge another one rent unless the conduct of the occupying co-owner was such as to make it impossible for them to live together (*Dennis v Macdonald* [1982] Fam 63 where the occupying co-owner was violent towards the other one). Section 13, TLATA gives guidance to the trustees about which beneficiary they should allow to occupy the premises (if more than one is entitled) and restrictions that they should impose. A prudent trustee will probably want to give the beneficiary a written document, similar in terms to a lease, specifying the care of the premises. Section 13(6) provides that, where a beneficiary is excluded by reason of the occupation of another entitled beneficiary, then the one in occupation should 'make payments by way of compensation' or forego other benefits under the trust in favour of the one excluded.

Section 9 allows trustees to delegate their functions (other than giving a good receipt for capital money) to a beneficiary or beneficiaries entitled in possession, and if more than one, the delegation may be to them either jointly or severally. Section 9A requires trustees to exercise the general duty of care applicable to all trustees under s. 1, Trustee Act 2000 as regards both the decision to delegate and overseeing and withdrawing if necessary the delegation.

The trustees must consult the beneficiaries of full age entitled in possession as to the exercise of their very wide powers (s. 11) unless there is a trust instrument dispensing with the requirement or the trust was created by a will made before 1 January 1997. The duty to consult does not apply to an express trust created before that date unless it is adopted by deed after that date. The exception to the requirement for consultation is where all the beneficiaries under the trust are of full age and capacity, in which case the trustees may decide to convey the land to them (s. 6(2)). Such beneficiaries may themselves decide to terminate the trust and require the trustees to convey the land to them, under the rule in *Saunders v Vautier* (1841) 4 Beav. 115.

One way of terminating co-ownership of land is (and always has been) for the co-owners of full age and capacity to agree to partition the land physically between them. If co-owners under a trust are all of full age and absolutely entitled to the trust property, then the trustees may agree with them to partition the land, dividing it physically between them (s. 7). This would, of course, be one way of applying the rule in *Saunders v Vautier* if the beneficiaries wanted the land instead of a share of the proceeds of sale.

In an expressly created trust, s. 8 allows the settlor to restrict the powers of the trustees under ss. 6 and 7 by requiring the consent of certain persons before such powers are exercised. As s. 6 gives the trustees all the powers of an absolute owner, this will include the power of sale. Any such restriction should be entered on the register of a registered title in order to warn a purchaser of its existence. The effect of s. 26, Land Registration Act 2002 is that a disponee of a registered title takes it free from any limitations that are not entered on the register, but that this does not affect the lawfulness of the disposition. This appears to put the beneficiaries in the same position as beneficiaries under a trust for sale, who could not impeach the sale but who could still sue the trustees for equitable compensation (damages) for a breach of trust if they failed to fulfil any requirements, such as obtaining a consent, before selling. A purchaser of unregistered land will take free from it unless he has actual notice of the restriction by virtue of s. 16, TLATA.

The beneficiaries can require a trustee to retire from the trusteeship (s. 19) or can designate any new trustee whom they would like to be appointed, unless the trust instrument prevents this. The new trustee cannot be appointed by the beneficiaries (who do not have the legal estate and so cannot vest it in him) and will be appointed by the existing trustees or the person (if any) to whom the trust instrument gives the power. Like the requirement for consultation in s. 11, these rights do not apply to a pre-1997 trust, unless adopted by deed made by the settlor or settlors.

Under s. 14, TLATA, a trustee or any person with an interest in the land may apply to the court for an order relating to any functions of the trustees, and the court may make such order as it thinks fit. Like the parallel s. 30, LPA relating to trusts for sale, this is a very widely drawn section and clearly includes a beneficiary. In addition obviously to a sale of the land, the section also specifically mentions the requirements of consultation (under s. 11) and to obtain any necessary consents (under s. 8). The Act then specifies, in s. 15, the matters that the court is to have regard to in determining what order to make. Subsections (2) and (3) reiterate the considerations that the trustees must have regard to in s. 13 in allowing a beneficiary entitled in possession to occupy the land, and the requirement to consider the views of the majority in value of the beneficiaries' interests in the event of a dispute. Section 15(1) appears to be a codification of the old case law on s. 30, LPA and will be primarily applicable in considering whether or not to make an order for the sale of the property. However, in *Mortgage Corporation v Shaire* [2001] Ch 743, Neuberger J had to consider the application for sale by a secured creditor, and took the view that the legislature had intended to widen the previous case law under which it was determined that an order for sale should be made on an application by a creditor, unless there were exceptional circumstances. Neuberger J's wider interpretation was not adopted by the Court of Appeal in *Bank of Ireland Home Mortgages v Bell* [2001] 2 FLR 809 (although on facts that would have caused considerably more hardship to a chargee than in *Shaire*) and has been criticised (see Pascoe [2000] Conv 315). Nevertheless, in *Edwards v Lloyds TSB Bank plc* [2005] 1 FLR 139, Park J took account of the fact that there was likely to be enough equity in the house for the bank to be repaid in full with interest for a few years, and ordered that a sale be postponed for five years until the youngest child attained the age of 18. An amendment was made by TLATA to the Insolvency Act 1986 by the addition of s. 335A, and s. 15(4) excludes the provisions of s. 15 if s. 335A applies. Section 335A provides that, on a bankruptcy, the court may have regard to all the circumstances set out therein in deciding whether or not to order a sale, but that, after one year, the interests of the unsecured creditors should be paramount and an order for sale should be made unless there are exceptional circumstances. It is perhaps curious that Neuberger J's approach would be less favourable to a secured creditor as against a beneficiary than s. 335A is to an unsecured creditor! *Dicta* in *Barca v Mears* [2005] 2 FLR 1, however, raise the possibility that the extent to which s. 335A leans in favour of a creditor might contravene Article 8 of the European Convention on Human Rights (respect for a home and family life), but in *Nicholls v Lan* [2006] EWHC 1255 (Ch) the court held that the criteria in s. 335A were not inconsistent with the rights in Article 8.

It is clear that, although the trustees of a trust of land are given very wide powers under TLATA, the beneficiaries are also given rights that enable them to control considerably the way in which the trustees exercise those powers. The abolition of the trust for sale under the LPA and substitution of a trust of land was necessary because the application of the doctrine of conversion, whereby the beneficiaries' interests were regarded as interests in the proceeds of sale and not in land, had led to some extraordinary and inconsistent decisions. There is still not much litigation involving the new Act—but this may perhaps be a testimony to its adequacy!

Question 2

Lucinda, who died recently, left a will appointing Tom and Tessa as her executors and trustees and including the following dispositions:

'(a) I devise my house Redroofs to my nephew Maurice for life, and on his death to his son Leopold absolutely;

(b) I devise my house Greengates to my nieces Annie (aged 22), Beryl (aged 20), and Connie (aged 16) in equal shares absolutely;

(c) I give my house Whitegables to my husband Harry but would like it to go to my daughter Jane on his death.'

How would your answer differ if the disposition had been 'to my husband Harry during his lifetime but on his death to my daughter Jane'.

Commentary

This question is straightforward and considers the operation of **TLATA** to certain dispositions (one of which creates a co-ownership situation rather than successive interests in land). Before the implementation of **TLATA** on 1 January 1997, the disposition in **(a)** would have created a settlement under **SLA 1925**, and the disposition in **(b)** a trust for sale under **LPA 1925**. The disposition in **(c)** required (and still requires) a consideration of **s. 22, Administration of Justice Act 1982**. Insofar as it could create successive interests in land, these would have taken effect under the **SLA** before 1997, but now take effect under **TLATA**.

Answer plan

(a) • This disposition would have created a settlement under the **SLA 1925** if the disposition had been made before 1997. After 1996, it creates a trust of land under **TLATA**.

(b) • This disposition creates co-ownership and **LPA 1925** imposes a trust, with Annie and Beryl as joint tenants at law and trustees. Before 1997, the trust would have been a trust for sale under the **LPA**, but, after 1996, all such trusts became trusts of land under **TLATA**.

(c) • Certain types of disposition giving an interest to a spouse and then to the testator's issue are interpreted as an absolute disposition to the spouse under **s. 22, Administration of Justice Act 1982**.

Suggested answer

(a) It is not possible to create a settlement under the SLA 1925 after 31 December 1996. The disposition will take effect as a trust of land under TLATA. The trustees will be Lucinda's personal representatives. Maurice, who has a life interest, is a beneficiary entitled in possession for the purposes of TLATA 1996 and Leopold, who has a fee simple remainder, has a future interest.

(b) Since the LPA 1925, co-ownership of land has always taken effect behind a trust with the legal estate vesting in the first four named co-owners of full age as joint tenants. They hold on trust for themselves and any other under-age co-owners in equity as either joint tenants or tenants in common. The legal estate in Greengates therefore vests in Annie and Beryl as joint tenants on a trust of land under TLATA. The legal estate can only be held as a joint tenancy, but in equity 'in equal shares' are words of severance which create a tenancy in common, so that they hold for themselves and Connie as tenants in common in equity. If the title is registered, Annie and Beryl will be the registered proprietors and a restriction will be entered in the proprietorship register after their names requiring any disposition of the land to be made by two trustees, thus protecting any interests under the tenancy in common in equity.

(c) This is the type of disposition that may arise in a homemade will. Before 1997, because there was no express trust for sale imposed, it had to take effect as a settlement under the SLA 1925, which meant that the surviving spouse (Harry in this case) could not dispose of the property until a vesting deed was executed (s. 13, SLA known as 'the paralysing section'). The legislature took the view that this was often an unintended and unforeseen result. To avoid the delay and expense of this, s. 22 Administration of Justice Act 1982 provided that a disposition by a testator to their spouse in absolute terms, which then goes on to make a gift on the spouse's death to their issue, shall take effect as an absolute gift to the spouse. Harry therefore takes Whitegables absolutely.

Section 22 only applies, however, as long as no contrary intention is expressed, so that, if the disposition states clearly that Harry is to have Whitegables only during his lifetime, then Jane will have a fee simple remainder. This disposition must therefore take effect behind a trust of land and the position is the same as in (a) above.

Question 3

James, who died earlier this year, appointed Tick and Tack as executors and trustees of his will and left all his property in trust for his wife Emma for life, and then to his two children John and Jane absolutely. His property included the Owl House, a listed building, and his will provided that this should not be sold without the consent of John and Jane.

Polly, who has always liked the house, made a good offer for it to the trustees which was in excess of its likely market value. She knew that Jane did not want to sell the house, but did not

know of the restriction on sale in James's will. Tick and Tack consulted Emma, who was keen to sell, but overlooked the fact that they should have consulted John and Jane. The trustees have now conveyed the house to Polly.

Advise John and Jane:

(a) if the title to the Owl House is unregistered;

(b) if the title to the Owl House is registered.

Commentary

The question requires you to have a knowledge of the different sections of **TLATA 1996** relating to the powers of trustees and the effect of a limitation on those powers. Because the sections impose a general fiduciary duty on the trustees, you also need to be aware of the general standard of care which applies to trustees.

It also requires a consideration of the effect on a purchaser of a breach of the limitation. As regards unregistered land, **s. 16, TLATA** specifically provides for this, but there was some argument as to the position of a purchaser in registered title. The **Land Registration Act 2002** resolves this.

Answer plan

(a)
- The Owl House will be held by Tick and Tack on a trust of land under **TLATA**, the definition of which is a trust which 'includes' land and does not have to be exclusively of land.
- **Section 6, TLATA** gives trustees of land all the powers of an absolute owner for the purpose of exercising their functions as trustees, and **s. 6(6)** says that their powers shall not be exercised in contravention of any rule of law or equity. They must therefore show the general standard of care required of trustees.
- **Section 8, TLATA** provides that a settlor may limit the very wide powers of the trustees in the disposition creating the trust, and that if consents are required to exercise their powers, then the powers shall not be exercised without the consents. **Section 11(1)** imposes a general requirement for the trustees to consult a beneficiary entitled in possession (Emma) as to the exercise of their powers. How compelling therefore are Emma's reasons for wanting to sell the Owl House?
- In the event of a required consent not being forthcoming (as likely here) the trustees may apply to the court under **s. 14, TLATA** to dispense with it. The court may make such order as it thinks fit and the matters which the court must consider are set out in **s. 15**.
- As regards Polly, we are told that she knew of Jane's opposition to a sale, but did not know of the limitation in the trust deed. **Section 16, TLATA** protects a purchaser of unregistered land who did not have 'actual notice' of the limitation. Although Polly's notice might possibly be regarded as constructive notice, it is not actual notice, and the sale is therefore valid.

- It is, however, a breach of trust by Tick and Tack for which they would be liable in damages to Jane.

(b)
- In registered title, the position under **TLATA** as to powers and consents is the same.
- As regards the protection given to a purchaser, however, **s. 16(7), TLATA** states that the section does not apply to registered title, but a restriction can be entered on the register to give a purchaser notice of any such limitation. The exclusion of **s. 16** to registered land caused some academics to argue that a power of consent, such as Jane's, might be an overriding interest if she were in actual occupation of the land, and so binding on a purchaser under **s. 70(1)(g), Land Registration Act 1925**.
- **Section 26, Land Registration Act 2002** now settles the matter by stating that the exercise by the trustees of their powers is to be taken as free from any limitation affecting the validity of the disposition unless the limitation is 'reflected by an entry in the register'.
- It is still a breach of trust for the trustees to sell without obtaining the requisite consents for which they could be liable in damages.

Suggested answer

(a) The disposition in James's will creates a trust of land under the TLATA 1996, which, by its definition in s. 1(1), is a trust of any property which 'includes' land, even though it also includes personalty. The trustees, Tick and Tack, have all the powers of an absolute owner for the purpose of exercising their functions 'as trustees' (s. 6(1)), but must have regard to 'any rule of law or equity' (s. 6(6)). These provisions suggest that trustees are under a general fiduciary duty and that the general standard of care applicable to all trustees applies to them. This is the standard of care established in the case of *Speight v Gaunt* (1883) 9 App Cas 1, and it requires a trustee to exercise the care which an ordinarily prudent man of business would apply in managing his own affairs (now given statutory effect in the Trustee Act 2000, s. 1(2)).

The policy of the Act is to give trustees very wide powers of management which may then be restricted by the settlor and s. 8(1) says that the very wide powers given to trustees under s. 6 do not apply if the trust provides that they shall not. Section 8(2) refers specifically to a provision which requires consent to be obtained for the exercise of any power, and states that the power shall not then be exercised without consent. (There is a provision also in s. 10(1) similar to s. 26(1) of the LPA 1925, that as regards a purchaser, any two consents shall be sufficient, but this of course will not apply to the present circumstances where the consent of a particular person is required.) Section 6(5) requires trustees to have regard to the rights of the beneficiaries in exercising their powers, and Tick and Tack have acted in breach of these sections.

Section 11(1), TLATA 1996 requires trustees to consult beneficiaries of full age and entitled to an interest in possession in the land. This general duty to consult would apply to Emma, but not to John and Jane who do not have an interest in possession.

Section 11(1)(b) requires trustees to give effect to the wishes of such beneficiaries, or the majority of them in value, but only 'so far as consistent with the general interest of the trust'. It may be that Emma has compelling reasons for wanting to sell the Owl House. Section 14 allows the trustees to make an application to the court for an order (*inter alia*) 'relieving them of any obligations to obtain the consent of ... any person in connection with the exercise of any of their functions'. Tick and Tack are therefore in breach of trust in selling without the consents of John and Jane or an order dispensing with them. Section 15 sets out the matters which the court should consider in making any order.

So far as the purchaser Polly is concerned, s. 16(1) relieves a purchaser of land with unregistered title of ensuring that the trustees have in fact had regard to the rights of any beneficiaries under the trust as they are required to do by s. 6(8). Section 16(2) provides that a contravention of s. 6(8) shall not invalidate the conveyance, if the purchaser does not have actual notice of it. Polly knew that Jane did not want to sell the Owl House and has made a very good offer for it, suggesting that she might have had constructive notice (i.e., the notice she would have had if she had made enquiries) of the restriction, or that as regards Jane she might not have acted entirely in good faith. Section 16 refers specifically to *actual* notice, however, which Polly did not have, and the transaction is therefore valid. It seems that a purchaser who knows that beneficiaries are opposed to a sale or other transaction is wiser not to ask too many questions!

The fact that Polly will obtain a good title if she does not have actual notice of the limitation does not relieve Tick and Tack from a breach of trust in that they have sold without first obtaining a requisite consent or an order dispensing with it. They are also in breach of s. 16(3)(a) (applicable only to unregistered land) which requires them to take all reasonable steps to bring any limitation on their powers to the notice of a purchaser. To have overlooked the requirement for consents to a sale of the Owl House is probably also a breach of the standard of care imposed upon trustees by s.1(2), Trustee Act 2000, and Jane would have an action for damages for breach of trust against them.

(b) Section 16(7) excludes the application of s. 16 to registered title however. Sections 40(2) and 40(3)(b), LRA 2002 allow for a restriction to be entered on the proprietorship register, the effect of which is to prohibit the registration of any disposition not complying with its requirement for the trustees to obtain the beneficiaries' consents. It is the duty of the trustees to apply for the registration of such a restriction (Land Registration Rules, 2003, r. 94(4), Schedule 4), but an application for entry of a restriction may also be made by any person with an interest in the registered estate (clearly John and Jane) (Land Registration Rules, 2003, r. 93(c)).

If a restriction has been entered, then the purchaser Polly will take subject to it, but if there is no restriction, then she will take free from the trustees' obligation to obtain consents (s. 26(1), LRA 2002). Section 26(3) makes it clear, however, that the purpose of the section is to give the purchaser a good title, notwithstanding that the disposition is in contravention of a limitation on the powers of the trustees, and 'it does not affect the lawfulness of a disposition'. So, although Polly would get a good title on sale without the requisite consents, it would still be a breach of trust for which John and Jane could sue the trustees for damages.

Question 4

Sydney, who died in 1996, was the registered proprietor of a house. In his will, he left his house to his son Bert 'subject to the right of my Aunt Agnes to live in it during her lifetime'. Agnes now wishes to sell the house and to use the proceeds to buy a small flat.

(a) Discuss.

(b) How would your answer differ if Sydney had died in 1997?

Commentary

Note the dates in this question—part **(a)** pre-dates the implementation of **TLATA 1996**, so that the **SLA 1925** would have applied, and part **(b)** falls within the regime of **TLATA**.

The question relates to the informal creation of a settlement in such cases as ***Bannister v Bannister* [1948] 2 All ER 133**, ***Binions v Evans* [1972] Ch 359** and ***Ungurian v Lesnoff* [1990] Ch 206**. You should be aware that the Law Commission Report, 'Transfer of Title, Trusts of Land' (Law Com. No. 181) makes unfavourable comments about the informal creation of settlements. There are also academic articles and Case Notes on the subject, one of which has been referred to in the Introduction to this chapter.

In part **(b)**, the **SLA** can no longer apply. The Law Commission's criticism of the use of settlements to give effect to these informal arrangements is because of the very extensive powers of management of the land which the **SLA** gave to a tenant for life, and this was the reason for Lord Denning MR's dissenting judgment in ***Binions v Evans***. The Law Commission's Working Paper No. 94 on Trusts of Land suggests that the court might use the new trust of land if it finds that an interest in land was intended to be granted, but otherwise some form of licence, and the Law Commission Report No. 181 echoes this thinking.

Answer plan

(a) • Before **TLATA** was in force, Sydney's disposition might have created a settlement under **SLA 1925**, the definition of which in **s. 1(1)** includes any instrument whereby land is 'limited in trust for persons by way of succession'. Many settlements under the **SLA** were created inadvertently.

- Had there been any dealings between Bert and Aunt Agnes which gave rise to an estoppel or a constructive trust in favour of Aunt Agnes, the court might also have imposed a settlement under the **SLA** to protect Aunt Agnes' interest. There are cases where a settlement under the **SLA** was used by the courts to protect an informal arrangement supported by an estoppel or a constructive trust.
- Settlements in existence when **TLATA** came into force on 1 January 1997 continue until they come to an end.

(b)
- **TLATA 1996** prevents the creation of any new settlements under the **SLA** after 1 January 1997 as it provides a general 'umbrella' for all trusts of land.
- It still remains to be seen as to how, if at all, the courts will apply **TLATA** to the informal arrangements to which they have applied the **SLA** in the past.

Suggested answer

(a) As Sydney dies prior to the implementation of the Trusts of Land and Appointment of Trustees Act 1996, it is necessary to consider the effect of the Settled Land Act 1925.

Under the Settled Land Act 1925, s. 1(1)(i), where land was limited in trust for persons by way of succession, a settlement arose. In Sydney's will, he purports to leave land to Bert subject to the right of Agnes to live in it during her lifetime. The question arises, therefore, whether this was sufficient to bring into play the Settled Land Act 1925. If it was, then Agnes became the tenant for life and, as such, was entitled to have the legal estate vested in her, and, in addition, acquired all the powers of the tenant for life under the Act. These include the power to sell the property, to lease and mortgage it.

In order to create a settlement expressly two documents were required. Where a settlement was created by will, a vesting assent by the personal representatives was required to convey the legal estate to the tenant for life. The will itself constituted the trust instrument, i.e., the document setting out the terms of the settlement. The issue in this problem is whether the words of gift in the will constituted the creation of a settlement. The words are loosely formulated and such a result may have been unintended by Sydney.

There are precedents where an informal arrangement has triggered the application of the Settled Land Act 1925 but they are usually to give effect to a constructive trust or an estoppel. In *Bannister v Bannister* [1948] 2 All ER 133, the defendant sold two cottages to her brother-in-law at a price below the market price and there was an informal arrangement that she could live in one of them rent-free for as long as she liked. It was held that the oral agreement created a constructive trust under which she was entitled to a life interest determinable on her ceasing to live in the property. The Court of Appeal held that the effect of creating a trust in this form was to make the defendant a tenant for life under the Settled Land Act 1925. This result is extraordinary in that an informal oral agreement was deemed sufficient to create a settlement, a result clearly unintended by the parties concerned. In *Binions v Evans* [1972] Ch 359, the ruling in *Bannister v Bannister* was applied by two of the Court of Appeal judges. In *Binions* a written agreement to permit the occupation of a property rent-free for the remainder of the defendant's life was held to create a settlement under the Act in order to give effect to a constructive trust which arose when the property was sold to the plaintiffs at well below the market price because of the defendant's occupation. Lord Denning MR dissented on the ground that s. 1(1)(i) required an express limitation of the land to persons in succession and an informal arrangement could not satisfy the requirement. He also felt that the agreement was never intended to give to the defendant the extensive powers of management, including the power to sell or lease the property, given to a tenant for life under the Settled Land Act. Therefore, in the particular circumstances of the case, he would have protected the interest of the defendant by imposing a contractual licence. Lord Denning MR's approach was criticised in *Griffiths v Williams* (1977) 248 EG 947, where the Court of Appeal found that the interest of the defendant amounted to a lease determinable on death which arose under the doctrine of estoppel. They specifically avoided the award of a life interest as it would create a settlement under the Act, a result unintended by the parties. Similarly in *Dodsworth v Dodsworth* (1973) 228 EG 1115, the court declined to protect the equity raised by an estoppel by imposing a life interest which might have created a Settled Land Act settlement since that would have awarded the defendants a greater interest than was envisaged. Whilst the results of *Bannister v Bannister* have been unfavourably received, they have been applied more recently in *Ungurian v Lesnoff* [1990] Ch 206 where an informal grant to a cohabitee of a right of residence for life in a flat, on the strength of which she had carried out much work to the flat, was held to create a tenancy for life under the Settled Land Act 1925. The Act was also applied in *Costello v Costello* (1995) 27 HLR 12, to give effect to a family arrangement between a mother and a son.

These cases concern informal grants. In the problem, the grant is in the form of a will and, albeit loosely worded, it does apparently create a succession of interests which could have constituted a settlement for the purposes of the Settled Land Act 1925, s. 1(1), particularly if Aunt Agnes were able to plead an estoppel or a constructive trust arising in her favour as a result of dealings between her and Sydney during Sydney's lifetime. Presumably such informal arrangements might now take effect under a trust of land under the TLATA 1996 and the courts may well use this form of trust to give effect to them in future.

As a tenant for life under a settlement, Aunt Agnes would have very wide powers of management of the settled land, including the power to sell it and to buy a small flat. The balance of the proceeds of sale would be capital moneys to be invested according to the Trustee Act 2000.

Although TLATA prevents the creation of any new settlements after 1 January 1997, it does not affect existing settlements which continue until they come to an end (in this case, on the death of Aunt Agnes).

(b) The cases referred to in (a) above have presented the courts with a problem—namely, how to protect the interest of a wronged party where there are circumstances which give rise to an estoppel or which justify the imposition of a constructive trust. These equitable doctrines are very much alive and developing (for a more recent extreme example of the application of estoppel, see *Gillett v Holt* [2000] 2 All ER 289) and there is no reason to think that the steady stream of litigation in this area will cease.

In seeking to protect the rights of wronged litigants by the application of these equitable principles, the courts will now presumably have to apply a trust of land under TLATA 1996. A beneficiary under such a trust has a right to occupy the land (s. 12(1)), and the trustees have an obligation to consult a beneficiary on the exercise of their 'functions' (s. 11(1)). Other sections of the Act (such as s. 9 giving the trustees power to delegate their functions, or ss. 19–21 giving the beneficiaries rights to retire or appoint trustees) are inappropriate to such trusts and would presumably be excluded. As mentioned in the Commentary to this Question, the Law Commission's Working Paper No. 94 has suggested that some form of licence (presumably with some sort of protection) might be an alternative to a trust of land if there were no intention to give the wronged person any actual interest in the land. Another alternative might be to follow the decision in *Griffiths v Williams* (*supra*) where a lease for life was ordered.

There are as yet no cases on this—so watch this space!

Question 5

Consider the effect of the following dispositions made last year:

(a) 'The Red House to Angela, founder of Ambridge Harassed Mothers Ltd in fee simple until such time, not exceeding 80 years, as it is no longer used as a day nursery for children under five years old resident in Ambridge.'

How (if at all) would your answer differ if the disposition had been to Ambridge Harassed Mothers Ltd with no additional words?

(b) 'The Broom House to my son James in fee simple, but if he shall marry a person of the Treeworshippers' Faith, then to my daughter Rachel.'

Commentary

This question arises from the definition of a fee simple absolute in possession in the **Law of Property Act 1925, s. 1(1)**, which states that such an estate is one of the two estates 'capable of subsisting or of being conveyed or created at law' after 1925. This meant that, after the Act came into force on 1 January 1926, conditional and determinable fees simple were necessarily only equitable with some unsatisfactory consequences which the **Law of Property (Amendment) Act 1926** sought to correct.

This is an area which your lecturer may or may not consider important. You should therefore be guided by your lecture notes and tutorials as to how large it should feature in your studies.

Answer plan

(a)
- Disposition to Angela is a determinable fee and so not 'absolute' and not capable of being a legal estate within **s. 1(1) LPA 1925**.
- The specific provision of a period not exceeding 80 years complies with the perpetuity rule and the disposition is therefore valid. It will now take effect as a trust of land under **TLATA**.
- **Section 7(2), LPA 1925** provides that a fee simple vested in a corporation shall be treated as a fee simple absolute notwithstanding that it may be liable to defeasance on the dissolution of the corporation.

(b)
- The disposition to James is a fee simple subject to a condition subsequent.
- Although not absolute and not within the definition of a legal estate in **s. 1(1) LPA 1925**, **s. 7(1), LPA 1925** provides that fees subject to a right of re-entry should be treated as absolute and therefore legal.
- Although such conditions subsequent are subject to the rule against perpetuities, there will be no problem with this disposition as the condition must occur (if at all) within the lifetime of James.

Suggested answer

(a) The disposition to Angela creates a determinable fee simple as there is an ultimate time specified for the existence of the estate. This prevents it from being a fee simple 'absolute', and so it is not capable of being a legal estate within the Law of Property Act 1925, s. 1(1). It must therefore take effect in equity behind a trust of land.

The limitation was one of those included in the Settled Land Act 1925, s. 1(1)(ii)(c), as a settlement. No new settlements under the Act can be created after 1996 when the Trusts of Land and Appointment of Trustees Act 1996 (TLATA) came into force on 1 January 1997. It will therefore take effect under a trust of land of which the grantor (or his personal representatives if the disposition is contained in a will) will be the trustees.

At common law, the reversionary interest is vested from the date the disposition is made, and is not therefore subject to the rule against remoteness of vesting. Statute changes this however: the reversionary interest under a determinable fee is made subject to the rule against perpetuities because the prior interest is treated, for the purposes of the rule, as subject to a condition subsequent (Perpetuities and Accumulations Act 1964, s. 12(1)(a)). A perpetuity period not exceeding 80 years may be specified by the instrument creating the interest (s. 1(1)).

If a disposition may vest (if at all) outside the perpetuity period, and so would be void at common law, it is possible, under the Perpetuities and Accumulations Act 1964,

s. 3, to wait and see if the interest does in fact vest within the perpetuity period. For this purpose, the perpetuity period will be the statutory life or lives in being plus 21 years, or in the absence of statutory lives, 21 years (s. 3(4)). Whereas under the common law rule in *Cadell v Palmer* (1833) 1 Cl & Fin 372, an interest was void *ab initio* if it was not bound to vest within the period, it is now treated as valid until such time as it becomes apparent that it cannot vest within the time.

Since the settlor has expressly provided that the event bringing about the limitation on the fee given to Angela must occur within a period of 80 years, the disposition is valid for the purposes of perpetuity at common law, as modified by the Perpetuities and Accumulations Act 1964, s. 1(1). There is, therefore, no need to wait and see. If the house ceases to be used as a day nursery within 80 years, the limitation will take effect: in this event, the fee will determine automatically, and will revert to the donor or to the donor's heirs. If, however, the limitation does not operate within the 80 years, the fee will become absolute so that the legal estate will then vest indefeasibly in Angela.

Had the disposition been to the Ambridge Harassed Mothers Ltd, it would have been a disposition to a corporation and liable to defeasance on the dissolution of the corporation. However, s. 7(2), LPA 1925 provides that a fee vested in a corporation is to be treated as a fee simple absolute in possession and is therefore a legal estate.

(b) The limitation in this disposition is a fee simple subject to a condition subsequent. The full fee simple has been granted, but it is liable to be prematurely cut short on the occurrence of a specified event.

It differs from a determinable fee only in its terminology, a difference which was said by Pennycuick V-C in *Re Sharp's Settlement Trusts* [1973] Ch 331 at p. 340 to be 'an extremely artificial distinction' and, referring to a dictum of Porter MR in an Irish case (*Re King's Trusts* (1892) 29 LR IR 401 at p. 410) 'little short of disgraceful to our jurisprudence'.

A conditional fee simple, which is subject to a right of re-entry, is again not an absolute one, and so necessarily became equitable after 1925. At that time, there were many freehold properties, in certain areas of the country, subject to a rentcharge (an annual charge on freehold property). The owner of the rentcharge would have a right of re-entry against the fee simple owner if the rentcharge was not paid, so that such fees simple were effectively conditional fees. The effect of the Law of Property Act 1925, s. 1(1), was to render all such fees simple equitable on 1 January 1926 when the legislation came into force, and so invoke the cumbersome machinery of the Settled Land Act 1925.

To deal with this problem, the Law of Property (Amendment) Act 1926 amended the Law of Property Act 1925, s. 7(1), by providing that 'a fee simple subject to a legal or equitable right of entry or re-entry is for the purposes of this Act a fee simple absolute'. Although the intention of the amendment was to deal primarily with the unhappy situation in which the owners of land subject to a rentcharge found themselves, the wording of the amendment is not confined to rights of re-entry on non-payment of a rentcharge, but extends to all fees simple subject to a right of re-entry. The amendment therefore appears to turn all fees simple which are subject to a condition subsequent into fees simple absolute, and thus legal estates within the Law of Property Act 1925, s. 1(1). James will therefore have a legal fee simple absolute in possession.

The determining event, if it occurs at all, must occur during James' lifetime, and so the disposition does not infringe the rule against perpetuities to which conditional fees are subject.

Although a total restraint against marriage would be a void condition as against public policy, a partial restraint such as this is acceptable and valid.

9

Co-ownership and trusts of land

Introduction

This chapter deals with co-ownership of land which, before January 1997, took effect under a statutory trust for sale. After 31 December 1996, all co-owned land is held on a trust of land under the new regime introduced on 1 January 1997 by the TLATA 1996. This Act is retrospective as regards trusts for sale with one exception, relating to certain wills made before 1 January 1997, illustrated in Question 2 of Chapter 8 and Question 1 of this chapter. Trusts for sale no longer exist unless expressly created after 1996. Even then, the provisions of the Act apply to them and it is not possible to exclude the implied power to postpone sale.

The chapter covers co-ownership arising expressly and from the conveyance of land to co-owners, as well as co-ownership under constructive and resulting trusts, which are also now included within the new regime of trusts of land under the TLATA 1996. Because there is a large area of overlap between these topics, they should ideally be studied together, and you should be prepared for questions which demand an ability to apply them together. Some of the questions in this chapter contain such overlaps. A general question on the aims and effects of the TLATA 1996 is to be found in Question 1 of Chapter 8 on Successive Interests and Trusts of Land.

Question 1 of this chapter deals with the mechanisms for governing co-ownership as a trust of land. It considers the rights of the beneficiaries, the functions of the trustees and the statutory guidance now given to the court under s. 15, TLATA 1996 in dealing with applications concerning the land held on trust for co-owners.

Question 2 is a longer-than-would-be-expected examination question which explores many issues of a joint tenancy and a tenancy in common, including severance of an equitable joint tenancy. In doing so, it picks up some of the points dealt with in Question 1. The law relating to the operation of the two forms of co-ownership has been left unchanged by the TLATA 1996.

Question 3 is concerned with how co-owners hold in equity, and Question 4 is essentially on constructive, hidden co-ownership. If you have read the area of law covered by the Questions 1 and 2 in Chapter 5, you will have realised that this type of co-ownership is of comparatively recent judicial development. The courts are keeping abreast of changing social patterns which have thrown up many problems, often involving an adjudication between the purchaser of land and a third party with rights in it. It is, of course, the achievement of a fair balance between the interests of a purchaser and a third party which is central to any system of land law.

Question 1

A testator who died recently devised his freehold four-bedroom house 'Dunroamin' to trustees upon trust for his three children Susan, Tom, and Ursula in equal shares. The will provides that should any of the three children wish to do so, they may live in the house.

Advise the trustees under the following circumstances:

(a) Tom, who is married with five children, would like to live in the house, but Susan and Ursula would like it to be sold with the proceeds of sale to be divided between them;

(b) If Tom and his family do go to live in the house, whether Susan and Ursula would be entitled to any rent for his occupation;

(c) Tom is single and aged 17 and wishes to occupy the house with his aunt and guardian, with whom he is now living.

How would your answer differ if there had been no provision in the will for any of the three children to live in the house if they so wished?

Commentary

This is a fairly straightforward question on the powers of the trustees and the rights of the beneficiaries under a trust of land. It requires a knowledge of the relevant sections of the **TLATA 1996**. Case law on the Act is slowly arising. Comparisons have been made in the suggested answer with the previous law on trusts for sale under the **Law of Property Act 1925**, which remains a point of reference when resolving disputes under the **1996 Act**.

Answer plan

(a)
- **Section 12(1) TLATA 1996** and the right to occupy land.
- **Section 11** consultation with beneficiaries.
- Possible application to court under **s. 14** by Ursula and Susan and relevant matters under **s. 15**.

(b) • Condition of occupation could be payment of compensation (**s. 13(5)**).

• Possible payment of rent by Tom (consider former case law).

(c) • **Section 15(1)** welfare of minor relevant factor for court to consider but consideration of suitability of house.

• Duty to consult and importance of majority view (**s. 11(1)**).

• Rights of occupation of other beneficiaries.

Suggested answer

(a) This disposition will take effect under the TLATA 1996 which came into force on 1 January 1997. Because there is no requirement to sell the property, it takes effect as a trust of land. It is recognised that the interests of the beneficiaries under trusts of land are interests in land rather than in the proceeds of sale of land as under the trust for sale under the Law of Property Act 1925 which the trust of land replaced.

Section 12(1), TLATA 1996 gives a beneficiary who has an interest in possession the right to occupy the land if the trust makes it clear that the property is to be available for occupation (as here), or the trustees hold land that is so available, and the land is not for any reason unsuitable. In *I.R.C. v Eversden* (2002) STC 1109, it was held that the 'purpose' of a trust is primarily to be found in the trust instrument, and even if the purpose is found outside the trust it must be consistent with it. A four-bedroom house might be regarded as reasonably suitable for a family with five children.

Section 11 requires the trustees to consult the beneficiaries of full age entitled to an interest in possession in the land and to give effect to their rights or the wishes of the majority of them in value. (In this respect, it is similar to s. 26(3) of the 1925 Act as it applied before 1997 to a statutory trust for sale, although narrower because it only requires consultation with the beneficiaries with an interest in possession.) This requirement of consultation may be excluded by the settlor, but does not appear to have been excluded here.

The trustees may not unreasonably exclude any beneficiary's entitlement to occupy land (s. 13(2)), but may impose reasonable conditions with regard to his occupation (s. 13(3)), including obligations with regard to the use of the land and payment of outgoings (s. 13(5)). In *Rodway v Landy* [2001] 2 WLR 1775, it was held that s. 13 allows trustees to divide a building between the beneficiaries. It has been pointed out by commentators on the Act that these provisions will almost certainly require the trustees to give to a beneficiary a written licence to occupy the property setting out the terms of occupation. Section 9 also allows trustees to delegate any of their functions (other than the receipt of capital money) to a beneficiary of full age entitled in possession, and if Tom is to occupy the house the trustees may wish to consider this. Any delegation must be done by a power of attorney to the beneficiary for a fixed or indefinite period.

Section 6 of the Act, which gives the trustees all the powers of an absolute owner of the land, also requires them to have regard to the rights of the beneficiaries in exercising those powers (s. 6(5)). They must also act 'as trustees' and not contrary to 'any rule of law or equity'. However, there is no presumption in favour of a right of sale under the Act, but only a power of sale. As the testator has specifically mentioned occupation by the beneficiaries as a possible purpose of the trust, it seems probable that they could decide to allow Tom and his family to occupy 'Dunroamin'. If Ursula and Susan are aggrieved by this decision, they can apply to the court under s. 14, whereby the court may make any order, including one not to sell (unlike the old s. 30 of the 1925 Act, where sale was often the required way to resolve any dispute unless the purposes for which the property was acquired were still extant). The matters to which the court must have regard in deciding what order to make are set out in s. 15 and include the intention of the settlor, the purpose of the property (as under s. 30), and the welfare of any minor. Presumably this might include Tom's five children, and possible occupation by a beneficiary being stated as a purpose might tilt the decision in Tom's favour.

(b) One of the conditions which the trustees may impose for occupation of the property under s. 13(5) is the payment of compensation to any beneficiary who is excluded from occupation, or that the beneficiary who occupies the property should forego other benefits under the trust. Under the old case law on co-ownership it was recognised that if one co-owner was effectively excluded from occupation, he could be awarded rent from the occupying co-owner (*Dennis v McDonald* [1981] 1 WLR 810, *Bernard v Josephs* [1982] Ch 391). Although Lady Hale cautioned in *Stack v Dowden* [2007] UKHL 17, at 94, that the criteria in the statute should be applied rather than the cases decided under the old law, she conceded that the results may often be the same. It is probable, therefore, that Susan and Ursula could require Tom to pay a rent presumably of two-thirds of the rack rent value of the house.

(c) If Tom were a minor and the aunt's house were unsuitable for him to live in for any reason, the trustees should consider very seriously allowing Tom and the aunt to occupy 'Dunroamin', bearing in mind that the welfare of any minor is specifically mentioned in s. 15(1) as a factor which the court should consider in making any order. However, in *Chan v Leung* [2003] 1 FLR 23, the statutory right of occupation was not available where the house was disproportionate to the needs of the beneficiary. So, Susan and Ursula may be able to argue that a four-bedroom house is unsuitable for only two people and that consideration of Tom's minority would only be for a further 12 months (although there are provisions in the Act for protecting a beneficiary who has taken up occupation from being disturbed: s. 13(7)). It remains the fact though that as Tom, at 17, is close to achieving majority, less weight will be given to consideration of his welfare than to a younger child (*Bank of Ireland Home Mortgages Ltd v Bell* [2001] 2 FLR 809 *per* Peter Gibson LJ at 816).

Had there been no specific provision in the will allowing any of the three children to live in the house if they so wished, the duty to consult and to have regard to the wishes of the majority in value under s. 11(1) applies, and the trustees might have to do what Susan and Ursula wish and exercise their power of sale. The trustees, or Tom's guardian on his behalf, could apply to the court under s. 14, but s. 15(2) specifically requires the court to have regard to the wishes of other beneficiaries entitled to occupy (Susan and Ursula), as well as to the welfare of any minor who 'might reasonably be expected to occupy [the property] as his home' (s. 15(1)). Given that Tom is a minor for only another year, and that a four-bedroom house may not be entirely suitable, it is possible that the wishes of Susan and Ursula might prevail.

Question 2

In 1994 Angus, Belinda, Connie and David, who were medical students, decided to buy a large house in which to live while they were studying. They contributed to the purchase price equally. Connie was only 17 at the time.

At the end of his first year at University, Angus unfortunately failed his examinations and, having decided that medicine did not suit him, went to Spain to train as a toreador. He wrote enthusiastically in 1995 to Belinda and Connie (then 18) about his life in Spain, but not to David. He said that as he did not feel he would have much use for the house in future, he would like them to buy his share or to sell the house.

In 1996, Belinda mortgaged her interest in the house to buy a horse. In 1998, Belinda was tragically killed in a riding accident. She had made a will in 1996 leaving all her realty to her sister Iris and all her personalty to her brother James.

David married in 2006, and while Angus was staying with them to attend the wedding, David took the opportunity to have dinner with Angus and Connie to discuss the future of the house. The occasion was a convivial one, and all three agreed that their shares in the property should be separate and distinct in future, although nothing was put into writing to this effect.

Sadly, Angus perished in 2008 on the horns of a bull. He had made a will earlier that year leaving all his realty to Ronnie and his personalty to Penny.

David would like the house to be sold; but Connie, who is working at a hospital nearby, would like to keep it.

(a) If the house is sold, how should the proceeds of sale be split?

(b) If the house is sold, who will be able to give a good title to it?

(c) Advise Connie as to whether she might successfully oppose a sale.

Commentary

This is a fairly typical examination-type question on co-ownership. Before you can say who will be entitled to the proceeds of any sale and who will be able to convey the legal estate to a purchaser, you will have to trace logically the devolution of both the legal estate and the equitable interests. You should do this in the answer to the question, of course, but you may find it easier to set it out first in diagrammatic form in rough, as set out opposite.

Legal title	Trust for sale	Equitable interests
1994 A, B, D as joint tenants		A, B, C, D as joint tenants.
1995 Angus' letter no change not an effective severance	Ditto	Ditto
1995 Connie 18 and can hold legal estate no change	Ditto	Ditto
1996 A, B, D as joint tenants	Ditto	A, C, D as joint tenants. B as tenant in common as to a one-quarter share.
1 January 1997 **TLATA 1996** comes into force		

Legal title	On a trust of land	Equitable interests
1998 A, D as joint tenants	Ditto	A, C, D as joint tenants. Iris as tenant in common as to B's one quarter share.
2008 If no severance D	Ditto	D, C joint tenants of a three-quarter share, and I as tenant in common as to B's one-quarter share.
If severance D	Ditto	D, C, I, and R as tenants in common with one-quarter share each.

In case your transcription to essay form is erroneous, it might be preferable to put only two or three lines through your rough working but still leave it legible! A kind-hearted examiner might be prepared to give some credit for a correct rough working erroneously transcribed.

Such questions will often involve circumstances which are problematic as to whether there has been an effective severance or not of the equitable joint tenancy. If so, you should be prepared to answer the question in the alternative, i.e. showing how the equitable interests devolve if there has been a severance and if there has not been. After all, you can hardly be expected to predict what the judge would decide in any particular circumstances!

Before 1 January 1997, co-ownership of land had to take effect behind a trust for sale under the **Law of Property Act 1925**. All such statutory trusts for sale were abolished by the **TLATA 1996** and become trusts of land instead. The question illustrates how the new Act would operate on an existing co-ownership situation. Apart from amending the form of trust under which co-ownership takes effect, the law of co-ownership is unchanged. The abolition of the doctrine of conversion however affects the devolution of a beneficiary's share as a tenant in common under wills such as those of Belinda and Angus leaving realty to one person and personalty to another.

Answer plan

(a)
- Diagram essential for tracing title in this sort of problem see above.
- Legal title vests in the first four named of full age (A, B, and D), equitable interest in all four equally as joint tenants. Their contribution to the purchase price is equal, so the presumption of tenancy in common (which arises where co-owners contribute unequally) is not applicable here.
- A's letter cannot amount to a notice of severance in equity within **s. 36(2), LPA 1925** as it has not been sent to all the other joint tenants.
- B's mortgage is an act operating on her own share and will effect a severance of her equitable share, but not of her legal joint tenancy as this cannot be severed after 1925. On her death her share of the legal estate accrues by survivorship to A and D. Although her will was made in 1996, before **TLATA 1996** came into force on 1 January 1997, her death was after then. There was a saving of a trust for sale in **TLATA** for wills of this sort which became effective on a death before 1 January 1997 so that an equitable interest passed as personalty and not realty, but this does not apply if the testator dies after 1 January 1997. B's equitable share therefore goes to I as realty.
- Although there appears to be an agreement between all three remaining equitable joint tenants, it is uncertain if this will be valid because of **s. 2(1), Law of Property (Miscellaneous Provisions) Act 1989**, which requires a contract for the disposition of an interest in land to be in writing and signed by both parties. ***Burgess v Rawnsley* [1975] Ch 249** was decided before **TLATA** when equitable interests under a trust for sale were personalty owing to the doctrine of conversion. Even if not a valid agreement, it might constitute severance by a course of dealing whereby all the joint tenants mutually recognised their interests to be severed (see again ***Burgess v Rawnsley***).
- On A's death, his share of the legal estate passes to D by survivorship. If there was a severance, then his equitable interest (since **TLATA**, an interest in land) passes to R as realty. If there was no severance, then it passes to the two remaining joint tenants, C and D.
- If there was a severance, then D,C,I, and R each have a one-quarter share of the proceeds. If there was no severance, then I has one-quarter share whilst D and C have three-quarters as joint tenants.

(b) • A purchaser cannot accept a conveyance or transfer of the house from D alone as there is still co-ownership in equity. D must appoint a second trustee to overreach the beneficial interests under the trust (**s. 2(1), LPA 1925**).

(c) • Any person with an interest in the land, or a trustee, may apply to the court under **s. 14, TLATA** and the court may make such order as it thinks fit as to (*inter alia*) the exercise by the trustees of their powers, including the power of sale.

- Although **s. 11(1), TLATA** requires trustees to consult the beneficiaries on the exercise of their powers, this does not apply unless expressly adopted by deed (**s. 11(3)**).
- Criteria for deciding whether to order a sale or not are set out in **s. 15, TLATA**, the relevant two subsections here being **s. 15(1)(a) and (b)**. There have been conflicting decisions as to how **s. 15** should be interpreted as to whether it is merely a codification of the old case law on **s. 30, LPA 1925** or whether the legislature intended to make changes. The Court of Appeal case (***Chan Pui Chun v Leung Kam Ho* [2002] EWCA Civ. 1075**) also considers the impact of **s. 12(2) TLATA** as to the suitability of property for a beneficiary to occupy.

Suggested answer

(a) As Connie was only 17 when the house was purchased in 1994, she could not hold a legal estate in land, and the legal estate will therefore be vested in Angus, Belinda, and David as joint tenants at law.

The Law of Property Act 1925, s. 34(2) and s. 36(1) imposed a statutory trust for sale wherever land was conveyed to joint tenants, so that Angus, Belinda, and David held it as joint tenants and trustees for sale for themselves and Connie in equity. Assuming that there are no words of severance in the conveyance (such as 'in equal shares') then they will be joint tenants in equity also as they contributed equally to the purchase price. The presumption of equity of a tenancy in common only applies where contributions to the purchase price are unequal.

It is possible that the content of Angus's letter in 1995 to Belinda and Connie might be sufficient to constitute a notice of severance for the purposes of the Law of Property Act 1925, s. 36(2). The section requires any such notice to be given to 'the other joint tenants', however, so that notice to only two of them would not be sufficient to sever Angus's share with regard to any of them, and the joint tenancy would continue in equity.

It is possible also that the letter might qualify as an act of severance being 'an act of any one of the persons interested operating on his own share' (*per* Page-Wood V-C in *Williams v Hensman* (1861) 1 John & H 546). A declaration of intention to sever by one party was accepted by Havers J in *Hawkesley v May* [1956] 1 QB 304 as a sufficient act of severance, and this was approved by Plowman J in *Re Draper's Conveyance* [1969] ChD 486, where he found that a summons and affidavit in support filed by a wife asking for the sale of the matrimonial home and division of the proceeds was sufficient to sever the joint tenancy held by her and her husband. The problem remains, however, that the letter to only two of the joint tenants cannot effect a severance with a third to whom there has been no 'declaration', as it would still lack the necessary element of mutuality for severance. If Angus's share is to be severed, it must be severed with all of them, and the letter, again, would therefore be ineffective.

Connie's attaining her majority in 1995 did not automatically make her a co-trustee and owner of the legal estate, which continued to be vested in Angus, Belinda, and David. For Connie to become a trustee and joint tenant at law, there would have to be a deed of appointment by the existing trustees vesting the legal estate in her and them as joint tenants.

Belinda's mortgage of her share in 1996 would certainly be an act operating on her own share within the dictum of Page-Wood V-C above. It therefore severs her equitable joint tenancy. The legal joint tenancy can never be severed however, so Belinda remains as a joint tenant of the legal estate with Angus and David. She becomes a tenant in common in equity, although the joint tenancy continues as regards the other joint tenants. So the position is that Angus, Belinda, and David hold the legal estate as joint tenants on trust for sale for Angus, Connie, and David as joint tenants in equity as to three-quarters, together with Belinda who is a tenant in common as to a one-quarter share.

On 1 January 1997, **TLATA 1996** came into force, so that the trust for sale under the **LPA** became a trust of land under **TLATA**. This was effected by amendment of **ss. 34(2) and 36(1), LPA**, which is retrospective so as to convert all existing trusts for sale into trusts of land and to abolish the doctrine of conversion (**s. 3, TLATA**). Apart from this, the law of co-ownership is basically unchanged by the Act.

The one saving for the doctrine of conversion was in relation to a will such as Belinda's which was made *before* the Act was effective (**s. 3(2), TLATA**), as there was then a trust for sale under which Belinda's share was personalty. This only applied, however, where the testator also *died* before 1 January 1997. On 1 January 1997, the trust for sale became a trust of land under **TLATA** and the doctrine of conversion no longer applies. Her share therefore passes as realty to her sister Iris.

The position in 1998 then is that Angus and David hold the legal estate as joint tenants (Belinda's share having accrued to them by the right of survivorship), and they hold as trustees of a trust of land for themselves and Connie as joint tenants in equity as to three-quarters, together with Iris as a tenant in common as to a one-quarter share.

Although the legal joint tenancy cannot be severed, as a tenancy in common cannot exist at law after 1925, the equitable joint tenancy may be severed either by notice (**Law of Property Act 1925, s. 36(2)**), or by any of the three ways described by Page-Wood V-C in ***Williams v Hensman*** (*supra*). (*Note*: the first, an act of any one of the persons interested operating on his own share, has already been considered in relation to the letter from Angus and Belinda's mortgage.) The other two ways of severance which should be considered in relation to the dinner party are severance by mutual agreement between the joint tenants, or a course of dealing sufficient to intimate to all the joint tenants that their interests were mutually to be regarded as being held under a tenancy in common in future.

Although all three joint tenants appear to have agreed upon a severance of the equitable joint tenancy, it is a purely oral agreement. In *Burgess v Rawnsley* [1975] Ch 249, Lord Denning MR expressed the opinion that severance of the equitable joint tenancy could be oral as it was not a contract for the sale or other disposition of land, and so did not have to comply with the Law of Property Act 1925, s. 40 (now repealed), or be a specifically enforceable contract. This was probably justified only by regarding the interests of the joint tenants as personalty because of the operation of the doctrine of conversion to a trust for sale. After 1 January 1997, the joint tenants have an interest under a trust of land, so that severance by agreement will probably have to comply with s. 2, Law of Property (Miscellaneous Provisions) Act 1989 as being 'a contract for the sale or *other disposition* of an interest in *land*'. Any such agreement will then have to be in writing and signed by all parties, so that the oral agreement over dinner would not suffice.

Even if the oral agreement is not effective, it may still operate as a severance if it can be regarded as a sufficient course of dealing to sever. This would essentially be a matter for the court to decide.

Assuming that there was no effective severance of the equitable joint tenancy, when Angus died the right of survivorship would operate to vest his legal share in the surviving joint tenant, David. Angus's equitable interest would pass, again by the right of survivorship, to Connie and David as joint tenants. If there was a severance of the equitable joint tenancy, when Angus died the right of survivorship would still operate to vest his legal share in David, but his equitable interest would pass under his will. Since the abolition of a trust for sale and conversion, a beneficiary's share in co-ownership is regarded as land, and Angus' share would therefore pass to Ronnie.

The division of the proceeds of sale therefore depends upon whether the dinner-party can be regarded as a course of dealing sufficient to sever the equitable joint tenancy. If not, then Angus' share will accrue to Connie and David by the right of survivorship, who will then be entitled to three-quarters equally between them, and Iris to one-quarter. If it is sufficient to effect a severance, then Ronnie will take Angus' one-quarter share under his will, whilst David, Connie, and Iris also each have one-quarter shares as tenants in common.

(b) Although David is the sole remaining trustee and owner of the legal estate, there is still co-ownership in equity. In order to overreach the equitable interests, therefore, a purchaser should require the appointment of a second trustee (who may be Connie or someone else) to give a good receipt for the purchase moneys (s. 2(1) LPA, 1925).

(c) One of the main purposes of the TLATA 1996 was to abolish the presumption in favour of a sale which applied to a trust for sale under the Law of Property Act 1925. Section 11(1), TLATA 1996 requires trustees to consult the beneficiaries as to the exercise of their extensive powers and to have regard to the wishes of the majority in value (as s. 26(3) of the 1925 Act required in the case of a statutory trust for sale before 1997). If there had been an effective severance and David, Angus's heir, and Iris all wanted the property sold, this would suggest that the property should be sold.

However, s. 11(3) states that the duty of consultation under s. 11(1) does not apply to 'a trust created before the commencement of this Act by a disposition' (as here) unless adopted by deed. This appears to reverse s. 26(3), LPA, and the only remedy would therefore be an application to the court under s. 14, TLATA.

If there was no severance so that David and Connie have equal shares then Iris' wishes could be decisive. Section 14 of the 1996 Act allows a trustee or a person with an interest in property to apply to the court for an order. The section is wider than s. 30 of the 1925 Act which it replaces, because whereas s. 30 allowed an application for sale, a s. 14 application can be for any order and would presumably allow Connie to apply for an order resisting sale.

Section 15, TLATA 1996 sets out statutory criteria which the court should consider when making an order under s. 14, and the two relevant ones here would appear to be 'the interests of the persons who created the trust' (s. 15(1)(a)), and 'the purposes for which the property subject to the trust is held' (s. 15(1)(b)). This latter subsection reflects the case law on s. 30 of the 1925 Act. There are two conflicting decisions at first instance on this that of Wroath J in *TSB Bank v Marshall* [1998] 2 FLR 769, who said that the previous case law under s. 30, LPA should apply, and that of Neuberger J in *The Mortgage Corporation v Shaire* [2000] 1 FLR 973, who found eight reasons for concluding that the legislature had not necessarily intended the courts to be bound by the previous case law (see Chapter 8, Question 1). *The Mortgage Corporation v Shaire* was cited with approval by the Court of Appeal in *Bank of Ireland Home Mortgages Ltd v Bell* [2001] 2 FLR 809 although the court took a relatively limited view of the discretion available under s. 14. More relevant to the circumstances here might be the Court of Appeal decision in *Chan Pui Chun v Leung Kam Ho* [2002] EWCA Civ. 1075, which considered the effect of s. 12(2) TLATA as to whether a particular property is suitable for a particular beneficiary to occupy. A house bought for four students to occupy might well not be suitable for Connie alone to live in.

Question 3

Consider the significance of the decision of the House of Lords in *Stack v Dowden* [2007] AC 432.

Commentary

This is a topical question, which gives the candidate scope to discuss the case both in the context of the previous law and also in the light of subsequent decisions. In this sort of book-work question on a particular case, it can be useful to set out the facts, the reasoning of the court, and the decision itself, and then to go on to consider the scope of the decision and to comment on it. The suggested answer builds its comments on an interesting lecture given by Lord Neuberger, who gave the only dissent in ***Stack v Dowden***. The suggested answer is framed by an introduction, which sets out the basic legal issue in the case, and a conclusion, which draws the discussion together. Candidates should remember that a conclusion should not be used to introduce new points not previously mentioned.

For interesting comments on ***Stack v Dowden***, see M. Dixon [2007] *Conv* 352, M. Pawlowski, 'Beneficial entitlement No Longer Doing Justice?' [2007] *Conv* 354, A. Moran, 'Anything to declare?' [2007] *Conv* 364, and M. Dixon, 'The Never-Ending Story' [2007] *Conv* 456.

Answer plan

- Introduction.
- ***Stack v Dowden***
  - Facts;
  - Lady Hale's speech;
  - Decision.
- Scope of ***Stack v Dowden***
  - Acquisition of interest where legal title in one name?
  - Size of beneficial interest;
  - Lord Neuberger's dissent in ***Stack v Dowden***;
  - Lord Neuberger's four extra-judicial concerns.
- Do parties intend right of survivorship?
- Meaning of 'domestic consumer context' (and effect on third parties, e.g. trustee in bankruptcy).
- Are factors mentioned by Lady Hale persuasive?
- Intention post-acquisition.
- Conclusion.

Suggested answer

The decision of the House of Lords in *Stack v Dowden* was narrowly concerned with the determination of the beneficial shares of cohabitees who had purchased in joint names a family home but without expressly declaring how they held in equity. The decision is of broader significance, however, because it is clear that the House of Lords intended their decision to be applicable to cases where both parties contribute to the purchase but the legal title is put into the name of one of them only.

The parties, Miss Dowden and Mr Stack, had cohabited since 1975, and had four children. In 1993 they bought a house for £190,000, which was transferred into joint names. The purchase moneys were raised as to £67,000 from the sale of a property in which they both had a beneficial interest, the balance being obtained by a mortgage loan from Barclays Bank. Over the next few years, Dowden (who was on a higher salary) paid over £38,000 towards the mortgage instalments, and Stack £27,000. They separated in 2002, and the question arose how they held the beneficial interest in the property. There was no express declaration of the beneficial interests in the transfer, although it was stated that the survivor could give a good receipt for capital moneys.

Lady Hale, giving the main speech of the majority, said that the determination of beneficial interests depended on the intention of the parties. She stated that, 'at least in the domestic consumer context, a conveyance into joint names indicates both legal and beneficial joint tenancy, unless and until the contrary is proved'. She said that it would require unusual circumstances if it were to be found, in the absence of any express agreement or declaration, that the beneficial interests were other than equal. Her Ladyship said that, in determining the parties' true intentions as to their respective beneficial shares, many factors other than merely financial contributions were relevant. She supplied a long list of factors including: advice and discussions at the time of purchase, the reasons for purchase in joint names, the purpose for which the home was acquired, the nature of their relationship, whether they had children for whom they both had responsibility to provide a home, how the purchase was financed (both initially and subsequently), how they arranged their finances (separately or together), and how they discharged their outgoings and their other household expenses. She added that the parties' individual characters and personalities might also be a factor in deciding where their true intentions lie.

Lady Hale considered that the circumstances of the case were unusual in that the parties kept their finances and expenditure rigorously separate. In the light of this, she held that the appropriate division was 65:35 in favour of Miss Dowden.

As a result of the case, there is now a strong presumption that a transfer of property into joint names in the context her Ladyship described creates a joint tenancy in equity. This is the new starting point, even if one of the parties makes no contribution to the purchase price. The previous starting point in cases of transfer into joint names, namely that of resulting trust according to financial contributions, has been abandoned in the context her Ladyship described, and therefore has no role to play. If the presumption were rebutted by evidence of the parties' contrary intentions, the parties would then hold on a constructive trust for themselves in unequal shares.

The ratio of *Stack v Dowden* is narrow, because the House of Lords was dealing with a case where the property had been transferred into joint names. Where the property is transferred into the name of one of the parties only (A), the starting point is different, as then the party whose name is not on the legal title (B) must first establish that he or she has acquired a share in equity in the first place. Nothing in *Stack v Dowden* affects the need for B to establish that he or she has acquired an equitable interest. It was established before *Stack v Dowden* that B might do this by producing evidence of a declaration of trust complying with the Law of Property Act 1925, s. 53(1)(b), by bringing evidence of an actual informal agreement that B was to have a share (supported by detriment through acting on the agreement), or, by showing that he or she made a direct contribution to the purchase price or to the mortgage instalments; in this last circumstance, the court might infer a common intention that B was intended to have a share: ***Lloyd's Bank plc v Rosset* [1991] AC 107**. Before ***Stack v Dowden***, B could have no equitable interest unless he or she could show the acquisition of such an interest by one of these methods, or in some other way, e.g. through proprietary estoppel or some general principle of restitution. Lord Walker in ***Stack v Dowden***, however, thought that the law had moved on since Lord Bridge in ***Rosset***, and that now the courts, in seeking to ascertain the parties' intentions, could take account of the parties' whole course of conduct, and that a common intention constructive trust might now be inferred from other than the direct contributions to which Lord Bridge had referred. Lady Hale approved this statement in delivering the advice of the Privy Council in ***Abbott v Abbott* [2008] 1 FLR 1451**. If these observations (which were strictly *obiter*) are interpreted widely, the decision in ***Burns v Burns* [1984] Ch 317**, where a woman acquired no beneficial interest through 17 years of housework and childcare, might now be different; see M Dixon [2007] *Conv* 456. It might therefore be that ***Stack v Dowden*** has the startling effect of broadening the circumstances in which a person may acquire a beneficial interest even where the title is in one name only. If this is what Lord Walker and Lady Hale intended, then their remarks are inconsistent with the earlier decisions of the House of Lords in ***Pettitt v Pettitt* [1970] AC 777** and ***Gissing v Gissing* [1971] AC 886**. More recently, however, in ***Thomson v Humphrey* [2009] EWHC 3576 (Ch)**, Warren J was unable to infer an agreement that the beneficial interest should be shared merely from the non-legal owner's taking care of the housekeeping; so it seems that the principle of ***Burns v Burns*** survives ***Stack v Dowden***.

There is no doubt, however, that Lady Hale's observations are relevant to the cases of purchase in a sole name, at the second stage: namely in ascertaining, in the absence of any express agreement between the parties, the size of B's share. Lady Hale was critical of Chadwick LJ's comment in ***Oxley v Hiscock* [2004] 3 All ER 703 (para. 69)** that the parties were each entitled to 'that share which the court considers fair having regard to the whole course of dealing between them in relation to the property'. Lady Hale emphasised that the search was for the parties' intentions, not what the court considered fair. Her Ladyship indicated that, whilst the starting point was different where the legal title was in the name of A alone from where it had been vested in A and B jointly, the same factors that she mentioned as relevant in determining the parties' true intentions should be applicable to both.

The application of the factors in ***Stack v Dowden*** is seen in ***Abbott v Abbott* [2008] 1 FLR 1451**. Land in Antigua had been transferred into the husband's sole name because, as his wife was not an Antiguan national, there were problems with putting her name on the transfer. The wife's financial contribution to the building of a house on the land was only 8.3%, but the Privy Council held her entitled to half the beneficial interest. It was significant that the parties had contributed to the property jointly, had a joint bank account and had joint legal liability for the mortgage repayments and insurance.

The fact that *Stack v Dowden* excludes the application of the doctrine of resulting trusts was of concern to Lord Neuberger, who delivered the sole dissenting speech in the House of Lords in that case. His dissent was not on the result, but on the majority's reasoning. His approach was to apply traditional property law principles. He said that the determination of the beneficial interests should depend initially on an application of the principles of the resulting trust, which might then be supplanted by the doctrine of constructive trust arising from an express or inferred agreement supported by detriment. It should also be noted that the size of the shares that the House of Lords determined in *Stack v Dowden* applying the factors that Lady Hale set out were about the same as the parties' overall financial contributions: in other words, the decision itself would have been the same even on a broader resulting trust approach (i.e. one that takes into account not merely the initial contributions to the purchase price, but also the payment of mortgage instalments).

Speaking extra-judicially, Lord Neuberger has since expressed four concerns about the decision in *Stack v Dowden*: see Lord Neuberger, 'The conspirators, the tax man, the Bill of Rights and a bit about the lovers', Chancery Bar Association Annual Lecture, 28 March 2008.

First, his Lordship doubted whether most couples can be taken to have intended a joint tenancy in equity, with the consequent right of survivorship. This seems to be a powerful criticism: indeed, it is somewhat ironic that the majority in *Stack v Dowden*, applying the Court of Appeal's decision in *Huntingford v Hobbs* [1993] 1 FLR 736, rejected the notion that, merely because the transfer provided that the survivor could give a receipt for capital moneys, the parties were joint tenants in equity. To a lawyer, this statement indicates a joint tenancy in equity, but the House of Lords took the view that this was not helpful, as there was no evidence that the parties themselves understood its legal implications.

Secondly, Lord Neuberger was concerned about what Lady Hale meant by suggesting that the principle she was laying down applied 'at least in the domestic consumer context'. This question has been considered in later cases. In each of *Fowler v Barron* [2008] EWCA Civ 377, and *Edwards v Edwards* [2008] All ER (D) 79 (Mar) (Ch), the joint legal owners had long-term sexual relationships, and there was insufficient evidence to rebut the strong presumption of joint beneficial ownership. Where the property is not bought for occupation by spouses or co-habitees, however, the position is less clear. In *Adekunle v Ritchie* [2007] EW Misc 5 (EWCC), the property had been bought by a mother and her son, and Judge Behrens in the county court proceeded on the basis that *Stack v Dowden* applied, even in the absence of a sexual relationship. In *Laskar v Laskar* [2008] 2 P&CR 245, the Court of Appeal (Lord Neuberger delivering the only reasoned judgment) considered that *Stack v Dowden* did not apply where a mother and daughter had bought the mother's council house as an investment (for letting rooms out) even though the mother lived there for a while after the purchase. If they were wrong on that, the Court of Appeal nevertheless held that there were factors rebutting the strong presumption, particularly the reason for the transfer into joint names and the investment purpose for which the house was acquired. In *Close Invoice Finance Ltd v Abaowa* [2010] EWHC 1920 (QB), a resulting trust approach was adopted of property bought as an investment (a buy to-let) and put into the daughter's name only.

Another potential difficulty with the majority reasoning in *Stack v Dowden* is, whilst the principle might be applicable as between domestic purchasers who take a transfer jointly, it is difficult to see why this should be binding on a trustee in bankruptcy of one of the parties. In such circumstances, it would seem that the trustee in bankruptcy could not seize the share of a solvent co-owner held under a resulting trust, but the trustee ought to be able to take any larger share arising from the presumption in *Stack v Dowden*, as such additional share would have been acquired under a voluntary disposition made by the bankrupt: cf. *Densham v Densham* [1975] 1 WLR 1519 and *Segal v Pasram* [2007] BPIR 881 (ChD).

Thirdly, Lord Neuberger was not persuaded by some of the factors that Lady Hale had mentioned as pointing away from a beneficial joint tenancy. If unequal contributions rebutted the presumption of equal beneficial shares, then the presumption was of no value, since the issue would arise only where the contributions were not equal. He was also doubtful whether the fact that the parties keep their finances separate was at all unusual; he thought that many couples probably do this.

Fourthly, he was concerned that the reference to the court's need to determine the parties' true intentions, and the list of factors that Lady Hale mentioned as relevant, tend towards uncertainty and will therefore lead to more, not less, litigation. This is a powerful criticism: the list of factors is long, and some of them—such as the parties' characters and personalities—are entirely subjective. The difficulties of determining the size of the shares are illustrated in *Adekunle v Ritchie* (2007), where the strong presumption of a joint beneficial tenancy was rebutted on the evidence, as the property had been put into the joint names of a mother and son only because the former could not otherwise obtain a mortgage to buy her council house at a discount. The son paid most of the mortgage instalments, and had contributed one-quarter of the overall purchase price; but the judge, applying the holistic approach favoured in *Stack v Dowden*, held that the son was beneficially entitled to one-third. Similarly, in *Hapeshi v Allnatt* [2010] EWHC 392 (Ch), Mrs Hapeshi bought her council house, which was transferred into the joint names of herself and one of her sons, Michael; she obtained a discount on the purchase price, the balance being obtained by a mortgage loan. On her death, another son, Kevin, claimed to be entitled to a half share under a common intention constructive trust. The judge could find no evidence of any common intention, but Kevin had paid some of the mortgage arrears. Applying the holistic approach approved in *Stack* and *Abbott*, the judge quantified Kevin's share as one-quarter. In neither of these decisions is it clear how the respective proportions were arrived at.

If the parties hold the property as beneficial joint tenants at the time of acquisition, to what extent, following *Stack v Dowden*, can those beneficial interests be subsequently varied? In the light of *Jones v Kernott* [2010] EWCA Civ 578, it appears that there can be no variation, absent evidence of an actual agreement or estoppel. In that case, the parties, who had already been living together, bought a house in 1985, which was transferred into their joint names. After eight years, they split up, and Mr Kernott moved out. It was agreed that at that time their beneficial interests were joint. For the next 14 years, however, Ms Jones paid all the mortgage interest and insurance premiums out of her own funds, as well as all the costs of bringing up their two children (to which Mr Kernott contributed nothing). The Court of Appeal, reversing the judge at first instance (who had declared Ms Jones entitled to a 90% share), held that Ms Jones remained entitled only to one-half, as there was insufficient evidence of any common intention by the parties after they split up that their beneficial interests should be anything other than joint. On a broader resulting trust approach, Ms Jones would probably have obtained much more than 50%. The application of *Stack v Dowden* in these circumstances, however, shows that even many years of financial input into mortgage payments by one party alone after the other has left is not enough to affect the size of their beneficial interests. In an extreme case like *Jones v Kernott*, this seems unfair. Indeed, Rimer LJ, whilst applying *Stack v Dowden*, was critical of Lady Hale's distinction between an 'inferred' and an 'imputed' agreement. It is understood that Ms Jones has been given leave to appeal to the Supreme Court.

Although it is now a few years since the controversial decision in *Stack v Dowden*, many issues remain unclear: first, what circumstances will be regarded as exceptional to rebut the strong presumption that it laid down; secondly, the extent to which the decision applies where the legal title is in one name only; and, thirdly, how the size of beneficial interests is calculated using the 'holistic' approach favoured by Lady Hale. More recently, the decision in *Jones v Kernott* has revealed not only the problem of when an agreement can be inferred, but also the difficulties that can arise in trying to establish that the beneficial shares have been varied post-acquisition. To date, therefore, whilst the decision in *Stack v Dowden* has shifted the nature of the legal arguments over beneficial interests in the family home, it has not produced clear legal principles that enable parties to settle their disputes without recourse to the courts. Indeed, the volume of litigation since the House of Lords' decision seems rather, as Lord Neuberger feared, to have increased.

Question 4

In 2000, Nancy bought a house of which she was the sole registered proprietor. Her father, who had been recently widowed, moved in with her. He gave her £10,000 for the deposit on the house and spent £5,000 of his life insurance money on adapting part of the ground floor so that he had a bedroom with en suite bathroom for his own use. In 2005, Nancy met and fell in love with Bill, who moved in with her. Bill, who was unemployed, spent a good deal of time on improving and renovating the house. He also did all the housework and cooking. He spent most

of his £5,000 redundancy money on the renovations and also contributed to the housekeeping bills. Last year, Nancy took out a mortgage on the house with the Fagin Finance Emporium in the sum of £125,000. Tiring of Bill's obsessive housekeeping, she bought a round-the-world air ticket and left. The Fagin Finance Emporium is now seeking possession of the house as a preliminary to sale.

(a) Advise Bill and Nancy's father.

How would your answer differ if:

(b) Nancy and Bill had been married?

(c) Nancy had been declared bankrupt?

Commentary

Although ***Stack v Dowden* [2007] AC 432** concerned the acquisition of beneficial interests where the title to domestic property was in joint names, it appears that the House of Lords intended the same principles to apply to cases where the legal title is in one of the parties' names only. How ***Stack v Dowden*** applies to the latter situation has not yet, however, been completely clarified, and the suggested answer draws attention to this. As ***Stack v Dowden*** established that, where the legal title is in joint names, there is a strong presumption that the beneficial interests are also held jointly, so it would seem to follow that, where the legal title is in one name, there is a strong presumption that the equitable interest is with the legal owner. If this is so, it seems to place a heavier burden on the non-legal owner to show that he or she has a beneficial interest than was the position before ***Stack v Dowden***. This is a problem question, so take advantage of it, and use the points in it as hooks on which to hang your argument.

Answer plan

(a) Nancy's father:

- Deposit as gift, loan or acquisition of beneficial interest?
  - acquisition constructive trust under ***Stack v Dowden.***
- Adapting ground-floor bedroom
  - a factor in determining size of share under acquisition constructive trust?
  - if not, nature of work depends on whether can infer common intention for post-acquisition constructive trust.

Bill:

- Housekeeping—no beneficial interest absent express agreement.
- Renovation—possible interest under post-acquisition constructive trust, depending on the nature of the work.

(b)
- Improvements—**Matrimonial Proceedings and Property Act 1970, s. 37.**
- Property adjustments on divorce—**Matrimonial Causes Act 1973.**

(c)
- **Insolvency Act 1986, s. 335A.**
- Exceptional circumstances?
- **Article 8 of ECHR.**

Suggested answer

(a) The Fagin Finance Emporium (the Emporium) may be seeking possession because the mortgage instalments are in arrears. Whether it will be able to obtain possession of the house depends, however, on whether Nancy's father and Bill (or either of them) has a beneficial interest in the house that is binding on the Emporium.

The legal title to the house is in Nancy's sole name, but her father may try to establish a beneficial interest on the basis that he provided £10,000 for the deposit, and spent £5,000 in adapting the ground floor. It is first necessary to determine the basis on which the £10,000 for the deposit was provided. If the evidence shows that it was intended to be a gift, the father will not have any beneficial interest in the house. Although the question says that he 'gave' her the money, it could be that the word is used loosely to mean merely 'transferred'. In the absence of evidence, the presumption of advancement will have applied to the transfer of the money, as it was a transfer from father to child; although that presumption is abolished by the Equality Act 2010, s. 199, the abolition is not retrospective, and so will apply here, as the father transferred the money to her in 2000. The presumption is easily rebutted, however, by evidence of surrounding circumstances; and in *McGrath v Wallis* [1995] 2 FLR 114, it was held that the presumption was rebutted by the fact that the person who had contributed to the purchase of a house was to share occupation with the legal owner. Another possibility is that the £10,000 was intended to be a loan; but, absent evidence to support this construction, it is unlikely.

As the legal title is in Nancy's sole name, there is a strong presumption that she has the entire beneficial interest: cf. *Stack v Dowden* [2007] AC 207. Nancy's father might be able to rebut this presumption by showing that he acquired a beneficial interest in the house by virtue of paying the £10,000 deposit. Before *Stack v Dowden*, this direct contribution to the purchase price would, in the absence of any agreement between them, have given him a proportionate share of the beneficial interest in the house; so that if, for example, it had been bought for £200,000, he would thereby have obtained a 5% share. In many instances, however, once it was established that the non-legal owner had a beneficial interest under a resulting trust, the court could infer that the parties had agreed that they were to share the beneficial interest, and could, where the non-legal owner had acted to his or her detriment in reliance on the common intention, award such person a larger share under a constructive trust: *Midland Bank v Cooke* [1995] 4 All ER 562. In practice, therefore, the resulting trust would usually be superseded in these sorts of cases by a constructive trust. In the House of Lords in *Stack v Dowden*, however, it was established that, in the domestic context, both the acquisition of a beneficial interest and the size of any interest obtained are to be determined, not according to principles of resulting trust, but in accordance with the parties' intentions, whether express or (more likely) inferred. In *Stack v Dowden*, the legal title was in the parties' joint names; but it is clear that the House of Lords intended the principles they laid down to apply also to cases where the legal title is (as in the question) in one person's name only. Even though there is no sexual relationship between Nancy and her father, the facts in this part of the problem indicate a domestic context within *Stack v Dowden*. On this basis, Nancy's father's payment of the £10,000 deposit would be treated both as evidence that he and Nancy had a common intention that he should have an interest in the property, and also that he had changed his position to his detriment in reliance on such agreement; these are the ingredients of a common-intention constructive trust, which would be outside the statutory formalities of the Law of Property Act 1925, s. 53(1)(b) by virtue of s. 53(2). In determining the size of the share, Lady Hale, with whose speech in *Stack v Dowden* the majority agreed, favoured a 'holistic' approach, and she listed the many factors that are to be taken into account, including the parties' individual characters and personalities. This being so, it is impossible to predict what the court might determine the size of Nancy's father's share to be. However, one factor which might be taken into account to enlarge his share under such constructive trust might be his later expenditure of £5,000 in adapting the ground floor for his bedroom.

If, however, the initial deposit was intended as a gift or a loan, the moneys spent on the bedroom later on might not give the father a beneficial interest. Much depends on whether the work amounts to an improvement that enhances the house's value. If it does, it may be evidence from which the court could infer that he and Nancy had agreed that he was to have an interest, but it is by no means certain that such an inference would be made. If it does not, it may be difficult for Nancy's father to show that he had an agreement with Nancy that he was intended to share the beneficial interest and that his expenditure was in reliance on that agreement.

In respect of Bill, the situation is different since he did not make a contribution at the outset. According to Lord Bridge in *Lloyds Bank plc v Rosset*, it is only in exceptional cases that a common intention can be deduced to share in the beneficial ownership at a date later than the time of acquisition. Bill's contribution is £5,000 to the renovation of the house and the payment of the housekeeping costs. It would seem extremely unlikely that a constructive trust would arise in the case of either of the contributions. The cost of the renovations and the housekeeping expenses would not amount to direct contributions to the purchase price, nor would they amount to the equivalent of purchase money (*Burns v Burns* [1984] Ch 317 and *Pettitt v Pettitt* [1970] AC 777). An indirect contribution could only act as a detriment where there was an express agreement or where the payment of the household expenses enabled Nancy to pay the mortgage (*Grant v Edwards* [1986] Ch 638). In the absence of an express agreement, a common-intention constructive trust can arise if there is detrimental reliance on an implied bargain. Bill could argue that the use of his redundancy money is clear evidence of detrimental conduct. His labour alone is unlikely to be sufficient to establish detrimental conduct. In *Eves v Eves* [1975] 1 WLR 1338, the woman's arduous work of renovation was held to have been carried out in reliance on a common intention that she should share the beneficial ownership. The conduct of the man in inducing her to agree that the property should be put in his name alone because she was under 21 was clear evidence of a common intention and her work would not have been carried out without such an agreement. However, in the present case, Bill's work may not fall into the same category. On its own, without any express agreement as to beneficial ownership, it might be viewed as solely an anxiety on his part to improve his living conditions. In *Lloyds Bank plc v Rosset* the woman's work in assisting in the renovation of the house was simply attributed to her anxiety to move the family in quickly. It was not sufficient evidence to point to an agreement as to shared beneficial ownership. On the other hand, Bill's work, coupled with his expenditure, might increase his chance of a successful claim (*Ungurian v Lesnoff* [1990] Ch 206). It would seem apparent, however, that his payment of the housekeeping expenses would have no relevance in establishing beneficial ownership in the absence of an express agreement (*Rosset*). In *Gissing v Gissing*, it was held that the wife's contribution to the household expenditure and her labour in caring for the family was insufficient evidence of detrimental conduct in reliance on a common intention to share beneficially in the ownership. It seems unlikely that Bill will be able to establish a constructive trust. Lord Walker in *Stack v Dowden* [2007] 2 AC 432 considered that the law had moved on since Lord Bridge in *Rosset*, and said that a common intention constructive trust might now be inferred from other than direct contributions. This view was approved by the Privy Council in *Abbott v Abbott* [2008] 1 FLR 1451. These observations, however, were made in cases involving a transfer into joint names, and it seems unlikely that they were intended to be inconsistent with *Pettitt v Pettitt* [1970] AC 777 and *Gissing v Gissing* [1971] AC 886, both of which rejected the possibility of imputing an agreement that the parties never made. The better view is that the observations are applicable only to determining the size of a beneficial interest the existence of which, but not the quantum, has already been established. They do not therefore affect the earlier case law that establishes whether the claimant has acquired a beneficial interest in the first place. The court will not therefore infer an agreement between Nancy and Bill that the latter should have a beneficial interest merely from his housework and cooking: *Thomson v Humphrey* [2009] EWHC 3576 (Ch).

If either Nancy's father or Bill has an equitable interest in the house, then, as they are both in actual occupation, this may constitute an overriding interest under the Land Registration Act 2002, Schedule 3, para. 2 provided they do not fall within the exceptions in paras 2(b) and (c). As the capital money is paid to only one trustee (Nancy) by the Fagin Finance Emporium, the doctrine of overreaching will not operate

(*Williams & Glyn's Bank Ltd v Boland* [1979] Ch 312). The Fagin Finance Emporium will, therefore, take subject to the rights of any beneficiaries.

The Fagin Finance Emporium will need to apply to the court for an order for sale under s. 14, TLATA 1996. The court must have regard to the matters set out in s. 15 which include the intentions of the person who created the trust, the purposes for which the property is held, the welfare of minors occupying as a home the trust property and the interests of secured creditors.

There is no indication in s. 15 of the relative weights to be given to the competing interests of the creditors and other parties with an interest. Each case must depend on its facts and it is for the court to make a value judgment (*Abbey National v Moss* [1994] 1 FLR 307, and *Re Domenico Citro* [1991] Ch 142). In a Court of Appeal decision (*Bank of Baroda v Dhillon* [1998] 1 FLR 524), the priority to be given to the interests of the creditors in preference to those of a spouse with an overriding interest, was recognised where an application for an order for sale under s. 30, Law of Property Act 1925 (now s. 14 of the Trusts of Land and Appointment of Trustees Act 1996) was made. Where, as in the present case, the family relationship has broken up, the purpose will be regarded as spent (*Re A; A v A* [2002] EWHC 611 (Admin/Fam); *First National Bank plc v Achampong* [2003] EWCA Civ 487).

In *Bank of Ireland Home Mortgages Ltd v Bell*, it was held that the issue of whether a creditor was being recompensed for being kept out of his money was a powerful factor to be considered.

If the Emporium obtained possession and sold the house, the issue would then be how much of the proceeds of sale they would have to pay to Nancy's father or to Bill. This depends on the extent to which their beneficial interests bind the Emporium. Lady Hale emphasised that the principle in *Stack v Dowden* applies in the domestic context. It is not clear, however, whether an action by a mortgagee against a beneficial owner has a domestic or a commercial context. If the context is domestic, the Emporium will first have to apply the sale proceeds in paying Nancy's father the share to which he is entitled under the constructive trust. If the context is commercial, the Emporium will have to pay him only the interest he will have acquired under the principles that apply outside *Stack v Dowden*: namely, his interest under a resulting trust (which might be smaller). In *Densham v Densham* [1975] 1 WLR 1519, a wife had contributed the original deposit on a house, this being one-ninth of the purchase price. The house was conveyed into the sole name of her husband, who later became bankrupt. It was held that the one-ninth share that she had under a resulting trust was binding on the trustee in bankruptcy, as it was obtained for valuable consideration before the bankruptcy. The larger share that she claimed under a constructive trust, however, was held voidable by the trustee in bankruptcy, as it involved an element of voluntary disposition. It may therefore be that Nancy's father would only be able to claim from the Emporium the share obtained under a resulting trust by his £10,000 payment of the deposit.

(b) If Nancy and Bill had been married, the Matrimonial Proceedings and Property Act 1970, s. 37 would have applied. This provides that if a husband or wife makes a substantial contribution in money or money's worth to the improvement of property, such person acquires a share, or an enlarged share, of the beneficial interest as the parties have agreed, or, in the absence of agreement, as the court in all the circumstances considers just. Bill's expenditure of £5,000 is a substantial contribution, but the work of renovation may merely involve repairs, redecoration and recarpeting, none of which would qualify as improvements. If his work did rank as an improvement, however, he might be able to use s. 37 to acquire an interest where he could not acquire one under *Stack v Dowden*. The difference is that, in order for Bill to obtain an interest under that case, he would need to provide evidence of a common intention, and this might be difficult to establish in the case of subsequent improvements; furthermore, in accordance with that case, the court cannot simply award him the share that it considers fair, but only the share that it can be inferred the parties intended him to have: *Stack v Dowden*, disapproving on this point of Chadwick LJ's observations in *Oxley v Hiscock* [2004] 3 All ER 703. In contrast, under s. 37, in the absence of agreement, the court will award Bill the share that it considers just.

The Matrimonial Causes Act 1973 applies only on divorce and so would not apply here. Where it does apply it gives a court very extensive powers of property disposition between the spouses, taking into account circumstances relevant to their conduct in the marriage as well as their contributions to the property (*LF v LF & W plc* [2001] 2 FLR 970).

The answer is unchanged as regards Nancy's father.

(c) Had Nancy been declared bankrupt, then, where an application is made by the trustee in bankruptcy to a court with jurisdiction over the bankruptcy, the Insolvency Act 1986, s. 335A (inserted by Schedule 3 of TLATA 1996) applies and s. 15, TLATA 1996 is excluded (s. 15(4)). The court shall make such order as it thinks just and reasonable having regard to the criteria set out in s. 335A(2). These criteria include the interests of the bankrupt's creditors and, where a dwelling-house is involved which is or has been the home of the spouse or former spouse, then the conduct of that spouse in contributing to the bankruptcy is to be considered. Further matters include the needs and financial resources of that spouse and the needs of any children, and all the circumstances of the case other than the needs of the bankrupt. This might presumably include the fact that the house is also Nancy's father's home. After one year, however, the interests of the creditors are to become paramount unless there are exceptional circumstances (s. 335A(3)). Exceptional circumstances are only likely to include extreme matters such as severe ill-health or terminal illness (*Claughton v Charalamabous* [1999] 1 FLR 740. In *Re Bremner* [1999] 1 FLR 912) where the bankrupt had a life expectancy of six months and was being cared for by his elderly spouse, the order for sale was postponed for three months after the bankrupt's death. His spouse was considered to have needs in these exceptional circumstances that justified the postponement of the sale. Other examples include the needs of a physically disabled child (*Re Bailey* [1977] 1 WLR 278), schizophrenia (*Re Raval* [1998] 2 FLR 718), and cancer (*Judd v Barr* [1999] 1 FLR 1191). No such circumstances appear to apply in the present case. The fact that the proceeds of the sale will be swallowed up in expenses is not an exceptional circumstance which would prevent an order for sale (*Harrington v Bennett* (2000) EGCS 41).

It is arguable that the test under s. 335A(3) is incompatible with Article 8 of the European Convention on Human Rights in that it interferes with the right to respect for family life and home although no case law currently supports this argument (*Barca v Mears* [2004] EWHC 2170 (Ch) and *Foyle v Turner* [2007] BPIR 24).

It is likely that the same considerations will be applied if Nancy and Bill are unmarried. In *Re Domenico Citro* [1991] Ch 142, Nourse LJ said that the case law relating to unmarried couples is the same as the statutory law relating to married couples, so the same considerations may well be taken into account by the court if Nancy and Bill are unmarried.

Further reading

Burn, E.H., and Cartwright, J., *Cheshire and Burn's Modern Law of Real Property*, 17th edn, Oxford, 2006, chapter 13.

Gardner (2004) 120 *LQR* 541.

Law Com. No. 728, Sharing Homes: A Discussion Paper (2002).

Lord Neuberger, 'The conspirators, the tax man, the Bill of Rights and a bit about the lovers', Chancery Bar Association Annual Lecture, 28 March 2008.

Oakley, A. J., *Constructive Trusts*, Sweet & Maxwell, 1997.

Smith, R. J., *Property Law*, 5th edn, Longman, 2006, chapters 8, 12, and 13.

Thompson, M. P., 'Constructive trusts, estoppel and the family home' [2004] *Conv* 496.

10

Proprietary estoppel

Introduction

There is a difficulty in seeking to establish separate categories for such topics as estoppel and licences and, indeed, constructive trusts, since in many of the cases they seem to be inextricably linked as cases such as *Yaxley v Gotts* [2000] All ER 71 demonstrate. In *Oxley v Hiscock* [2004] 3 All ER 703 it was held that, in respect of the rules as to the quantification of the parties' respective shares, there was no difference in outcome whether the true analysis lay in constructive trust or estoppel. Question 3, a mixed question, attempts to tackle this overlap. In so far as the doctrine of proprietary estoppel has a separate existence it deals with the situation where a party attempts to renege on an agreement in breach of equitable principles. There is no single judicial pronouncement on the doctrine, although the classic exposition is normally considered to have been that of Lord Kingsdown in *Ramsden v Dyson* (1866) LR 1 HL 129 at 170. There are further developments of the doctrine in *Crabb v Arun District Council* [1976] Ch 179 and *E. R. Ives Investment Ltd v High* [1967] 2 QB 379. There is a development of the case law which has evolved the doctrine, so that the modern approach, confirmed by *Taylors Fashions Ltd v Liverpool Victoria Trustees Co Ltd* [1982] QB 133, shows a broader direction without the requirement of satisfying a number of strict prerequisites established in some of the earlier cases. This approach is confirmed by the many cases which have recently been decided under this doctrine. Examples of these include *Gillett v Holt* [2000] 2 All ER 289; *Matharu v Matharu* (1994) 68 P & CR 93; *Mollo v Mollo* [1999] EGCS 117; *Jennings v Rice* [2003] 1 P & CR 8; *Yeoman's Row Management Ltd v Cobbe* [2008] UKHL 55 and *Thorner v Major* [2009] UKHL 18. However, it remains necessary to know the essentials for establishing the doctrine, i.e. the assurance of entitlement given by the owner, the reliance on the assurance by the claimant, and the detriment caused by that reliance.

Questions relating to the topic of licences usually bear upon one (or both) of two issues. The first is the question of the nature of the interest. Does it create a mere personal permission to use land in a certain way or does it have a proprietary dimension? The second question flows from the first. Can a licence bind third parties? It is necessary to be able to distinguish between the different types of licences—bare, coupled with an interest and contractual. Then there follows the question of the manner of protection of the equity raised by the estoppel, and an abundance of case law providing a variety of examples of the way that this dilemma can be resolved. This is an area where there is much judicial doctrinal debate and the precedents need to be read with care. A useful article on the Contracts (Rights of Third Parties) Act 1999 is: S. Bright [2000] 64 *Conv* 398.

The effect of s.116 Land Registration Act 2002 on an equity arising out of an estoppel is also considered.

Question 1

'The overwhelming weight of authority shows that detriment is required. But the authorities also show that it is not a narrow or technical concept. The detriment need not consist of the expenditure of money or other quantifiable financial detriment, so long as it is something substantial. The requirement must be approached as part of a broad enquiry as to whether repudiation of an assurance is or is not unconscionable in all the circumstances' (*per* Robert Walker LJ in *Gillett v Holt* [2000] 2 All ER 289).

To what extent have the strict requirements set out in *Willmott v Barber* (1880) for establishing the equitable doctrine of proprietary estoppel been modified by subsequent cases?

Commentary

This essay question requires a knowledge of the classic exposition of the equitable doctrine of proprietary estoppel and its subsequent development through judicial precedent. There has been an increasing number of cases which have rested on the application of this doctrine and the quotation from one of them, ***Gillett v Holt* [2000] 2 All ER 289** provided an opportunity in the Court of Appeal for a review of the doctrine. The decisions in ***Yeoman's Row Management Ltd v Cobbe* [2008] UKHL 55** and ***Thorner v Major* [2009] UKHL 18**, also provided the opportunity for the House of Lords to deliberate on the doctrine. However, the pivotal point in the discussion is probably the dictum of Oliver J in ***Taylors Fashion Ltd v Liverpool Victoria Trustees Co Ltd* [1982] QB 133** where a clear break was made with the strict classical exposition of the doctrine which can be found in ***Willmott v Barber* (1880) 15 ChD 96**.

This area has not been without controversy and cases such as ***Re Basham* [1986] 1 WLR 1498** and ***Taylor v Dickens* [1998] 1 FLR 806** have been criticised both in subsequent cases and in some of the many articles spawned by this area. Interestingly, the decision in ***Gillett v Holt*** appears to resolve some of these conflicts in that it criticises ***Taylor v Dickens*** but appears to vindicate the decision in ***Re Basham***.

For some examples of relevant articles see M. Thompson [1998] *Conv* 210, W. J. Swadling [1998] *Restitution Law Review* 220, and M. Dixon [1999] *Conv* 46. Many other articles deal with this doctrine: G. Battersby [1991] *Conv* 36 is a particularly good example.

Answer plan

- Modern approach in ***Taylors Fashions Ltd v Liverpool Victoria Trustee Co Ltd* [1982] QB 133**.
- Strict fivefold criteria.
- Decision in ***Gillett v Holt***.
- Analysis of modern approach:
  - the promise;
  - detrimental reliance;
  - unconscionability.

Suggested answer

The extract from the judgment in *Gillett v Holt* demonstrates that the equitable doctrine of proprietary estoppel has moved from a rigid requirement for proof of strict elements to a broader approach depending ultimately on the unconscionability of the action.

Proprietary estoppel is an equitable doctrine whereby an owner of real property is prevented from insisting on his strict legal rights in relation to that property, when it would be inequitable for him to do so, having regard to the dealings which have taken place between the parties (*Hughes v Metropolitan Railway Co* (1877) 2 App Cas 439).

Modern case law appears to show that there has to be some assurance of an individual's rights and some detrimental reliance on those rights. This approach was confirmed in *Taylors Fashions Ltd v Liverpool Victoria Trustees Co Ltd* [1982] QB 133 where Oliver J said (*obiter*) that it is necessary to ascertain whether, in the particular circumstances, 'it would be unconscionable for a party to be permitted to deny that which, knowingly, or unknowingly, he has allowed or encouraged another to assume to his detriment'. This was to be preferred to an attempt to fit every conceivable case within the strictures of some preconceived formula.

The formula to which Oliver J was referring is to be found in *Willmott v Barber* (1880) 15 ChD 96 which followed the views of Lord Kingsdown (in a dissenting opinion) in *Ramsden v Dyson* (1866) LR 1 HL 129. These criteria were necessary, according to Fry J, in order to establish that it would be tantamount to fraud for individuals to assert their strict legal rights. This fraudulent conduct comprised the legal owner remaining silent in the face of someone else's mistaken belief. In this case it was considered that the mistake must be unilateral; i.e. only that of the person who believes he has a right.

The strict criteria are fivefold:

(a) the claimant must have made a mistake as to his legal rights;

(b) the claimant must have spent money or done some act on the faith of his mistaken belief;

(c) the defendant, as holder of the legal right, must know of the existence of his own right which is inconsistent with the right claimed by the claimant;

(d) the defendant must know of the claimant's mistaken belief; and

(e) the defendant must have encouraged the claimant in his expenditure of money or the other acts performed, either directly or by abstaining from asserting his legal right.

Originally, these criteria were followed diligently and there have been some cases which have continued to follow this approach, such as *Matharu v Matharu* (1994) 68 P & CR 93, although these have been criticised. In general, the approach adopted in *Taylors Fashions Ltd v Liverpool Victoria Trustees Co Ltd* [1982] QB 133 is considered to be the preferred approach and this is borne out by the decision in *Gillett v Holt* [2000] 2 All ER 289 which cites with approval the earlier decisions in *Re Basham* [1986] 1 WLR 1498, *Jones v Watkins* [1987] CAT 1200 and *Wayling v Jones* [1993] EGCS 153. Further, the House of Lords' decision in *Yeoman's Row Management Ltd v Cobbe* [2008] UKHL 55 confirms that a claim to a proprietary interest by virtue of the application of the doctrine of proprietary estoppel requires 'clarity as to what it is that the object of the estoppel is to be estopped from denying, or asserting, and clarity as to the interest in the property in question that the denial, or assertion, would otherwise defeat' (Lord Scott at 28). If there is no mistake by the claimant as to their legal rights then no claim in proprietary estoppel can be made out.

In *Gillett v Holt*, a close relationship developed between a prosperous gentleman farmer, the defendant, and a schoolboy, the claimant, which lasted over 40 years and extended to include the family of the claimant once he grew up and married. The relationship which developed was both on a social and a business basis, the boy going to work for the farmer and also becoming a surrogate son to him. Over the years many unambiguous and public assurances were given that the claimant would become the owner of the estate. The claimant relied on these assurances investing all his life in the business of his employer and friend until the relationship eventually broke down when the defendant came to rely instead on someone else.

The Court of Appeal held that the claim had been made out. In reaching this decision they considered that the assurances that were made were tantamount to a promise even though they amounted to a promise to make a testamentary disposition in itself a revocable act. On this point they criticised the earlier case of *Taylor v Dickens* [1998] 1 FLR 806 (which has since been compromised on appeal), where it had been held that since the promise was revocable, the estoppel claim could not be made out. The criticism was made on the point that the very nature of every such promise is that it is revocable; it is the subsequent detrimental reliance which makes it irrevocable.

Thus, the first requirement under the modern broad approach to a successful claim is the establishment of an unambiguous promise by the defendant to the claimant that he would acquire some interest or benefit over his real property. This is described in the earlier cases as 'encouragement or acquiescence' (*Ramsden v Dyson* (1866) LR 1

HL 129) and was one of the elements that was missing in *Yeoman's Row Management Ltd v Cobbe* [2008] UKHL 55. The promise does not have to be the exclusive reason why the claimant acted to his detriment in reliance on it (*Amalgamated Property Co v Texas Commerce International Bank* [1982] QB 84).

The promise could take the form of a written assurance (*Dillwyn v Llewelyn* (1862) 4 De GF & J 517) or an oral one (*Pascoe v Turner* [1979] 1 WLR 431; *Gillett v Holt*; *Jennings v Rice and Others* [2003] 1 P & CR 100). It could include a request to act in a particular manner (*Plimmer v Mayor of Wellington* (1884) 9 App Cas 699), or passive encouragement (*Ward v Kirkland* [1967] Ch 194) where the defendant knows that the claimant mistakenly believes he will obtain an interest. However, if the promise is not clearly made then it will be insufficient to support the claim. So, where, in *James v Evans* (2000) EGCS 95; (2000) 42 EG 173, negotiations for the grant of a ten-year tenancy had been undertaken 'subject to contract' there was no basis for an estoppel claim. A similar result was reached in *Attorney-General of Hong Kong v Humphreys Estate (Queen's Gardens) Ltd* [1987] AC 114. In *Yeoman's Row Management Ltd v Cobbe*, the claimant, a commercial property developer, entered into an oral agreement with the defendant that he would purchase a block of flats for £12 m, would develop it, and then split the profits with the defendant. Relying on this agreement, the claimant then spent 18 months drawing up plans, engaging architects and other professional consultants and applying for planning permission. When planning permission was eventually granted, the defendant refused to honour the oral agreement. The House of Lords made it clear that, as a commercial person, the claimant knew that there was no legally enforceable contract and therefore knew that he 'was free to discontinue the negotiations without legal liability that is liability in equity as well as at law' (Lord Walker at 91).

Shortly after *Cobbe,* the House of Lords heard another estoppel case, *Thorner v Major* [2009] UKHL 18, the facts of which were similar to those of *Gillett v Holt*. In the case, Peter, a taciturn farmer, by conduct and laconic statements over many years, led a younger relative, David, to believe that he would inherit the farm on his death; in reliance on this, David worked for 15 years on the farm without pay. The House of Lords held that the minimum equity to satisfy the estoppel was to declare David entitled to the farm. Lord Neuberger's speech clearly distinguished *Cobbe*, most importantly on the ground that the parties were not business people and had never even contemplated entering into a contract for the disposition of the farm on Peter's death. Peter simply made an assurance over a period of years and David had acted on it to his detriment over a long period.

The second essential ingredient of the doctrine is that the claimant must show that he relied to his detriment on the promise. There must be a link between this promise and the detrimental reliance (*Wayling v Jones* [1993] EGCS 153; *Eves v Eves* [1975] 1 WLR 1338). This link can be demonstrated by the bare link between the owner encouraging the claimant to incur expenditure on his land as in *Inwards v Baker* [1965] 2 QB 29 where a father allowed his son to build a bungalow on his land.

But the requirement for detrimental reliance is not narrow. It must simply consist of something substantial. In *Mollo v Mollo* [1999] EGCS 117, it consisted of both the time (valued at £11,900) and the money (£31,900) that the claimant had spent renovating property held in his wife's name. Similarly, in *Yaxley v Gotts* [2000] All ER 711, the claimant undertook the refurbishment and conversion of a property into three flats in reliance on a promise that he would have the ground floor flat.

The detriment relied on must, however, be more than minimal expenses and must be something substantial and long-lasting (*Dr Kong Bok Gan v Wood & Choudhury* (1998) EGCS 77, CA). The reliance can be inferred from the conduct of the claimant as where a former servant looked after a family without pay relying on the promise that she could stay in the house for life (*Greasley v Cooke* [1980] 3 All ER 710; [1980] 1 WLR 1306). In *Jennings v Rice*, it consisted of years of unpaid work comprising gardening, shopping, maintenance, and nursing care. There must be sufficient conduct on the part of the claimant for the inducement to detrimental reliance to be inferred. Once this hurdle has been cleared then the burden of disproving it shifts to the defendant.

Ultimately, the test as to whether the detriment is sufficiently substantial to be relied on is determined on the basis of whether it would be unjust or inequitable to allow the owner to renege on the assurance given in the particular circumstances of the case—the test of unconscionability.

In *Gillett v Holt* the claimant relied on: his continued employment with the defendant and refusal of offers elsewhere; his contributions beyond that of an ordinary employee; his failure to take any other steps to secure his future wealth, such as through a pension; and, his expenditure and labour on the defendant's farmhouse which he occupied. It was argued that the claimant was simply acting as an employee and that, had he moved on, he might have done no better than staying under the protection of his employer and benefactor. However, the court considered that it was sufficient that the family deprived themselves of the opportunity of trying to better themselves. This clearly draws the test for detrimental reliance very wide.

The fact that the claimant also derives benefit from the acts of reliance does not preclude there being a detriment; in assessing whether there is sufficient overall detriment, any advantages are weighed against the disadvantages: *Jennings v Rice,* approved in *Henry v Henry* [2010] UKPC 3, 51.

The third requirement of the doctrine is that of unconscionability. This is a broad requirement which underpins the other elements and generally informs the doctrine of proprietary estoppel. It must be shown that it would be unconscionable for the owner of the land to deny the claimant the benefit he has promised him and on which he has relied to his detriment. This element might be traced back to the earliest exposition of the doctrine in *Ramsden v Dyson* (1866) LR 1 HL 129 where Lord Kingsdown opined that the doctrine of estoppel could arise where there was a fostering of an expectation in the minds of the parties which, once acted upon, it would be unconscionable to deny later.

In *Gillett v Holt*, this element was considered to have been made out by the very fact that the claimant had devoted himself for more than 40 years both at an employment level and a social one, to the betterment of the defendant's life. There must be a broad enquiry as to the circumstances which it is alleged give rise to the unconscionability although this does not permit the judge to exercise a 'completely unfettered discretion' according to his notion 'of what is fair in any particular case' (*Jennings v Rice* [2003] 1 P & CR 8, *per* Robert Walker LJ). Nor does it permit a claimant to rely on a promise that he clearly knows (perhaps because of his commercial expertise) not to be legally binding (*Yeoman's Row Management Ltd v Cobbe*). Thus, the particular circumstances of each case will be the pertinent factors to decide whether the tests for unconscionability have been made out and whether there has been an assurance given and sufficient detrimental reliance resulting from it for that promise to become irrevocable. The fact that the property has since passed into the hands of a purchaser might be a factor affecting unconscionability: *Henry v Henry* [2010] UKPC 3.

Question 2

Cyril was the registered proprietor of Acacia Lodge. Five years ago, he told his Aunt Agatha that she could live there rent-free for as long as she wanted provided she did any necessary repairs. Agatha gave up her council flat and moved in. Agatha was very nervous about intruders so she spent £2,000 on security locks and a burglar alarm. Cyril only found out about this when he visited her one day and accidentally set off the alarm.

Last year, Cyril sold Acacia Lodge to Derek at half the market value for a vacant property of that type. Cyril told Derek about the arrangement with Aunt Agatha and Derek assured him that he was looking at the property as a long-term investment.

Earlier this year, Aunt Agatha decided to replace the windows as the house was very cold. She had double-glazed units installed at a cost of £5,000 which absorbed practically all of her life-savings. When Derek came to visit Acacia Lodge, he told her he was absolutely delighted about the windows. He said: 'As long as you carry on paying for all the outgoings and repairs you can do what you want with the place as we agreed'.

Derek was killed in a road accident last week. The devisee of Acacia Lodge now wishes to sell it with vacant possession. Advise Aunt Agatha.

Commentary

It can be difficult to decide whether the circumstances presented give rise to a constructive trust, to a contractual licence or to the doctrine of proprietary estoppel. If in doubt, go in with all guns firing. Separate out the arguments for each type of equitable remedy or you might shoot yourself in the foot. There are overlaps, but it is easier to handle the issues if you keep the points separate. This is a question that requires the inclusion of a lot of case law to illustrate the points.

Answer plan

- Contractual licence:
  - *Binions v Evans*, per Lord Denning MR;
  - not an interest in land;
- Constructive trust:
  - If agreement gave rise to a trust of land, Derek took subject to Agatha's rights through her actual occupation;
  - As Derek took expressly subject to Agatha's right to occupy and paid a reduced price;
  - By virtue of Agatha's expenditure on property?
    - common-intention constructive trust?
    - (or mere restitutionary claim for reimbursement of expenditure?)
- Proprietary estoppel:
  - unconscionability;
  - proportionality between acts of reliance and remedy.

Suggested answer

There are several potential causes of action based upon a contractual licence, a constructive trust and the doctrine of proprietary estoppel.

Contractual licence

Agatha was told by Cyril that she could live in the property rent-free provided she undertook repairs. Such an agreement is capable of forming the subject-matter of a licence. However, the property was subsequently transferred to Derek so the issue is whether this licence is enforceable against Derek's devisee as a successor in title who was not a party to the licence agreement. The facts suggest that when Acacia Lodge was sold to Derek, it might have been sold subject to her rights, as reflected by the low price. In ***Binions v Evans* [1972] Ch 359**, it was agreed between the trustees of the Tredegar Estate that Mrs Evans should occupy a cottage on the estate for the rest of her life. The trustees sold the cottage to purchasers who bought at less than the market price because they took expressly subject to Mrs Evans' rights of occupation. All three judges agreed that the purchaser could not evict Mrs Evans, but the legal reasoning of Lord Denning MR was different from that of the majority. He considered that the agreement between Mrs Evans and the trustees gave her a right to reside in the cottage for the rest of her life, and that this conferred on her an equitable interest that was binding on the purchasers as they took with notice. In Lord Denning's judgment, therefore, the contractual licence was an interest in land. Lord Denning MR's view is inconsistent with the earlier House of Lords' authority of *King v David Allen & Sons (Billposting) Ltd* [1916] 2 AC 54, and the *dicta* in *Ashburn Anstalt v Arnold* [1989] Ch 1, that a licence cannot be an interest in land, although it is in line with *Errington v Errington* [1952]

1 KB 290. The view that contractual licences do not bind land has been confirmed in further cases such as *Camden LBC v Shortlife Community Housing* (1992) 90 LGR 358, *Canadian Imperial Bank of Commerce v Bello* (1992) 64 P & CR 48, *Nationwide Building Society v Ahmed* (1995) 70 P & CR 381, and *Lloyd v Dugdale* [2002] 2 P & CR 167. In the light of these authorities, it cannot now be contended that the contractual licence is itself an interest in land; thus Agatha's contractual licence cannot *per se* bind the purchasers. However, it will now be considered whether her licence might become binding by reason of a constructive trust.

Constructive trust

In *Bannister v Bannister* [1948] 2 All ER 133, the defendant agreed to sell two cottages to the plaintiff on the basis that she was to be able to live in one of them rent-free for the rest of her life. The sale, which was at a considerably lower price than market value, was completed, and then the plaintiff tried to turn her out. The Court of Appeal held that, as the defendant had obtained the title to the cottages only because he had agreed that the defendant should be able to live there rent-free, it would be fraud on him to rely on the absolute nature of the conveyance. As the agreement intended to confer a beneficial interest on her, it held that the defendant held the cottage in which she was living on a constructive trust for her for her life, determinable on her ceasing to live there. The effect was that she became a tenant for life under the Settled Land Act 1925.

In *Binions v Evans*, the majority of the Court of Appeal applied *Bannister v Bannister*, and held that the agreement between Mrs Evans and the Tredegar Estate gave her a beneficial interest, which meant that she became a tenant for life under the Settled Land Act 1925. If the agreement between Agatha and Cyril is construed in a similar way, it would give her a beneficial interest under a trust for land under the TLATA 1996. This beneficial interest would bind Derek because, although not protected by a restriction in the charges register, Agatha was in actual occupation when Acacia Lodge was transferred to Derek: LRA 2002, Schedule 3, para. 2. Derek's estate would continue to be bound by this interest after Derek's death, as it could be in no better position than Derek.

Lord Denning MR in *Binions v Evans* took a different view from the majority. As an alternative to his holding that the contractual licence created an equitable interest (a view which now seems untenable) he argued that, as the purchaser took the cottage expressly subject to Mrs Binions' licence to occupy, and at a reduced price, it would be fraud on the purchasers to attempt to turn her out. He quoted with approval the statement of Cardozo J in *Beatty v Guggenheim Exploration Co* (1919) 225 NY 380, 386: '[a] constructive trust is the formula by which the conscience of equity finds expression'. Lord Denning would have held that in the circumstances the purchasers would have taken the conveyance subject to a constructive trust under which Mrs Evans had a right to remain in the cottage for the rest of her life. Lord Denning's constructive trust analysis was later applied in *Lyus v Prowsa Developments Ltd* [1982] 2 All ER 953. As Derek paid half price for Acacia Lodge, it might be inferred that this was because he had agreed to take it subject to Agatha's occupation rent-free for life. He might therefore have taken the transfer of Acacia Lodge subject to a constructive trust under which Agatha would be a beneficiary under a trust of land with a right to reside there for life, and such trust would continue to bind his estate after his death.

There is another way in which Agatha might possibly be able to argue that she has an interest under a constructive trust, and so can resist eviction: this is if she can establish that she has acquired a beneficial interest in Acacia Lodge through having spent £2,000 on the security lock and burglar alarm, and £5,000 on double-glazing. In order to establish this, Agatha would have to show, that there was an agreement, either express or inferred, with either Cyril or Derek (or both), that she was to have a beneficial interest in the property, and that she acted to her detriment by spending her life-savings in reliance on such agreement. As there appears to be no express agreement, she would have to argue that the court could infer an agreement merely from her expenditure on the cottage. The court cannot impute an agreement that the parties never made merely because it thinks it fair, and the onus is on Agatha to establish a common intention that can lead to the imposition of a common-intention constructive trust: *Stack v Dowden* [2007] UKHL 17. As there is a strong presumption that the beneficial ownership follows the legal title, it may be difficult, on the facts of the problem, for Agatha to establish a common intention that secures for her a post-acquisition beneficial interest. If the works have increased the value of the property, the most that Agatha might therefore hope for is that Derek's estate would be unjustly enriched were it to take the benefit of her expenditure, and that she might therefore be awarded compensation on a restitutionary basis for her expenditure on Acacia Lodge.

Proprietary estoppel

To rely on the doctrine of proprietary estoppel, Aunt Agatha must show that it would be unconscionable for her to be evicted from the property when she has been encouraged or allowed to assume to her detriment that she will be permitted to remain there for as long as she wished (*Taylors Fashions Ltd v Liverpool Victoria Trustees Co Ltd* [1982] QB 133). Her mistaken belief appears to fall into the category of domestic cases envisaged in *Yeoman's Row Management Ltd v Cobbe* [2008] UKHL 55. She could rely on the promise made by Cyril and the assurance given her by Derek. Her actions in giving up her council flat and spending money on Acacia Lodge could amount to the detrimental conduct in reliance on the representations, which is necessary for her to establish to succeed under this head (*Crabb v Arun District Council* [1976] Ch 179).

It is not necessary to show a written agreement as the requirements contained in s. 2 of the Law of Property (Miscellaneous Provisions) Act 1989 need not be satisfied when the elements of proprietary estoppel are made out (*Yaxley v Gotts* [2000] All ER 711). Aunt Agatha is an example of 'the typical domestic claimant' personified by Lord Walker, at 68 in *Yeoman's Row Management Ltd v Cobbe*, who does not know that some further legal formality is necessary to complete title.

The court will take account of the proportionality between the remedy and the detriment it is designed to avoid. In *Sledmore v Dalby* (1996) 72 P & CR 196, the plaintiff, an elderly woman in need of a home, sought possession of a house which her son-in-law had occupied for 30 years undertaking improvements in the belief that it would be left to his wife. The son-in-law had other accommodation, however, and was not in such need of the house as the plaintiff. The Court of Appeal held that it was inequitable to allow any expectation raised earlier to be defeated in the circumstances of the case. In *Bawden v Bawden* (CA) [1997] EWCA Civ 2664 (7 November 1997) it was accepted that the court needed to adopt a flexible approach, that is, the minimum required to do justice in the case. It would therefore be appropriate to consider the balance in Aunt Agatha's case between her interest and that of the devisee of Derek's estate.

Once Aunt Agatha has established the doctrine, an equity arises and the court would seek a way to satisfy her claim on the basis of proportionality and justice. In *Dodsworth v Dodsworth* (1973) 228 EG 1115, the defendants spent £700 on improvements to a bungalow in the expectation that they would be able to remain there for as long as they wished. The Court of Appeal held that the defendants would be allowed to remain in occupation until their expenditure was reimbursed. A more extreme example can be found in *Pascoe v Turner* [1979] 1 WLR 431, where the Court of Appeal ordered that the fee simple should be conveyed to the defendant who had spent £1,000 on the property in reliance on the promise that the property was hers. However, it is also possible for the court to award compensation (*Gillett v Holt* [2000] 2 All ER 289; *Wayling v Jones* [1993] EGCS 153; *Campbell v Griffin* [2001] EWCA Civ 990; *Jennings v Rice* [2003] 1 P & CR 100).

Prior to the implementation of the Land Registration Act 2002 there remained an unsettled question as to whether the inchoate equity created an equitable proprietary right which could constitute an overriding interest, or, whether that would only arise once the right had been crystallized by the court (*Birmingham Midshires Mortgage Services Ltd v Sabherwal* Court of Appeal (2000) 80 P & CR 256). Section 116 of the Land Registration Act 2002 resolves this point as it confirms the proprietary status of an equity arising by estoppel in relation to registered land. It can therefore be protected by entry of notice on the register or (if the claimant is in actual occupation) it will be protected without the need for registration provided it falls under Schedule 3, para. 2, Land Registration Act 2002.

Thus, Aunt Agatha may seek to rely on the doctrine of proprietary estoppel and any interest so protected would bind Derek's devisee. As the devisee intends to sell Acacia Lodge, however, Agatha should be warned that, although her estoppel interest will bind any purchaser (LRA 2002, s. 116) provided she remains in actual occupation (ibid. Sch. 3, para. 2), the test for unconscionability might need to be considered afresh if the property has since passed into the hands of a third-party purchaser. In *Henry v Henry* [2010] UKPC 3, the Privy Council did not rule this out, but they did not comment further as the point had not been pleaded: paras 46–68, 56.

Finally, the argument that to evict her from her home would be in breach of the Human Rights Act 1998 appears not to be available (*Albany Home Loans v Massey* [1997] 2 All ER 609; [1997] 2 FLR 305; *Birmingham Mortgage Services Ltd v Sabherwal*; and, *Harrow London Borough Council v Qazi* [2003] 3 WLR 792.)

Question 3

'The Court of Appeal [in *Ashburn Anstalt v Arnold* [1989] Ch 1] put what I hope is the quietus to the heresy that a mere licence creates an interest in land. They also put the quietus to the heresy that parties to a contractual licence necessarily become constructive trustees' (*per* Sir Nicholas Browne-Wilkinson in *IDC Group Ltd v Clark* [1992] 1 EGLR 187, at 189).

Discuss.

Commentary

This is one of those academic arguments which have huge practical conveyancing implications. You need to be completely familiar with all those property concepts that you studied early in your course such as personal rights and proprietary rights, rights *in personam* and rights *in rem* and so on. The cases are difficult, not least because the judgments may contain different arguments with which you need to be familiar. There are also differences between the cases which may mean that they are distinguishable and there may be room for reading into some of the judgments a more profound interpretation than they are sometimes accorded. The Court of Appeal judgment in ***Ashburn Anstalt v Arnold*** is sometimes said, for instance, to have brought an end to Lord Denning's development of the contractual licence. Read Fox LJ's judgment for yourself and form your own view.

For additional reading see 'Licences and Third Parties', Wade (1952) 68 *LQR* 337; Sheridan (1953) 17 *Conv* 440; Crane (1967) 31 *Conv NS* 332; Thompson [1983] *Conv* 50; Moriarty (1984) 100 *LQR* 376; Dewar (1986) 49 *MLR* 741, to name but a few articles from the many written on this subject. This is an erudite topic which has spawned many commentaries.

For a view on the impact of the **Contracts (Rights of Third Parties) Act 1999** on this area see: S. Bright [2000] 64 *Conv* 398.

Answer plan

- Rights *in personam* and description of different types of licences.
- Intervention of equity.
- Development of contractual licence.
- Position of third parties.
- Discussion of ***Errington v Errington*** and ***Binions v Evans***.

Suggested answer

The original concept of a licence was that it created a right *in personam* which bound the immediate parties. A gratuitous or bare licence is one that gives a mere permission to use land in a certain way. Such permission may be withdrawn at any time by the licensor. A contractual licence is one that is supported by consideration. Again, it was originally thought only to bind the parties to the contract under the doctrine of privity of contract. If it were withdrawn, then an action for damages might lie. It may be possible that an injunction would be available where, on the proper construction of the contract, the licence was irrevocable (*Winter Garden Theatre (London) Ltd v Millenium Productions Ltd* [1948] AC 173). Thus, as between the parties to the contract, equity might intervene in order to preserve the bargain.

However, such equitable intervention in itself does not necessarily extend to the creation of an interest in land. Such a development would lead to the result that a contractual licence would bind a third party. Earlier cases are clear on the point that a contractual licence is not capable of being a proprietary right and cannot, therefore, bind third parties. The earliest statement of this view was expressed by Vaughan CJ in *Thomas v Sorrell* (1674) Vaugh 330: 'A dispensation or licence properly passeth no interest nor alters or transfers property in anything, but only makes an action lawful, which without it had been unlawful.' Further cases such as *Edwards v Barrington* (1901) 85 LT 650 and *Frank Warr & Co Ltd v London County Council* [1904] 1 KB 713 confirmed this view and were followed by the decision of the House of Lords in *King v David Allen & Sons (Billposting) Ltd* [1916] 2 AC 54, which concluded that a licence to affix advertisements to the side of a cinema wall did not bind the successors in title to the original contracting party. This view was followed by the Court of Appeal in *Clore v Theatrical Properties Ltd* [1936] 3 All ER 483. The subsequent development of judicial authority on this point has, unfortunately, not followed the clarity of this line of reasoning and there are two cases which can be cited as standing for the proposition that a contractual licence can bind a third party.

The first of these is *Errington v Errington* [1952] 1 KB 290. In this case the Court of Appeal held that a son and daughter-in-law were licensees of a house subject to the condition that they paid the mortgage instalments. Since the breach of this contractual licence could have been restrained by the intervention of equity, this had the effect of creating an interest in equity which was vested in the licensees. This equitable interest bound third parties, in this case, the licensor's widow who had inherited the house. This principle was also followed in *E. R. Ives Investment Ltd v High* [1967] 2 QB 379, where a licence was created which was binding on a purchaser for value and this decision has been referred to with approval in *Thatcher v Douglas* (1996) 146 *NLJ* 282.

Secondly, the case of *Binions v Evans* [1972] Ch 359, further strengthened this development of the contractual licence. In this case, a contractual licence was enforced against a purchaser who took a conveyance of land expressly subject to it. Mrs Evans had entered into a written agreement with the Tredegar Estate trustees whereby she was permitted to remain in a cottage on the estate for the rest of her life free of rent and rates. The conveyance to purchasers was expressed to be subject to this condition and this was reflected in the price. The purchasers then sought to gain possession of the cottage on the ground that they were not bound by her interest. The Court of

Appeal were unanimous in deciding that Mrs Evans was protected as a constructive trust arose. Two of the judges considered that the agreement entered into created a settlement under the Settled Land Act 1925 and Mrs Evans was the tenant for life. Lord Denning MR, however, argued that since the purchasers took expressly subject to her rights, her contractual licence was protected. A licence bound a third party where a constructive trust arose and such a trust would arise where a person took land expressly subject to it. He distinguished the earlier decisions in *King v David Allen & Sons (Billposting) Ltd* and *Clore v Theatrical Properties Ltd* on the ground that actual occupation would be required before a contractual licence could bind a third party. This viewpoint was accepted in *DHN Food Distributors Ltd v Tower Hamlets London Borough Council* [1976] 1 WLR 852 where an irrevocable contractual licence was said to give rise to a constructive trust which gave the licensees a sufficient interest in land to qualify for compensation for disturbance. In addition, in *Re Sharpe* [1980] 1 WLR 219 an irrevocable licence to occupy a house until a loan was repaid was held to bind the trustee in bankruptcy.

Although there is no House of Lords decision which is a direct authority in this area, views have been expressed in various cases. In *National Provincial Bank Ltd v Ainsworth* [1965] AC 1175 the view that a contractual licence could be converted into a proprietary interest was treated with reluctance. In *National Provincial Bank Ltd v Hastings Car Mart Ltd* [1964] Ch 665 the Court of Appeal took the traditional view that a contractual licence creates no more than a personal right and, as such, cannot bind a purchaser regardless of notice. In *Ashburn Anstalt v Arnold*, Fox LJ, *obiter*, could not accept that, where land was sold expressly subject to a licence a constructive trust should, as a general proposition, be imposed. The fact that a purchaser may have notice of a contractual licence was not, he considered, enough to subject him to it. He considered that the decision in *Errington v Errington* was in conflict with earlier authority including the decisions of the House of Lords in *King v David Allen & Sons (Billposting) Ltd* and *Clore v Theatrical Properties Ltd*. However, Fox LJ does appear to leave open the possibility that there may be occasions where the conscience of the purchaser is affected and that in a situation where a purchaser takes title subject to another's rights and, in consequence, takes at a lower price (as in *Binions v Evans*), a constructive trust will be imposed. Fox LJ's remarks, although *obiter*, have been referred to as authoritative in *Habermann v Koehler* (1996) 72 P & CR D10 and the view that a contractual licence creates an interest in land has been rejected in *Camden LBC v Shortlife Community Housing* (1992) 90 LGR 358, *Canadian Imperial Bank of Commerce v Bello* (1992) 64 P & CR 48, *Nationwide Building Society v Ahmed* (1995) 70 P & CR 381, and *Lloyd v Dugdale* [2001] EWCA Civ 1754; [2002] 2 P & CR 167.

So, although it has been argued that the Court of Appeal in *Ashburn Anstalt* put the quietus to the heresy and 'finally repudiated the heretical view that a contractual licence creates an interest in land capable of binding third parties' (*per* Millett J at 373, *Camden LBC v Shortlife Community Housing Ltd*) there does remain some doubt. It would seem unlikely that it could be said with certainty that there are no circumstances where a contractual licence would create a proprietary interest and, thus, be capable of binding third parties. The strict view of the earlier cases has clearly been eroded. The effect of the decisions in ***Errington v Errington*** and ***Binions v Evans*** has not been clearly laid to rest by the *dicta* in the more recent cases such as ***Ashburn Anstalt v Arnold* [1989] Ch 1**. (Although ***Ashburn Anstalt*** was overruled by ***Prudential Assurance Co Ltd v London Residuary Body* [1992] 2 AC 386** on other grounds, the *dicta* were not discussed and may be considered as authoritative.)

Further developments relating to the impact of licences on third parties may well be anticipated once the first cases begin to appear as a result of the implementation of the **Contracts (Rights of Third Parties) Act 1999**. It may be possible to argue under this Act that a contractual licence binds a purchaser from a licensor where the contract between purchaser and licensor purports to confer a benefit on the licensee.

Further reading

Burn, E.H., and Cartwright, J., *Cheshire and Burn's Modern Law of Real Property*, 17th edn, Oxford, 2006, pp. 814–25.

Megarry & Wade, *The Law of Real Property*, 7th edn, Sweet & Maxwell, 2008, chapters 16 and 34.

Smith, R.J., *Property Law*, 5th edn, Longman, 2006, chapter 9.

11

Leases and licences

Introduction

The questions in this chapter have caused the writers a considerable headache! The reason for this is that it is difficult to know exactly what should be included under this heading and what may safely be left out.

You will doubtless have seen on the library shelves whole textbooks on the subject of landlord and tenant, and land law courses vary enormously as to the depth in which they deal with the subject. Most textbooks on landlord and tenant divide the subject into the general law of leases and the statutory law. Some land law courses may include some of the statutory law, although the majority will probably only touch lightly upon it, if at all.

Even the general law of leases is very wide however as it deals with the effect of a number of different covenants which are frequently found in leases. The advice on this topic must therefore be to *listen to your lecturer*! If your lecturer deals in depth with repairing covenants and practically ignores covenants against assignment, then you should do the same. You must be guided by the lectures and tutorials you are given as to which covenants you should pay attention to, and the depth in which the lecturer expects you to know some particular aspect of the subject. Be sure, too, that you look at the current year's lectures and tutorials—lecturers may get bored with a topic they have covered in some depth for a year or two and decide to have a change!

Having said that, Questions 1 and 3 are old favourites for examiners in some form or another. A perusal of Question 2 and its answer should give you a basic understanding of the nature of different types of leases; Question 6 and its answer give some idea of the complexity (and injustices) of the rules which governed the enforceability of covenants against the original parties to a lease and between successors in title to the original parties; different rules have replaced them for leases made on or after 1 January 1996 to which the Landlord and Tenant (Covenants) Act 1995 applies. The old rules will continue to apply to long leases made before 1996, but certain sections of the Act also apply to these leases to give some relief to a tenant. In Questions 4 and 5 we have dealt with the different forfeiture procedures. With regard to forfeiture of leases, the Law Commission have issued Consultation Paper No. 174 (2004) 'Termination of tenancies for tenant default' with a view (*inter alia*) to establishing uniformity in forfeiture procedure for breach of any covenant in a lease, instead of the present distinction between forfeiture for non-payment of rent and forfeiture for breach of any other covenant. The Government are still considering (at the time of writing) whether or not to take any further action. We have also selected some particular covenants in leases for consideration. Therefore it is in answering these two questions that you need to consider the extent to which your lecturer has dealt with these particular covenants.

Both Question 4 and Question 5 deal with the assignment or sublease of the term of a lease, and Question 5 deals with the assignment of the landlord's reversion. It is quite possible for a truly sadistic examiner, perhaps labouring under the stresses of academic life, to dream up an extremely complicated problem involving the devolution of title to the lease and the reversion and the consequent enforceability of covenants between different parties. Although such a question may sound totally confusing on a first reading, *keep calm*! It is usually possible to reduce such questions to a diagrammatic form which clarifies the situation immediately. You should therefore do a rough diagram before embarking upon your answer. Once you have achieved this, you may be surprised at how comparatively simple the whole question becomes.

The diagrammatic form (used in some textbooks also) is to indicate a lease or a sublease by a vertical line and an assignment by a horizontal one. Thus the following sequence of dispositions is represented by the diagram below it.

L leases to T. T assigns to T1. T1 assigns to T2. T2 sublets to S. S assigns to S1. L assigns the reversion to L1.

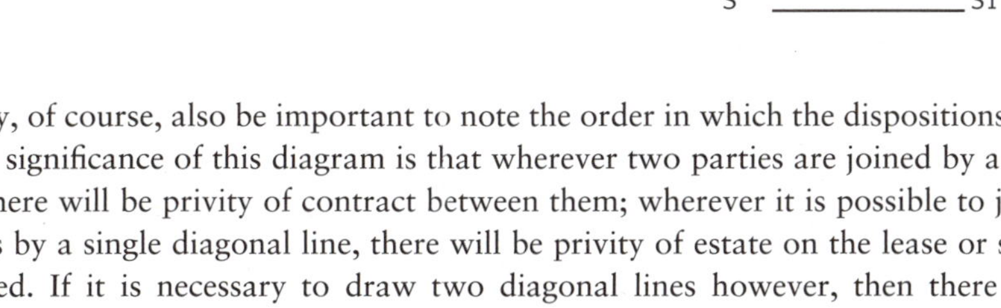

(It may, of course, also be important to note the order in which the dispositions occur.)

The significance of this diagram is that wherever two parties are joined by a vertical line, there will be privity of contract between them; wherever it is possible to join two parties by a single diagonal line, there will be privity of estate on the lease or sublease assigned. If it is necessary to draw two diagonal lines however, then there will be no privity of estate or of contract. In the diagram above, there is privity of contract between L and T on the head lease and between T2 and S. There is privity of estate on the headlease between L1 and T2, and on the sublease between T2 and S1. There is no privity of contract or estate between L1 and S or S1.

Once you have identified what privity, if any, exists between the parties, then you will be well on the way to determining what covenants are enforceable between them. The diagram should also help you to consider what possible indemnities may arise between the parties. You should remember, however, that these rules have changed for leases made on or after 1 January 1996, and there is now a very much more limited liability under the **Landlord and Tenant (Covenants) Act 1995**.

Question 5 is one where a diagram of this sort helps to clarify the situation and one has been included in the introduction to the question.

The general rule is that where there is neither privity of contract nor privity of estate (as with a headlessor and a subtenant) then there will be no rights of action on covenants (except that a headlessor may sue a subtenant on restrictive covenants in the lease which bind all occupiers of the land). It is possible that the **Contracts (Rights of Third Parties) Act 1999**, which came into force on 11 May 2000, may change this situation in an appropriately worded lease or sublease. There are, as yet, no cases on this so far as the writers are aware.

The **Land Registration Act 2002** made some significant changes to the registration of leases and to leases which are overriding interests. Leases exceeding seven years (formerly 21 years) are now registrable substantively with their own title number, and leases not exceeding seven years become overriding interests under **Schedule 3, para. 1**. Equitable leases and options, which might have been binding as the rights of a person in actual occupation under **s. 70(1)(g), Land Registration Act 1925** may still be binding, but may be excluded by the more restrictive wording of the new 'occupation' section, **Schedule 3, para. 2**.

Question 1

A year ago, George inherited a large Victorian house which he decided to convert into three flats from which he might derive an income. He therefore made the following arrangements:

(a) He completed the conversion of the ground floor flat. On 1 May he signed a 'licence' giving Annie the right to occupy the flat for a payment of £200 per month. On 2 May, he signed an identical 'licence' giving Bob the right to occupy the flat with Annie or any other person whom George should select for a payment of £225 per month.

(b) He completed the conversion of the small one-bedroomed attic flat and gave Joe and Linda a licence to occupy it at a fee of £400 per month. They both signed identical licence agreements which bore the same dates. The licence agreement also reserved the right to George to nominate another occupier or to occupy the flat himself. Linda recently vacated the flat, since when George has accepted only £200 fee per month from Joe.

(c) The conversion of the basement flat is not yet completed but his niece, Marie, who recently left her husband and had nowhere to live, moved in last month and is paying a rent of £20 per week. George has kept a key to the premises in order to supervise the workmen and has entered the premises a few times for this purpose.

George has now received a very attractive offer for the freehold of the house from Horace. Advise Horace as to whether he will be able to obtain vacant possession of the flats.

Commentary

This question is on an area of law which has been the source of much litigation. The reason for this was the extensive rent control and security of tenure given to tenants for many years by legislation. The courts recognised that this could affect a landlord unfairly as he could find that he had inadvertently created a tenancy, which became protected, by letting an occupier into his premises under circumstances of exigency or kindness on his part.

With the demise of strict security of tenure and rent control, it is possible that we shall see fewer of these types of cases. The fundamental distinction between a lease and a licence (that the former is an interest in land whilst the latter is not) will nevertheless remain important in determining whether rights granted to an occupier will bind a third party or not. Moreover, a licence will not give a business tenant a right to extend his occupation under the **Landlord and Tenant Act 1954, Part II**, whereas a lease will generally do so.

Answer plan

- Difference between a lease (an estate in land capable of binding third parties such as Horace) and a licence (a purely personal right to occupy land and not binding on third parties).
- Definition of a lease by Lord Templeman in ***Street v Mountford* [1985] AC 809**—the reality of the arrangement is the determining factor and courts must be wary of 'sham' agreements.
- Exclusive possession and sharing cases. If one occupier leaves, do the others or the landlord have the right to choose another occupier? Is the rent a joint liability of all the occupiers, or individual liabilities of each occupier?
- Distinguish the exclusive possession of a tenant from the exclusive occupation of a licensee.
- The landlord's retention of a key to perform services will indicate a licence and not a lease, but a key for other reasons may not do so.
- Certain agreements made in circumstances of friendship or family arrangement may mean that the agreement was not intended to create legal relations at all and is therefore not a lease; little or no rent may be indicative of this.

Suggested answer

(a) In *Street v Mountford* [1985] AC 809 Lord Templeman said that wherever exclusive possession of premises is granted for a term at a rent, then *prima facie* a lease will be created. He warned that judges must be wary of 'sham' agreements, where a lease is disguised as something else, such as a licence or a service occupancy. In *Street v Mountford* itself, the agreement purported to be a licence and the landlord expressly reserved the right to enter the room to inspect and maintain it and to read the meters. It was held however that the reality was that a lease had been created whereby the tenant had exclusive possession for a term at a rent. The landlord's express reservation of rights of entry for certain purposes merely emphasised the tenant's right to exclusive possession.

Exclusive possession means however that the tenant may exclude everyone else, including the landlord, from the premises. Where premises are shared therefore, it is necessary to consider the nature of the sharing arrangements to decide whether the occupiers all have equal rights and interest in the whole of the property, in which case they may be joint tenants, or whether they all have different individual rights to parts of the property, which would be incompatible with a joint tenancy. Again, it is the reality of the arrangement which should be considered if this differs from the arrangement which the agreement purports to create.

In *Antoniades v Villiers* [1988] 3 WLR 1205 the two occupiers of a small one-bedroom flat paid equal contributions to payments of rent. It was held that the landlord's purported right to occupy was merely a sham, so that together they had exclusive possession and were tenants. On the other hand, in *AG Securities v Vaughan* [1988] 3 WLR 1205 four occupiers who signed different licence agreements on different dates and for different terms and different individual payments were held to be licensees of a four-bedroom flat as the necessary four unities were not present to make them joint tenants. Although they each had an exclusive right to occupy the flat with the other three, they did not collectively have a total exclusive possession.

Although Annie and Bob between them occupy the whole of the flat, the different agreements on different dates and for different payments would suggest that, as in *AG Securities v Vaughan*, they are licensees rather than joint tenants. George's right to select another occupier would also suggest that they do not have the necessary exclusive possession for a tenancy, unless this is in reality a 'sham'.

(b) The fact that the agreement between George and Joe and Linda is called a licence is inconclusive (*Addiscombe Garden Estates v Crabbe* [1957] 3 WLR 980). Where possession of premises is given for a term at a rent, it will *prima facie* create a lease (*Street v Mountford*). Moreover, the intention of the parties is to be determined from the reality of the arrangement rather than any formal agreement. In his judgment in *Street v Mountford*, Lord Templeman warned the judges that they must be wary of 'sham' agreements.

One of the essentials of a valid lease is that the lessee must have exclusive possession. If there are joint tenants, then they may collectively have exclusive possession between them. If this is the situation, then if one joint tenant leaves the premises, the other joint tenants will be able to choose a successor if they so wish. If, however, there is a right reserved for the landlord to share the accommodation, or to put in another occupier, then this would tend to negate the notion of a joint tenancy. In *Antoniades v Villiers*, where a landlord reserved the right to occupy a small one-bedroom attic flat, it was held that this was unrealistic, and the arrangement therefore amounted to a tenancy and not a licence. The identical licence agreements to commence on the same date, and the fact that Joe and Linda pay equal contributions to the 'fee' of £400 per month, all suggest that they are joint tenants.

In *Mikeover v Brady* [1989] 3 All ER 618 however, identical licence agreements required two occupiers to take responsibility for their own payments of £86.66 per month. Although the fee was exactly the same for both of them, the Court of Appeal held that as it was not a joint liability, the necessary unity of interest for a joint tenancy did not exist. The fact that George has accepted only the original £200 which Joe was liable to pay suggests that Joe and Linda were separately liable for a share of the 'fee', and this could mean that they were indeed licensees and not joint tenants.

(c) The fact that George retains a key to the basement flat might suggest that Marie does not have exclusive possession, but only exclusive occupation. In *Luganda v Service Hotels Ltd* [1969] 2 Ch 209, where the landlord retained a key to enter a room and carry out certain minimal services such as cleaning, the occupier was held to have exclusive occupation, which enabled him to exclude everyone except the landlord, but he did not have exclusive possession as against the landlord, and did not therefore have a tenancy. In *Abbeyfield (Harpenden) Society Ltd v Woods* [1968] 1 WLR 374, although the occupier had exclusive possession of a room, the various services provided made the agreement as a whole a licence.

In *Family Housing Association v Jones* [1990] 1 All ER 385 however the retention of a key for purposes not related to shared occupation, but in order to discuss rehousing and inspect the state of repair of the premises, was not sufficient to negate exclusive possession. It may well be therefore that George's retention of a key for purposes not relating to his agreement with Marie does not detract from her exclusive possession so that she could have a lease.

Although Lord Templeman said in *Street v Mountford* that exclusive possession of premises for a term at a rent would *prima facie* create a lease, he did recognise that the circumstances of certain arrangements might mean that they were not intended to create legal relations at all. These could well be the types of agreement referred to earlier by Lord Denning MR in *Facchini v Bryson* [1952] 1 TLR 1386 which are affected by 'circumstances such as of family arrangement, and an act of friendship or generosity or such like'. If the rent which Marie pays is substantially below the market rent, and in fact is merely a nominal rent, then the arrangement may fall within this category. However, a small rent paid to a relative is not necessarily conclusive of a licence rather than a tenancy (see *Ward v Warnke* [1990] 22 HLR 496, where a son-in-law who paid a small rent to his parents-in-law was held to be a tenant of a holiday cottage which he occupied). In *Ashburn Anstalt v Arnold* [1989] Ch 1 the Court of Appeal confirmed that rent is not essential for a lease, so that presumably such an arrangement without any rent at all could still constitute a lease. In practice however, the higher the rent, the more difficult it will be to draw the inference that the agreement was in fact affected by any of Lord Denning MR's circumstances.

If the arrangements made by George have merely created licences then, because as the Court of Appeal confirmed in *Ashburn Anstalt* a licence is not an interest in land, the licensees will not have any rights binding upon Horace. As the premises are dwelling-houses however, the Protection from Eviction Act 1977, s. 5 requires that Horace should nevertheless give 28 days' notice to vacate the premises.

If the arrangements created leases, then these would be periodic tenancies and would be legal interests under the Law of Property Act 1925, s. 54(2). As such, they would be binding on Horace as purchaser.

The type of periodic tenancy is determined by the period by which the rent is expressed to be payable rather than the periods when it is actually paid, so that Annie and Bob would have a monthly tenancy terminable by one month's notice to terminate at the end of the month, and Marie would have a weekly tenancy, terminable by a week's notice. The Protection from Eviction Act 1977, s. 5, which applies to the occupation of dwelling-houses, requires however that Marie should be given 28 days' notice.

Question 2

Consider the validity and effect of the following dispositions:

(a) A grants to B a lease of a flat for one day.

(b) The grant of a lease to B for 20 years 'if he so long lives' at a rent of £1,000 per annum.

(c) A lease of Black House to B for 20 years or until A should marry.

(d) A grants B a lease for seven years with an option to renew on exactly the same terms as the present lease.

(e) An oral agreement to grant a lease of Red House to B for two years at a market rent of £5,000 per annum to take effect in possession.

(f) A grants B a yearly tenancy of White House not to be terminated by A unless B becomes unemployed.

Commentary

This is a straightforward question on leases if you know your general basic law on the subject well.

The different parts of the question require a knowledge of the operation of case law and statutory provisions on certain grants. It is the type of question to which you will either know the answer or not.

You would be unwise (unless desperate!) to attempt a question with six parts unless you are fairly sure of the answer to at least four parts of it. Unless your exam paper specifically states that all parts of the question merit equal marks, some parts may be worth more than others. Part **(c)** of this question, for instance, is a very short point on the wording of the **Law of Property Act 1925, s. 149(6)**, whereas part **(f)** involves a fundamental point of law on the nature of leases, reaffirmed by the House of Lords in 1992, upsetting the decision in ***Re Midland Railway Co's Agreement* [1971] Ch 725** which had stood since 1971. Part **(f)** gives a student the opportunity to show an understanding of the decision and its effect, and to pick up more marks than may be possible on part **(c)**. It would be a strange examiner who did not regard an explanation of this as deserving of more marks than the short point in part **(c)**!

Answer plan

- Certainty of term and rent.
- Effect of **s. 149(6), LPA 1925** on leases terminable on death or marriage.
- Options to renew and perpetually renewable leases under **LPA 1922**.
- Formalities for an agreement for a lease within **s. 54(2), LPA 1925**.
- Certainty of term applied to periodic tenancies.

Suggested answer

(a) One of the essential requirements of a lease is that it must be for a certain term. Although the technical name for a lease is 'a term of years' the Law of Property Act 1925, s. 205(1)(xxvii) specifically includes in the definition 'a term for less than a year'. It is therefore possible to have a lease for just one day. The same definition section also says 'whether or not at a rent', so that it could still be a lease if no rent were reserved, although this is a factor which might suggest that it is instead a licence.

As the lease is for less than three years, it may also be a legal lease provided that it fulfils the other requirements of the Law of Property Act 1925, s. 54(2), i.e. it is at the best rent obtainable (a market rent) and takes effect in possession.

(b) A lease determinable upon death is for an uncertain duration and is therefore *prima facie* void. The Law of Property Act 1925, s. 149(6), states that a lease 'determinable with life or lives' at a rent or for a fine shall become a term of 90 years terminable by one month's written notice on the death. Although the section states that consideration for the lease is necessary, in *Griffiths v Williams* (1977) 248 EG 947 it was applied to a gratuitous lease in order to satisfy an estoppel. Presumably consideration would be necessary however for it to apply to an expressly created lease. Lack of any consideration would have given B a life tenancy under a settlement before 1 January 1997, and presumably a life interest under a trust of land on or after that date (TLATA 1996).

The grant to B for 20 years determinable on his death is therefore converted to a term of 90 years, which may be determined by the grantor or B's personal representatives by one month's written notice on B's death.

Note that s. 149(6) was applied in *Skipton Building Society v Clayton* (1993) 66 P & CR 223 to an agreement which called itself a 'licence' but which the court found in reality to be a lease for life for a premium.

As the lease is for a period exceeding seven years, it will not operate at law until it is registered substantively with its own title number (s. 27(1) and s. 27(2)(b)(i), Land Registration Act 2002).

(c) This grant is also for an uncertain duration and is therefore *prima facie* void. Although the Law of Property Act 1925, s. 149(6) rescues leases terminable on the *tenant's* marriage and converts them into a term of 90 years, it does not apply apparently to leases terminable on the marriage of anyone else. It would not therefore apply here and the grant would be void.

(d) The grant of a lease containing an option to renew on exactly the same terms gives to B the right to require another lease with the same option to renew, and therefore contains the seeds of its own perpetual reproduction.

The Law of Property Act 1922, s. 145 converted such leases into terms of 2,000 years. The tenant alone has a right to terminate the lease by giving 10 days' notice to terminate on a date when the lease would have terminated but for its conversion into a 2,000-year term. The tenant must give notice of any assignment to the landlord, and such leases differ from other leases with regard to the privity of contract rule. Once the tenant has assigned the lease, he is no longer liable to the landlord on the covenants in the lease under privity of contract.

In construing a renewal option in a lease however, the courts will lean against interpreting it as giving a right to perpetual renewal. In *Marjorie Burnett Ltd v Barclay* (1980) 258 EG 642 the provision for review of rent on renewal was said to be inimical to the creation of a 2,000-year term and the lease was construed as giving only one further right to renew after the first renewal.

As in (b) above, the lease for 2,000 years exceeds seven years and so must be registered substantively in order to operate at law. If however this is construed as an option to renew the lease for one period only, then the lease for seven years will not be registrable substantively but will be an overriding interest under Schedule 3, para. 1.

(e) A lease for two years at a market rent which takes effect in possession will be a legal lease within the Law of Property Act 1925, s. 54(2), notwithstanding that it is 'parol'.

Before the Law of Property (Miscellaneous Provisions) Act 1989 there was an anomaly in that even though such a lease could be validly granted orally, an agreement for such a lease had to satisfy the Law of Property Act 1925, s. 40, and was only enforceable if evidenced in writing or supported by part performance. Section 2(5)(a) of the 1989 Act removes this anomaly by providing that an agreement for such a lease does not have to comply with s. 2(1) of the 1989 Act and is therefore valid even though oral.

(f) A periodic tenancy satisfies the requirement that a lease must be for a fixed and definite duration as it is regarded as being a lease for the period which is automatically renewed and runs on from one period to the next unless notice is given by either party. In *Breams Property Investment Co Ltd v Stroulger* [1948] 2 KB 1 a restriction prohibiting the landlord from giving notice to quit during the first three years was, however, accepted as valid.

In *Re Midland Railway Co's Agreement* [1971] Ch 725, a provision that the landlord would not give notice to quit unless it required the demised premises for the purposes of its undertaking was also accepted as valid. In *Prudential Assurance Co v London Residuary Body* [1992] 2 AC 386, however, the House of Lords affirmed the rule in *Lace v Chantler* [1944] KB 368 that the duration of a lease must be certain. They expressed the opinion that *Midland Railway* had been wrongly decided as the restriction on one party to give a notice to quit was governed by events which were uncertain, thus rendering the duration of the whole term uncertain. In *Prudential Assurance Co Ltd*, a local authority had granted a lease of land until it was 'required by the Council for the purposes of the widening of Walworth Road and the street paving rendered necessary thereby'. It was held that the grant was void as a lease as the term granted was of uncertain duration. The tenant therefore had a yearly tenancy, which arose by reason of his occupation and payment of rent on a yearly basis.

A's grant of the yearly tenancy would therefore be void for uncertainty of term, although B might acquire an implied yearly periodic tenancy if he occupies the White House and pays rent annually.

Question 3

(a) **'There is now no distinction . . . between a lease and an agreement for a lease' (Field J in *Re Maughan* (1885) 14 QBD 958). Discuss.**

(b) **Leslie is the registered proprietor of two cottages, Nos 1 and 2 Sycamore Terrace, which he inherited from his aunt.**

A year ago, he agreed in writing to let No. 1 to Abigail for five years at a rent of £2,500 per annum. Both he and Abigail signed the agreement. Abigail took possession and has paid rent monthly. However, Abigail has been away visiting relatives in Australia for the last three months.

Six months ago, Leslie alone signed an agreement to let No. 2 to Bodgem Ltd for two years at £20 per month, the term to begin one month thereafter. The low rent was because the agreement stated that Bertram, the managing director of Bodgem Ltd, was to occupy the cottage on behalf of the company and that the company would carry out certain modernisations. Leslie allowed Bertram to move into the cottage three months ago, in order to begin the work.

Leslie has now sold the freehold of both the cottages to Percy who wants to know whether the agreements are binding upon him.

Would your answer differ if the title to the two properties were unregistered?

Commentary

Part **(a)** of this question is a straightforward book question, the answer to which is to be found in most textbooks on land law. It does however illustrate the vital differences between a legal estate in land and an equitable one, and so is quite fundamental to an understanding of land law.

In the course of your answer, you would probably mention the case of ***Walsh v Lonsdale*** **(1882) 21 ChD 9**, which was one of the first cases to apply the **Judicature Act 1875, s. 25(11) (now the Senior Courts Act 1981, s. 49(1))**. This provides that in the event of a conflict between common law and equity, equity shall prevail. The result is that where there is a valid contract to create or transfer an interest in land of which equity will grant specific performance, the contract itself creates an equitable interest. The principle is not confined to leases, but is generally applicable in land law, and a reference in your answer to the broader principle would be appropriate as showing a general understanding of property law.

Part **(b)** of the question gives you an opportunity to apply this fundamental knowledge. Although the question asks about the binding effect of different arrangements on a purchaser, it is essential to decide first what interests, if any, the agreements or arrangements create before you are able to decide whether they will bind a purchaser or not. So your answer should address this question first.

It is not unusual for questions on land law papers to ask about the effect of a transaction in both registered and unregistered title, and you should be prepared for this if your course has considered the binding effect of equitable interests in unregistered land.

Answer plan

(a)
- Formality requirements for a legal lease and a contract for a lease.
- Doctrine of ***Walsh v Lonsdale*** **(1882) 21 ChD 9**—contract creates an interest protected by equity.
- Discretionary grounds on which equitable remedy of specific performance will be granted.
- Effect of an equitable lease as between the parties to it and their assignees.
- Binding effect of legal and equitable leases on a purchaser of the reversion in registered and unregistered title.

(b)
- Effect of Leslie's agreement with Abigail and Abigail's taking possession and paying rent.
- Does the agreement for a periodic tenancy bind a purchaser of the reversion (Percy) (i) in registered title (ii) in unregistered land?
- The effect of the agreement between Leslie and Bodgem Ltd.
- Whether this agreement will be binding on Percy as in (i), and (ii) above.

Suggested answer

(a) A deed must be used in order to create, or to convey, a legal estate or a legal interest in land (Law of Property Act 1925, s. 52(1), re-enacting an earlier provision in the Conveyancing Act 1881). The exception to this is a lease not exceeding three years which complies with the requirements of the Law of Property Act 1925, s. 54(2) (at the best rent obtainable without a fine and taking effect in possession), which may be legal notwithstanding that it is created by parol.

A *contract* for the 'sale or other disposition' of an interest in land will be enforceable however if it complies with certain formal requirements. The Law of Property (Miscellaneous Provisions) Act 1989, s. 2, requires such contracts, created after 26 September 1989, to be actually in writing and signed by both parties, or in two parts with one part signed by each party, and the two parts exchanged, as in a normal conveyancing transaction. The 1989 Act repeals the Law of Property Act 1925, s. 40 (the former statutory provision applicable to contracts), and it probably also abolishes the doctrine of part performance, although a purely oral estoppel has been recognised as making a contract enforceable where it is affected by this, or where the circumstances justify the imposition of a constructive trust—see *Yaxley v Gotts* [1999] 3 WLR 1217.

Where the actual lease, conveyance, or other document purporting to create or to convey a legal estate or interest is in writing but has not been executed as a deed, then provided it complies with s. 2 of the 1989 Act as to signatures, it will create a valid contract to create or convey the estate or interest. Under the doctrine of *Walsh v Lonsdale* (1882) 21 ChD 9 the grantee has an equitable estate or interest, that is, one which equity will recognise and give effect to by means of an order for specific performance.

A legal lease must therefore be created either by deed, or fall within the Law of Property Act 1925, s. 54(2) but equity may be prepared to grant specific performance of a valid contract for a lease requiring the lessor to execute a valid legal lease.

It should be remembered, however, that the equitable remedy of specific performance is discretionary and will be awarded only according to equitable principles. One of these is the well-known equitable maxim that the party seeking an equitable remedy 'must come to equity with clean hands'. Therefore if the tenant is at fault in any way, for example, in arrears with the rent or in breach of some other covenant in the agreement, then the remedy will not be available to him. Thus in *Coatsworth v Johnson* (1886) 54 LT 520 a tenant who was in breach of his covenants under an equitable lease was unable to obtain specific performance of it. Nor will the remedy be granted if the order would cause the lessor to be in breach of an agreement with a third party. In *Warmington v Miller* [1973] QB 11 the court refused to grant a decree of specific performance of an agreement for a sublease where the headlease contained a covenant against subletting, as an order to execute a sublease would necessarily have caused the tenant to be in breach of his covenant with the head lessor in the headlease.

As between the two contracting parties to an agreement for a lease, the agreement will in most respects be as good as a lease itself. The Law of Property Act 1925, s. 62, will not apply, however, to give to the tenant as easements the benefit of rights previously enjoyed by the demised premises. This is because s. 62 applies only to a 'conveyance', and it was held in *Borman v Griffith* [1930] 1 Ch 493 that a contract for a lease is not within the definition of a conveyance in the Law of Property Act 1925, s. 205, as 'an assurance of property or an interest therein'. It could not therefore operate to pass to an equitable lessee a right of way over a drive; although, on the facts of the case, it was held that he obtained the right under the rule in *Wheeldon v Burrows* (1879) 12 ChD 31, which will apply to a contract, such as an equitable lease. In *Wright v Macadam* [1949] 2 KB 744, s. 62 was held to apply however to a two-year written agreement for a lease within the Law of Property Act 1925, s. 54(2), as this was within the definition of a conveyance in s. 205, although a purely oral lease would not have been.

Furthermore, on the assignment of an equitable lease or the landlord's reversion, the equitable lease may not be as good as a legal lease as regards the passing of the benefit and burden of its covenants. If the equitable tenant assigns his equitable lease, he is merely assigning the benefit of a contract and not a legal estate. There cannot therefore be any relationship of privity of estate where there is an assignment of the equitable lease or of the reversion on it.

The general rule is that it is possible to assign the benefit of a contract, but not the burden. So in *Manchester Brewery v Coombs* [1901] 2 Ch 608, the purchasers of a brewery became the assignees of the reversion of an hotel. They were able to enforce a covenant by the *original* tenant to buy beer only from the brewery, as the benefit of the covenant passed to them. In *Purchase v Lichfield Brewery Co* [1915] 1 KB 184, however, the plaintiff landlords were unable to claim rent against the assignee by mortgage of an equitable tenant, as the burden of the covenants in the equitable lease did not pass to the mortgagee.

As regards equitable leases created on or after 1 January 1996, however, the Landlord and Tenant (Covenants) Act 1995, which applies also to equitable leases, changes this situation as it provides for the benefit and burden of all covenants (other than purely personal ones) to pass to assignees.

In unregistered title, legal leases are rights *in rem* which bind everyone. This position pertains in registered title also, where legal leases exceeding seven years are registrable substantively, and legal leases not exceeding seven years are overriding interests under the Land Registration Act 2002, Schedule 3, para. 1.

A further disadvantage of an equitable lease is the one common to all equitable interests—that it may not necessarily bind a purchaser of the legal freehold estate in the land.

In unregistered title, the equitable lease is an estate contract and is registrable as a Class C(iv) land charge under the Land Charges Act 1972. If it is so registered, it will be binding against a purchaser of the legal estate for money or money's worth; if it is not so registered, it will not be binding, even if the purchaser has *actual notice* of the equitable lease (*Midland Bank Trust Co v Green* [1981] AC 513).

In registered title, an equitable lease is neither registrable substantively, nor an overriding interest under the Land Registration Act 2002, Schedule 3, para. 1. The wording of this paragraph is the same as the wording of s. 70(1)(k), LRA 1925 and refers to the 'grant' of a lease not exceeding seven years, which was held to include legal leases, but not equitable ones arising from a contract (*City Permanent Building Society v Miller* [1952] Ch 840). An equitable lease is a minor interest and may be protected as such by notice on the register. It may, of course, also become an overriding interest under the Land Registration Act 2002, Schedule 3, para. 2, if the tenant is in actual occupation and satisfies the requirements of the paragraph, so that it is more likely to be binding than in unregistered title.

Nevertheless, it is possible under both systems for an equitable lease not to bind a purchaser of the legal estate.

(b) Leslie's agreement to let No. 1 to Abigail cannot be a legal lease as it was not made by deed, and so did not comply with the formality requirement to create a legal estate in the Law of Property Act 1925, s. 52. As the agreement is in writing and signed by both of them however, it will be a valid agreement complying with the Law of Property (Miscellaneous Provisions) Act 1989, s. 2(1). Assuming that equity will grant specific performance of the agreement, then Abigail has an equitable lease.

If such equitable lease is registered as a minor interest, then it will bind the purchaser, Percy. Even if not so registered, it would bind Percy if Abigail were in occupation for the purposes of the Land Registration 2002, Schedule 3, para. 2. It is not entirely clear what degree of occupation is necessary to claim an overriding interest under Schedule 3, para. 2. The underlying rationale for the section and its predecessor, s. 70(1)(g), Land Registration Act 1925, is that in most cases actual occupation of property will amount to notice to a purchaser of the occupier's interest. If Abigail's furniture and personal possessions are still in the cottage, therefore, this might well be sufficient occupation to give her an overriding interest under Schedule 3, para. 2, notwithstanding that she is not physically present when Percy buys. It is not clear whether Schedule 3, para. 2 of the 2002 Act will change the case law on what amounts to sufficient occupation, but there is an exclusion under para. 2(c)(i) for a person whose occupation would not have been obvious on a reasonably careful inspection of the land. It remains to be seen if this additional wording will have any significant impact on the case law.

In addition to her equitable lease, Abigail would also have a periodic tenancy by reason of occupying premises and paying rent. The type of periodic tenancy would be determined by reference to the period by which she pays rent (*Adler v Blackman* [1953] 1 QB 146). The rent is expressed as a figure per annum, and she would therefore have a yearly periodic tenancy. All periodic tenancies are legal under the Law of Property Act 1925, s. 54(2), and are overriding interests under the Land Registration Act 2002, Schedule 3, para. 1, being legal leases not exceeding seven years. The legal periodic tenancy would therefore be binding in any event on Percy, who would have to give six months' notice to terminate it at the end of the year.

If the title to the cottages were unregistered, the five-year equitable lease would be binding on Percy if it were registered as a Class C(iv) land charge under the Land Charges Act 1972, but not otherwise. The legal periodic tenancy would however be binding, as legal estates and interests are rights *in rem* and binding against everyone. It could, of course, be determined by six months' notice as before.

Percy will not be bound by the agreement to let No. 2 to Bodgem Ltd if the agreement is void for non-compliance with the formalities of the Law of Property (Miscellaneous Provisions) Act 1989, s. 2(1). It is clear that such formalities are not satisfied, since the agreement was not signed by both parties.

A contract for a lease for a term of three years or less without taking a fine and at the best rent reasonably obtainable is not, however, subject to the formalities of s. 2(1), and can be made informally: Law of Property (Miscellaneous Provisions) Act 1989, s. 2(5). The only doubt in the problem is in regard to the rent. Although the monetary sum to be paid by Bodgem Ltd is low, at common law 'rent' can include the performance of services. The undertaking of the work by Bodgem Ltd can therefore comprise part of the rent, and so bring the agreement within s. 2(5) as being an agreement for a lease within the Law of Property Act 1925, s. 54(2).

In that event, Bodgem Ltd has a valid estate contract with Leslie, which will bind Percy if protected by registration as a minor interest. Even if it is not so protected, it may bind Percy as the right of a person in actual occupation under the Land Registration Act 2002, Schedule 3, para. 2. Under the doctrine of separate corporate personality, Bodgem Ltd ranks as a person, albeit an artificial one. It can also be treated as being in actual occupation through Bertram, its managing director (*London & Cheshire Insurance Co Ltd v Laplagrene* [1971] Ch 499—a case on s. 70(1)(g), Land Registration Act 1925).

Notice, however, that in *Lloyd v Dugdale* (2001) 48 EGCS 129 occupation by a company did not protect an overriding interest of the managing director of the company personally.

Question 4

Frieland Ltd is the freehold owner of a shop and separate flat above it.

In 2006 Frieland Ltd granted a 14-year lease of the shop to Curlywig, a firm of hairdressers. The lease includes covenants not to assign, sublet or part with the possession of the whole or any part of the property without the consent in writing of the landlord, to pay the rent of £20,000 per annum, and not to use the premises for any purpose other than that of a hairdressing business.

Post 1996

In 2007 Frieland Ltd granted a yearly tenancy of the flat above the shop to Susie.

Two years ago Curlywig applied in writing to Frieland Ltd for consent to assign the lease of the shop to Kingpin, a hairdresser, but some four months later had received no reply, in spite of repeatedly reminding Frieland Ltd of their application. Kingpin refused to wait any longer, so Curlywig assigned the lease to him, and Kingpin has paid the rent ever since to Frieland's agents.

A year ago, Kingpin started to have financial problems and so allowed Minnie to use part of the shop premises in the evenings as a massage parlour in return for a money payment. Kingpin is now three months in arrears with the rent.

Susie has been disturbed by unpleasant clients of the massage parlour ringing her bell and leaving the shop premises as late as 2.00 am.

The staircase to Susie's flat is in a bad state of repair and the metal window frames are badly rusted through condensation.

Advise:

(a) Frieland Ltd

(b) Susie

as to what possible remedies they may have.

Commentary

This question requires you to consider the effect of certain covenants commonly found in leases. It requires a consideration of the different forfeiture procedures for non-payment of rent and for breach of any other covenant in a lease. You also require some knowledge of landlord's covenants which are implied into a lease, including the statutory obligations relating to dwelling-houses. Although most land law courses will include these, this is one of the more peripheral areas of the subject (mentioned in the introduction to this chapter) and it is possible that some courses may omit it. You will have to be guided on this by your lecture notes and tutorials.

Although there is an assignment, it is not an immensely complicated question with a series of dispositions, so that a diagram is probably unnecessary. A diagram, following the technique suggested in the introduction to this chapter, would appear as follows:

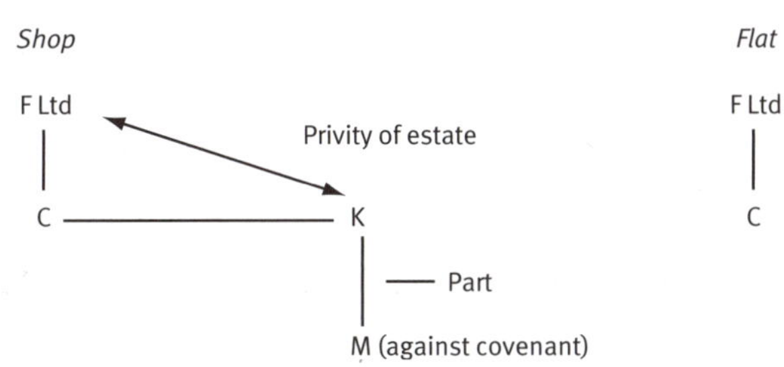

The question concerns a lease made after 31 December 1995 to which the **Landlord & Tenant (Covenants) Act 1995** will apply. Had the lease been made before then, the benefit and burden of the covenants would still have passed as covenants 'having reference to the subject matter of the lease' or 'touching and concerning the land' under **ss. 141 and 142, LPA 1925** and the rule in ***Spencer's Case***.

Answer plan

(a)
- Nature of covenant against assignment, etc.—qualified. Therefore **Landlord and Tenant Act 1927** applies and consent must not be unreasonably refused. **Landlord and Tenant Act 1988**—landlord must give reasons in writing for a refusal within a reasonable time.
- Effect of assignment in breach of covenant—privity of estate.
- Forfeiture proceedings for any covenant other than payment of rent—notice under **s. 146, LPA 1925**.
- Enforceability of restrictive covenants in leases.
- Forfeiture proceedings for non-payment of rent—**Common Law Procedure Act 1852**.
- Right of recovery of rent from original tenant Curlywig under the **Landlord and Tenant (Covenants) Act 1995** and procedure for this.

(b)
- Implied covenant by landlord to repair under **s. 11, Landlord and Tenant Act 1985** and implied obligations under ***Liverpool City Council v Irwin* [1977] AC 239**.
- Tenant's remedies for breach of a repairing covenant.
- Landlord's implied covenant for quiet enjoyment and its limitations.

Suggested answer

(a) A covenant not to assign or sublet without the consent of the landlord is a qualified form of such a covenant and is therefore subject to the Landlord and Tenant Act 1927, s. 19(1), which implies that such consent shall not be unreasonably withheld. The Landlord and Tenant Act 1988 provides that where a tenant applies in writing for such consent, the landlord must give his decision in writing to the tenant within a reasonable time, stating any reasons for refusing consent. The burden of proof to show that he has complied with the Landlord and Tenant Act 1988 is on the landlord, and Curlywig could have had a claim for damages for breach of the statutory duty imposed by the Act if Frieland Ltd have delayed unreasonably in replying. Recent cases indicate that what constitutes a reasonable time will vary according to the complexity of the circumstances that the landlord has to consider (*NCR Ltd v Riverland Portfolio No. 1 Ltd* [2004] 16 EG 110 (CS)) but that, in a fairly straightforward matter, it should be no more than a few weeks, so that four months would seem to be an unreasonable delay for which Frieland Ltd could have been liable in damages.

However, Curlywig have gone ahead and assigned the lease, so that they may not have suffered any actual loss giving rise to a claim for damages. As Frieland Ltd's agents have accepted rent from Kingpin, Frieland Ltd will be deemed to have waived any breach of covenant. The assignment, in any event, is effective to dispose of the lease, and the landlord must proceed against the assignee Kingpin, for any breach of covenant and not against Curlywig (*Old Grovebury Manor Farm v W. Seymour Plant Sales & Hire Ltd (No. 2)* [1979] 1 WLR 1397).

In allowing Minnie to use part of the premises, Kingpin may be in breach of the covenant not to part with the possession of the whole or any part of the premises without the landlord's consent. In *Akici v L.R. Butlin Ltd* [2005] EWCA Civ 1296, however, Neuberger LJ held that sharing possession of premises was a different breach of covenant from parting with the possession of part of premises. If this is correct and Kingpin is using the premises during the daytime, then it may be that Kingpin is not in breach of the covenant at all. If there is a breach, however, this is a landlord and tenant covenant, the burden of which would pass to Kingpin, and Frieland Ltd would therefore be able to sue Kingpin for forfeiture or damages or both.

If they decide to sue for forfeiture, they must first serve a notice under the Law of Property Act 1925, s. 146, informing Kingpin of the breach complained of, requiring it to be remedied and requiring compensation for it. The notice need not require the breach to be remedied if it is irremediable. In *Scala House & District Property Co Ltd v Forbes* [1974] QB 575, the Court of Appeal held that a breach of covenant against assignment was irremediable, although in *Akici* Neuberger LJ, whilst accepting that he was bound by *Scala House*, expressed doubts about this. The notice need not require compensation if the landlord does not want this (*Governors of Rugby School v Tannahill* [1935] 1 KB 87). An immoral user of the premises may well be irremediable (*Rugby School v Tannahill*). Kingpin may apply for relief against forfeiture under the Law of Property Act 1925, s. 146(2), although he would be unlikely to obtain it. Breach of a covenant against assignment without consent is an irremediable breach.

The covenant not to use the premises for any purpose other than that of a hairdresser's business is a restrictive covenant. It is therefore binding upon anyone who occupies the premises, including a squatter, other than a *bona fide* purchaser for value of the lease without notice of it. (*Re Nisbet and Potts' Contract* [1905] 1 Ch 391). Frieland Ltd may therefore seek an injunction against Minnie to restrain the breach of the covenant. Under the Senior Courts Act 1981, the court may award Frieland Ltd equitable damages against Minnie either in lieu of, or in addition to, an injunction.

Frieland Ltd may also forfeit the lease for non-payment of the rent, but the procedure here is entirely different from that for forfeiture for breach of any other covenant. It is not necessary to first serve a s. 146 notice, as it is for breach of any other covenant.

Forfeiture for non-payment of rent is governed by the Common Law Procedure Act 1852. Unless the lease provides otherwise (as most leases do) the landlord must first make a formal demand for rent. Such demand is however unnecessary if at least half a year's rent is in arrear, and there are insufficient goods on the premises available for distress to satisfy the amount due (Common Law Procedure Act 1852, s. 210 (High Court); County Courts Act 1984, s. 139 (county court)).

If Frieland Ltd brings its action in the High Court, and at least half a year's rent is in arrear, Kingpin has an automatic right to relief if, before the trial, he pays off all the arrears and costs. Failing this, if Frieland Ltd re-enters under an order of the court, Kingpin has six months after re-entry in which to pay off the arrears and costs and to apply for relief. The court has a discretion to grant relief, and it would not be granted if this will prejudice the position of a *bona fide* purchaser of the lease without notice of Kingpin's right to seek relief. After six months, any application for relief is barred (Common Law Procedure Act 1852, s. 210).

If Frieland Ltd brings its action in a county court, the procedure, though differing in detail, is broadly similar in effect. If Kingpin fails to pay off the arrears and costs within the period specified by the court, he may apply for discretionary relief for six months after Frieland Ltd's re-entry (County Courts Act 1984, s. 138(9A)). If Kingpin does not apply within this time, he is barred from all relief both in the county court and in the High Court (*Di Palma v Victoria Square Property Co Ltd* [1986] Ch 150).

If Frieland Ltd peaceably re-enters without a court order, the High Court has an inherent equitable jurisdiction to grant relief (*Howard v Fanshawe* [1895] 2 Ch 581). Although there is no statutory time limit, in practice the court will not be prepared to grant relief unless the application is made within six months (or a few days exceeding six months) of the re-entry (*Thatcher v C.H. Pearce & Sons (Contractors) Ltd* [1968] 1 WLR 748).

Under a lease made before 1996, Frieland Ltd would also have been able to sue the original tenant Curlywig for any arrears of rent and for damages for breach of the user covenant as the privity of covenant between them made an original tenant liable to a landlord on covenants in the lease throughout the term. The main purpose of the Landlord and Tenant (Covenants) Act 1995 was to limit an original tenant's liability once he had assigned the lease. Provided the assignment is a lawful assignment with the landlord's consent, then the original tenant will be released from his liability on covenants in the lease under privity of contract. However, the landlord may be able to require the assigning tenant to give an authorised guarantee agreement guaranteeing the performance of the covenants by his immediate assignee. (See the suggested answer to Question 6 for a more detailed consideration of the application of the 1995 Act.)

If however the assignment is unauthorised or occurs by operation of law (e.g. on the death of the tenant) then the assigning tenant's liability will continue until there is an authorised assignment. In the circumstances of this question, Frieland Ltd would appear to have been in breach of their obligation under the Landlord & Tenant Act 1988 to consent to a proposed assignment or to give reasons for their refusal to consent within a reasonable time, in spite of repeated requests from Curlywig. So the assignment may be treated as authorised and Frieland Ltd would no longer have any right of action against Curlywig.

Even if the lease had been made before 1996, Frieland Ltd could only have recovered the rent from Curlywig if they had first served a notice under s. 17, Landlord and

Tenant (Covenants) Act 1995 within six months of Kingpin's default. A tenant against whom a landlord proceeds to recover rent on the default of an assignee (whether the lease was made before or after the Act came into force) has a right under s. 19 to require the landlord to grant him an overriding lease, effectively making him the immediate (intervening) landlord of the defaulting assignee.

(b) Susie's lease, being a yearly tenancy, is within the Landlord and Tenant Act 1985, s. 11(1), which applies to residential leases of less than seven years. The section requires a landlord to maintain the structure and exterior of a dwelling-house, and installations for water, gas, electricity, sanitation, and space and water heating. The section was extended by the Housing Act 1988, s. 116, to include the common parts of a building of which the dwelling-house forms only part, and any installations used by all the tenants, such as a central heating boiler. The staircase would now be within this section and Frieland Ltd would be liable to repair this.

Frieland Ltd would also be liable under the principle of *Liverpool City Council v Irwin* [1977] AC 239. In this case, the House of Lords said that there is an implied obligation on a landlord to maintain essential access and services to premises without which the premises would be unusable.

In *Quick v Taff Ely BC* [1986] QB 809, however, condensation caused by metal window frames was held to be outside s. 11, as it was due to a design fault rather than to any lack of repair.

A tenant's remedies for breach of a repairing covenant are damages, which might include the cost of temporary accommodation elsewhere, storage of furniture if necessary while the repairs are carried out, and cleaning and redecoration afterwards (*McGreal v Wake* (1984) 1 EG 42). Susie may also carry out the repairs herself and set off the cost against future rents (*Lee-Parker v Izzet* [1971] 1 WLR 1688) although she should first give notice to Frieland Ltd that she intends to do this. She may also sue Frieland Ltd for specific performance of the covenant, which extends to common parts of the building (Landlord and Tenant Act 1985, s. 17). Under the Environmental Protection Act 1990, a tenant of premises which are in such a bad state of repair as to make them 'prejudicial to health' or a nuisance may apply to a magistrates' court for an order to repair the premises, but it has been said that only reasonable orders should be made (*Southwark LBC v Ince* (1989) 21 HLR 504, dealing with noise abatement), and in view of the decision in *Quick*, it is unlikely that Susie would obtain such an order with regard to the windows.

As regards the disturbance from the use of part of the shop premises as a massage parlour, Susie would have had an action for breach of the landlord's implied covenant for quiet enjoyment of the premises if the user were by the landlord himself or the breach of the covenant was due to the lawful user by another tenant of the landlord's. The covenant does not extend to the illegal user of another tenant however (*Sanderson v Berwick-upon-Tweed Corporation* (1884) 13 QBD 347) and such an action will probably not be available. She would of course have an action for nuisance in tort against Kingpin himself and Minnie.

Question 5

Leonora, the freehold owner of an old house in an area of London which has recently become more fashionable, leased the house to Tony for 40 years in 1985. The lease included a covenant to keep the house in good repair, to use it only as a private dwelling-house, and an option for Tony to purchase the freehold reversion.

In 1986 Leonora assigned the reversion to Rita. In 1987 Tony assigned the lease to Alice and in 1988 Alice assigned it to Albert. Last year, Albert sublet the house to Sam for three years.

A garden wall belonging to the property and a shed leaning against it have collapsed and require complete rebuilding. The other houses in the street have been renovated and improved over the last few years and Rita would like to replace the windows and the door so that the house is more in keeping with the neighbourhood.

Rita has recently discovered that Sam is running a mail order business from the house.

Advise Rita what causes of action she may have, and what rights of relief, if any, the parties may have.

Consider whether anyone may exercise the option to purchase the freehold reversion.

Commentary

This question requires first a consideration of the enforceability of covenants in leases against the successors in title to the original parties to the lease, and secondly a discussion of the scope and extent of repairing covenants. As mentioned in the Introduction to this chapter, a landlord's right to sue an original tenant or guarantor has been largely abrogated as regards post-1995 leases by the **Landlord and Tenant (Covenants) Act 1995**. Also, the Act applies to all 'landlord and tenant' covenants and not just to those 'touching and concerning the land' or 'having reference to the subject-matter of the lease' (the types of covenant enforceable wherever there was privity of estate between the parties on a pre-1996 lease).

The enforceability of covenants against successors in title is dealt with more fully in essay form in Question 6, but it arises in this question in problem form. It is therefore a question on which you might usefully apply the type of diagram given in the introduction to this chapter. It should then look something like this:

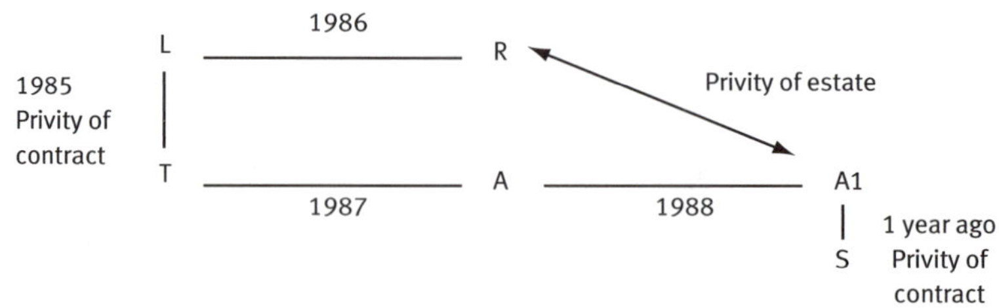

Answer plan

- Diagram to show dispositions of lease and reversion.
- Privity of estate and passing of benefit and burden of covenants in a pre-1996 lease.
- **Section 146** notice and counter-notice under **Leasehold Property (Repairs) Act 1938**.
- Limitations on damages for breach of a repairing covenant.
- Rita's remedy for breach of user covenant and possibility of Albert's getting relief from forfeiture for Sam's breach.
- Albert can sue Sam for breach of any user covenant in sublease as there is privity of contract between them.
- Rita can sue Sam directly for an injunction and damages for breach of the user covenant as it is a restrictive covenant.
- Standard of repair under a repairing covenant and scope of a repairing covenant—case law on this.
- Passing of benefit and burden of an option to purchase the reversion in unregistered and registered title.

Suggested answer

The passing of the benefit and burden of covenants in a lease made in 1985 is governed by the law before the Landlord and Tenants (Covenants) Act 1995 came into force. On assignment of the reversion, the benefit of covenants 'having reference to the subject-matter' of the lease passes to the assignee of the reversion (Law of Property Act 1925, s. 141), as does the burden (s. 142).

There is privity of estate between Rita, the landlord for the time being, and Albert, the tenant for the time being. The benefit and burden of covenants which 'touch and concern the land' pass to Albert (*Spencer's Case* (1583) 5 Co Rep 16a). Section 141 LPA 1925 provides that covenants which 'have reference to the subject matter of the lease' pass on an assignment of the reversion by the landlord. The statutory phrase 'having reference to the subject-matter of the lease' means much the same as the words used in *Spencer's Case*, so that where there is privity of estate between the parties, the benefit and burden of covenants which affect the user and enjoyment of the demised property and the relationship of landlord and tenant, will pass. This will include the repairing covenant and the user covenant, but not the option to purchase the reversion, which is a purely personal covenant. (In a post-1995 lease, the benefit of such an option would pass to the tenant's assignee—see Question 6.)

Rita may therefore sue Albert on the repairing covenant and on the user covenant. If there is a forfeiture clause (and it would be a very badly drawn lease which did not include a right of re-entry for breach of covenant!) then before forfeiting, she must first serve a notice on Albert under the Law of Property Act 1925, s. 146, informing him of the breach, requiring it to be remedied and requiring any compensation.

The lease, being for at least seven years with three years left to run, is within the provisions of the Leasehold Property (Repairs) Act 1938. Any s. 146 notice for breach of the repairing covenant would therefore have to inform Albert of his right to serve a counter-notice under the 1938 Act. If Albert does so, then Rita may not proceed any further in an action for forfeiture without the consent of the court. To obtain this consent, Rita will have to show that one of the five circumstances set out in s. 3(5) of the Act apply, and since *Associated British Ports v Bailey plc* [1990] 2 AC 703, the landlord needs to show more than just a *prima facie* case.

Rita could also sue for damages for breach of the covenant, but any damages for breach of the *repairing* covenant would be limited to the diminution in the value of the reversion (Landlord and Tenant Act 1927, s. 18(1)). Moreover, as the lease is within the 1938 Act, Rita must comply with the procedure under the Act also in order to claim damages.

If Rita were to seek forfeiture on the breach of the user covenant, she would similarly have to serve a s. 146 notice on Albert. If Albert was unaware of Sam's breach of the covenant however, and immediately took steps to stop it, it is likely that he would obtain relief against forfeiture under the Law of Property Act 1925, s. 146(2) (*Glass v Kencakes Ltd* [1966] 1 QB 611).

Even though there is no privity of contract or estate between Rita and Sam, Rita could sue Sam directly for an injunction or for damages in lieu for breach of the user covenant, which, although expressed positively, is a restrictive covenant. A restrictive covenant binds any occupier of the land, which includes a subtenant (*Mander v Falcke* [1891] 2 Ch 554). Restrictive covenants in leases are not registrable under the Land Charges Act 1972 or on the freehold title of registered land, but are binding nevertheless.

If the sublease includes the same covenants as the headlease (which it will certainly do if it has been well drafted) then Albert will be able to sue Sam on the covenants in the sublease as there is privity of contract and privity of estate between them. He may recover damages and forfeit the lease if there is a forfeiture clause.

It is uncertain whether the rebuilding of the wall and shed and the replacement of the windows and door would be within the scope of the repairing covenant. In *McDougall v Easington DC* (1989) 58 P & CR 201, the Court of Appeal reviewed the cases on what is within the scope of a repairing covenant. The court identified three guidelines for deciding whether any particular work was a 'repair' or not. First, the work should not affect the whole, or substantially the whole, of the building. Secondly, the work should not result in the building being a totally different building from that leased. Thirdly, the cost of the work should not be a disproportionate part of the value of the building when repaired.

'Repair' was defined by Buckley LJ in *Lurcott v Wakeley & Wheeler* [1911] 1 KB 905, as 'renewal of a part ... restoration by renewal or replacement of subsidiary parts of a whole'. A total rebuilding of a structure might be outside this definition, although it is of course only part of the premises as a whole. In *Halliard Property Co Ltd v Nicholas Clarke Investments Ltd* (1984) 269 EG 1257 a tenant was held not liable under a repairing covenant to reconstruct a jerry-built structure at the rear of the premises which had collapsed. To require him to do so would have been to give the landlord a very different building from that leased.

The replacement of the windows and the door to fit in with the neighbourhood may well be outside the scope of the repairing covenant, as this would seem to be the substitution of something different. The standard of repair imposed by a repairing covenant was laid down in *Proudfoot v Hart* (1890) 25 QBD 42, and is to be determined by the age, character and locality of the demised property *when the lease was granted*. Rita will only be able to expect the standard of repair which would have been appropriate therefore in 1985, and not a higher standard because the neighbourhood has improved. A curious anomaly (noted by the Law Commission) is that any repairing covenant contained in the sublease granted last year would therefore require a different standard of repair from the one contained in the headlease.

Although the option to purchase the reversion is a personal covenant and the benefit will not pass to Albert under privity of estate, it creates an equitable interest which may be assigned to him. In *Griffith v Pelton* [1958] Ch 205, the lease defined 'lessee' to include 'her executors administrators and assigns', and it was held that the benefit of an option to purchase the reversion therefore passed to an assignee of the lease. Even if there is no such definition in the lease, it was held in *Re Button's Lease* [1964] Ch 263 that such an option may be assigned to an assignee of the lease, provided that it is not expressed to be personal to the tenant only. Provided that the option to purchase is given to the tenant under the lease and not to Tony personally, then Albert will probably obtain the benefit of it.

As Rita is an assignee of the reversion, it will not be exercisable against her unless it has been registered as an estate contract Class C(iv) land charge under the Land Charges Act 1972 in unregistered title. In registered title, it will be binding if it has been registered as a minor interest, or may become binding as an overriding interest under the Land Registration Act 2002, Schedule 3, para. 2, if the tenant is in actual occupation (*Webb v Pollmount Ltd* [1966] Ch 584, a case on s. 70(1)(g), Land Registration Act 1925). Here, however, Albert is no longer in occupation, and so could not have an overriding interest under Schedule 3, para. 2.

Question 6

(a) Describe the rules relating to the passing of the benefit and the burden of covenants in leases made before 1 January 1996, indicating the problems which led to the passing of the Landlord and Tenant (Covenants) Act 1995.

(b) Describe the provisions of the Act applicable to:
  (i) leases created after 1995; and
  (ii) leases created before 1996.

Commentary

This was a very complicated area of the law where there were a number of cases defining the limits of liability of assignees of the original landlord and of the original tenant.

Because the rules could operate very harshly on an original tenant and his guarantor, who could find themselves liable under privity of contract for rent on a lease many years after the tenant had assigned it, it was also an area of law where there was strong social pressure for reform. The insolvency of many business tenants during the recession of the late 1980s and early 1990s exacerbated and highlighted the unfairness of the law. The Law Commission Report No. 174 (1988) and draft Bill proposed measures for dealing with this. However, articles occasionally appeared pleading for the preservation of the value of a landlord's investment property, and nothing was done initially to implement the reforms, reflecting no doubt the strong 'landlord' lobby in Parliament. The **Landlord and Tenant (Covenants) Act 1995** was therefore originally introduced as a private member's Bill although subsequently adopted by the (then) Government. Its main aim is to limit the possible liability of an assigning tenant to the default of his immediate assignee only in leases made on or after 1 January 1996, and this provision cannot be contracted out of. There are some sections of the Act which apply also to pre-1996 leases, however, so affording some relief to tenants and guarantors of these earlier leases.

There are two preliminary points which the student should bear in mind when approaching this topic, whether in relation to pre-1996 or post-1995 leases.

First, privity of estate, which is still relevant to pre-1996 leases, exists only between the landlord for the time being and the tenant for the time being. Therefore, if the tenant, instead of assigning the original term, subleases it, then, even if the sublease is for only one day less than the whole of the remainder of the term, there will be no privity of estate between the head-landlord (or his assignee) and the subtenant (or his assignee).

Secondly, the assignment of the lease is the disposition of a legal estate and must therefore be effected by deed, even if the lease itself is within the **Law of Property Act 1925, s. 54(2)** and so capable of being created by word of mouth (***Crago v Julian* [1992] 1 WLR 372**).

An equitable lease is contractual in nature and does not create a legal estate in the land. The rules applicable to the transmission of the benefit and burden of covenants in pre-1996 leases do not, therefore, apply to pre-1996 equitable leases. Therefore, applying the ordinary principles of contract law, the assignee of an equitable lease cannot enforce the tenant's obligation to pay rent: ***Purchase v Lichfield Brewery Co* [1915] 1 KB 184**. This is an application of the ordinary principles of the law of contract that the burden of a contract cannot (without novation) be imposed on a third party. The transmission rules applicable to post-1995 leases do, however, apply to post-1995 equitable leases, because the **1995 Act** defines a lease to include an agreement for a tenancy (**s. 28(1)**), and so includes an equitable lease.

Answer plan

(a) pre-1996 leases:

- impact of privity of contract;
- liability on assignment of reversion and lease;
- harshness of continuing liability;
- possibility that liability might increase through variation of terms?
- statutory and other indemnities for tenant;
- impact of privity of estate;
- 'touching and concerning' covenants;
- personal covenants.

(b) (i) provisions of LT(C)A 1995 applicable to post-1995 leases:

- passing of benefit of landlord and tenant covenants (**s. 3**);
- personal covenants;
- release of tenant on authorised assignment;
- authorised guarantee agreements;
- assignor-tenant's guarantors cannot guarantee an assignee;
- no increased liability for variations (**s. 18**);
- landlord of commercial lease may stipulate grounds for reasonable refusal of consent to assign;
- no automatic release of landlord on assignment of reversion (**s. 8**).

(b) (ii) provisions of LT(C)A 1995 applicable to pre-1996 and post-1995 leases:

- statutory default notice (**s. 17**);
- no increased liability for variations (**s. 18**);
- overriding leases (**ss 19–20**).

Suggested answer

(a) A lease is essentially a contract, albeit one which creates an estate in land, and privity of contract between the original landlord and the original tenant means that all the covenants contained in a pre-1996 lease should be enforceable by and against each of them throughout the term of the lease.

As regards these leases, after assignment of the reversion the original landlord's right to sue the original tenant is limited to personal covenants. This is the result of the interpretation in *Re King* [1963] Ch 459 of the Law of Property Act 1925, s. 141(1), which provides that the benefit of all those tenant covenants 'having reference to the subject-matter' of the lease passes with the reversion to the landlord's assignee. Therefore the original landlord has no right to sue on such covenants after assignment of the reversion, even if the breach occurred before such assignment (*Arlesford Trading Co Ltd v Servansingh* [1971] 1 WLR 1080, where the assignee of the landlord's reversion was able to recover arrears of rent which became due before the assignment). Conversely, the original tenant, after assignment of the lease, may still sue the original landlord for a breach of the landlord's covenants occurring before the tenant assigned (*City and Metropolitan Properties Ltd v Greycroft Ltd* [1987] 1 WLR 1085). In *Greycroft* the tenant recovered damages for breach of a repairing covenant from the original landlord after assignment where the breach had caused him to lose a purchaser of a term under a long lease. These rules are, to say the least, quite complex.

The real harshness of the privity of contract rule is in the continuing liability of the tenant and any surety of his on all the covenants in the lease throughout the term of the lease. An assignee who enters into a direct covenant with the landlord (which the terms of a lease often require him to do) may also remain liable under privity of contract. Many tenants of pre-1996 leases are under the delusion that once they have parted with the term of their lease, they are no longer liable on its covenants. This is, unfortunately for them, not generally true. Privity of contract means that if an assignee of the lease defaults on payment of rent, the landlord (even by assignment of the reversion) may sue the original tenant and his surety for arrears on a covenant to pay rent. He may also sue a previous assignee of the lease if he had entered into a covenant directly with the landlord. Moreover, the original tenant may be liable too for any increases in the rent agreed between the landlord and an assignee of the lease (*Centrovincial Estates plc v Bulk Storage Ltd* (1983) 46 P & CR 393), assuming that a rent increase was contemplated by a rent-review clause in the original lease (*Friends Provident Life Office v British Railways Board* [1996] 1 All ER 336). This Court of Appeal decision ameliorated the position of original tenants and earlier assignees to some extent in that it held they are liable only to the extent of the contractual obligations they have undertaken, and not for additional obligations due to an unauthorised variation of the lease, such as improvements contrary to the terms of the lease by a subsequent assignee.

The result of this rule during the recession meant that, on the insolvency of an assignee, many original tenants were sued by landlords for rent on leases which they had assigned many years before and had forgotten all about! An original tenant who is made to pay may be able to recover on an indemnity from assignees of the lease and their guarantors, under an express or statutory indemnity covenant, or under the rule in *Moule v Garrett* (1872) LR 7 Ex 101. However, an indemnity against an insolvent assignee is of little value; and even if there is a solvent assignee further down the chain, it was decided in *RPH Ltd v Mirror Group (Holdings) Ltd* [1993] 1 EGLR 74, that a tenant cannot insist that an insolvent assignee should sue such a solvent assignee.

Under a pre-1996 lease, once the original parties have assigned the lease or the reversion, or both, there will be privity of estate only between the landlord for the time being and the tenant for the time being, and not privity of contract. The new landlord by assignment will of course have the benefit of the tenant's covenants having reference to the subject-matter of the lease by the operation of the Law of Property Act 1925, s. 141(1); and s. 142(1) of the same Act provides that he is subject to the burden of the original landlord's covenants. He will not be liable, however, for breaches of covenant which occur before the assignment to him (*Duncliffe v Caerfelin Properties Ltd* [1989] 2 EGLR 38).

The tenant for the time being will have the benefit and the burden of covenants which 'touch and concern the land'. This principle is known as the rule in *Spencer's Case* (1583) 5 Co Rep 16a, and it has been held that such covenants are effectively the same as the covenants defined in the Law of Property Act 1925, ss. 141 and 142, as 'having reference to the subject-matter' of the lease.

The effect of *Greycroft* (*supra*) would appear to be, however, that the tenant for the time being cannot sue for breaches of covenant which occur before the assignment to him.

The covenants which pass under ss. 141 and 142 and the rule in *Spencer's Case* are those which affect the landlord *qua* landlord and the tenant *qua* tenant (*Cheshire and Burn's Modern Law of Real Property*, 16th edn, ed. E. H. Burn, 2000). It was held by the House of Lords in *P & A Swift Investments v Combined English Stores Group plc* [1989] AC 643, that a surety's covenant to pay rent on the default of a tenant is such a covenant, so that the benefit of it will pass to an assignee of the reversion. In *Hua Chiao Commercial Bank Ltd v Chiaphua Industries Ltd* [1987] AC 99, however, the Privy Council held that a landlord's covenant to repay a security deposit made by the original tenant was a purely personal one, the burden of which did not pass under s. 142(1) to an assignee of the reversion. As mentioned in the answer to Question 5, an option to purchase the freehold reversion is also a personal covenant.

(b) (i) As regards new leases made on or after 1 January 1996, the Landlord and Tenant (Covenants) Act 1995 instituted a new regime which considerably limits a tenant's liability for the default of a future assignee.

Section 3 provides that the benefit and burden of *all* 'landlord and tenant covenants' shall pass on assignment of the lease or the reversion. Sections 141 and 142, Law of Property Act 1925 and the rule in *Spencer's Case* are therefore abolished. This means that an assignee of a landlord or a tenant has no rights relating to the time before the assignment, and reverses the old law in *Re King*, so that a previous landlord and not a new landlord has a right to sue for arrears of rent. The law for a tenant is unchanged and remains as in *City & Metropolitan Properties v Greycroft*.

Section 3 does not apply to a covenant 'which (in whatever terms) is expressed to be personal': s. 3(6)(a). It is not clear what will now be regarded as a purely personal covenant which will not pass with the lease or reversion. Presumably one where the tenant or the landlord enters into a covenant in their own name which does not in any way concern their relationship as landlord and tenant might qualify, but what about a covenant to repay a tenant's rent deposit which was held to be personal and unenforceable by the tenant's assignee against the landlord's assignee in *Hua Chiao Commercial Bank Ltd v Chiaphua Industries Ltd* [1987] AC 99?

The question of what is a personal covenant which does not pass under the Act was considered in *First Penthouse Ltd v Channel Hotels and Properties (UK) Ltd* [2004] 1 EGLR 16. Lightman J said that: 'The tenancy does not have to spell it out in terms that the covenant is to be personal. The intention may be expressed explicitly or implicitly.' This begins to look similar to the old 'touching and concerning' distinction that the Act sought to abolish.

The main provision of the new Act is that a tenant is *automatically* released from liability on covenants in the lease after assignment. There can be no contracting out of this provision, and it applies *except* for:

(a) existing breaches of covenant;

(b) where it is not an authorised assignment, i.e. where assignment is in breach of covenant, or by operation of law (on death or bankruptcy of the tenant).

It may be reasonable in some circumstances for a landlord to require an authorised guarantee agreement (AGA) as a condition for consent to assign, but not necessarily so. (*Wallis Fashion Group Ltd v CGU Life Assurance Ltd* [2000] 27 EG 145.) Under it, the tenant guarantees the performance of the covenants by his immediate assignee, but not for any other later assignees. Where (a) or (b) above applies, the tenant's liability will continue until the next authorised assignment takes place.

Where the tenant lacks sufficient covenant strength, the landlord may require one or more guarantors. However, even though a landlord may be able to require a tenant who assigns to enter into an AGA, it has recently been held in *Good Harvest Partnership LLP v Centaur Services Ltd* [2010] EWHC 330 (Ch) that if the assignor tenant's guarantor purports to guarantee the obligations of the assignee, such guarantee is void as breaching the anti-avoidance section of the 1995 Act, namely s. 25. As a result, landlords granting leases might now prefer that a person who would formerly have been required to act as a guarantor is now made one of the tenants instead, so that an AGA can be required of such person when the lease is assigned. It remains unclear whether a guarantor can be required, when the lease is assigned, to guarantee the assignor's AGA (by way of a sub-guarantee), although the judge in the *Good Harvest* case thought that he could not.

An amendment was made to s. 19(1), Landlord and Tenant Act 1927 as regards commercial leases, and a new s. 19(1A) was inserted by s. 22. Whereas it had hitherto not been possible for a landlord to specify what would be reasonable grounds for his refusal of consent to an assignment (*Re Smith's Lease* [1951] 1 All ER 146), it is now possible for a landlord to specify this. There would therefore now appear to be two types of reasons for which a landlord may refuse his consent—factual ones (rent deposit, an assignee to have certain net profits, the outgoing tenant to give an AGA), and discretionary ones (that the assignee is not financially viable, or would be in competition with another tenant of the landlord's)—to which the 'reasonable' test of s. 19(1) will still apply.

A tenant who gives an AGA is liable as a guarantor and the general law as to guarantees applies to him. This means that his liability as guarantor would end if it was varied even slightly without his consent. Section 18, which applies also to old leases created before 1 January 1996, provides that in any event a tenant will not be liable for any substantial variation in the lease not contemplated by its terms. (This had of course already been judicially decided by the Court of Appeal in *Friends Provident Life Office v British Railways Board*.)

Under the general law of guarantees, a guarantor who pays out on the default of the debtor whom he has guaranteed has a right of recovery against him. The indemnities implied on an assignment for value under s. 77, Law of Property Act 1925 and s. 24, Land Registration Act 1925 (whether for value or not) are therefore no longer necessary, and these sections have been repealed as regards post-1995 leases. The repeal of these sections presumably also protects any intermediate assignee from a claim, and the rule in *Moule v Garrett* (1872) LR 7 Ex 101 would also appear to become otiose.

The Act does not provide for an automatic release of the landlord from his liabilities on assignment of the reversion. He may, however, serve a notice on each tenant within four weeks of the assignment requesting a release (s. 8). If the tenant objects, the landlord can apply to the court for a release, which the court may grant if it considers it reasonable to do so. If the landlord does not serve a notice, or is not released, he remains liable on the landlord's covenants in the lease along with the new landlord, and could be liable if the new landlord defaults on repairs or services. He may apply again for release on the occasion of the next assignment of the reversion. A release under this procedure does not release the landlord from personal covenants: *BHP Petroleum Great Britain Ltd v Chesterfield Properties Ltd* [2002] Ch 194 (CA). The aim of the legislation, that a landlord's liability on landlord covenants should continue after assignment of the reversion unless there is compliance with the s. 8 procedure, has been effectively undermined by the House of Lords in *Avonridge Property Co Ltd v Mashru* [2006] 1 P & CR 25, which held (Lord Walker dissenting) that the 1995 Act does not prevent the lease from expressly limiting the landlord's liability on landlord covenants to the period that it remains landlord.

The effects of the Act are felt mainly in the area of commercial leases; it was commercial tenants who suffered most from the harshness of the privity of contract rule. Some commentators have predicted that it will result in more subleases rather than assignments. The recent trend in commercial leases has been for tenants to require shorter leases, and this has been reinforced with the introduction of Stamp Duty Land Tax whereby stamp duty is payable now on the aggregated amount of rent payable throughout the term of the lease.

(b) (ii) Certain sections of the new Act apply to older pre-1996 leases as well as to new ones. Section 18, which applies to both, has already been mentioned above.

After 1 January 1996, a landlord who wishes to proceed against a former tenant or guarantor must first serve a default notice within six months of the default for which he is seeking to recover (s. 17). The default must be for a fixed sum such as rent, service charges or liquidated damages, such as a debt for repairs carried out by the landlord.

Any person who then pays on a default notice may, within 12 months, require the landlord to grant to him an overriding lease (s. 19). This is a reversionary lease of up to three days longer than the term of the lease on which the tenant has defaulted. He thereby becomes the landlord of the defaulting tenant and has a power of forfeiture so that he may obtain possession and so seek to recover some of his losses.

The landlord must grant the reversionary lease within a reasonable time. If more than one person requests an overriding lease, it should be granted to the first person to make the request. If the landlord receives more than one request on the same day, previous tenants have priority over previous guarantors and earlier tenants over later tenants.

12

Easements and profits

Introduction

The law of easements is a relatively discrete topic, so that questions which mix this with other areas of land law are somewhat uncommon. Lectures on easements generally work through the subject in a systematic way, starting with the nature of and requirements for an easement, then the methods by which an easement can be created (distinguishing between legal and equitable easements), followed by fluctuations in user, and finishing with the means by which an easement may be discharged. You should not, however, imagine that every answer you give to a question on easements needs to work through all aspects of the subject, nor in the same sequence. You must answer the question asked, not write everything that you know. You will need to identify the particular areas of the law of easements which give rise to difficulties, and apply the law to the facts. You should not spend time considering points of law which, on the facts, do not cause problems.

Take, for instance, the requirements for an easement as laid down in *Re Ellenborough Park* [1956] Ch 131, where it was held that:

(a) there must be a dominant and a servient tenement;

(b) the easement must accommodate the dominant tenement;

(c) the dominant and servient owners must be different persons; and

(d) the right must be capable of forming the subject-matter of a grant.

A question on easements on your examination paper may require you to deal with all, some, or indeed none, of these requirements—it may after all be a question largely or exclusively on some other aspects of easements. If the question does involve one or more of the requirements in *Re Ellenborough Park* you should deal with those that are relevant to the problem only. Question 1 in this chapter, for instance, deals (amongst other things) with (b) and (d). Question 2 also deals with them (more briefly); and Questions 3 and 4 merely touch on (d) only (in regard to the point on *Phipps v Pears* [1965] 1 QB 76 and *Copeland v Greenhalf* [1952] Ch 488 respectively). In each case it is unnecessary and, indeed, a waste of time and effort, to state all the requirements laid down in *Re Ellenborough Park*, and then to consider whether these are met. A right of way is clearly capable of comprising an easement: it would have been a waste of time to have discussed this matter in Question 3.

Question 5 is a general question involving a consideration of the requirements for an easement, acquisition by implied grant and prescription and the extent of easements so acquired (an area where there has been quite a lot of recent litigation), and the acquisition of a profit.

Just because your examiner has been clever enough to dream up some new and novel right which you decide will not qualify as an easement as it lacks one of the essential requirements under *Re Ellenborough Park* do not put down your pen and regard that as the end of your answer! You cannot know for sure what a court would decide, and your examiner will expect you to go on to consider whether the possible (though unlikely) easement has been acquired in any of the ways recognised by the law for the acquisition of easements.

Keep your powder dry for the issues which really do matter in a question. All of the problems in this chapter also involve, in varying degrees, other aspects of the law of easements. It is important to identify the areas which would in practice give rise to legal argument, so that your answer gives sufficient attention to each. Writing 'out of time' at the end of an answer does not secure any extra marks: it merely draws attention to the fact that you fell down on time management.

Question 1

In 1997, Miranda was the owner of a plot of freehold land. At one end of the plot, and adjoining the main road, stood a house and garden. In the middle of the plot there were tennis courts and a shed, and beyond that was a muddy wood which adjoined a lane. Miranda and her tennis partners often searched the wood for their lost balls.

In 1998, Miranda contracted to sell the house and garden to Silvia, and permitted Silvia to go into immediate possession. Miranda (who had herself never used the shed) also allowed Silvia to store her diesel lawnmower in the shed. The subsequent conveyance to Silvia contained a reservation of a right of way from the main road across the garden to the tennis courts.

In 1999, Miranda conveyed the middle part of the plot (containing the tennis courts and the shed) to Ophelia, who began hiring out the tennis courts for club matches. Over the years, the frequency of such hirings has increased steadily. Miranda is concerned that the increased foraging for lost balls in the wood is damaging the rare plant species which grow there. Furthermore, whilst in the past visitors to the tennis courts have crossed the garden on foot, they have recently started to traverse it in minibuses and coaches. When Silvia complained to Ophelia last week, Ophelia demanded that Silvia remove her lawnmower from the shed.

Advise Miranda and Silvia.

Commentary

The problem involves separate aspects of the law of easements: whether certain rights can exist as easements; implied easements; whether the burden of an easement affects a person who takes a conveyance of the burdened land; and increase in intensity of user. The suggested answer tackles these matters as follows:

(a) whether there can exist an easement to forage for balls; and, if so, whether, and by what means such an easement was created;

(b) whether there can exist an easement to store a lawnmower in a shed; and, if so, whether, and by what means, such an easement was created; and

(c) the scope of an easement by reservation, and increase in the intensity of its user. There have been some recent cases on the extent of easements. This has to be considered in relation to the way in which the easement is claimed, that is, by express or implied grant.

You will find it helpful to draw a diagram in your rough notes, which should look something like this:

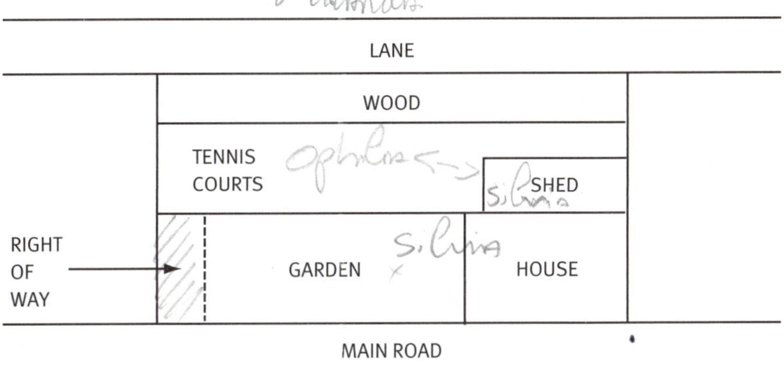

The decision of the Court of Appeal in ***P & S Platt Ltd v Crouch* [2004] 1 P & CR 18** has cast doubt upon what had been considered a settled point: namely, that for an easement (other than an easement of light) to be created in favour of a grantee under **LPA 1925, s. 62 (1)**, there had to be diversity of ownership or occupation before the conveyance to the grantee. The reason for this is that the sub-section speaks of 'liberties and privileges'; but a person who uses one part of their land for the benefit of another cannot be said to be exercising a 'liberty' or a 'privilege' over their own land—their right to use it is an ordinary incident of land ownership. Rather they are said to be exercising a quasi-easement, and a quasi-easement can become an easement on a contract or conveyance under the rule in ***Wheeldon v Burrows***. **Section 62 (1)** can however operate where the *grantee* is already enjoying a liberty or privilege (e.g. a licence) before the conveyance. That **s. 62 (1)** contains this implicit requirement was revealed in ***Long v Gowlett* [1923] 2 Ch 177** (which considered its statutory predecessor), and was accepted without qualification by the House of Lords in ***Sovmots Investments Ltd***

***v* Secretary of State for the Environment [1979] AC 144**. It was also later approved by the Court of Appeal in ***Payne v Inwood* (1997) 74 P & CR 42**.

There was one clear exception to this requirement: namely, easements of light, as laid down in ***Broomfield v Williams* [1897] 1 Ch 602**. Rights of light are distinguishable, however, because **s. 62 (2)** specifically provides that a conveyance of land with buildings 'includes . . . lights . . . enjoyed with . . . the . . . houses'. This distinction was accepted in ***Long v Gowlett***. Megarry and Wade, in the previous edition of their leading text, had accepted that the easement of light was an exception, noting that that easement 'is an exception to many rules': *The Law of Real Property*, 5th edn, Stevens, 1984, p. 866. In an article in (1977) 41 *Conv* 415, however, Charles Harpum argued that continuancy and apparency is an alternative requirement to prior diversity of ownership or occupation (as had been accepted by Sargant J in ***Long v Gowlett*** itself). This view was supported in the sixth edition of Megarry and Wade, which Harpum edited: *The Law of Real Property*, 6th edn, Sweet & Maxwell, 2000, para. 18–114, and it may be that it was this exposition of the law that influenced the Court of Appeal in ***P & S Platt Ltd v Crouch***.

If Harpum's view, now supported by ***P & S Platt Ltd v Crouch***, is correct, so that **s. 62** applies to quasi-easements, then **s. 62** is much wider than had generally been thought, and leaves little scope for the operation of the rule in ***Wheeldon v Burrows***. It should be remembered that the section is wider than ***Wheeldon v Burrows***, in that it can turn licences into easements even if they are not necessary for the reasonable enjoyment of the land granted. It is therefore questionable whether any extension of the scope of **s. 62** is desirable, and it is to be hoped that the contrary view expressed in ***Sovmots*** (the higher authority) is held to prevail.

Answer plan

(a) Easement to forage for lost balls?

- Requirements for easement:
  - definite in scope (***Re Ellenborough Park***; ***Mulvaney v Jackson***)?
- Means of acquisition:
  - by implication under ***Wheeldon v Burrows***?
  - by implication under **s. 62, Law of Property Act 1925**?
  - (but no prior diversity of occupation: ***Long v Gowlett***; contrast ***P & S Platt Ltd v Crouch***).

(b) Easement for storage of lawnmower

- Too extensive to qualify (***Copeland v Greenhalf***; ***Grigsby v Melville***; ***Wright v Macadam***)?
- Means of acquisition:
  - **s. 62, Law of Property Act 1925** (***Sovmots v Secretary of State***; ***Goldberg v Edwards***);
  - implied easement under ***Wheeldon v Burrows***?

(c) Right of way

- O takes benefit of right of way (**Law of Property Act 1925, s. 62**).
- Scope of reservation?
  - construction against purchaser (**Law of Property Act 1925, s. 65**) (***St Edmundsbury and Ipswich Diocesan Board v Clark***).
  - evidence from physical nature of access (***White v Richards***).
- Increase in intensity:
  - scope of express easement determined at time of grant (***Jelbert v Davis***);
  - but easement not lost through excessive user (***Graham v Philcox***).

Suggested answer

Miranda, as the owner of the wood, will be able to prevent the foraging for balls unless Ophelia and her visitors have a legal right to forage. As Miranda does not appear to have given a contractual licence for such purpose, such right, if one it be, can exist only as an easement. To be valid, an easement must accommodate the dominant tenement, i.e. it must benefit it as a piece of land. The right claimed must not be merely a personal benefit to the owner; *Hill v Tupper* (1863) 2 H & C 121. As the benefited land comprises tennis courts, this will probably be satisfied. More difficult to surmount, however, is the requirement that the right claimed be of definite scope, which thus excludes a mere right to wander at will over another's land (*ius spatiandi*). In *Re Ellenborough Park* [1956] Ch 131, the right to walk at will in a garden qualified as an easement because there were defined pathways: the visitors could not walk over the flower-beds. In *Mulvaney v Jackson* [2002] EWCA Civ 1078, the right to use a backyard as a communal garden for recreational and amenity purposes was similarly confirmed. A right to forage for lost balls may pose greater difficulties because there is no apparent restriction on the right claimed (since the balls could land anywhere). It is therefore unlikely that such a right could exist as an easement. If this is so, Miranda can sue the foragers in trespass, and she may be able to obtain injunctive relief to prevent future foraging.

If, however, such a right is held capable of existing as an easement, it is necessary to determine if such easement was acquired in any of the ways recognised by the law. It might have been created impliedly. When Miranda owned the tennis courts, her foraging for lost balls may be considered to be the exercise of a quasi-easement over the wood for the benefit of the tennis courts. Unless Miranda excluded implied easements from the conveyance to Ophelia, the grant would have been effective to vest in Ophelia all those quasi-easements over the retained land which are continuous and apparent, necessary to the reasonable enjoyment of the land granted, and which were, at the time of the grant, used by the grantor for the benefit of the part granted (*Wheeldon v Burrows* (1879) 12 ChD 31). These are cumulative, not alternative, requirements: *Wheeler v J. J. Saunders Ltd* [1996] Ch 19 (CA). 'Continuous' means a right which does not require personal activity for its enjoyment. Strictly, this excluded a right of way, but such a right has been held to pass under this doctrine (*Borman v Griffith* [1930] 1 Ch 493). 'Apparent' means a right which is discoverable by inspection of the land. Since the wood is muddy, there may be evidence of the foragers' footprints, which would meet this requirement. The quasi-easement could not, however, pass to Ophelia under the Law of Property Act 1925, s. 62, because, when Miranda herself foraged, she did so as owner of the wood, not through the exercise of a 'liberty' or 'privilege' (as established in *Long v Gowlett* [1923] 2 Ch 177) which effectively requires diversity of occupation of the quasi-dominant and quasi-servient tenements immediately prior to the conveyance for s. 62 to operate. *Payne v Inwood* (1997) 74 P & CR 42 suggests that even a short time of common occupation of the two tenements (in that case one week) may be enough to make s. 62 inoperative. Prior diversity of occupation was not considered necessary in *P & S Platt Ltd v Crouch* [2004] 1 P & CR 18 (CA), but the court did not review the earlier authorities, particularly *Sovmots v Secretary of State for the Environment* [1979] AC 144.

Ophelia will not be able to prevent Silvia from continuing to store her lawnmower in the shed if Silvia has an easement to do so. The right claimed as an easement must not be so extensive as to amount to possession of any part of the servient tenement (*Copeland v Greenhalf* [1952] Ch 488). In *Grigsby v Melville* [1972] 1 WLR 1355 (affirmed [1974] 1 WLR 80) a claim to store bottles in a cellar failed because, on the facts, it amounted to a claim to exclusive user. If the owner is excluded from possession for short periods only, however, a right can be an easement (*Miller v Emcer Products Ltd* [1956] Ch 304 (use of a lavatory); *London & Blenheim Estates Ltd v Ladbroke Retail Parks Ltd* [1994] 1 WLR 31 (limited right to park a car)). Similarly, provided it is limited in extent, a right of storage can also qualify (*Wright v Macadam* [1949] 2 KB 744 (storage of coal in a shed)). Whether Silvia's claim to store her lawnmower can comprise an easement will therefore depend upon the comparative sizes of the mower and the shed, and the manner of storage. If the mower fills the shed or otherwise prevents reasonable user by Ophelia, the claim will probably fail. If it succeeds, it will include the ancillary right of way across Ophelia's land in order to fetch and return the mower.

Even if the storage of the mower can comprise an easement, Silvia must still establish that such an easement was acquired. When she went into possession of the house and garden between contract and completion, she had merely a licence from Miranda to use the shed for storing the mower, and such licence could have been withdrawn at any time. However, unless it provided otherwise, the conveyance would have passed to Silvia, as legal easements, all 'liberties' and 'privileges' at the time of the conveyance enjoyed with the land (Law of Property Act 1925, s. 62). As mentioned above, if diversity of ownership or occupation is required at the time of the conveyance (as established in *Long v Gowlett* [1923] 2 Ch 177 and approved in *Sovmots v Secretary of State for the Environment* [1979] AC 144 (HL), although a contrary view was taken in *P & S Platt Ltd v Crouch* (2004) where it was said that diversity of occupation was not necessary where the exercise of the right claimed was continuous and apparent), that is satisfied, in any event, because Silvia was in possession prior to completion. The permission to store could thus be transformed, on the conveyance, into a legal easement (cf. *Goldberg v Edwards* [1950] Ch 247).

An alternative claim to an easement of storage based on the doctrine of *Wheeldon v Burrows* is less likely to succeed. Although Miranda may be considered, before completion, to be exercising, through Silvia, a quasi-easement, the requirement that the right claimed be necessary for the reasonable enjoyment of the dominant tenement is unlikely to be satisfied: there are many other places where the mower could be stored, and Miranda herself never found it necessary to use the shed for this purpose.

The burden of any easement of storage will bind Ophelia, the present owner of the servient tenement: in land with unregistered title, because it is a legal interest; in land with registered title, because it is an overriding interest under the Land Registration Act 1925, s. 70(1)(a), which was in force at the time of the transfer to Ophelia. If Ophelia transfers her plot in the future, the easement will bind a purchaser for value as an overriding interest only if one of three criteria is satisfied, namely: if the purchaser has actual knowledge at the time of the disposition; if the easement would at that time have been obvious on a reasonably careful inspection of the land; or if it can be proved that the easement was exercised within the period of one year before the disposition was made: LRA 2002, Schedule 3, para. 3.

By virtue of the Law of Property Act 1925, s. 62, Ophelia will take the benefit of the right of way. Miranda expressly reserved a right of way over Silvia's garden. Therefore, whether Silvia can prevent large numbers of Ophelia's guests crossing her garden in motor vehicles depends upon the scope of such reservation. If the reservation does not specify whether the right is one to cross on foot only, or by some other means, it will be construed against the grantor. Before 1926, a reservation took effect by way of a re-grant and was thus construed against the purchaser. After 1925, a reservation operates without any re-grant (Law of Property Act 1925, s. 65). Nevertheless, there are *dicta* of the Court of Appeal to the effect that a post-1925 reservation is also to be construed against the purchaser (*St Edmundsbury and Ipswich Diocesan Board v Clark (No. 2)* [1975] 1 WLR 468). Evidence relating to the physical nature of the access may give some indication of the easement's scope. In *White v Richards* (1998) 68 P & CR 105, the grant of the user of an unmade-up track 8′10″ wide 'with or without motor vehicles' was held not to extend to up to fourteen heavy lorries a day, and the Court of Appeal said that the extent of the user should be determined in the light of the physical characteristics of the track at the time of the grant. In the absence of any evidence, however, the reservation will be construed in favour of Ophelia, i.e. to include the use of motor vehicles.

Although there does not appear to have been any change in user of the right of way, it seems that there has been increased intensity of user. In contrast to an easement acquired prescriptively (*British Railways Board v Glass* [1965] 1 Ch 538) the scope of an express easement is determined at the time of the grant (*Jelbert v Davis* [1968] 1 WLR 589). Silvia can therefore restrain any increase in intensity beyond what could have been contemplated in 1998. Excessive user does not itself, however, cause the easement to be lost (*Graham v Philcox* [1984] 1 QB 747).

Question 2

In 1965 Joe, the fee simple owner of Greenacre, agreed with one of his neighbours, Celia, that she might park her car from time to time on a corner of one of his fields near to her house.

In 1972 Joe erected a large greenhouse on the boundary of one of his fields and started to grow in it tomatoes for sale. In connection with this, and at about the same time, he put up a sign on the wall of a neighbouring cottage, which belonged to Harry, advertising the sale of fresh eggs and produce. Also in 1972, Joe installed a water butt to catch the rain from the greenhouse roof. When Joe was not about, Celia used to cross on to Joe's land to draw water from the butt in order to wash her car when it was parked on her own land.

In 1975 Harry leased his cottage to Tommy for a term of years which expired nine months ago. After the termination of this lease, Harry conveyed his cottage to William, who has now obtained planning permission to erect a house that, when built, will block direct sunlight to Joe's greenhouse. William is also objecting to the presence of Joe's sign on his cottage wall.

Celia has now concreted over the area of the field where she parks her car. Joe wishes to prevent any further user of this area for parking, and to stop Celia drawing water from his butt.

Advise Joe.

Commentary

This question requires the candidate to have a good knowledge of the acquisition of easements by long user, or (as it is technically called) prescription. Many students have difficulty in seeing how the three methods of prescription relate to each other, so a brief explanation here may help.

Prescription at common law is based on the notion that the easement was granted before 1189 (this being the accession of Richard I and the date of legal memory). Because it was virtually impossible to prove user for such a long period, the courts began to accept evidence of user within living memory, and eventually began to accept evidence of 20 years' user as sufficient (probably by analogy with what used to be the period required to bar a title to land by adverse possession). A claim to an easement at common law could, however, be defeated in various ways. First, it could be defeated by evidence that showed that the right claimed had not been enjoyed *nec vi, nec clam* and *nec precario* (without force, without secrecy, and without permission). Secondly, it could be defeated if it could be shown that it could not have existed before 1189—which meant that most prescriptive claims at common law failed.

In order to overcome this (usually fatal) weakness of prescription at common law, the courts began to accept a pure fiction that an easement had been granted in the more recent past, but the deed of grant had been lost. The loss of such deed would not, of course, mean the loss of the easement itself. The courts were willing to accept this fiction (of a lost modern grant) if there was evidence of user for a period of 20 years (which seems to have been a borrowing from the 20-year period for prescription at common law). Many claims to easements by prescription thus succeeded under this doctrine that would have failed at common law. Nevertheless, the doctrine of lost modern grant has two defects: first, it is a blatant fiction; secondly, since *any* period of 20 years' user suffices, there may be evidential difficulties where the relevant period on which a claim is based is many years in the past.

In essence, it might be said that the **Prescription Act 1832** was intended to preserve the notion of 20 years' user forming the basis for a prescriptive claim, but without either of the drawbacks just mentioned of the lost modern grant. So the **1832 Act** established a basic period of 20 years' user for acquisition of easements, but required that the period be 'next before action' (thereby ensuing that any evidence of user is fresh). It also basically preserved the notion that a claim is defeated unless the use was *nec vi, nec clam*, and *nec precario*. Of course the **1832 Act** went much further than this, by introducing, amongst other things, a separate period of prescription of 40 years, and by having different provisions for easements of light and for profits. Unfortunately, the Act is badly drafted, and has been much criticised for its confusing nature and its unnecessary complexity.

It is not only the **1832 Act**, however, that is under threat, but rather the whole idea that easements should be capable of being acquired by prescription. Although prescription is different from adverse possession (in that it operates positively to confer a right, whereas adverse possession operates negatively to remove a right), both doctrines share the same idea that property rights can be affected (created or destroyed) in certain circumstances by the passing of time. This idea seems to be contrary to the spirit of land registration, which is moving from the concept of registration of title to what might be called 'title by registration'. Thus, in registered land, the **2002 Act** has effectively neutered the doctrine of adverse possession (see Chapter 4, Introduction). Although that Act still recognises prescription as a means of acquisition of easements, it is possible that prescription may at some time in the future go the same way as adverse possession in the registered land context. At a more detailed level, it must also be admitted that the doctrine of lost modern grant sticks out like a sore thumb in the context of registered land, where the equivalent would be a lost registration! The Law Commission is currently looking into the acquisition of easements by prescription, and published a Consultation Paper in 2008 proposing extensive reform (Law Commission CP No. 186, *Easements, Covenants and Profits à Prendre*); it hopes to publish its final report (with a draft Bill) in spring 2011.

The question raises (*inter alia*) the issue considered in ***Pugh v Savage* [1970] 2 QB 373**, of prescription under the statute where the servient tenement has been subject to a lease during the 20 years next before action. The question does not, however, deal with the same issue in relation to user for a period of 40 years. This is considered in the answer to Question 3 of this chapter.

In studying the law of easements you may also deal with profits, and the extent of the knowledge you need about profits for the purpose of your examinations may be gauged from how extensively they are treated in your course. If the treatment is fairly extensive, you may be asked detailed questions about profits, and you might be asked to compare them with easements. The answer to the present question touches on profits only briefly.

Answer plan

Easement of parking?

- Criteria for easement (***Re Ellenborough Park***):
  - right to park anywhere in field could be easement (***Newman v Jones***);
  - but not if particular space (exclusive possession) (***London & Blenheim Estates Ltd v Ladbroke Retail Parks Ltd***).
- Creation?
  - no prescription at common law (not enjoyed since 1189).
  - **Prescription Act 1832, s. 2** (40 years' actual user).
    - no written consent or agreement;
    - *nec vi, nec clam*;
    - 'next before action'.
  - lost modern grant?

    twenty years' enjoyment *nec vi, nec clam*, and *nec precario*.

Right to draw water from butt for washing of car?

- Not a *profit à prendre* (not soil or produce thereof) (***Alfred F. Beckett Ltd v Lyons***).
- Easement?
  - accommodates a dominant tenement (***Re Ellenborough Park***)?
  - or mere personal benefit to C (***Hill v Tupper***)?
  - even if qualifies, secrecy precludes claim based on prescription.

Easement of light to greenhouse?

- Criteria for easement?
  - specially high degree of light can qualify (***Allen v Greenwood***).
- Creation?
  - **Prescription Act 1832, s. 3** (20 years' uninterrupted actual enjoyment):
    1. – no written consent or agreement;
    2. – letting to T not stop period running (***Simper v Foley***).

Easement for sign?

- Criteria for easement?
  - accommodates a dominant tenement (***Moody v Steggles***)?
- Creation?

- **Prescription Act 1832, s. 2**:
  - twenty-year period begins against fee simple owner, H;
  - so can include period when land leased to T (***Pugh v Savage***).

Suggested answer

Joe will be unable to prevent Celia from parking her car in the corner of his field if she has acquired an easement to do so. The first issue, whether a right to park a car in a specified parking bay can be an easement, remains a matter of some dispute. In the recent Scottish appeal to the House of Lords in *Moncrieff v Jamieson* [2008] 1 P & CR 21 (HL), Lord Scott thought that it could, because he considered the correct test to be whether the servient owner retains possession and control. He pointed out that the servient owner would still be able to build above or below a designated parking space, or place advertising hoardings on the walls. Lord Neuberger in the same case, however, was more cautious, and was not prepared to abandon the test established in *Copeland v Greenhalf* [1952] Ch 488. These were the only two members of their Lordship's House to comment on the English law on this point, and it therefore seems that the test remains that laid down in *Copeland v Greenhalf*. This being so, there can be no easement of parking in a specified parking bay, since this would amount to a claim to exclusive possession, and would thus deprive the servient owner of the reasonable use of that part of his land (*London & Blenheim Estates Ltd v Ladbrooke Retail Parks Ltd* [1994] 1 WLR 31). For the same reason, a right effectively to fill the parking area with vehicles cannot exist as an easement (*Batchelor v Marlow* [2003] 1 WLR 764; *Central Midlands Estates Ltd v Leicester Dyers Ltd* [2003] 2 P & CR DG1). However, a right to park a car anywhere within a larger area (*Newman v Jones*, unreported, 22 March 1982) or within any one of several parking bays (*Hair v Gilman* (2000) 80 P & CR 108, CA) is capable of being an easement and of accommodating the dominant tenement (*Re Ellenborough Park* [1956] Ch 131). More evidence is therefore needed in the problem to ascertain whether Celia's claim is one merely to park anywhere within a larger defined area in a corner of Joe's field, or in a particular space: the concreting suggests the latter. In any event, a mandatory injunction will be available to compel Celia to remove the concreting.

If Celia's right were to park anywhere within a defined area and were thus considered capable of existing as an easement, she would still need to establish that such easement had been created. As there was no express grant, any such right could arise only by prescription or by presumed grant. Like all the other possible easements in the problem, it could not arise by prescription at common law, since it is easy to establish that it could not have been enjoyed since 1189 (*Bury v Pope* (1588) Cro Eliz 118).

Under the Prescription Act 1832, s. 2, where the claim to an easement (other than an easement of light) has been actually enjoyed without interruption for 40 years, the right is deemed absolute and indefeasible unless it was enjoyed by written consent or agreement. The user must still, however, have been *nec vi* (not by force) and *nec clam* (nor by stealth) (*Gardner v Hodgson's Kingston Brewery Co Ltd* [1903] AC 229; *Smith v Brudenell-Bruce* [2002] 2 P & CR 4), which appears to have been the case here. Under general principles, even oral permission defeats a claim to an easement. The effect of s. 2 is that any permission given *during* the running of the 40-year period defeats the claim. If, however, permission is given only *before* that period, it will defeat the claim if it is written, but not if it is merely oral: *Gardner v Hodgson's Kingston Brewery Co Ltd*. There is no evidence of such consent here.

The user that Celia must establish is user 'next before action'. Thus any rights she has under the statute are inchoate until recognised in court proceedings. If, therefore, Joe interrupts the user, and Celia acquiesces in it for a period of at least one year, Celia's inchoate rights will be lost (Prescription Act 1832, s. 4).

If Joe were able so to destroy a claim under the statute, Celia might, as a last expedient, claim a presumed easement of parking under the doctrine of lost modern grant. Twenty years' enjoyment *nec vi, nec clam, nec precario* (not by force, nor by stealth, nor by permission), which does not need to be next before action, raises a presumption that in the past there was a grant (since lost) (*Bryant v Foot* (1867) LR 2 QB 161). Even evidence that no such grant was made is ineffective to rebut the presumption (*Tehidy Minerals Ltd v Norman* [1971] 2 QB 528). In practice, Celia would probably claim an easement under both the Prescription Act 1832 and the doctrine of lost modern grant.

Although a right to remove something from the land of another must generally fall within the category of *profits à prendre*, a right to draw water cannot be a profit because, even though water collected in a butt is capable of ownership, water is not part of the soil or the produce of the soil (*Alfred F. Beckett Ltd v Lyons* [1967] Ch 449). If the claim is therefore to rank as an incorporeal hereditament, it must be capable of comprising an easement. A right to take water to wash one's car would not appear to satisfy the requirements of *Re Ellenborough Park* [1956] Ch 131, since it seems not to accommodate the alleged dominant tenement, but merely to be a personal benefit to the owner of the car (cf. *Hill v Tupper* (1863) 2 H & C 121). In any event, Celia's apparent secrecy (*clam*) in drawing the water will preclude her from claiming that any such alleged easement was acquired by prescription.

Joe will be able to prevent the construction of the house in the way proposed if he can establish an easement of light to his greenhouse. A right to receive a specially high degree of light for growing plants in a greenhouse was held to comprise an easement in *Allen v Greenwood* [1980] Ch 119. Under the Prescription Act 1832, s. 3, an easement of light can be acquired by 20 years' uninterrupted actual enjoyment (next before action) unless with written consent or agreement. In this instance, therefore, the user does not have to be as of right. For the same reason, the general requirement that acquisition must be by a fee simple owner against a fee simple owner does not apply to the acquisition of an easement of light under the statute. Thus, the time during which Harry's cottage is let to Tommy does not stop the period of 20 years from running (*Simper v Foley* (1862)

2 J & H 555). It would therefore appear that Joe could, by action, both establish the acquisition of an easement of light and also obtain an injunction to prevent William's building on his land so as to interfere with such easement.

A right to have a signboard affixed to the wall of another's house is capable of being an easement (*Moody v Steggles* (1879) 12 ChD 261 (sign advertising a public house). Although Joe's sign relates to his business, it will probably be held (as in *Moody v Steggles*) to accommodate the dominant tenement, in this case, Greenacre. Twenty years ago, Harry's cottage was leased to Tommy. This will not, however, prevent the period of 20 years next before action required under the Prescription Act 1832, s. 2, from running, since Joe's sign had been affixed at a time when the fee simple owner (Harry) was in possession (*Pugh v Savage* [1970] 2 QB 373).

Joe may alternatively plead that he has acquired either or both the easement of light and the easement relating to his sign under the doctrine of lost modern grant. This is possible since the period of 20 years' user that gives rise to the presumption may include a period during which the servient land was tenanted where (as here) there was initial user against a fee simple owner (*Pugh v Savage*).

Question 3

In 1962, Abbey was the fee simple owner of Fox's Farm, which comprised two adjacent plots: Greenacre to the east and Redacre to the west. Two semi-detached cottages stood on Fox's Farm: one on each plot. Access to Redacre was via a public lane which abutted the western boundary of Redacre. Adjacent to Greenacre, and lying between it and the main road to the east, was Pinkacre. From 1963, with the oral consent of Ben, the fee simple owner of Pinkacre, Abbey began using the footpath on Pinkacre in order to gain access from Greenacre to the main road.

In 1984, Ben leased Pinkacre to Colin for a term which expired two years ago. In 1986, Abbey conveyed Redacre to Derek, who had been a tenant of Redacre for the preceding year. The conveyance did not reserve for Abbey a right of way over Redacre to reach the lane, and since then Abbey has not sought to cross Redacre for this purpose. While a tenant, Derek had kept sheep on Redacre, and Abbey had allowed him to graze them on Greenacre.

Ben is now refusing Abbey the use of the footpath. Without access through either Pinkacre or Redacre, Greenacre is landlocked. To add to Abbey's problems, Derek has demolished the cottage on Redacre and has refused to provide shoring to support the exposed wall of Abbey's formerly adjoining cottage, which is now suffering from instability and exposure to the weather. Derek is also claiming the right to graze his sheep on Greenacre.

(a) Advise Abbey.

(b) How (if at all) would your advice differ if, in 1963, Ben had executed a deed by which he conferred on Abbey what was described as a 'licence' to use the footpath over Pinkacre in order to reach the main road from Fox's Farm?

Commentary

This question covers a lot of different points, which means you are not expected to linger very long over any one of them. Those candidates who insist on writing 'all they know' type answers will fare very badly.

You will find it useful to draw a sketch:

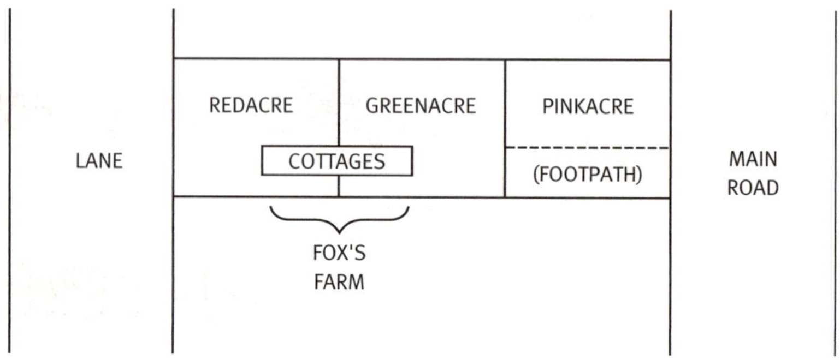

Although the question is in two parts, it should be apparent that the larger share of the answer (perhaps 80 per cent or more) needs to be devoted to the first part. In part **(b)** the questioner is testing your knowledge and understanding of specific points, i.e. that arising in ***IDC Group Ltd v Clark* [1992] 2 EGLR 184**, and the impact of written permission on the acquisition of an easement by prescription under the **Prescription Act 1832**. The variation of facts indicated in part **(b)** does indeed suggest that the advice would differ in some respects from that in part **(a)**. Do not, however, assume that the answer to: 'Would your advice be different if . . . ?' is always yes.

The only difficult aspect in the problem is that involving the lease to Colin. This involves not merely (as in Question 2), an appreciation of the issues raised in ***Pugh v Savage* [1970] 2 QB 373**; but, because the 40-year period is relevant here, also a knowledge of the effect of the **Prescription Act 1832, s. 8**. The law on this would appear to be as follows:

(a) if the user begins at a time when the servient tenement is leased, the period of 40 years cannot begin to run until the lease comes to an end (as in ***Pugh v Savage***);

(b) if the user begins at a time when the fee simple owner is in possession of the servient tenement, a claim under the 40-year period will not be defeated merely because, 40 years next before action, the servient tenement was subject to a lease (also as in ***Pugh v Savage***);

(c) however, where the lease was one for a term of at least three years, even if user began as in (b), if the fee simple owner brings an action within three years of the expiration of the lease, the time during which the land was leased is to be discounted from the period of 40 years (**Prescription Act 1832, s. 8**). Thus the time during which the land was leased is counted only if no such action is brought within three years of its termination.

It is (c) which is relevant to the present problem.

Answer plan

(a) Advice to Abbey

- Acquisition of an easement to use Pinkacre footpath (**Prescription Act 1832**):
  - twenty-year period: defeated by oral consent;
  - forty-year period: not defeated by oral consent given only *before* 40 years next before action;
  - acquisition against fee simple owner: lease to Colin;
  - deduction under **Prescription Act 1832, s. 8**.
- Implied easements: reservations:
  - necessity: Greenacre landlocked;
  - mutual: easement of support, but not against weathering.
- Ben's access to Pinkacre to effect works (**Access to Neighbouring Land Act 1992**).
- Derek's sheep-grazing: acquisition of profit—implied grant:
  - not ***Wheeldon v Burrows***;
  - **Law of Property Act 1925, s. 62**: diversity of occupation.

(b) Ben's 'licence'

- Despite deed, probably merely permissive.
- Permission by deed destroys claim to easement by prescription even under 40-year period of **Prescription Act 1832**.

Suggested answer

(a) Abbey will have a right to use the footpath over Pinkacre if he has acquired an easement by prescription. A claim that an easement was acquired under the Prescription Act 1832, s. 2, by virtue of 20 years' user next before action will be defeated by the oral permission that Ben gave Abbey in 1963. Unless there is evidence (which is not apparent from the question) that the permission was revoked before such 20-year period began, Abbey cannot show that the relevant period of user was *nec precario* (*Healey v Hawkins* [1968] 1 WLR 1967). The fact that consent was given from the outset will also defeat a claim based on lost modern grant (*Bryant v Foot* (1867) LR 2 QB 161). By contrast, oral consent will not defeat a prescriptive claim based on the 40-year period if such consent was given only *before* the 40 years started to run, and was not given again during that period: *Gardner v Hodgson's Kingston Brewery Co Ltd* [1903] AC 229. Only a written consent has this effect: Prescription Act 1832, s. 2. As there is no evidence in the question that the oral consent was repeated during the 40 years next before action, the oral consent given in 1963 will not defeat the claim under that period.

An easement can be acquired prescriptively only by and against a fee simple owner. In the problem, the user of the footpath over Pinkacre began while Ben was in possession. The mere fact that for some of the period comprising the 40 years 'next before action' Pinkacre was leased to Colin will not, therefore, itself prevent Abbey from claiming under the 40-year period in s. 2 (*Pugh v Savage* [1970] 2 QB 373). However, if Abbey claims under the 40-year period, Ben will (provided he resists Abbey's claim within three years of the termination of Colin's lease) be able to deduct the period during which Pinkacre was leased to Colin from the computation of the period of 40 years (Prescription Act 1832, s. 8). Since Colin's lease ended two years ago, Ben will have one year in which to resist. If he does so, Abbey's claim will fail, since he will be able to establish user for merely 23 years, i.e. 21 years before the grant of the lease, and two years after its termination. If Ben fails to resist within one year, however, Abbey will be able to include the period of the lease, and therefore should be able to establish 40 years' user 'next before action'.

It is unclear whether anything short of legal proceedings (such as blocking the right of way) suffices for a claim to be 'resisted' within s. 8. However, if Ben were to prevent Abbey's user of the path, and Abbey were to submit to it or to acquiesce in it for a year, there would be an interruption which would destroy Abbey's claim (s. 4).

Because of the general rule that a grant is construed in favour of the grantee, the reservation of an easement to a grantor will not be readily implied: it will usually need to be express. One exception, however, is where the conveyance by the grantor would leave his retained land landlocked. In such circumstances, a reservation of a right of way will be implied in favour of the grantor, unless the conveyance contains a contrary intention (*Nickerson v Barraclough* [1981] Ch 426). No such contrary intention appears from the problem. Such an easement of necessity can arise even where (as in the problem) some of the surrounding land (Pinkacre) belongs to a third party (Ben) (*Barry v Hasseldine* [1952] Ch 835). The necessity must exist at the time of the grant. In 1986, when Abbey conveyed Redacre, his use of the footpath over Pinkacre was merely permissive: such precarious user will not preclude the implication in the conveyance to Derek of an easement of necessity over Redacre (*Barry v Hasseldine*). Similarly, once acquired, the easement of necessity will not be destroyed by Abbey's subsequent acquisition of a right of way over Pinkacre.

Abbey's non-exercise of his right of way over Redacre since its acquisition in 1986 will not cause it to be lost, because even a long period of non-user (175 years in *Benn v Hardinge* (1992) 66 P & CR 246) is not enough to show abandonment. There has to be something to show that the only explanation of non-user is that the dominant owner intended to release his rights: *Swan v Sinclair* [1924] 1 Ch 254, 266; aff'd [1925] AC 227. On the facts, Abbey may have simply found it more convenient to use the permissive way over Pinkacre. Assuming that Abbey has an easement of necessity over Redacre, he may select any convenient route over Redacre to reach the lane (*Bolton v Bolton* (1879) 11 ChD 968). Once selected, the route cannot be changed (*Deacon v South Eastern Railway* (1889) 61 LT 377).

Another exception to the rule against implied reservation is where a grantor conveys one of two houses supported by one another. From such circumstances, where there is clear reciprocity, the courts will readily infer a common intention to grant and reserve easements of support, which will be implied (*Richards v Rose* (1853) 9 Exch 218).

Therefore Abbey will be able to compel Derek to provide the necessary shoring to stabilise the remaining cottage. A right to have a wall protected from weathering, however, is incapable of existing as an easement (*Phipps v Pears* [1965] 1 QB 76). Abbey cannot therefore compel Derek to provide weatherproofing for the exposed wall or sue Derek for damages for his loss. Abbey will need to execute and pay for such works himself.

If Abbey needs to enter upon Redacre to carry out such works, and Derek denies access, Abbey may apply for an access order under the Access to Neighbouring Land Act 1992, s. 1. The court must be satisfied that such works are reasonably necessary for the preservation of Greenacre, and that they cannot be carried out (or would be substantially more difficult to carry out) without access to Redacre. Since these works comprise the maintenance, repair, and (perhaps) renewal of a building, they rank as 'basic preservation works' (s. 1(4)), and are therefore treated as reasonably necessary for the preservation of Greenacre.

Derek will have a right to graze his sheep on Greenacre if he has acquired a *profit à prendre* to do so. He may have acquired such a profit by implied grant. A profit probably cannot be acquired under the rule in *Wheeldon v Burrows* (1879) 12 ChD 31 since it lacks the qualities of continuity and apparency, and of being reasonably necessary for the enjoyment of the land. It can, however, be acquired under the Law of Property Act 1925, s. 62(1), which, on a conveyance, converts into a legal right that which, prior to the conveyance, was merely a 'liberty' or a 'privilege' enjoyed with the land. The requirement that there be prior diversity of occupation (*Long v Gowlett* [1923] 2 Ch 177) is satisfied, because Derek had, until the conveyance, been grazing the sheep permissively on Greenacre while a tenant of Redacre. In any event, the requirement for diversity of occupation where the right claimed is continuous and apparent appears to have been affected by the decision in *P & S Platt Ltd v Crouch* (2004). Unless, therefore, the conveyance contains a contrary intention, it will convert Derek's quasi-profit of grazing into a legal profit, which Abbey will be unable to restrain.

(b) Although the document executed by Ben in 1963 was in the form of a deed, the use of the term 'licence' suggests that, rather than granting an easement, the document merely gave a permissive user. Whereas in the context of residential accommodation the use of the term 'licence' is not decisive against the grant of a lease (*Street v Mountford* [1985] AC 809), in the case of commercial interests over land (such as the right to pass over it) the courts are more willing to accept the parties' own description of the right conferred as decisive. This is particularly the case where the parties both had legal advice (*IDC Group Ltd v Clark* [1992] 2 EGLR 184 and *Clear Channel UK Ltd v Manchester City Council* [2006] 1 EGLR 27). Furthermore, if he has not provided consideration for the licence, Abbey will not be able to sue for damages for its revocation. A written consent, moreover, even if given only before the beginning of the period of user, will defeat a claim to the acquisition of an easement under the 40-year period (Prescription Act 1832, s. 2). Abbey will therefore be unable to establish an easement to use the footpath, and Ben may lawfully revoke his licence to do so.

Question 4

In 2005, Clement and Bailey were the adjoining freehold owners of Nos. 3 and 5 Shoreditch Lane respectively. Clement had difficulty parking his car in the garage of No. 3 without using the driveway of No. 5. Following discussion between them, Clement and Bailey in November that year entered into a written contract (signed by each of them) whereby, in consideration of Clement's paying Bailey the sum of £5,000, Bailey agreed that Clement and his successors in title were to have a right in perpetuity to use the driveway of No. 5 for the purpose of parking a motor vehicle in the garage of No. 3.

Three months ago, Bailey sold and conveyed the freehold title of No. 5 (which was at the time unregistered) to Stepney, who knew nothing of the agreement between Clement and Bailey. Stepney has now objected to Clement's use of the driveway of No. 5.

(a) Advise Clement.

(b) To what extent would your advice differ if the title to No. 5 had been registered when Bailey had acquired it?

(c) To what extent would your advice in (a) and (b) differ if the agreement of 2005 had been oral only?

Commentary

Easements can be either legal or equitable. It is surprising how many students seem to find an equitable easement where none exists. Equitable easements arise in somewhat narrow circumstances only. First, a legal easement can exist only if it is held for a period equivalent to an estate in fee simple absolute in possession, or for a term of years absolute (**Law of Property Act 1925, s. 1(2)(a)**). An easement for any other period (such as an easement for life) can exist as an equitable easement only. Secondly, a valid contract to grant a legal easement gives rise to an equitable easement; this is dealt with in part **(a)** of the answer. It should be remembered that, whereas the rule in ***Wheeldon v Burrows* (1879) 12 ChD 31** can apply on a contract to convey a legal estate (in which event it will give rise to an equitable easement), the **Law of Property Act 1925, s. 62**, can create an easement only upon a conveyance—which means that any such easement will be a legal one.

Part **(b)** deals with the position in registered land, where it is clear that the equitable easement needs to be protected by entry of a notice on the charges register of the burdened title.

Part **(c)** raises the difficult issue of proprietary estoppel, and whether such a right is binding on a third party purchaser. There is a significant difference here between unregistered and registered titles. In unregistered titles, it appears that a third party is bound unless able to establish the defence of *bona fide* purchaser for value of the legal estate without notice of the equity by estoppel. In registered titles, the equity should be protected by entry of a notice on the charges register. In the absence of the entry of a notice, the equity will not bind a transferee for value unless the person claiming it is in actual occupation.

In the question, it cannot seriously be argued that Clement is in actual occupation of the land over which he is claiming a right, since his use of the driveway of No. 5 to park his car on No. 3 is very transient. The answer to parts **(b)** and (so far as it pertains to registered land, part **(c)**) might have been different if the question had involved Clement's having a licence to *park* his car on No. 5. There is authority to support the proposition that the regular parking of a car on the servient land pursuant to an equitable easement to do so can amount to actual occupation by the dominant owner: ***Kling v Keston Properties Ltd* (1983) 49 P & CR 212** (parking of car in a garage). The regular parking of a car pursuant to an equity by estoppel would similarly appear to be capable of amounting to actual occupation. Under the **Land Registration Act 2002**, however, the interest of a person in actual occupation cannot be an overriding interest under **Schedule 3, para. 2**, if the occupation would not have been obvious on a reasonably careful inspection of the land at the time of the disposition where the disponee did not have actual knowledge of the interest at that time. In many instances, no doubt, the mere act of parking a car will not make the occupation obvious, since a purchaser might reasonably assume that a car parked on the land belongs to the vendor or to the vendor's family.

Answer plan

Unregistered title

- Equitable easement?
  - valid contract for easement (**Law of Property (Miscellaneous Provisions) Act 1989, s. 2**)?
  - if so, creates equitable easement: ***Walsh v Lonsdale***.
- Binding on third party (S)?
  - depends on registration as Class D(iii) land charge.

Registered title

- Equitable easement created after **LRA 2002** in force.
- Binding on S if protected by notice at time of transfer to S.
- Cannot argue overriding interest under **Schedule 3, para. 2** (no actual occupation).

Agreement oral only

- No valid contract to create an equitable easement (**LP(MP)A 1989, s. 2**).
- But C might acquire rights by proprietary estoppel (on payment of the £5,000).

- If *unregistered* title, seems estoppel is proprietary interest, and whether binds S depends on equitable doctrine of notice (***Ives v High***).
- if *registered* title, estoppel binds S only if entered as notice on charges register (cannot argue overriding interest under **Schedule 3, para. 2**, since no actual occupation).

Suggested answer

(a) Assuming that the written agreement satisfies the requirements of the Law of Property (Miscellaneous Provisions) Act 1989, s. 2, it is a valid contract to create a legal easement. A valid contract to grant a legal easement itself creates an equitable easement according to the maxim that equity looks upon as done that which ought to be done (cf. *McManus v Cooke* (1887) 35 ChD 681 and the principle of *Walsh v Lonsdale* (1882) 21 ChD 9). It would therefore seem that, from the agreement made in 2005, Clement acquired an equitable easement to use the driveway for the purpose of parking his car in his own garage.

The difficulty for Clement, however, is that the servient land has since been conveyed to a third party, Stepney. The issue is therefore whether Clement's equitable easement is binding on Stepney. If it is, Clement will be able, if necessary, to obtain an injunction to prevent Stepney from interfering with the exercise of such right.

As the title to No. 5 was unregistered when it was conveyed to Stepney, it is important to ascertain whether the equitable easement was protected by registration against the name of Bailey (the estate owner at the time the easement was created) as a Class D(iii) land charge under the Land Charges Act 1972, s. 2(5), before the completion of Stepney's purchase. If it was so protected, the easement is binding on Stepney. If it was not, it is void against Stepney if he was a purchaser of the legal estate for money or money's worth (s. 4(6)).

(b) If the title to No. 5 had been already registered when Bailey acquired it, then whether the easement is binding upon Stepney depends upon the principles of registered land. As the equitable easement was created after the Land Registration Act 2002 came into force (13 October 2003), it cannot be an overriding interest in its own right. Under that Act, the only easements created on or after that date that are capable of being overriding in their own right are legal easements, and even these can be overriding only in limited circumstances: LRA 2002, Schedule 3, para. 3. It would be difficult to argue that Clement had an overriding interest for the purposes of Schedule 3, para. 2 of that Act, since his transient use of the driveway of No. 5 could hardly amount to actual occupation. The equitable easement will be binding on Stepney, therefore, only if it was already protected by the entry of a notice on the charges register of No. 5.

(c) If the agreement entered into in 2005 had been oral, it would not have satisfied the requirements for a valid contract for the creation of an interest in land under the Law of Property (Miscellaneous Provisions) Act 1989, s. 2. This section requires (*inter alia*) a contract for the sale or other disposition of an interest in land to be made in writing incorporating all the terms. The oral agreement would not therefore have created an equitable easement. However, as Clement paid Bailey £5,000 under the void contract, the requirements for proprietary estoppel appear to be satisfied, in that Clement acted to his detriment in reliance upon Bailey's representation that Clement would have a right to use the driveway of No. 5 in perpetuity. As s. 2(5) of the 1989 Act expressly states that the section does not apply to constructive trusts, but does not make any saving for estoppel, the estoppel may arise under a constructive trust: *Yaxley v Gotts* [2000] Ch 162 (CA).

If the title to No. 5 had been unregistered when acquired by Bailey, there is some uncertainty whether an estoppel, being inchoate in nature, is capable of binding a third party purchaser for value. In *ER Ives Investment Ltd v High* [1967] 2 QB 379, the Court of Appeal considered that rights arising by proprietary estoppel are outside the machinery of what is now the Land Charges Act 1972 and so bind a purchaser according to the equitable doctrine of notice. In the view of Lord Denning MR in that case, such a right arising by proprietary estoppel is not an 'equitable easement' within Class D(iii), since such a right was not one capable of being conveyed or created at law before 1926.

Ives v High was controversial at the time, since it seemed to be giving proprietary effect to a licence, and an argument was advanced that the decision rested more soundly on the alternative basis on which the Court of Appeal relied, namely the doctrine of mutual benefits and burdens: Crane (1967) 31 *Conv* (NS) 332. Furthermore, in *United Bank of Kuwait plc v Sahib* [1997] Ch 107, Peter Gibson LJ explained *Ives v High* as turning on the joint application of the principles of mutual benefits and burdens and proprietary estoppel. His Lordship did not however refer to the slightly earlier decision of *Lloyds Bank plc v Carrick* [1996] 4 All ER 630, 642, where Morritt LJ, whilst not expressing a concluded view, thought that, in the light of *Ives v High*, it would be difficult to maintain that an equity by estoppel cannot bind a successor in title with notice.

On the authority, therefore, of *Ives v High*, the estoppel would be binding on Stepney unless he could establish the defence of *bona fide* purchaser for value of the legal estate without notice of the estoppel. The positioning of Clement's garage might put Stepney on notice that Clement has some rights to use No. 5 as an access when parking his car, but this is a matter of evidence. Ironically, therefore, Clement might have rights binding on Stepney (through the equitable doctrine of notice) if the agreement is void for non-compliance with s. 2 of the 1989 Act.

The uncertainty that exists in unregistered titles as to the proprietary status of an equity by estoppel before the court has awarded a remedy, no longer arises in registered titles, as the matter has been dealt with expressly in the Land Registration Act 2002. Thus, if the title to No. 5 had already been registered when acquired by Bailey, the equity by estoppel would have created a proprietary interest capable of binding successors in title from the time the equity arose: LRA 2002, s 116. The time the equity arose would have been the date Clement paid the £5,000. The equity could (and should) then have been protected by a notice in the charges register of Bailey's title. It is the nature of informal agreements of this kind, however, that they tend not to be so protected. If such agreement was not so protected, it will not bind Stepney, as rights by estoppel are not overriding interests in their own right. It can also hardly be argued that Clement's equity by estoppel is protected as an overriding interest under Schedule 3, para. 2, of the 2002 Act, since (as stated in the answer to part (b) above), Clement can scarcely be considered to be in actual occupation of that part of the drive of No. 5 that he used in order to park on No. 3.

Question 5

The Archer family have farmed Willow Farm for many generations. Dan, the current owner in fee simple of the farm, lives in the farmhouse, access to which is obtained along a narrow lane which belongs to the farm. Dan's son Herbert had lived in a house which Dan had built beside the lane, about half way between the road to which the lane leads, and Willow Farm, but in 1972, Herbert decided that country life was not for him and moved up to London. Dan then sold the house to Jim. The conveyance to Jim did not mention any rights to be enjoyed in connection with the house.

Jim and his family have two cars, and Jim and his wife have, since 1972, used the lane as access to the house, although the house can also be reached by a shorter unmade-up track from the road. As there is only a single garage with the house, they have been in the habit of parking one of their cars on a piece of land belonging to the farm beside the house. They like riding, and when they bought the house in 1972, Dan agreed orally that they could graze a horse in a field adjoining the house, which they have done ever since. They have also kept the horse in a disused barn at the corner of the field in bad weather.

Two years ago, Jim and his family bought three more horses, which they have also grazed in the field and kept in the barn. About this time, they started to show the horses and to give riding lessons to children. In connection with these activities, there are now far more cars, horse boxes and vans using the lane. There are often cars parked in the lane near the house, which makes access difficult for the farm lorries. About six months ago, Dan objected to the vans and cars with riding pupils using the lane; he asked Jim to remove all his horses from the disused barn, and not to use the field for grazing them. In view of the problems with car parking, he has also asked Jim not to park his own car at all on the plot of land beside the lane. Jim has so far not complied with these requests. Advise Dan.

Commentary

This is a fairly simple question geographically, so a plan is not really necessary. It requires consideration of three different possible easements (a right of way, parking and user of a barn) and a profit (grazing a horse). The possible methods of acquisition are implied grant and prescription.

The question also requires some discussion of whether parking and user of a barn fulfil the requirements for an easement, and the extent of an easement acquired in these ways. Not a question for someone who has tried 'question-spotting' as it requires a fairly wide knowledge of the subject!

Answer plan

Basic requirements

- For easements:
  - right of way;
  - parking?
  - use of barn?
- For profits:
  - grazing horses.

Method of creation

- Implied easements:
  - necessity;
  - intended;
  - ***Wheeldon v Burrows***;
  - **Law of Property Act 1925, s. 62**.
- Easement by prescription:
  - **Prescription Act 1832, s. 2** (20 years' user next before action);
  - lost modern grant (***Bridle v Ruby***).
- Profit by prescription:
  - **Prescription Act 1832, s. 1** (30 years' user next before action);
  - lost modern grant.

Change in nature and intensity of user

- Increase in use where easement by prescription (***BRB v Glass***).
- But restricted to nature of user at time of grant (***Jobson v Record***).
- May not excessively interfere with others' rights (***Jelbert v Davis***).

Suggested answer

Whether Dan can prevent Jim from using the lane (for his business as well as his personal use), parking his car and using his barn, depends upon whether Jim has acquired any rights as easements. Whether Dan can prevent Jim from grazing his horses depends on whether Jim has acquired a *profit à prendre* to do so.

For a right to exist as an easement, it must comply with the four criteria laid down in *Re Ellenborough Park* [1956] Ch 131. A right of way is a well recognised easement (*Borman v Griffith* [1930] 1 Ch 493). A right to park a car and a right to keep horses in a barn might each be capable of existing as an easement provided that the right claimed in each case does not amount to exclusive possession or occupation (*London & Blenheim Estates Ltd v Ladbroke Retail Parks Ltd* [1992] 1 WLR 1278, on parking of a car), and accommodates the dominant tenement. A claim by Jim to keep one horse in the barn might meet the criteria, but a claim to keep four there might fail to satisfy the requirement that the easement accommodates the dominant tenement. It might be argued that such activity instead accommodates Jim's business use, and is therefore merely a personal benefit to Jim (*Hill v Tupper* (1863) 2 H&C 121).

Provided that they meet the general requirements for easements, Jim may have acquired a right of way over the lane and an easement to park by implied grant when he bought the house. The sale of the house was the sale of the quasi-dominant tenement, so there are four possibilities for the acquisition of easements by this means: easements of necessity, intended easements, the rule in *Wheeldon v Burrows* (1879) 12 ChD 31, and the Law of Property Act 1925, s. 62.

As there is an alternative access over an unmade-up track, so that the house is not landlocked, there can be no easement of necessity in the strict sense. There is a garage with the house, however, and it might be possible to infer from this that a right of access by car was intended, and that this would be along a lane rather than over an unmade-up track. An easement could be acquired under the Law of Property Act 1925, s. 62, if Dan's son, Herbert, had used the lane for access by car (unless acquisition by such means was expressly excluded in the conveyance to Jim). For s. 62 to apply, under the rule in *Long v Gowlett* [1923] 2 Ch 177 (confirmed in *Sovmots v Secretary of State for the Environment* (1979)), it was considered that there had to be diversity of ownership or occupation before the conveyance. In *P & S Platt Ltd. v Crouch* (2004), however, it was held that such diversity was not necessary where the right claimed was continuous and apparent. In any event, Herbert does have prior occupation and user so the point does not arise.

An easement to use the lane might also have been acquired under the rule in *Wheeldon v Burrows* if the lane access could be regarded as necessary for the reasonable enjoyment of the land (although see *Wheeler v J. J. Saunders Ltd* [1996] Ch 19, where a similar claim to an easement was rejected when there was a viable alternative access). The acquisition of an easement to park a second car on a piece of land adjoining is more dubious. It could not be acquired under s. 62 unless Herbert had parked there, and it might not be regarded as necessary for the reasonable enjoyment of the land under *Wheeldon v Burrows*.

Alternatively, as Jim has enjoyed access over the lane and parking for 20 years, he may have acquired these rights as easements by prescription. Under the Prescription Act 1832, s. 2, 20 years' user as of right next before action will give rise to a claim for an easement, although the right is inchoate until an action is brought by the owner of the dominant tenement. Dan's objections over the last six months will not amount to an interruption under the Act, as this must subsist for a year to be effective (Prescription Act 1832, s. 4). In any event, to amount to an interruption, the acts of the owner of the servient tenement must be overt, such as physically blocking up a right of access or commencing an action for an injunction.

An easement by prescription is usually claimed by lost modern grant as an alternative to a claim under the Prescription Act 1832. This is the legal fiction devised to avoid defeat of a claim by prescription at common law where user back to 1189 was impossible to establish! There is a presumption of lost modern grant after 20 years' user, so that this might apply to the right of access over the lane (*Bridle v Ruby* [1989] QB 169), and also to the parking of the car if it is capable of being an easement.

Jim and his wife were given oral permission by Dan to graze their horse in his field in 1972. Assuming that they have continuously grazed a horse in the field since then, from 2002 onwards they will be able to claim a *profit à prendre* as they will be able to show 30 years' user next before action (Prescription Act 1832, s. 1). The acquisition of a profit, like an easement, must be as of right, and the shorter periods under the Act of 20 years for an easement and 30 years for a profit may be defeated by mere oral permission (*R (Beresford) v Sunderland CC* [2004] 1 AC 889). Any claim to a profit may therefore fail on this ground. Although a claim by lost modern grant may also be made for a profit, and the period is shorter (20 years), this also must be user as of right, and might possibly fail on the same ground. In practice, claims to profits using lost modern grant are rare.

A right of way acquired by prescription will not be exceeded by a mere increase in use (*British Railways Board v Glass* [1965] 1 Ch 538), but the user must be of the same kind, so that the domestic user acquired by prescription would not extend to business user.

Therefore, even if the right of access over the lane by car has been acquired as an easement, this could not have been for business user as the dominant tenement was not used for these purposes when purchased. *Jobson v Record* [1998] 1 EGLR 113 (a case on express grant) is authority for the proposition that the grant of an easement is restricted to the user at the time of the grant. *Jelbert v Davis* [1968] 1 WLR 589 (again a case on express grant of an easement) held that the user of a driveway must take into account the rights of other persons to use it and could not be so excessive that it interfered with their rights. The same principles would seem to be applicable to the acquisition of easements by implied grant, whether from a presumed intention or under the rule in *Wheeldon v Burrows*. The Law of Property Act 1925, s. 62 would not apply as Herbert had not enjoyed any such rights before the sale.

Further reading

Burn, E.H., and Cartwright, J., *Cheshire and Burn's Modern Law of Real Property*, 17th edn, Oxford, 2006, chapter 18.

Haley, M., 'Easements, exclusionary use and elusive principles: the right to park' [2008] *Conv* 244.

Smith, R.J., *Property Law*, 5th edn, Longman, 2006, chapter 20.

13

Freehold covenants

Before you start to write your answer to a problem involving the running of the benefits and burdens of freehold covenants, you might find it easier if you first clarify the position by drawing a diagram showing the various relationships between the parties. This is best done in your rough notes rather than in the answer itself, as many examiners prefer to read words than to look at pictures. You should adapt (as appropriate) the following basic diagram, which represents the following transactions.

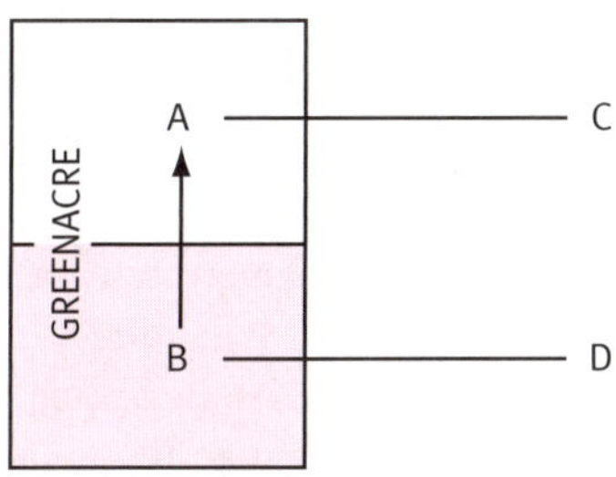

Greenacre

A, who owns Greenacre, sells and conveys the shaded part of it to B, taking a covenant from B in the conveyance. (The arrow represents the covenant, showing the burden flowing from B (the covenantor) to A (the covenantee).) A subsequently sells and conveys his remaining part of Greenacre to C, and B sells and conveys his part to D.

There are four possible actions for breach of the covenant:

(i) A can sue B for a breach of the covenant (which is a breach of contract) by B while he retains the benefited land. If the covenant is negative in nature, he may also be able to obtain an injunction in equity.

(ii) After A has sold to C, C can sue B if he can show the benefit of the covenant has passed from A to him. As the benefit will usually pass at common law (subject to certain conditions being satisfied), C will be able to sue for breach of a positive covenant as well as breach of a negative covenant. There is no need to show the passing of the burden as B is the original covenantor.

(iii) A (if he still retains his part of Greenacre) can sue D for breach of the covenant if the burden of the covenant has passed from B to D. The burden of a covenant never passes at common law and so this must be shown by applying the rules in equity (the rule in *Tulk v Moxhay* (1848) 2 Ph 774), and these apply only to negative covenants.

(iv) C can sue D for breach if he can similarly show that the burden has passed to D, and can additionally show that the benefit has passed from A to him. As it is necessary to show the burden passing under the rules in equity however, C must also show the benefit passing under the equitable rules, and the common law and equitable rules must never be mixed.

Once you have sorted out where you need to show the passing of the benefit and burden of a covenant in order for someone to sue on it, then you are half way to getting the right answer! You then have to apply the appropriate set of rules. Most questions on covenants will involve the passing of the burden as well as the benefit, but a good student will mention briefly (in no more than one sentence) that because it is necessary to show the passing of the burden, then the common law rules on the passing of the benefit are of no assistance, before proceeding to apply the rules in equity.

Since the Chancery Amendment Act 1858 it has been possible for equitable damages to be awarded in lieu of, or in addition to, an equitable remedy. This power, now contained in the Senior Courts Act 1981, s. 50, is discussed in Question 4 in this chapter. Since the burden of a restrictive covenant in equity binds the land rather than the covenantor's estate in the land, the burden of such a covenant is enforceable in equity against anyone who comes to the land (other than a *bona fide* purchaser). This includes a person who does not have the same estate in the land as the covenantor, including, therefore, an adverse possessor. An injunction may therefore be sought against an adverse possessor whose actions are in breach of a restrictive covenant. In such a case, the claimant may seek damages against the adverse possessor in addition to an injunction (or as an alternative should the court refuse to make an order for injunctive relief). The result is that damages in equity may be awarded against a person who could not have been liable in damages for breach of covenant at common law.

If the benefit has not been annexed to the land, so as to pass in equity, it may nevertheless have passed to the claimant by assignment, or by operation of law. Both of these methods are considered in Question 2 in this chapter.

A building scheme is a further means by which the benefits and burdens of restrictive covenants can pass in equity. Such schemes are considered in Question 3 in this chapter.

Question 4 in this chapter is a problem involving the possible discharge of a restrictive covenant. This is an area which has seen most of the recent litigation concerning restrictive covenants. There have been a number of applications to the Lands Tribunal and the courts on the interpretation of the Law of Property Act 1925, s. 84 (as amended by the Law of Property Act 1969). There is an article by Harold Wilkinson considering some of these in (2000) 150 *NLJ* 1523 and 1623. He concludes the article by quoting two conflicting statements from members of the Tribunal as to whether applications for discharge of restrictive covenants have to be treated specifically and individually, or in the context of a scheme of restrictive covenants! Given these conflicting views, there may well be more applications to the Tribunal.

As regards covenants entered into on or after 11 May 2000, the Contracts (Rights of Third Parties) Act 1999, s. 1(3) gives to a third party 'expressly identified in the contract by name, as a member of a class or as answering a particular description but [who] need not be in existence when the contract is entered into' the right to enforce a contract (including a land contract) in his own right. E. H. Burn and J. Cartwright in *Cheshire & Burn's Modern Law of Real Property*, 17th edn, Oxford, 2006, take the view that this wording would clearly cover 'successors in title' in a restrictive covenant and that such successors would have the benefit of a covenant both at common law and in equity. They also take the view that, as the Act deals with contractual rights, it would not be restricted at common law to covenants touching and concerning the land or benefiting the 'dominant' land. The wording of the section would extend rights to future owners of land affected by a covenant, and the restriction placed on s. 56 of the LPA 1925 by *Re Ecclesiastical Commissioners Conveyance, Re* [1936] Ch 430 (mentioned in the answer to Question 2) that the section can only apply to identifiable persons in existence at the time of the covenant will not apply to the Act.

Many possible applications of the Act may well have been rendered otiose by the courts' liberal interpretation of LPA 1925, s. 78 on annexation of the benefit of a covenant. Its significance remains to be seen from the cases!

Question 1

In the summer of 1989 Pip was the fee simple owner of a plot of some 5,000 acres, the title to which was unregistered. The plot slopes gently from north to south. The southern half of the plot (called Fruitlands) comprises orchards; the northern half (called Homestead) comprises a dwelling-house and extensive gardens. In the autumn of 1989, Pip conveyed Fruitlands to Squeak. In the conveyance to him, Squeak covenanted with Pip 'for the benefit of Pip's adjoining land':

(a) to maintain the drainage ditches on Fruitlands in order to prevent the flooding of Homestead; and

(b) to use Fruitlands for agricultural purposes only.

As Fruitlands was not at the time in an area of compulsory registration of title, the second of these covenants was immediately registered against Squeak's name as a land charge, Class D(ii).

In 1995, Pip conveyed Homestead to Cherry. The following year, Squeak conveyed Fruitlands to Wilfred.

Wilfred has neglected to repair the drainage ditches on Fruitlands, with the result that Cherry's land is periodically flooded. Wilfred also intends to build a block of flats on part of Fruitlands.

Advise Cherry.

Commentary

This question raises the issue of the extent to which the benefit and burden of both positive and negative covenants run with the land of the covenantee and the covenantor respectively. A sketch of the contractual position is as follows:

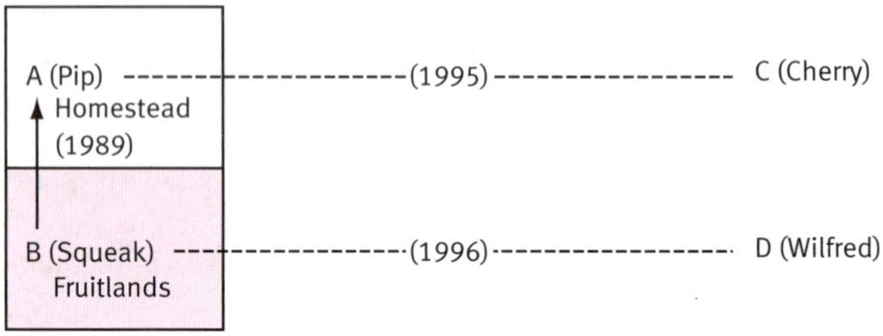

You will find it useful to consider the benefit and burden separately. In the absence of any evidence in the problem of any assignment of the benefit, the only issue to consider on the benefit side is whether the benefit has been effectively annexed. Annexation has caused much difficulty in recent years. It would have been simpler if equity had simply followed the law, and treated the benefit as being annexed to the land in those cases in which it can pass at common law. However, at least in the past, it appeared that the equitable rules relating to annexation were different from, and (unfortunately) more technical than, the rules relating to annexation at common law (see ***Rogers v Hosegood* [1900] 2 Ch 388**, and ***Re Ballard's Conveyance* [1937] 1 Ch 473**). ***Federated Homes Ltd v Mill Lodge Properties Ltd* [1980] 1 WLR 594** may have changed this, both by extending the scope of implied annexation in the **Law of Property Act 1925, s. 78**, and by casting doubt upon the correctness of ***Re Ballard's Conveyance***. The decision in ***Federated Homes*** has also considerably reduced the importance of assignment.

Most candidates will be able to point out that the burden of covenants cannot run at common law, whereas the burden of negative covenants is enforceable in equity against most persons coming to the land, provided equity's other requirements are met. The student should not, however, forget that the effect of the common law rule is that the original covenantor remains liable in damages for breaches of covenant which occur even after he has conveyed the burdened land. Although Cherry's bringing an action for damages against Squeak for breach of the covenant to maintain the drainage ditches does not itself ensure that those ditches are repaired, it may indirectly (through a chain of covenants) have this effect.

The present question does not involve covenants entered into before 1926. These are subject to the **Conveyancing Act 1881, s. 58**, which deems (pre-1926) covenants relating to land to be made with the covenantee and his *assigns*. This was assumed to mean assigns of the *covenant*, rather than of the land—a view confirmed in ***J. Sainsbury plc v Enfield LBC* [1989] 1 WLR 590**. For annexation to occur, it was therefore still considered necessary that the covenant itself used words indicating an intention that the benefit was to run with the land. Such intention was evinced by words indicating that the covenant was to enure for the benefit the covenantees, their assigns and others claiming under them as owners of the lands for the benefit of which the covenant was taken (***Rogers v Hosegood* [1900] 2 Ch 388**).

Post-1925 covenants, such as the one in the present problem, are governed by the **Law of Property Act 1925, s. 78**. This deems a covenant relating to land of the covenantee to be made with the covenantee and (*inter alia*) his successors in title. This expression is deemed to include the owners and occupiers for the time being of the *land* of the covenantee intended to be benefited. Given the clear difference in wording between this section and that of its predecessor of 1881, it is hardly surprising that the Court of Appeal in ***Federated Homes*** considered that the law relating to annexation had been changed by **s. 78**.

A final point for candidates to note is the date the covenants were entered into. Since this was in 1989, the **Contracts (Rights of Third Parties) Act 1999** does not apply to them.

Answer plan

Drainage covenant (*positive* covenant)

- Burden cannot run at common law or in equity.
- If benefit runs at common law, C can sue S for damages:
  - requirements for running of benefit at common law:
  - annexation (**LPA 1925, s. 78** and ***Federated Homes***);
  - chain of indemnity covenants?

Agricultural covenant (*negative* covenant)

- Burden can run to W in equity if certain conditions met (***Tulk v Moxhay***):
  - intention that burden run (**LPA 1925, s. 79**).
- Does *benefit* pass to C in equity:
  - equitable annexation (**LPA 1925, s. 78** and ***Federated Homes***);
  - annexation to each and every part (***Ballard***, ***Federated Homes***)?
- If both benefit and burden run, C can obtain injunction against W.

Suggested answer

Neither Cherry nor Wilfred were the original parties to the covenants contained in the conveyance of 1989. If, therefore, Cherry is to obtain injunctive relief against Wilfred for breach of either covenant, he must establish both that he is entitled to the benefit of each covenant and that Wilfred is subject to the burden of each.

The initial problem for Cherry is that, at common law, the burden of a covenant does not run with the burdened land (*Austerberry v Corporation of Oldham* (1885) 29 ChD 750 (CA), affirmed by the House of Lords in *Rhone v Stephens* [1994] 2 AC 310). Neither covenant therefore binds Wilfred at common law. In equity, the burden of a covenant can bind (*inter alia*) the covenantor's successor in title, but only if the covenant is negative in substance and the other requirements of the rule in

Tulk v Moxhay (1848) 2 Ph 774 are satisfied. A positive covenant (i.e. one which requires the expenditure of money to prevent its being breached) cannot be enforced against such successor in equity. The covenant to maintain the drainage ditches is clearly a positive covenant as it requires expenditure of money. Thus, regardless of whether he can show that the benefit of the covenant has passed to him, Cherry will not be able to compel Wilfred to maintain the ditches.

The corollary of the principle of *Austerberry v Corporation of Oldham* is that the original covenantor remains liable on a covenant at common law even after he has parted with the land. Cherry will therefore be able to sue Squeak for damages for breach of covenant (a) if he can show that he has acquired the benefit of such covenant at common law.

In order for the benefit of a covenant (whether positive or negative) to run with the land at common law (i.e. to be annexed to the land), the covenant must satisfy several requirements. First, it must touch and concern the covenantee's land; evidence that the value or occupation of Homestead is improved by the restriction upon the user of Fruitlands will suffice. Secondly, both the covenantee and his successor in title must have a legal estate in such land; this is clearly the case here. Thirdly, there must be an intention when the covenant is made that the benefit is to run with the land.

This third requirement has been the subject of much recent judicial analysis. The Law of Property Act 1925, s. 78, deems a covenant relating to land of the covenantee to be made with the covenantee and (*inter alia*) his successors in title, which expression is deemed to include the owners and occupiers for the time being of the land of the covenantee intended to be benefited. It does not, therefore, matter that Squeak expressly covenanted with Pip alone, because Pip's successors in title are statutorily included: *Federated Homes v Mill Lodge Properties Ltd* [1980] 1 WLR 594. The section does not apply where the covenant makes it clear that the benefit is not annexed (*Roake v Chadha* [1984] 1 WLR 40), but no such exclusion is contained in the covenant entered into by Squeak. The Court of Appeal in the *Federated Homes* case left open, however, the question of whether the covenant must identify the benefited land by express words or by necessary implication, or whether it is sufficient if the identity of the benefited land can be gleaned from the document itself or from evidence outside the document. In the more recent decision in *Crest Nicholson Residential (South) Ltd v McAllister* [2004] 2 EGLR 79, the Court of Appeal held that the former interpretation is the correct one. Thus, in the *Crest* case itself, it was held that the benefit of restrictive covenants had not been annexed by conveyances that did not identify the benefited land. A case where there had been sufficient identification was *Whitgift Homes Ltd v Stocks* [2001] 48 EG 130 (CS), where the reference in the conveyances was to 'the Vendor's Estate at Croydon'. The expression 'for the benefit of the Pip's adjoining land', which is similar to the descriptions used both in *Federated Homes* and in *Rogers v Hosegood* [1900] 2 Ch 388, is therefore sufficient to effect annexation.

Cherry can therefore sue Squeak, the original covenantor, for damages for breach of the covenant. If, as would be usual, Squeak obtained an indemnity covenant from

Wilfred when he conveyed Fruitlands to Wilfred, Cherry's threat to sue Squeak for damages, which would in turn induce Squeak to sue Wilfred for damages, might be sufficient to induce Wilfred to repair the ditches. No such indirect method of enforcement will avail Cherry, however, if Squeak did not take an indemnity covenant, or if he is untraceable or bankrupt, or if he has died and his estate has been wound up.

Covenant (b), by contrast, is negative in substance, so Cherry may be able to obtain an injunction against Wilfred to prevent the building under the doctrine of *Tulk v Moxhay* (1848) 2 Ph 774. For this to occur, it must be shown that the original parties to the covenant intended that the burden of the covenant should run with the land of the covenantor. Although Squeak appears to have expressly covenanted on his own behalf only, the effect of the Law of Property Act 1925, s. 79, is (subject to a contrary intention) to treat the covenant as being made by the covenantor on behalf of himself and (*inter alia*) his successors in title. Assuming there are no other covenants made by Squeak specifically for himself and his successors in title, which might then give rise to an inference that a covenant with him alone was not intended to bind successors (*Morrells Ltd v Oxford United Football Club Ltd* [2001] Ch 459), then this requirement is also met. If covenant (b) satisfies these and the other requirements for *Tulk v Moxhay* (1848) 2 Ph 774 (i.e. that it touches and concerns the land, and was taken for the benefit of the covenantee's land), it will be binding upon Wilfred since it was protected by registration as a land charge. Had the title to Fruitlands been registered, the covenant would have been protected if it had been registered as a minor interest in the charges register of the title at the HM Land Registry for the area.

As Cherry must rely upon the rules in equity to pass the burden of the covenant he will also have to establish that the benefit of covenant (b) has been passed to him in equity. Broadly, the requirements for equitable annexation are the same as those for annexation at common law, discussed above, except that in equity it suffices if the claimant has merely an equitable interest in the benefited land. In *Federated Homes*, the burdened land remained in the ownership of the covenantor. Nevertheless, because the claimant sought an injunction, an equitable remedy, the case appears to have concerned annexation in equity. In any event, in *Roake v Chadha*, where there had been a change in the ownership of the burdened land, the judge proceeded on the basis that the principle in *Federated Homes* was equally applicable to annexation in equity (see Todd [1984] *Conv* 68). It is therefore likely that the benefit of covenant (b) has been annexed in equity.

An additional complexity in relation to equitable annexation was, however, added in *Re Ballard's Conveyance* [1937] 1 Ch 473, in which Clauson J held that if the benefit of the covenant were expressed to be for the benefit of the vendor's retained land, it would not be annexed to each part of it. Therefore, unless the covenant touched and concerned the whole land, there would be no annexation at all. Since Homestead presumably comprises some 2,500 acres, the absence of appropriate words of annexation to each and every part would appear to be fatal to Cherry.

However, Brightman LJ in *Federated Homes* cast doubt on the soundness of the reasoning in *Ballard*, and considered it inconsistent with both *Williams v Unit Construction*

Co Ltd (1951) 19 *Conv* 262 and *Smith and Snipe's Hall Farm v River Douglas Catchment Board* [1949] 2 KB 500 (although these both concerned annexation at common law). Brightman LJ's *dicta* are more sensible, and will probably be followed. It would therefore seem that the benefit of covenant (b) has been annexed in equity to Homestead, and is enforceable by Cherry, who will be able to prevent Wilfred from building.

Question 2

In 1974 Clifford, the fee simple owner of Whiteacre, the title to which was unregistered, conveyed part of it to Arlington. In the conveyance, Arlington covenanted on behalf of himself and his successors in title with Clifford and with the other owners for the time being of land adjoining Whiteacre not to use the land thereby conveyed to him (*inter alia*) as a fish-and-chip shop. The conveyance expressly stated that the benefit of the covenant was not to pass to any subsequent owner of the benefited land except by assignment.

At the time of the conveyance from Clifford to Arlington, Buckingham was the fee simple owner of an adjacent plot, Blackacre. In 1980, Buckingham conveyed Blackacre to Ashley. This conveyance did not contain an express assignment of the benefit of Arlington's covenant; but in the negotiations preceding the conveyance to Ashley, Buckingham represented to Ashley that he would have the right to enforce the covenant.

In 1985, Arlington conveyed his part of Whiteacre to Lauderdale, who has recently expressed the intention of opening a fish-and-chip shop on that land. Ashley died last month. By his will, he gave all his property to Godolphin, whom he also appointed his executor.

Advise Godolphin if he can prevent Lauderdale from opening the fish-and-chip shop.

Commentary

As in the previous question, both the benefited and the burdened land have been assigned. Since the covenant is negative in substance, the answer needs to state that the burden can be enforced against Lauderdale, the successor in title to the original covenantor, provided it was protected by registration. This question is, however, primarily concerned with the passing of the benefit and whether the benefit of the covenant has passed to, and is enforceable by, Godolphin. This requires showing that the benefit of the covenant was acquired by Buckingham in the first place (explaining the impact of the **Law of Property Act 1925, s. 56**), and was then passed on from him to Ashley (by assignment), and then from Ashley to Godolphin (through operation of law). Annexation, it should be noted, is inapplicable, both because no benefited land is identified (***Crest Nicholson Residential (South) Ltd v McAllister* [2004] EWCA Civ 410**) and because it is, in any event, expressly excluded by the wording of the covenant, as it was in ***Roake v Chadha* [1984] 1 WLR 40**. You should not therefore spend too long on annexation: it is sufficient to show why it is that annexation cannot be relied upon in this question.

Since the covenant was entered into in 1974, the **Contracts (Rights of Third Parties) Act 1999** does not apply to it.

Answer plan

Passing of burden of negative covenant

- Requirements for running of burden in equity.
- Protection as a Class D (ii) land charge?

Passing of benefit in equity to Ashley?

- As original covenantee (**LPA 1925, s. 56**)?
- As successor in title:
  - annexation (ibid., **s. 78**) excluded;
  - assignment (express or implied)?

Passing of benefit in equity from Ashley to Godolphin?

- Assignment by operation of law?
- Implied assignment?

Suggested answer

If Godolphin is to succeed, he must establish both that Lauderdale is subject to the burden of the covenant, and that he has himself acquired, and is entitled to enforce, the benefit of the covenant (*Dano Ltd v 8th Earl of Cadogan* [2003] EWHC 239 (Ch)). As the burden of a covenant will never pass at common law (*Rhone v Stephens* [1994] 2 AC 310), it will be necessary to consider the rules for the passing of the burden and the benefit in equity.

First, the burden. Since the covenant in the problem is negative in substance, it may bind Lauderdale, as successor in title to the original covenantor, under the doctrine of *Tulk v Moxhay* (1848) 2 Ph 774. For this doctrine to operate, the covenantee (or his successors) must, both at the time of the covenant and subsequently, own nearby land for the protection of which the covenant was entered into—which is the case here. The restrictive covenant must also 'touch and concern' the dominant land, i.e. affect its mode of occupation or value. This requirement may also be satisfied, if, for example, it may be inferred that the covenant was taken in order to benefit Whiteacre and adjoining plots from the smells emanating from a fish-and-chip shop. Evidence may therefore be needed to show whether Blackacre is in fact capable of benefiting from such covenant. It must also be shown that the burden was intended to run with the land: this is satisfied by Arlington's having covenanted on behalf of himself and his successors in title.

Even if these requirements are met, however, if Lauderdale was a purchaser of the legal estate for money or money's worth, he will still take free of the covenant unless it was registered against the name of the estate owner of the burdened land, Arlington, before the completion of his purchase, as a land charge, Class D(ii). This is the case even if, at that time, he knew of the covenant's existence (*Midland Bank Trust Co. v Green* [1981] AC 513).

Secondly, the benefit. If Godolphin has to show the passing of the burden of the covenant in equity and is to enforce the covenant by means of an injunction against Lauderdale, he must show that he has acquired the benefit of the covenant in equity. This requires him to establish that he acquired it as Ashley's executor, and that Ashley had in turn himself acquired it from Buckingham.

Buckingham was not named as a party to the 1974 conveyance, i.e. he was not an express covenantee. Nevertheless, by virtue of the Law of Property Act 1925, s. 56, a person may take (*inter alia*) the benefit of any covenant respecting land, although he be not named as a party to the conveyance. In effect, the section enables a person who could have been a party to the conveyance to be an original covenantee, provided that he can be identified. In *Re Ecclesiastical Commissioners for England's Conveyance* [1936] Ch 430, where the covenant was made (*inter alia*) for the benefit of the owners for the time being of land adjacent to that conveyed, it was held that such owners, being identifiable, could have enforced the covenant. It would therefore seem that, since he can be similarly identified from the wording of the covenant, Buckingham, as owner for the time being of land adjoining Whiteacre, could likewise have enforced the covenant made by Arlington.

Only owners for the time being can take the benefit of the LPA 1925, s. 56, and this therefore excludes Ashley, who acquired Blackacre only subsequently. It might be argued that the benefit passed to him through annexation under the LPA 1925, s. 78(1), which deems a covenant relating to any land of the covenantee to be made with the covenantee and (*inter alia*) his successors in title. For two reasons, however, such an argument will fail. First, although the point was left open in *Federated Homes v Mill Lodge Properties Ltd.* [1980] 1 WLR 594, it has since been held that there can be statutory annexation under this section only where the benefited land is identifiable (as in *Federated Homes* itself), either expressly or by necessary implication, from the conveyance: *Crest Nicholson Residential (South) Ltd v McAllister* [2004] 2 EGLR 79. No benefited land is identifiable in this way in the conveyance from Clifford to Arlington. Secondly, it was held in *Roake v Chadha* [1984] 1 WLR 40 that, whilst s. 78 does not permit the range of persons with whom the covenant is made to be reduced, statutory annexation can be excluded by the covenant itself. The wording of the covenant in the problem, expressly limiting the passing of the benefit to assignment, has this effect. Annexation is therefore excluded.

If, therefore, the benefit of the covenant passed to Ashley, this can only have been through assignment. The requirements for a valid assignment in equity are five-fold, and were laid down by Romer LJ in *Miles v Easter* [1933] Ch 611, thus:

(a) the covenant must have been taken for the benefit of land of the covenantee;

(b) the land must be indicated with reasonable certainty;

(c) the dominant land must be retained in whole or in part by the plaintiff; and

(d) be capable of benefiting from the covenant; and

(e) the assignment of the covenant and the conveyance of the land to which it relates must be contemporaneous.

In the question the first three requirements of *Miles v Easter* appear to be satisfied. The fourth requirement is satisfied if the covenantee is thereby enabled to dispose of his land to advantage, i.e. if it increases the value of his land (*Miles v Easter* at p. 631). Assuming therefore (as discussed earlier) that the covenant 'touches and concerns' the benefited land, the fourth requirement is satisfied also.

Unless the assignment is contemporaneous with the conveyance—the fifth requirement—the benefit of the covenant is lost in equity. Thus, in the absence of an express assignment to Ashley, the fifth requirement is met only if a contemporaneous assignment can be implied. In *Miles v Easter* itself, there are conflicting *dicta*, both at first instance and in the Court of Appeal, regarding the need for the assignment to be (as in that case) express. Other authorities, however, suggest that the assignment may be implied, i.e. that it is enough that the vendor stated in the contract for the sale of the land, or represented to the purchaser in the negotiations preceding the sale, that the latter would have the right to enforce the covenant (*Renals v Cowlishaw* (1878) 9 ChD 125, at pp. 129–31, and *White v Bijou Mansions* [1937] Ch 610, at p. 622). It would therefore appear from the facts of the problem that Ashley acquired the benefit of the covenant by implied assignment effected at the same time as the conveyance to Ashley.

The final issue is therefore whether the benefit of the covenant has passed from Ashley to Godolphin. An express assignment by Ashley to Godolphin as his personal representative is obviously unnecessary. The benefit of the covenant is personal property of the deceased, and will pass to his executor by operation of law (*Ives v Brown* [1919] 2 Ch 314; *Newton Abbot Cooperative Society Ltd v Williamson and Treadgold Ltd* [1952] Ch 286). After he has administered the estate, Godolphin will, in due course, no doubt execute a vesting assent of the retained portion of Whiteacre in favour of himself (*Re King's Will Trusts* [1964] Ch 542) together with an assignment of the benefit of the covenant. Even if not expressly assigned to himself as beneficiary, the benefit of the covenant would presumably be thereby assigned impliedly. Indeed, even in the absence of an assignment in the strict sense, the same result would ensue were he treated as retaining the benefit of the covenant as executor, since he would be holding it on a bare trust for himself as beneficiary (cf. *Earl of Leicester v Wells-next-to-the-Sea UDC* [1973] Ch 110). Whatever his present capacity, therefore, Godolphin will be able to enforce the covenant.

Question 3

'The requirements for a building scheme are merely indicia of an intention to create a community of interest with reciprocity of obligation. Where such intention is found, equity is willing to read the covenants in the light of the surrounding facts. A building scheme is therefore no more than a species of implied annexation, and the law relating to such schemes is purely evidential. The notion of reciprocity of rights and obligations is the only characteristic which a building scheme shares with the doctrine of mutual benefits and burdens laid down in *Halsall v Brizell* [1957] Ch 169.'

Discuss.

Commentary

One or two questions on your examination paper may ask you to discuss a quotation. The quotation may be a genuine one; but sometimes (as here) it will have been specially written for the purposes of the question. It is always important to address every matter with which the quotation deals; and you should be prepared to disagree with statements which you consider incorrect—and, of course, to explain why.

In the present question, the examiner is evidently trying to elicit from you a discussion of the juridical basis underlying building schemes and the quotation itself usefully provides a ready-made structure for your answer. The quotation comprises four sentences and it will be seen that each of them requires you to deal with a distinct point. The first invites you to consider whether the requirements for a building scheme are indeed no more than indications of an intention to create a community of interest. The second calls for a discussion of equity's approach to the construction of covenants once a building scheme has been found. The third effectively asks you to consider whether a building scheme is no more than a form of implied annexation. The last expects you to compare the principles underlying building schemes with the doctrine of mutual benefits and burdens.

You are probably unlikely to have a question involving these issues unless your lectures or tutorials have directed you to consider them. The present method of approach, however, may be taken to apply to all questions which take the form of lengthy quotations. The examiner will probably see many scripts written by candidates who choose to ignore the substance of the quotation, and treat the question as if it began 'Write all you know about . . .'. Relatively few, in the writers' experience, will be the number of answers which really do seek to discuss the particular points raised in the light of the relevant law. For candidates prepared to apply and direct their knowledge, the higher marks are there just waiting to be earned.

Answer plan

- Traditional requirements for a building scheme (***Elliston v Reacher***).
- Equity's approach to construction of covenants in a scheme.

- Building scheme as a form of implied annexation.
- Comparison with doctrine of mutual benefits and burdens.

Suggested answer

The classic requirements for a building scheme (or scheme of development as it is sometimes known) were laid down by Parker J in *Elliston v Reacher* [1908] 2 Ch 374. The requirements are fivefold:

(a) the plaintiff and the defendant should have derived their titles from a common vendor;

(b) before the sale of the plots, the common vendor must have laid out his estate for sale in lots subject to restrictions intended to be imposed on all the lots;

(c) the restrictions were intended by the common vendor to be and were for the benefit of all the lots sold;

(d) the original purchasers must have bought their lots on the understanding that the restrictions were to enure for the benefit of the other lots; and

(e) (added in *Reid v Bickerstaff* [1909] 2 Ch 305) the geographical area to which the scheme extends must be clear.

In *Elliston v Reacher* Parker J considered that, where all the points were established, 'the community of interest imports in equity the reciprocity of obligation which is in fact contemplated by each at the time of his own purchase'. In more recent years, the courts have tended to emphasise this broader element of reciprocity (see *Brunner v Greenslade* [1971] Ch 993, and *Jamaica Mutual Life Assurance Society v Hillsborough Ltd* [1989] 1 WLR 1101). They have therefore been less concerned to find that all five requirements have been met. In *Baxter v Four Oaks Properties Ltd* [1965] Ch 816, for instance, Parker J's second requirement was not satisfied, but the court found an intention to create mutually binding covenants and held that this sufficed to create a scheme. Further, in *Re Dolphin's Conveyance* [1970] Ch 654, the court considered that both the first and second requirements were unnecessary. Nevertheless, an intention to create a community of interest with reciprocity of obligation is not in itself sufficient; the fifth requirement must always be met (*Lund v Taylor* (1975) 31 P & CR 167; *Jamaica Mutual Life*). The vendor may, however, retain the right to exempt part of his retained land from the stipulations (*Allen v Veranne Builders Ltd* [1988] (unreported)).

Where the requirements of a building scheme are met, the court simply treats the covenants as being mutually enforceable amongst the owners of the lots. This suggests that the basis for enforceability is something other than annexation or assignment—that building schemes create their own rights and obligations through the principle of reciprocity. Extrinsic evidence is admissible in order to show that the requirements, and the element of reciprocity, are present; such evidence could be of the parties' acts and statements before conveyance (which might include, for instance, details of sales advertisements), and even evidence from the common vendor's predecessor in title (*Kingsbury v LW Anderson Ltd* (1979) 40 P & CR 136).

It is sometimes contended that it is possible to achieve by a building scheme what cannot be achieved by annexation, i.e., the creation of reciprocal mutual rights amongst successive purchasers of lots. It is true that 'neither annexation nor assignment can enable the covenantee to distribute the benefits of later covenants to earlier purchasers' (Gray, *Elements of Land Law*, 4th edn, London: Butterworths, 2006). Even outside a building scheme, however, earlier purchasers can take the benefit of the covenants entered into by later purchasers if the covenants are expressed to be made, not merely with the common vendor for the benefit of his retained land, but also with existing owners of previously sold plots for the benefit of such plots (Law of Property Act 1925, s. 56). By this means, the benefit of later purchasers' covenants are annexed to the land of earlier purchasers.

If, however, in the foregoing circumstances, a building scheme exists, earlier purchasers can enforce in equity the covenants entered into by later purchasers even if they are not made covenantees under the Law of Property Act 1925, s. 56. An earlier purchaser's equity could be treated as arising merely through the application of the principle of reciprocity. It could, alternatively, be treated as deriving from covenant. Under the latter analysis, where equity finds an intention to create mutually enforceable obligations, it will readily infer the intention to make earlier purchasers original covenantees of later purchasers' covenants and to annex the benefit to their land.

Implied annexation therefore means that, once there is sufficient evidence to show the existence of the scheme itself, extrinsic (or further extrinsic) evidence can be used to show that the covenants are annexed to the land. The older cases proceeded on this footing, and established that, where a building scheme exists, the court will construe the covenants with a view to ensuring that the benefit of each purchaser's covenant is annexed to the lots of all the others (*Spicer v Martin* (1889) 14 App Cas 12, HL). Similarly, in *Rogers v Hosegood* [1900] 2 Ch 388, both Farwell J (at first instance) and the Court of Appeal treated a building scheme as merely exemplifying the general rule that a deed is to be construed in the light of surrounding circumstances (see Bailey [1938] *CLJ* 339, at p. 364).

Although implied annexation appears to explain the earlier decisions on building schemes, the importance attached in modern times to the underlying principle of reciprocity of obligations has made it more difficult to reconcile some recent cases with any form of annexation. Thus, it has been held that, if two or more of the lots come into common ownership, the covenants are not destroyed, but will, upon severance, become once again enforceable amongst their owners *inter se* (*Brunner v Greenslade; Texaco Antilles Ltd v Kernochan* [1973] AC 609, PC). Furthermore, a Commonwealth court has expressed its preparedness to uphold a building scheme purely on the basis of intention, even if the conveyances contain not a single covenant (*Re Louis and the Conveyancing Act* [1971] 1 NSWLR 164).

The law relating to building schemes appears therefore to have outgrown its origins in the equitable rules pertaining to the construction of deeds. In this respect, its development is not unlike that of the doctrine of mutual benefits and burdens. This doctrine also developed from a principle relating to deeds, namely that if a person is named as a party to a deed and takes a benefit under it with knowledge of the facts, then he is bound by it, even though he does not execute it (*R v Houghton-le-Spring* (1819) 2 B & Ald 375). From this narrow basis, the law moved a long way so that, in *Tito v Waddell (No. 2)* [1977] Ch 106, at pp. 301–3, Megarry V-C was able to refer to the 'pure principle' of benefits and burdens, namely that a person who takes the benefit of a deed must also take it subject to the burdens it contains. In *Rhone v Stephens* [1994] 2 AC 310, however, the House of Lords retreated from such wide formulation, and stated that the doctrine can apply only where the benefits and burdens are reciprocal and not independent of each other; the benefit cannot therefore be the whole benefit taken under the deed. Even within such confines, however, the doctrine can result in a subsequent purchaser of land being bound by a covenant made by a predecessor in title (*Hopgood v Brown* [1955] 1 WLR 213).

As the quotation states, the notion of reciprocity of obligations underpins both building schemes and the doctrine of mutual benefits and burdens, but there are considerable differences. First, a purchaser of a lot subject to a building scheme cannot escape from the obligations it imposes by choosing to forego the benefits it confers; whereas a purchaser who does not wish to take a benefit under a deed cannot be subjected to a reciprocal burden. Secondly, the only obligations that can be enforced in a building scheme are those which are negative or restrictive in nature; whereas, under the mutual benefits and burdens doctrine, even a positive obligation (such as the payment of a levy for the use of roads and sewers as in *Halsall v Brizell* itself) can be enforced. Thirdly, the obligations imposed by a building scheme are probably enforceable against subsequent purchasers only if protected by registration as a land charge or by notice; whereas the burdens imposed by the doctrine of *Halsall v Brizell* are not, as such, registrable as land charges (*Hopgood v Brown*).

Question 4

Two years ago, Isabella purchased Udolpho, a large freehold property with extensive gardens in Gloucestershire. The property was subject to a restrictive covenant created in 1900 in favour of the owners of the adjoining properties and their successors in title. By the terms of the covenant, no further buildings were to be erected on Udolpho. Isabella, however, recently obtained planning permission to build a block of flats in the back garden of Udolpho.

The owners of adjoining properties, Catherine and Eleanor, have threatened to seek an injunction to prevent the building in breach of the covenant. Catherine is concerned that any building in the back garden of Udolpho would prevent her house receiving the benefit of

evening sunshine. Although Eleanor's property does not itself enjoy a view over the valley, she is concerned that the building would obstruct the view of the valley from a lane one hundred yards from her property. This spot affords a prospect of Northanger Abbey surrounded by extensive oak woods. Isabella feels inclined to ignore her neighbours' objections and to begin the work of construction.

Advise Isabella.

Commentary

This question is concerned both with the remedies for a breach (or a threatened breach) of a restrictive covenant and also with the possible means by which such a covenant might be discharged. The latter aspect mostly involves going through the relevant grounds in the **Law of Property Act 1925, s. 84** explaining how they have been interpreted by the courts, and applying them to the facts. The point of view, it should be noted, is that of the successor in title to the covenantor, rather than that of the objectors. Candidates who have worked at this area, particularly if they have their statute book (rather than a laundry list) in the examination room, should not find this question the Gothic horror that it might otherwise be.

A useful note on the benefit of a view in relation to an application to discharge or modify a restrictive covenant is Polden, 'Views in Perspective' [1984] *Conv* 429.

Answer plan

- Criteria for award of damages in lieu of an injunction.
- Discharge or modification of restrictive covenant:
  - alteration in character of neighbourhood (***Chatsworth Estates Co. v Fewell***) ;
  - acquiescence (***Gafford v Graham***);
  - application to Lands Tribunal under **LPA 1925, s. 84**:
  - statutory criteria:

    para (a) (obsolete?);
    para (aa) (impede reasonable user?) provided:
    secures practical benefits of substantial value or advantage;
    or contrary to the public interest; and
    plus money adequate compensation?

Suggested answer

The proposed building would breach the restrictive covenant; so that, assuming the covenant is binding upon Isabella, and that the benefit of it has passed to Catherine and Eleanor (or to either of them), they could seek an injunction against Isabella to prevent her building. If Isabella were unwise enough to begin building in breach of the covenant, Catherine or Eleanor could seek a mandatory injunction requiring her to demolish any building put up in breach.

Where a restrictive covenant is breached, the court has had power (since the Chancery Amendment Act 1858) to award damages in lieu of an injunction. In a case of nuisance, it has been laid down that damages in lieu of an injunction will be awarded only if the injury to the claimant's legal rights is small, if it can be estimated in money, if it can be adequately compensated by a small money payment, and if it would be oppressive to the defendant to grant an injunction (*Shelfer v City of London Lighting Co Ltd* [1895] 1 Ch 287). In *Wakeham v Wood* (1981) 43 P & CR 40, CA, these criteria were held to apply to determine whether damages should be granted in lieu of an injunction where there had been a breach of a restrictive covenant. In that case, the defendant had flagrantly breached a covenant against building in a way that would obstruct a view of the sea. The Court of Appeal granted the plaintiffs a mandatory injunction, and Waller LJ expressed the opinion that the value of a view could not be estimated in monetary terms, and therefore could not be compensated by a small money payment. Although Eleanor's property does not itself enjoy the view, the court might adopt a similar stance. The value of evening sunshine to Catherine's property would similarly appear to be inestimable. Isabella would therefore be running a considerable risk should she begin building in breach of covenant.

A restrictive covenant cannot be enforced if the character of the neighbourhood has been so altered since the covenant was entered into that it is now of no value to the claimant and it would be inequitable and senseless to enforce it (*Chatsworth Estates Co. v Fewell* [1931] 1 Ch 224). These criteria are unlikely to be satisfied in the problem, since the benefit of the evening sunshine and the protection of the view are of continuing value to Catherine and Eleanor respectively. Also, if there have been long-standing breaches of the covenant in which the owners of the benefited land have acquiesced, they will be deemed to have waived the benefit of the covenant, but this would not seem to be applicable here.

If Isabella actually starts building and Catherine and Eleanor fail to make any interlocutory application for injunctive relief, then they may subsequently be restricted to the remedy of damages (*Gafford v Graham* [1999] 3 EGLR 75), such damages to be what Isabella might reasonably have been expected to pay for the lifting of the restriction (*Jaggard v Sawyer* [1995] 1 WLR 269, applying *Wrotham Park Estates Co Ltd v Parkside Homes Ltd* [1974] 1 WLR 798 and *Hugh Small v Oliver & Saunders (Developments) Ltd* [2006] EWHC 1293 (Ch)).

Isabella's best course of action, therefore, is to apply to the Lands Tribunal to have the covenant modified or discharged under the Law of Property Act 1925, s. 84, as amended by the Law of Property Act 1969. If it were to make an order discharging or modifying the restrictive covenant, the Tribunal could also direct Isabella to pay such consideration as it thinks just to any persons entitled to the benefit of the covenant—which could clearly include Catherine and Eleanor.

Before making any order, however, the Tribunal must be satisfied that one of several sets of circumstances is fulfilled, these being set out in the Law of Property Act 1925, s. 84(1) paras (a)–(c). The only paragraphs which might be relevant to the problem are (a) and (aa). The circumstances in para. (a) are that, by reason of the change in the character of the property or the neighbourhood or other material circumstances, the restriction ought to be deemed obsolete. Evidence of such changes in character would need to be produced; but, given that the covenant still protects the view over the valley and affords Catherine the benefit of evening sunshine, it is unlikely that Isabella will succeed under this paragraph.

Isabella might be able to make out a better case under para. (aa), which was added by the Law of Property Act 1969. This paragraph enables the Tribunal to discharge or modify the covenant if its continued existence would (or unless modified would) impede some reasonable user of the land. The Lands Tribunal may not discharge or modify the covenant under this paragraph, however, unless it is satisfied that the restriction does not secure to persons entitled to the benefit of it any practical benefits of substantial value or advantage to them, or is contrary to the public interest. It must also be satisfied that, in either case, money will be an adequate compensation for any loss or disadvantage that any such persons will suffer from the discharge or modification: Law of Property Act 1925, s. 84(1A). In determining whether a case falls within s. 84(1A) and whether a restriction ought to be discharged or modified, the Lands Tribunal must take into account (*inter alia*) the development plan and any pattern for the grant or refusal of planning permission in the relevant areas.

The fact that Isabella has obtained planning permission to erect the block of flats is persuasive (but not decisive) evidence that the proposed user is reasonable (*Re Bass Ltd's Application* (1973) 26 P & CR 156). Assuming that the covenant impedes that user, the next matter to be determined (in accordance with *Re Bass*) is whether the proposed user secures practical benefits to the objectors. In *Re Bellamy's Application* (1977) JPL 456 the enjoyment of evening sunshine in a sun-lounge was held to be a practical benefit. A view can also be a practical benefit (*Gilbert v Spoor* [1983] Ch 27).

Although Eleanor does not have a view over the valley from her property, the view from the road near her property may enhance the enjoyment of her property. In *Gilbert v Spoor* [1983] Ch 27, a similar objection was made: namely, that the building would obscure a view enjoyed only from a road adjoining the objectors' property. The Court of Appeal rejected the argument that the benefit sought to be protected must be one that is capable of touching and concerning the benefited land; although, on the facts, it concluded that the covenant did touch and concern the objectors' land. In the problem, therefore, it would be open to the Tribunal to find that the view from the road is a practical benefit to Eleanor.

If this requirement is met, the Tribunal must then be satisfied that the benefits secured by the restrictive covenant are of substantial 'value or advantage'—a phrase which indicates that money value is not the only thing to be taken into account (*Re Bass*). In *Re Banks' Application* (1976) 33 P & CR 138 it was stated that a direct view of the sea was of immense value, and, in *Gilbert v Spoor* Eveleigh LJ considered that a power to preserve a magnificent view was of substantial value or advantage. If, as appears from the problem, the view over the valley is a particularly fine one, and the lane is easily accessible, this criterion might also be met. The enjoyment of evening sunshine is also capable of satisfying this criterion. It is essentially a matter of fact for the Tribunal. Evidence that the objector has never personally admired the view, though relevant, is not fatal to the objection (*Gilbert v Spoor*).

It is very difficult to establish that the continued existence of the covenant is contrary to the public interest: in only two applications has such argument succeeded. In the first, *Re SJC Construction Co Ltd's Application* (1974) 28 P & CR 200, there was a scarcity of building land, and unless the restriction were modified, £47,000 worth of building work would have to be destroyed. In the light of *Wakeham v Wood* (discussed above), the latter factor may now be of lesser significance. In the second, *Re Lloyd's and Lloyd's Application* (1993) 66 P & CR 112, a user covenant was modified to permit the premises to be used as a community care home. The restriction was considered contrary to the public interest because of the government's policy of care in the community and the acute need for such a home in the area. There is nothing in the problem, however, to suggest that a public interest argument could be made out there.

Finally, if the Tribunal finds that the restriction does not secure practical benefits of substantial value or advantage, it must consider whether money will be an adequate compensation to the objector. In *Re Carter's Application* (1973) 25 P & CR 542 a covenant against erecting more than one dwelling-house on the plot was modified to permit infilling with a bungalow. The objectors' properties enjoyed merely glimpses of the sea, which was held not to be a substantial value or advantage. The objectors were awarded compensation of between £100 and £200. The applicant's offer to reduce the height of the bungalow by 2 ft 6in was made a condition of the modification order.

If, therefore, the benefits of the view and evening sunshine are held not to comprise practical benefits of substantial value or advantage, it will be open to the Tribunal to discharge or modify the covenant, and to require Isabella to pay compensation to Catherine and Eleanor. It might also assist Isabella's application in such circumstances if she is prepared to modify her building plans so that the view and the sunshine, whilst reduced, are not entirely lost. It is completely at the discretion of the Lands Tribunal whether to order modification or discharge of a restrictive covenant (*Re University of Westminster's Application* [1997] 1 EGLR 191). If, however, the restriction is considered to secure practical benefits of substantial value or advantage, the Tribunal cannot permit discharge or modification of the covenant, even on payment of large amounts of compensation.

Further reading

Burn, E.H., and Cartwright, J., *Cheshire and Burn's Modern Law of Real Property*, 17th edn, Oxford, 2006, chapter 19.

MacKenzie, J. A., and Phillips, M., *Textbook on Land Law*, 12th edn, Oxford University Press, 2008.

14

Mortgages

The law of mortgages is a topic usually dealt with towards the end of a land law course. This is because you need first to understand leases, land charges and the difference between legal and equitable interests, which are all relevant to mortgages.

For a really sound understanding of the subject, some slight background knowledge of the nature of mortgages before 1926, and of how and why equity intervened to assist the oppressed mortgagor, will be an advantage. This is touched upon in Question 1(a), which also describes the relevant provisions of the Law of Property Act 1925 (LPA 1925) and the Land Registration Act 2002 (LRA 2002). The different ways in which an equitable mortgage of freehold land may be created are dealt with in Question 4, which also considers the remedies available to such an equitable mortgagee.

The two main topics for questions on mortgages are probably restrictions on the equity of redemption ('clogs' on the equity), and the remedies of a mortgagee in the event of the mortgagor defaulting.

The first topic has been subject to a considerable change in the attitude of the courts since the early cases, where it was established that equity would intervene to mitigate the harshness of a bargain forced upon an oppressed mortgagor. Cases such as *Knightsbridge Estates Trust Ltd v Byrne* [1939] Ch 441 and *Kreglinger v New Patagonia Meat & Cold Storage Co Ltd* [1914] AC 25, referred to in Question 2, reflect a readiness by the courts to perceive a mortgage as part of a wider commercial transaction where appropriate; they have been prepared to depart from the strict maxims of equity against clogs on the equity of redemption where they have felt that they operated unfairly.

A mortgagee's remedies on default of the mortgagor are to be found in both case law and statute law. The recession of the early 1990s led to an unprecedented decline in property values, and led to some interesting adaptations of the power of sale in cases such as *Palk v Mortgage Services Funding plc* [1993] Ch 330 and *Target Home Loans Ltd v Clothier & Clothier* (1992) 25 HLR 48, referred to in Question 3. There have been cases on a mortgagee's or receiver's duties on a sale, and an entirely new interpretation of 'reasonable time' in s. 36, Administration of Justice Act 1970 (*Cheltenham & Gloucester Building Society v Norgan* [1996] 1 WLR 343).

Question 5 highlights a problem area for mortgagees which arises from co-ownership of, and sureties for, mortgaged property. There has been a steady stream of cases in the wake of the House of Lords' decision in *Barclays Bank plc v O'Brien* [1994] 1 AC 180. This is hardly surprising given that what is at stake is the co-mortgagor's or surety's home, and that the validity of the mortgage against a lender depends upon two factors which necessarily have to be determined on the particular facts of each case—that the co-mortgagor or surety was acting under the undue influence of the borrower (dispelled or not by the advice which they received), and that the lender had notice (constructive or imputed) of this. The decision in *Royal Bank of Scotland v Etridge (No. 2)* [2002] 2 AC 773 on undue influence forms the basis of the question.

Question 1

(a) Discuss the ways in which a legal mortgage may now be created in registered land.

(b) David is the tenant of a 50-year lease of a shop. Five years ago, he borrowed £20,000 from Quickslip Bank plc in order to expand his business, and the sum was secured by a legal charge on the leasehold property. Quickslip Bank plc have recently discovered that David has had financial problems, as a result of which he had become in arrears with his rent, and the landlord has forfeited the lease. The landlord says that he had no notice of the mortgage to Quickslip Bank plc, and that the mortgage would, in any event, have been prohibited by the terms of the lease, which includes a covenant not to assign or sublet without first obtaining the landlord's consent in writing.

Advise Quickslip Bank plc.

Commentary

Mortgages of registered land can be made only by a legal charge: **s. 23(1)(a), LRA 2002** prohibits mortgages made by demise or subdemise. Nevertheless, the legal charge is not complete and freestanding in its own right, and reference must be made to **s. 87(1), LPA 1925** for the powers and remedies of a mortgagee by way of legal charge. Part **(b)** concerns forfeiture of a lease and its effect on the mortgagee. It also raises a problem which has beset mortgagees of leaseholds who may not have notice of forfeiture proceedings brought by a landlord until it is too late.

Answer plan

(a) • Creation of mortgage: charge by way of legal mortgage.

(b) • Possible breach of covenant against assignment and subletting.

- Effect of **s. 146(4) LPA 1925**.
- Method of forfeiture.
- Relief from forfeiture in equity.

Suggested answer

(a) Important changes to mortgages of registered land were introduced in the LRA 2002. Since the date that Act came into force (13 October 2003), a legal mortgage of registered land (whether freehold or leasehold) can be created *only* by legal charge: LRA 2002, s. 23(1)(a). However, although the method of mortgaging by demise can no longer be used, this makes little practical difference, since even before the 2002 Act came into force, mortgages were virtually always made by legal charge. If a registered proprietor were now to attempt to create a mortgage by demise, the registrar would simply reject the application for registration.

A charge does not transfer any legal estate to the mortgagee, but merely designates certain property as security for the debt. However, the LPA 1925, s. 87(1) gives to a mortgagee by way of legal charge 'the same protection, powers and remedies' as if he were a mortgagee by way of demise. His position is further strengthened by the inclusion of charge by deed by way of legal mortgage as a legal interest in the LPA 1925, s. 1(2).

The charge takes effect as a *legal* charge only on registration: LRA 2002, s. 27(1), (2)(f). The chargee must therefore be entered in the register as the proprietor of the charge: LRA 2002, Schedule 2, para. 8. Until registration, the charge takes effect only in equity, and so needs to be protected by a notice on the charges register. Failure to register the legal charge leaves the chargee at risk of being subject to subsequently created legal estates and interests: *Barclays Bank plc v Zaroovabli* [1997] Ch 321. This is another instance of the registration gap, which will disappear when e-conveyancing is introduced, so that the creation and registration of the legal charge will be simultaneous.

(b) A legal charge of the leasehold property does not constitute a breach of a covenant against assignment or subletting as it is not a disposal of the leasehold term. Therefore, unless the covenant in the lease were more comprehensive and specifically mentioned charging, the execution of the legal charge to Quickslip Bank plc by David will not be a breach of this covenant.

The LPA 1925, s. 146(4), states that, where the lessor is proceeding by action or otherwise to forfeit a lease for breach of covenant or for non-payment of rent, an underlessee, including an underlessee by way of mortgage, may apply to the court to have the lessee's estate vested in him upon such conditions as the court thinks fit. If the court makes such an order, a new lease is created between the lessor and the underlessee or mortgagee. Although Quickslip has a mortgage by way of legal charge, it has a right to apply under this subsection, because the LPA 1925, s. 87(1), gives a mortgagee by way of legal charge the same 'protection, powers and remedies' as a mortgagee by way of demise or subdemise (*Grand Junction Ltd v Bates* [1954] 2 QB 160).

The problem does not state whether the landlord forfeited the lease pursuant to a court order or merely by taking peaceable re-entry. The method of forfeiture is, however, crucial to Quickslip, because it has a right to apply for relief under the LPA 1925, s. 146(4), only while the landlord is 'proceeding by action or otherwise' to forfeit the lease. Similar words are used in s. 146(2), which enables relief to be sought by the tenant. It has been held that, once a landlord has re-entered pursuant to a court order, he is no longer 'proceeding', so that the tenant's right to seek relief under s. 146(2) is lost (*Rogers v Rice* [1892] 2 Ch 170). However, if the landlord re-enters peaceably without a court order, he can still be considered to be 'proceeding' and the tenant is not precluded from applying for relief (*Billson v Residential Apartments Ltd* [1992] AC 494). Given the similarity of the wording of the two subsections, the same principles probably govern the right of a mortgagee to seek relief under s. 146(4).

Where the forfeiture is made for non-payment of rent, other forms of relief may be available to the mortgagee. If the landlord has re-entered pursuant to an order of the High Court under the Common Law Procedure Act 1852, s. 210, the mortgagee has six months after such entry to apply for relief. Such relief, if granted, takes the form of a new lease; but it will be granted only if the mortgagee pays all the arrears of rent, costs and damages. At the end of six months, the right to apply for relief is barred.

The Common Law Procedure Act 1852 applies, however, only if all the requirements of s. 210 are satisfied, and one such requirement is that the rent is six months or more in arrears. If, therefore, the arrears were less, the mortgagee's right to apply for relief derives from the equitable jurisdiction of the Court of Chancery, now exercisable by the High Court under the Senior Courts Act 1981, s. 38(1). Relief under this section will also be available if the landlord peaceably re-enters. The court will generally require an application to be made within six months of re-entry but it may accept an application made slightly after such period (*Thatcher v C. H. Pearce & Sons (Contractors) Ltd* [1968] 1 WLR 748, where the application was permitted even though made six months and four days after re-entry).

If the landlord has re-entered for non-payment of rent pursuant to an order of a county court, an underlessee (including a mortgagee) may apply for relief under the County Courts Act 1984, s. 138. The application for relief must be made within six months of the re-entry (County Courts Act 1984, s. 138(9A)). The High Court has no inherent jurisdiction to relieve a mortgagee whose application is made after the statutory period of six months (*United Dominion Trust Ltd v Shellpoint Trustees* [1993] 35 EG 121, CA).

The problem contains, however, one further twist, as it would appear that the Quickslip Bank plc did not receive any notification of the landlord's forfeiture proceedings. A landlord seeking an order of forfeiture from the High Court is obliged (under the Civil Procedure Rules) to serve a copy of the proceedings upon any underlessee or mortgagee of whom it is aware. A parallel obligation applies if the landlord is proceeding in a county court. These rules do not help Quickslip if the landlord had not been notified of Quickslip's legal charge. If, however, the landlord had been notified, and nevertheless failed to serve a copy of the proceedings upon Quickslip, the latter may be able to apply for relief in equity independently of statute (*Abbey National Building Society v Maybeech Ltd* [1985] Ch 190). Indeed, if the landlord deliberately refrained from notifying Quickslip, the latter might be able to claim relief even after six months of re-entry on the ground that the landlord should not be permitted to use the statutory time-limit as an engine of fraud. There is no direct authority to this effect, however, and the status of *Maybeech* is not entirely free from doubt (see *Smith v Metropolitan City Properties Ltd* [1986] 1 EGLR 52).

Subject to the foregoing caveat, therefore, if the landlord in the problem has re-entered pursuant to an order of the court, Quickslip will be able to seek relief only if it applies within six months of the re-entry. If the landlord has re-entered peaceably without a court order, Quickslip will need to apply for relief within a reasonable time. In any event, relief will not be granted which would prejudice the interests of a third party, e.g. a *bona fide* purchaser for value of a legal estate without notice of the right to apply for relief (*Fuller v Judy Properties Ltd* [1992] 1 EGLR 75).

Question 2

Ten years ago, Quentin purchased a 50-year lease of a market garden with the aid of a loan of £100,000 from Sunnyveg plc secured by a legal mortgage over the property. At that time, it was difficult to obtain finance and Quentin agreed to pay interest at 10 per cent above the bank base rate.

The mortgage deed provides that the capital outstanding should be recalculated annually to align with the retail prices index, and that Quentin shall not redeem the mortgage for 25 years. Quentin further undertook in the mortgage deed that for the 25 years he would first offer to sell to Sunnyveg plc any asparagus produced by the market garden at the market price before selling it elsewhere.

Quentin has now obtained a more favourable offer of finance and would like to redeem the mortgage.

Advise him whether this might be possible, as to the terms of the mortgage generally, and whether the agreement relating to the asparagus crop is enforceable against him.

Commentary

The equity of redemption and 'clogs on the equity' is one of the favoured areas of mortgages for examination questions.

You should be aware of the different provisions which may be regarded as clogs on the equity. You should also be aware of the underlying principles which determine whether or not the court will be prepared to intervene—terms in the mortgage deed which are oppressive and unconscionable to the mortgagor.

There are a number of old cases which establish the principle. (Many of these should be of special interest to beer drinkers as they concern the 'tied house' provisions in the mortgages of public houses!) There are also some more recent cases which confirm it.

As with so much of land law, the area reflects changing social circumstances, and illustrates the way in which equity is able to adapt broad principles to specific circumstances. There is a recognition that present-day mortgages may be part of wider agreements made between parties 'of equal bargaining power'. The down-trodden mortgagor of the nineteenth century, who was so frequently the object of equity's intervention, is very much less evident in the cases nowadays. The mortgagor has, of course, been given statutory protection too by the **Consumer Credit Act 1974**. This question does not cover the **1974 Act**, but if your lecturer has given any prominence to it, then you should familiarise yourself with its provisions and the few cases there have been on it. It has now been confirmed that the **Unfair Terms in Consumer Contracts Regulations 1999** apply to land transactions (***R (Khatun) v Newham LBC* [2005] 1 QB 37**) and a recent case on the Act is ***Falco Finance Ltd v Gough* (1999) CCLR 16**.

Answer plan

- Equitable principle that equity will not allow a clog on the equity of redemption.
- Effect of postponement of right to redeem.
- Unconscionability.
- Collateral advantage.

Suggested answer

Equity has traditionally protected the mortgagor from the exploitation of his weaker position by an unscrupulous mortgagee. One of the ways in which this protection was effected was by the inviolability of the mortgagor's equity of redemption; this arises as soon as the legal date for redemption has passed.

Equity takes the view that the essential nature of a mortgage is a security for a loan, and that on repayment of the loan, the mortgagor is entitled to have back his property freed from all obligations arising under the mortgage. This requirement of freedom from any encumbrances imposed in a mortgage deed is expressed in the equitable principle that 'equity will not allow a clog on the equity of redemption'.

One possible clog on the equity would be an undue postponement of the right to redeem the mortgage. Any such postponement which renders the right to redeem illusory will be void. Thus in *Fairclough v Swan Brewery Ltd* [1912] AC 565 a clause which provided that a mortgage was redeemable only one month before the expiration of the mortgagor's lease, leaving the mortgagor with no property worth redeeming, was held to be void.

Postponement, of itself, may not necessarily be bad however. In *Knightsbridge Estates Trust Ltd v Byrne* [1939] Ch 441, Greene MR said that a postponement would not be bad unless it was in some way oppressive or unconscionable. In that case, a postponement of the right to redeem for 40 years was upheld. The mortgagee had provided the mortgagor with finance at a time when credit was difficult to obtain. The parties were two large business associations and there was a reciprocal agreement that the mortgagee would not call in the loan for the period of postponement.

In this case, Quentin would still have 25 years of his lease left if he were to redeem after 25 years, so that the postponement would not appear to render the equity of redemption illusory as in *Fairclough*. However, Quentin does not appear to be a large commercial undertaking, as in *Knightsbridge Estates*, and there is no evidence of any reciprocal arrangement by Sunnyveg. It may therefore be possible for Quentin to obtain a declaration from the court that the postponement is oppressive and therefore void.

As part of its protection of the equity of redemption, equity has been anxious to ensure that a mortgagor should not have to pay an excessive rate of interest. Thus in *Cityland v Dabrah* [1968] Ch 166 a lump sum payment, which would have meant that the purchaser paid an interest rate of 57 per cent when spread over the period of the mortgage, was varied to give a rate of 7 per cent. This principle has been given statutory force with regard to certain qualifying mortgages within the Consumer Credit Act 1974 if the terms of the mortgage are 'oppressive and unreasonable'. A rate of 10 per cent above the base rate might well be oppressive and it might be possible to obtain an order varying it.

However, it will not necessarily be oppressive or unconscionable to link both capital and interest to a particular index. In *Multiservice Bookbinding Ltd v Marden* [1979] Ch 84 outstanding capital was recalculated according to the exchange rate with the Swiss franc which, after inflation and devaluation of sterling, more than doubled the original loan! As the provision was made to protect the mortgagee and was not intended to take advantage of the mortgagor, it was upheld. Further, in *Paragon Finance v Nash* [2002] 1 WLR 685, it was held that where a mortgagee is entitled to vary an interest rate he does not have an unfettered discretion to do so. Nevertheless where he raises it over and above the market rate to head off his own financial difficulties that may be reasonable. It is probable therefore that the recalculation of capital outstanding on Quentin's loan will be valid.

The provision giving Sunnyveg a first refusal on any asparagus crop produced by Quentin for 25 years may be regarded as a collateral advantage obtained from the transaction by Sunnyveg. Such an advantage continuing after the redemption of the mortgage would undoubtedly be void as repugnant to the equity of redemption, as the mortgagor is entitled to have back his property in an unencumbered state (*Noakes v Rice* [1902] AC 24). However, unless Quentin is able to redeem the mortgage before the period of 25 years specified in the mortgage has elapsed, this principle would not apply here, as the agreement is to subsist for 25 years (the duration of the mortgage) only. In *Biggs v Hodinott* [1898] 2 Ch 307, a mortgagor who agreed to buy only the mortgagee's beer for five years, and thereafter for as long as the loan was outstanding, and where the mortgagee agreed not to call in the loan for five years, was held to be bound by the agreement.

Collateral advantages were discussed by the House of Lords in *Kreglinger v New Patagonia Meat & Cold Storage Co Ltd* [1914] AC 25. In that case, part of the consideration for a loan by wool brokers to a meat-preserving company was a right of pre-emption on any sheepskins for five years. As in *Biggs v Hodinott*, there was a reciprocal agreement not to call in the loan for five years. The House of Lords felt that the rigid application of the doctrine of 'no clogs on the equity of redemption' was inappropriate to what was essentially a commercial contract between two business parties, and Lord Mersey referred to the doctrine as 'an unruly dog, which, if not securely chained to its own kennel, is prone to wander into places where it ought not to be'. More recently, Lord Phillips MR has said that the doctrine, like the appendix, no longer serves any useful purpose and should be excised: *Jones v Morgan* [2002] 1 EGLR 125, 136 (CA). In *Warnborough Ltd v Garmite Ltd* (2004) 1 P & CR D 18, the vendor of property left the purchase moneys outstanding on a mortgage he held and the purchaser granted him an option to purchase the property. Jonathan Parker LJ, applying the dictum of Lord Haldane in *Kreglinger*, said that the option granted by the purchaser did no more than to raise the question as to whether the rule on 'clogs' applied but that, in each case, the court must look at the substance of the transaction to decide its true nature. In this case, the option could have been part of the sale and purchase transaction rather than the mortgage.

It is difficult to see that the asparagus agreement is in any way unconscionable or unfair to Quentin as it is merely a right of first refusal at market value. However, the arrangement does not appear to give any reciprocal rights to Quentin as in *Biggs* and *Kreglinger*, and so may be voidable.

In *Esso Petroleum v Harper's Garage* [1968] AC 269 the House of Lords held that any restrictions on trade contained in a mortgage deed are also subject to the general common law rules as to restraint of trade, so that an alternative way in which Quentin might be able to avoid this agreement is to show that it is excessive under the common law rules. As at common law, it is possible to sever the part of the mortgage agreement which is bad as an excessive restraint on trade (*Alec Lobb (Garages) Ltd v Total Oil Great Britain Ltd* [1985] 1 WLR 173).

Question 3

Some years ago, when the property market was buoyant, Robin and Anne purchased the freehold of a desirable residence, Orchard Cottage, for £250,000 with the assistance of a loan of £175,000 from the Quickslip Bank secured by a legal mortgage over the property. Robin unfortunately became redundant a year ago and he and Anne began to experience problems in keeping up the mortgage repayments. They obtained planning permission for two bungalows on plots which are part of the orchard, being part of the cottage grounds, hoping to ease their financial problems by selling these off.

They are now six months in arrears with the mortgage repayments and the bank is seeking immediate possession of the property in order to sell it. The agents instructed by the bank have

prepared particulars of sale which do not mention the planning permission, although the bank has been told of it.

(a) Advise Robin and Anne of the bank's rights of possession and sale of the property.

(b) How would your advice differ, if at all, in the following circumstances:

(i) The bank has already contracted to sell the property to Cuthbert, but Robin and Anne have since received a higher offer for the property from Denis, and intend to contract to sell to him;

(ii) Robin and Anne want to sell to avoid mounting debt on the interest payable on the loan, but the bank refuses as the depreciation in property prices means that the likely sale price will not cover the amount of the loan?

Commentary

This question concerns the remedies of a mortgagee where the mortgagor defaults. It is an area of the law where, for the first time since the 1925 property legislation, the courts have had to consider entirely new social circumstances.

Until the late 1980s, in the main, property prices had only ever risen, so that it was extremely unusual for the sale price of the property not to cover the mortgage debt. Unfortunately, many people who purchased during the property 'boom' in 1987 subsequently found they had a 'negative equity'. The recession exacerbated this position, resulting in large numbers of repossessions by mortgagees. The remedies of a mortgagee on the default of the mortgagor have always, hitherto, been regarded as available solely for the mortgagee's benefit and he might choose how and when to exercise the chosen remedies. His only duty was to act in good faith. There are cases now indicating that the mortgagee owes a duty of care in equity to the mortgagor and any subsequent encumbrancer on the exercise of his powers. There are recent cases, too, in which the courts have interpreted the applicable legislation on sale more generously towards a mortgagor, recognising that even though a mortgagor has defaulted, his interest should not be entirely disregarded in granting a remedy to the mortgagee.

Lastly, ***Cheltenham & Gloucester Building Society v Norgan*** **[1996] 1 WLR 343** gives an entirely new interpretation of what may be regarded as a 'reasonable time' (in **s. 36, Administration of Justice Act 1970**) to postpone a possession order and allow the mortgagor to pay off arrears.

Persons having problems keeping up their mortgage repayments may wish to lease the mortgaged property so as to have a rent that they can use towards the mortgage repayments. Often such mortgagors (in breach of their mortgage agreement) simply let the property without informing the mortgagee. Such a lease (often an assured shorthold tenancy) will be subject to the prior mortgage, and the tenant has until recently had no protection in the event of the mortgagor's defaulting. The position of the tenant in these circumstances has recently been improved by the **Mortgage Repossessions (Protection of Tenants etc) Act 2010**. This statute enables the court to postpone a mortgagee's possession action against a tenant of a dwelling house where the mortgagee's interest is not subject to the tenancy. There is no discussion of this in the problem, but it is another possible variation in a question of this nature, which candidates should look out for.

Answer plan

(a) • Legal mortgagee's right to possession.
- Mortgagor's default.
- **Section 36, Administration of Justice Act 1970**; **s. 8, Administration of Justice Act 1973**.
- Power to suspend order for 'reasonable time'.
- Exercise of mortgagee's statutory power of sale, **s. 101, LPA 1925**.
- Duty to take reasonable care.

(b)(i) • Priority between mortgagee and third party.

(b)(ii) • Court's discretion to order sale under s. 91(2), **LPA 1925**.

Suggested answer

(a) Unless there is a provision in the mortgage deed to the contrary, a legal mortgagee has a common law right to possession of the mortgaged property 'before the ink is dry on the mortgage deed' (*per* Harman J in *Four-Maids Ltd v Dudley Marshall (Properties) Ltd* [1957] Ch 317). This is because the mortgagee has a legal lease of the property, or, if he has a legal charge, he has all the same rights as if he had a legal lease (LPA 1925, s. 87(1)).

In practice, a mortgage deed will often provide that the mortgagee's right of possession shall arise only on the mortgagor's default. The courts may be reluctant to limit this to a default on the mortgage repayments, however, and in *Western Bank Ltd v Schindler* [1977] Ch 1 (where the mortgage had been defectively drafted), it was held that the mortgagee still had a right to possession where he had no other rights. In that case, the mortgagor had not defaulted on the mortgage repayments as no repayment was due until a life policy matured, thereby providing the capital and interest to repay the loan. The mortgagor had defaulted on the payments due under the life policy. Although the power of sale was not exercisable, it was held that the mortgagee had a right of possession. Buckley LJ said 'It is a common law right which is an incident of his estate in the land. It should not, in my opinion, be lightly treated as abrogated or restricted'. It was held (Goff LJ dissenting) that the Administration of Justice Act 1970, s. 36, still applied to allow the court to postpone possession for a limited period.

If the mortgaged property is a dwelling-house, as in this question, then, where a mortgagee brings an action in which he claims possession, his right to possession will be restricted by the Administration of Justice Act 1970, s. 36, and by the Administration of Justice Act 1973, s. 8. It would seem that s. 36 is operable only where court proceedings for possession take place (*Ropaigealach v Barclays Bank plc* [2000] QB 263). So, the mortgagee's right to possession could be exercised by peaceable entry without the assistance of the court. This is regulated by s. 6(1) of the Criminal Law Act 1977, which would prevent the use of threatening behaviour or force. But, a right of peaceable possession of unoccupied premises without a court order is possible. Section 36 is only triggered where the mortgagee of a dwelling-house 'brings an action in which he claims possession'. However, as it would seem that Robin and Anne are in occupation, the bank is likely to seek a court order for possession thus bringing into play the effect of s. 36. If , however, the bank were to sell the property and it were the purchaser who brought an action for possession, Robin and Anne would not be able to rely on s. 36, as the action would have been brought but someone other than the mortgagee. In *Horsham Properties Group Ltd v Clark* [2008] EWHC 2327 (Ch), the court rejected an argument that the purchaser's possession action breached the mortgagor's right to peaceable enjoyment of her possessions under Article 1 of the First Protocol to the European Convention on Human Rights.

If it is the bank that brings an action for possession, s. 36(2) of the 1970 Act gives the court a discretion to suspend an order for possession if it appears to the court that the mortgagor is likely to be able to pay off any sums due within a reasonable period. If the prospect of such repayment is merely speculative, the court is unlikely to exercise its discretion. In *Bristol and West plc v Dace* [1998] EWCA Civ 1468 (CA), the court refused to exercise its discretion where the mortgagor was resting his hopes of repayment on the prospect of winning a legal action against his neighbour and then selling the property. Robin and Anne's plans to sell the building plots would have to be considered in the light of this. It may be that, on the facts, this is not considered speculative but a real method of repayment.

Section 8(1) of the 1973 Act provides that the court may treat as sums due such instalments of the mortgage as the mortgagor would have been expected to pay by the date of the hearing, and may effectively ignore any provision in the mortgage deed making the whole of the mortgage debt due on default on any one instalment.

Section 36, however, gives the court power only to suspend an order for possession for 'such period or periods as the court thinks reasonable'. Such suspension must be for a specified time and cannot be an indefinite adjournment (*Royal Trust of Canada v Markham* [1975] 1 WLR 1411). The ground for the suspension is that the mortgagor is likely to make good any defaults, or remedy any other breach of obligation in the mortgage deed, within a reasonable time. In *Realkredit Danmark v Brookfield House Ltd* [1999] EWCA Civ 630 the Court of Appeal held that the size of the arrears and the defendant's inability to pay were relevant factors for the judge to have taken into account in granting a possession order.

The courts had always regarded a 'reasonable time' as anything between two and four years, and the guidance on s. 36(2) in the *Supreme Court Practice* referred to 'at least two years'. However, in *Cheltenham & Gloucester Building Society v Norgan* [1996] 1 WLR 343, Waite LJ said 'the court should take as its starting point the full term of the mortgage' and ask 'would it be possible for the mortgagor to maintain payment-off of the arrears by instalments over that period?' This effectively puts lenders in a position of having to show why a lesser period should be adopted, instead of the borrower having to persuade the court that he could catch up on payments within a set period of between two and four years. Evans LJ, who gave a concurring judgment, suggested eight questions which the county court judges should ask in deciding whether or not to exercise this discretion. These include such matters as how the arrears accumulated, whether the borrower's difficulties are temporary, the type and terms of the mortgage, how much remains owing, and any factors affecting the security which should influence the period of repayment.

In *Norgan* the security was valued at a sum of £100,000 in excess of the debt and so was a very adequate security. In this question, the amount of security is not as great proportionately as in *Norgan*, which may justify a lesser period than the whole of the mortgage term.

Even if Robin and Anne are not able to persuade the court to reschedule their repayments over a very much longer period, they may be able to persuade the court that they have every possibility of paying off the arrears by selling the plots with planning permissions, and the court might then be prepared to exercise its discretion in their favour.

In *Target Home Loans Ltd v Clothier & Clothier* (1992) 25 HLR 48 the Court of Appeal used the power to suspend a possession order under the 1970 and 1973 Acts for four months to enable the mortgagor to sell the property while in possession. It was accepted that this would be likely to realise a higher sale price than if the mortgagee repossessed and then sold a vacant property. It is possible therefore that Robin and Anne may be able to achieve a stay of any possession order on the ground that they themselves are trying to sell the property and have a realistic chance of doing so.

The case of *Clothier* was considered, however, in *National & Provincial Building Society v Lloyd* [1996] 1 All ER 630, where Neill LJ (referring to the judgment of Waite LJ in *Norgan*) said that the court must be even-handed between the mortgagor and the mortgagee. In *Lloyd* the court refused to suspend a possession order on the mortgagor's claim to be able to sell parts of the property (two barns) to pay off only part of the debt. It was said that there was no reason why the mortgagee should have to accept piecemeal sales of parts of the property from time to time.

In practice, a mortgagee will usually seek possession only in order to sell the mortgaged property with vacant possession. A mortgagee who seeks to occupy the property is strictly accountable to the mortgagor for profits which *might* have been made as well as for those which were *actually* made, and therefore is not in a very happy position (*White v City of London Brewery Co* (1889) 42 ChD 237, where the mortgagee of a public house was liable to the mortgagor for the difference in rent which he might have received if he had let it as a free house and not as a 'tied' house).

The mortgagee's statutory power of sale is contained in the LPA 1925, s. 101, and applies to all mortgages made by deed, unless there is a contrary intention stated. It only *arises* however when the mortgage moneys have become due, that is, when the legal date for redemption has passed. It only becomes *exercisable* under one of the three circumstances set out in the LPA 1925, s. 103. These are that the mortgagee has demanded repayment of the capital outstanding and the mortgagor has defaulted for three months, that the mortgagor is two months in arrear with interest payments under the mortgage, or that the mortgagor is in breach of some other covenant in the mortgage deed, such as a covenant against letting the property. The legal date for redemption is usually inserted, quite unrealistically, into a mortgage deed as six months after the date of the mortgage. This is not because anyone imagines for a moment that the mortgagor will be able to repay the whole of the loan and interest at that time, but so that the remedy of sale is available to a mortgagee fairly early on. Assuming that the legal date for redemption in their mortgage deed has passed, as Robin and Anne are six months in arrears with the interest payments, the power of sale has become exercisable.

If the title to Orchard Cottage had been registered, any limitations on the chargee's powers of sale (such as a postponement of the legal date for redemption) should have been entered as restrictions on the freehold title. By virtue of LRA 2002, s. 52(1), the chargee of a registered charge has the power of sale of a legal mortgagee subject only to entries on the register. This provision seems to be intended to protect a purchaser against the risk that the property is transferred to him before the power of sale has arisen. Smith has pointed out that the subsection is defective, however, in that the statutory power of sale of a legal mortgagee is contained in LPA 1925, s. 101(1)(i), and so does not, in any event arise, until the mortgage moneys have become due: Smith, *Property Law*, 5th edn, Longman, 2006, at p. 590.

In exercising a power of sale, a mortgagee must take reasonable care to obtain a proper market price for the property. In *Cuckmere Brick Co v Mutual Finance Ltd* [1971] Ch 949, the mortgagee instructed estate agents to sell. The estate agents were told that planning permission had been obtained for 35 houses, but were not informed that planning permission had also been obtained for 100 flats. The auction advertisements therefore mentioned only the houses. The mortgagor drew the mortgagee's attention to this and requested a postponement of sale to allow the property to be correctly advertised. Evidence was given that house developments are very different from flat developments, the latter involving a larger initial outlay but yielding higher profits. Developers involved in flat developments would not bother to attend an auction of land for housing development. The estate agents received a surveyor's letter indicating that the valuation of the land with planning permission for flats might be approximately double (£70,000) the valuation with planning permission for houses only (£35,000). The mortgagor wrote to the mortgagee on the question of valuation. The auction nevertheless went ahead. It was held that the mortgagee had not taken reasonable care to obtain the market value of the property and was liable to the mortgagor in damages for the difference between this and the price actually obtained. Such a claim by the mortgagor must be brought within six years (*Raja v Lloyd's TSB Bank plc* (2001) Lloyd's Rep Bank 113).

Although it was suggested in *Standard Chartered Bank Ltd v Walker* [1982] 1 WLR 1410 (CA) that the duty owed by mortgagees in exercising the power of sale is one in the tort of negligence, this was doubted by the Privy Council in *Downsview Nominees Ltd v First City Corp Ltd* [1993] AC 295, which preferred the view that the duty to obtain a proper market price is a duty in equity. The significance of the duty existing only in equity is that it is narrower in scope than the duty of care in negligence. Thus, it does not include any duty on the mortgagee to take steps to improve the value of the property, such as by obtaining planning permission, carrying out improvements, or letting: *Silven Properties Ltd v Royal Bank of Scotland* [2004] 1 WLR 997. There are also equitable duties of good faith and due diligence in relation to any dealings with capital moneys: *Medforth v Blake* [1999] 3 WLR 922 (CA), stating the duties of a receiver, which in this context were held in the *Silven* case to be identical to those of a mortgagee. It is now clear that the equitable duty extends to the mortgagor and anyone else interested in the equity of redemption, including later mortgagees and (as held in *Barclays Bank plc v Kingston* [2006] EWHC 533 (QB)) the mortgagor's guarantor.

Nevertheless, if Robin and Anne remind both the bank and the agents of the planning permissions, which will obviously increase the market price of the property, it might be questionable whether the bank will have acted in good faith if the sale then goes ahead without mention of this. They would have an action for equitable compensation against the bank, which must also be liable for any negligence of the agents instructed by it.

(b)(i) The fact that Robin and Anne have received a higher offer for the property might suggest that the bank has not complied with its duty to take reasonable care to obtain the 'true market value' at the date of the sale: *Cuckmere Brick Co Ltd v Mutual Finance Ltd* [1971] Ch 948. Whether the bank has complied with this duty would therefore be a matter of evidence.

It might appear from *Cuckmere Brick* that the Lords Justices were referring to a duty of care in tort; but (as discussed in part (a) above) later cases, notably *Downsview Nominees Ltd v First City Corp Ltd* [1993] AC 295, have clarified that it is only a duty of care in equity. The practical significance of this in the problem is that there is no wider duty e.g. to sell at the best time from the mortgagor's point of view. Thus in *China & South Sea Bank Ltd v Tan Soon Gin* [1991] 1 AC 536, the Privy Council held that a mortgagee is under no duty to delay exercising the power of sale until market conditions are more favourable. Robin and Anne cannot therefore argue that the bank is in breach of its equitable duty merely because the market value of the house has risen since the bank entered into the contract for sale.

The mortgagor's equity of redemption is extinguished when the mortgagee, in the exercise of its power of sale, enters into a valid contract for sale of the mortgaged property: see the judgment of Millett LJ in *National & Provincial BS v Ahmed* [1995] 2 EGLR 127. A contract of sale by the mortgagors, Robin and Anne, cannot put their purchaser, Denis, into a stronger position *vis-à-vis* the mortgagee than they are in themselves. Therefore, even if Denis were to protect his estate contract by entry of a C(iv) Land Charge (if the title to Orchard Cottage is unregistered) or by a notice in the charges register (if the title is registered) before Cuthbert had taken similar steps to protect his own estate contract, the bank's sale and subsequent conveyance or transfer to Cuthbert would be unaffected: ***Duke v Robson*** **[1973] 1 WLR 267**. Assuming therefore that the power of sale has arisen, upon the bank's contracting to sell to Cuthbert, Robin and Anne's equity of redemption is replaced merely by an equitable interest in the property. Any contract of sale by Robin and Anne to Denis would therefore be merely a sale of such equitable interest. This equitable interest would then be statutorily overreached on the subsequent conveyance or transfer by the mortgagee (**LPA 1925, s. 2(1)(iii)**) and become instead an equitable interest in any surplus remaining after the bank has applied the sale moneys in accordance with the **LPA 1925, s. 105**. Under that section, the bank would hold such surplus in trust for Denis (as the person entitled to the mortgaged property).

(b)(ii) In ***Palk v Mortgage Services Funding plc*** **[1993] Ch 330** the mortgagor wanted to sell the mortgaged property for approximately £80,000 less than the mortgage debt. Not unsurprisingly, the mortgagee objected to this and applied for possession of the property, intending to let it and sell at a later date when the property market had improved.

The **LPA 1925, s. 91(2)**, provides that the court may make an order for sale on the request of the mortgagee or 'any person interested in... the right of redemption'. Notwithstanding that the section had only ever been used in its long history (at least as far back as the **Conveyancing Act 1881**) to order a sale rather than foreclosure, and that this had only been done where the sale proceeds would cover the mortgage debt, the Court of Appeal in ***Palk*** held that it had a wide and unfettered discretion under **s. 91(2)**, to order a sale.

In exercising this discretion, the court in ***Palk*** said that it could take into account not only the interests of the mortgagee (considered by Lord Templeman in ***China & South Sea Bank Ltd v Tan Soon Gin*** **[1990] 1 AC 536** to be paramount), but also the interests of the mortgagor. In ***China & South Sea Bank Ltd***, Lord Templeman said that it was a matter for a mortgagee which of his possible remedies he chose to pursue on default, and it was accepted that the mortgagee could be made to accede to a sale by the mortgagor or his surety only if the proposed sale price covered the whole of the mortgage debt. But in ***Palk*** it was pointed out that a mortgagee still has the right to sue a mortgagor on a personal covenant to pay for any monies still outstanding after sale.

There were circumstances in ***Palk*** however which would have made refusing the mortgagor's application for sale particularly harsh on her whilst only giving the mortgagee a possibility of future benefit. The rental income from the property would not have covered the mounting interest debt, so that the mortgagor would be steadily increasing her indebtedness by some £43,000 per annum. Kerr LJ conceded that generally a mortgagee's wishes should be given preference, and if there had been a 'real possibility' even of an increase in price (due, for example, to the possibility of obtaining planning permission for development) then it might have been more reasonable to postpone the sale. There was no immediate realistic certainty that a postponement of sale would produce a better sale price however—it was merely speculative optimism on the part of the mortgagee. It was said that it would be unfair to the mortgagor for the mortgagee to speculate on the property market at her expense, and that if it wished to do so, it could do so by purchasing the property from the mortgagor herself (the proposed sale being by the *mortgagor* and not therefore being a sale by the *mortgagee* to itself). The mortgagor was therefore allowed to sell the property.

The court may, however, take into account the fact that the mortgagor may attempt to delay matters, and it may not suspend an order pending sale where the sale proceeds will not be enough to discharge the debt: *Cheltenham & Gloucester plc v Krausz* [1997] 1 WLR 1558.

It is clear, then, that the court regards itself as having an unfettered discretion under the LPA 1925, s. 91(2), whether to order a sale or not, and how it exercises such discretion will depend upon the circumstances of each particular case. The factors to be taken into account in determining whether Robin and Anne are likely to obtain an order for sale are the likely shortfall between the sale price and the mortgage debt, whether any rental income from the property would cover the interest payments on the mortgage, and whether there are any other factors, such as the sale of further plots of the orchard with planning permissions, which might realistically offer an increase in the sale price.

Question 4

Explain how an equitable mortgage of freehold land is created, and consider what remedies are available to an equitable mortgagee of freehold land.

Commentary

This might appear to be a simple type of bookwork question, but it conceals much uncertainty and complexity. The enactment of the **Law of Property (Miscellaneous Provisions) Act 1989, s. 2**, has been held to have put an end to the creation of informal equitable mortgages by deposit of title deeds. An equitable mortgage of freehold land can now be created only by a valid contract complying with **s. 2 of that Act**.

It is important to note the scope of the question. The first part does not ask the candidate to explain how equitable mortgages of all types of property are created, but only equitable mortgages of freehold land. This narrows the scope of the question, since it effectively relieves the candidate of having to discuss the other ways in which equitable mortgages can arise.

There are two other ways in which an equitable mortgage can arise. First, it can be created of an *equitable* interest in land, such as a beneficial interest under a trust of land, under which the beneficiary assigns his or her equitable interest to the mortgagee. Such an assignment must be in writing and signed by the mortgagor or the mortgagor's authorised agent: **LPA 1925, s. 53(1)(c)**. Secondly, an equitable mortgage can arise where one of two joint tenants of a freehold estate forges the signature of the other in a purported legal mortgage of the legal estate. The forgery invalidates the legal mortgage, but it operates as an equitable mortgage of the forger's beneficial interest in the property (thereby severing any joint tenancy of the equitable interest under the trust of land): ***First National Securities Ltd v Hegarty* [1985] QB 850**; ***Edwards v Lloyds TSB Bank plc* [2004] EWHC 1745 (Ch)**. Neither of these types of equitable mortgages is discussed in the answer, because neither involves an equitable mortgage of a freehold estate, but rather the mortgage of an equitable interest.

Answer plan

- Creation of equitable mortgage of freehold land:
  - **LP(MP)A 1989, s. 2**;
  - **LRA 2002**.
- Remedies of an equitable mortgagee of freehold land:
  - foreclosure;
  - possession;
  - sale;
  - appointment of a receiver.

Suggested answer

An equitable mortgage of freehold land is created by a valid and specifically enforceable contract to create a legal mortgage. A contract to create a legal mortgage of land is a contract relating to the disposition of an interest in land; therefore, before 27 September 1989, such a contract had to comply with the LPA 1925, s. 40(1), i.e. it had to be evidenced in writing, or, in the absence of such written evidence, it could be supported by a valid act of part performance. The cases had established that an act of sufficient part performance was the deposit by the mortgagor of the title deeds with the mortgagee by way of security. Such a deposit was taken to be both evidence of a contract to create a mortgage and part performance of that contract. The effect was that the mere deposit of title deeds could create an equitable mortgage without any writing. A creation of an equitable mortgage in this way went back to the eighteenth century: *Russell v Russell* (1783) 1 Bro CC 269.

Section 40, was repealed, however, by Law of Property (Miscellaneous Provisions) Act 1989, s. 2. The new provision requires a contract for the disposition of an interest in land to be in writing, and has thereby abolished the doctrine of part performance. There was some doubt in the first few years after s. 2 was enacted whether the informal deposit of title deeds might still create an equitable mortgage on the basis that such mortgages might be treated as *sui generis*; but such argument was rejected in *United Bank of Kuwait v Sahib* [1997] Ch 107, where the Court of Appeal held that s. 2 now precludes the informal creation of an equitable mortgage in this way. A contract for a mortgage of land must therefore now be in writing to comply with s. 2.

In registered land, the equivalent principle to the creation of an informal mortgage by deposit of title deeds used to be the creation of an equitable lien over the land by the deposit of the land certificate with the lender as security. After the decision in *Sahib*, however, there was no reason to preserve this method in registered land, and it has been abandoned in the LRA 2002.

The formality requirements in s. 2 of the 1989 Act do not, however, apply to the creation or operation of constructive trusts: LP(MP)A 1989, s. 2(5)(c). This leaves the possibility that, if the circumstances gives rise to an estoppel, the court might impose a constructive trust, thereby effectively circumventing the formality requirements: *Yaxley v Gotts* [2000] Ch 162. Alternatively, the court might find that the circumstances lead to the imposition of a constructive trust without the need for establishing an estoppel. Whether, in this context, estoppel and constructive trust are identical concepts remains unclear. In *Kinane v Mackie-Conteh* [2005] EWCA Civ 45, an informal agreement to create a charge over a house as security for a loan was held not to fall foul of s. 2 because the lender had insisted that he needed security for the loan, and the borrower had represented to him that the agreement for the charge was both valid and binding. The Court of Appeal held that this gave rise to a constructive trust within s. 2(5)(c). The decision is very wide, and has the potential to undermine the formality requirements of s. 2.

The primary remedy of an equitable mortgagee is foreclosure, which requires a court order. Since an equitable mortgagee has no legal estate, the foreclosure order directs the mortgagor to convey the property to the mortgagee free from the right to redeem. Foreclosure, however, is nowadays very rare. There are three reasons for this. First, if a mortgagee applies for foreclosure, the mortgagor (or anybody else interested in the equity of redemption) can request the court to make an order for sale instead: LPA 1925, s. 91(2). A sale would therefore normally be ordered at the behest of the mortgagor where the value of the property exceeds what is due to the mortgagee, as in those circumstances foreclosure would give the mortgagee an unmerited windfall. Secondly, foreclosure extinguishes the mortgagee's right of action on the personal covenant to repay. A mortgagee is therefore unlikely to seek foreclosure where the value of the property falls short of what it is owed. Thirdly, a purchaser from a mortgagee who has foreclosed may not be safe, since the court has power to *re-open* such an order to allow the mortgagor to redeem at a later date: *Campbell v Holyland* (1877) 7 ChD 166.

An equitable mortgagee is generally considered to have no *right* to possession, although the court may award an order for possession: see *Barclays Bank Ltd v Bird* [1954] Ch 274, and he may take possession if the mortgage so provides. It is of course correct that such a mortgagee, having no legal estate in the land, has no right to possession at law; but Megarry & Wade, *The Law of Real Property* (6th edn, 1999, at

p. 1214, para. 19–087), argue that, since an equitable mortgage is a contract for a legal mortgage, and equity looks upon that as done which ought to be done, an equitable mortgagee should be able to take possession under the doctrine of *Walsh v Lonsdale* (1882) 21 ChD 9.

A mortgagee has the statutory power of sale under LPA 1925, s. 101, only where the mortgage is made by deed. For this reason, an equitable mortgage is often made by deed. However, s. 101(1)(i) enables the mortgagee to sell 'the mortgaged property', and in *Re Hodson and Howe's Contract* (1887) 35 ChD 668, it was held that this means that the mortgagee can sell only the interest that he has, which in the case of an equitable mortgage is merely the equitable interest. This narrow interpretation was doubted by Lord Denning MR in *Re White Rose Cottage* [1965] Ch 940, but in view of the doubt, it is usual for an equitable mortgagee to make sure it can convey the legal estate by using one of two conveyancing devices. First, the mortgage deed may contain a power of attorney, empowering the mortgagee to convey the legal estate. Secondly, the mortgage deed may contain a declaration of trust, under which the mortgagor declares that he holds the legal estate in trust for the mortgagee and gives the latter the power to appoint himself or his nominee a trustee in place of the mortgagor. The mortgagee can therefore vest the legal title in a purchaser by appointing the purchaser a trustee in substitution for the mortgagor.

If the equitable mortgage is not made by deed, the mortgagee cannot himself sell, but he can still *apply to the court* for a sale under LPA 1925, s. 91(2), and the court can (*inter alia*) make a vesting order conveying the land to the purchaser: ibid., ss. 90(1), 91(7).

An equitable mortgagee has an inherent right in equity to apply to the court for the appointment of a receiver in an appropriate case, e.g. where interest is in arrears. This power is now contained in the Senior Courts Act 1981, s. 37. If, however, the mortgage is by deed, the equitable mortgagee has the power to appoint a receiver under LPA 1925, s. 101(1)(iii). This is clearly better for the mortgagee, since it avoids the need to apply to the court.

Question 5

'The furthest a bank can be expected to go is to take reasonable steps to satisfy itself that the wife has had brought home to her, in a meaningful way, the practical implications of the proposed transaction. This does not wholly eliminate the risk of undue influence or misrepresentation. But it does mean that a wife enters into a transaction with her eyes open so far as the basic elements of the transaction are concerned.'

(*per* Lord Nicholls, *Royal Bank of Scotland plc v Etridge (No. 2)* [2002] 2 AC 773)

Explain the effect that the House of Lords' decision in *Etridge* has had in the light of the case law that followed their Lordships' decision in *Barclays Bank plc v O'Brien* [1994] 1 AC 180.

Commentary

This question deals with two authoritative decisions of the House of Lords in conjoined appeals, ***Barclays Bank plc v O'Brien* [1994] 1 AC 180**, and ***CIBC Mortgages plc v Pitt* [1994] 1 AC 200**. These cases dealt with the question as to the extent to which one co-owner, A ('the surety'), who has mortgaged property jointly owned with another, B, or solely owned by A, can set aside the mortgage on the basis that A entered into the transaction by reason of undue influence or misrepresentation.

Since these cases, there has been a plethora of decisions dealing with a variety of permutations of the facts raised by them. In ***Royal Bank of Scotland plc v Etridge (No. 2)* [2002] 2 AC 773**, a case in which eight conjoined appeals were heard, the House of Lords laid down general guidelines. The eight appeals were all concerned with wives who had charged the matrimonial home to secure their husband's liability to the bank. The key issue in all the cases was whether the bank had taken sufficient steps to avoid being fixed with constructive notice of any undue influence by the husband. In six of the eight cases the wife's appeal was allowed.

To some extent these appeals have resolved a number of issues arising in such cases and each of the eight cases raises an interesting application of the principles to a set of facts. The question asks for a discussion, so what is required is a clear exposition of the requirements for liability in the light of the House of Lords' decision in ***Etridge***.

Answer plan

- Explanation of the decision in ***Barclays Bank plc v O'Brien* [1994] 1 AC 180**.
- The principle of undue influence—case.
- The test of 'manifest disadvantage'.
- The requirement for the bank to be 'put on inquiry'.
- The application of the equitable doctrine of notice and its unconventional use.
- The steps a bank is required to take to ensure that the surety understands the risk.

Suggested answer

Since the decisions of the House of Lords in *Barclays Bank plc v O'Brien* [1994] 1 AC 180 and *CIBC Mortgages plc v Pitt* [1994] 1 AC 200, a number of cases have come before the courts which have applied the principles set out in those decisions to a variety of different facts.

In *O'Brien* and *Pitt*, which were conjoined appeals, it was decided that, where undue influence or misrepresentation occurs so as to induce a wife to charge the matrimonial home by way of security for her husband's liability to the bank, then the wife will, in certain circumstances, have a right to avoid her obligation. The House of Lords' decision in *O'Brien* and *Pitt* confirmed the principle that where there was a relationship between two persons where one has some influence over the other, then the dominant person will not be permitted to take advantage of that dominant position.

This followed from earlier case law largely established in the nineteenth century. In *Bainbrigge v Browne* (1881) 18 ChD 188, for example, the relationship was between a father and his children. He influenced them so as to charge their interests under a marriage settlement with his debts. This transaction was avoided because of the father's undue influence over his children. In *Allcard v Skinner* (1887) 36 ChD 145, this relationship was described as one where one party has a duty to advise the other and in *Zamet v Hyman* [1961] 1 WLR 1442, the duty owed by the dominant party was one of candour and protection. Other relationships which might give rise to this situation have included that between banker and customer, *National Westminster Bank plc v Morgan* [1985] AC 686; and employer and employee, *Credit Lyonnais Bank Nederland NV v Burch* [1997] 1 All ER 144. The House of Lords in *Royal Bank of Scotland plc v Etridge (No. 2)* [2002] 2 AC 773 accepted that the principle of undue influence has been widened in that the types of relationship which may fall into this category are wide and various. The consequence of this decision is that banks will always be put on inquiry as to the possible existence of undue influence in all cases where they are dealing with a tripartite situation where the surety appears to derive no benefit from the guarantee. The only limitation is that it applies only to non-commercial cases. In commercial cases it may be supposed that those engaged in business are capable of dealing with the risks involved.

The general rule is that whether a transaction was brought about by the exercise of undue influence is a question of fact. The burden of proof rested on the person who claimed to have been wronged. The nature of the evidence required to establish that the claimant was unduly influenced includes the relationship between the parties and the nature of the transaction. The first element requires the complainant to show that she placed trust and confidence in the dominant partner in relation to their financial affairs. The second element is that the transaction calls for some explanation. Once these hurdles have been crossed, then a *prima facie* case has been made out that the dominant party abused his position of trust. At that point, a presumption arises that undue influence was brought to bear on the complainant and, as a result, the burden of proof falls to the defendant to prove that he did not unduly influence the complainant (*Bainbrigge v Browne*). In other words, there is a rebuttable evidential presumption of undue influence.

The House of Lords in *Etridge* considered that discussion in the case law post *O'Brien* of the distinction between 'presumed undue influence' and 'actual undue influence' (as described in *Bank of Credit & Commerce International SA v Aboody* [1990] 1 QB 923) was confusing. They considered that, even where the transaction does not of itself call for an explanation so that the presumption of undue influence does not arise, it is still open for the complainant to be able to establish that there was, in fact, undue influence.

In the post-*O'Brien* cases, the classic relationship involved has been that of husband and wife. The House of Lords in *Etridge* confirmed that the spousal relationship does not belong to the class of cases where the very nature of the relationship gives rise to the irrebuttable presumption of undue influence (*Yerkey v Jones* (1939) 63 CLR 649). Thus, although a presumption may arise if the circumstances are right, that presumption is rebuttable.

The second element required for the presumption to arise is that some explanation is required as to the transaction. In other words, the transaction is not one which is in the interest of the weaker party. In *Allcard v Skinner*, the donor gave away nearly all her property to someone who was in a dominant position in the relationship. This was said to call for an explanation since it could not reasonably be accounted for on ordinary grounds of friendship and so on. The post-*O'Brien* cases have typically dealt with situations where the wife, who has a proprietary interest in the house, has acted as surety for the husband's debt using the house as collateral. In the circumstances which have transpired, the debts have not been repaid and the mortgagee bank has sought a possession order of the house. Patently, the transaction has not turned out to be for the advantage of the wife. In *National Westminster Bank plc v Morgan* [1985] AC 686, the House of Lords held that there must be a disadvantage which is sufficiently serious to give rise to the presumption of undue influence. The court in *Etridge* concurred with this view.

Some of the post-*O'Brien* case law had found difficulty with the principle that the wife must show that the transaction was to her 'manifest disadvantage'. The transaction may be one which preserves the husband's creditworthiness, for example, so as to ensure that the family business prospers. This will be also in the wife's interest. Can it be said that the transaction is, therefore, to her manifest disadvantage? The House of Lords in *Etridge* adopted the approach that the label 'manifest disadvantage' is not the appropriate test. They indicated that it was necessary to show 'a disadvantage sufficiently serious to require evidence to rebut the presumption that in the circumstances of the parties' relationship it was procured by the exercise of undue influence'. The test is to see whether the transaction calls for some explanation and, in the ordinary course of things, such a transaction is not to be regarded without more as being subject to the presumption that undue influence has been exercised. A narrow test is not appropriate.

These principles relating to undue influence are not entirely new. As can be seen they date from earlier case law. What was novel about the decision in *O'Brien* was the extent to which the mortgagee was deemed to have notice of the fact that the vulnerable party was unduly influenced by the dominant party so as to act as surety in the transaction. The existence of the presumption of undue influence puts the mortgagee on inquiry and he is, therefore, imputed with constructive notice of the rights of the wife.

This application of the equitable doctrine of notice has been considered to be unconventional. Its conventional use relates to the transfer of a legal estate or interest in property where the transferee acquires a title to that property either subject to or free from another person's interest. The transferee takes the legal title free from equitable interests where he did not know nor ought to have known of their existence. In the *O'Brien* case, the mortgagee in acquiring the legal title takes it subject to the wife's interest where the mortgagees ought to have known of the existence of the undue influence or misrepresentation. The steps prescribed by the courts in these cases are directed not at preventing the mortgagee from taking subject to the wife's interest but instead at preventing the wife from being subject to the undue influence. The steps are proactive in preventing the undue influence from operating rather than being reactive in protecting the mortgagee. The fact that they do have the effect of protecting the mortgagee is coincidental.

The point at which a mortgagee is put on inquiry is considered in *Etridge* to be a low one. It arises whenever a wife (or, in another relationship, the vulnerable party) stands surety for her husband's debts rather than for their joint debts in a non-commercial context. Earlier case law (including the Court of Appeal decision in *Etridge*) had put the threshold higher and had required that the bank should know that the parties were cohabiting or that the surety placed implicit trust and confidence in the debtor. The House of Lords in *Etridge* considered that this introduced too much uncertainty into the law.

One of the main areas of contention in the case law has been as to what steps a bank should take where undue influence is presumed. This part of the decision in *O'Brien* is new so no earlier case law is instructive on this point. For the future, *Etridge* has clarified the situation by deciding that a bank would satisfy the requirements to take steps to bring to the wife's attention the risks of standing as surety if it insisted that the wife attended a private meeting with a representative of the bank. At that meeting she would be told of the extent of her liability as surety, warned of the risk she was running, and urged to take independent legal advice. In subsequent decisions in *Lloyds TSB Bank plc v Holdgate* [2003] HLR 335 and *First National Bank plc v Achampong* [2004] 1 FCR 18, it was not enough for the bank simply to know that the wife was being advised by a solicitor. It must know that the wife is being advised as to the nature and effect of the transaction. In exceptional cases, the bank, to be safe, had to insist that the wife was separately advised. The House of Lords set out the core minimum content of the legal advice that the solicitor advising the wife should give. This should be in the context of a face-to-face meeting, in the absence of the husband, and in suitably non-technical language. The solicitor should explain the transaction and its implications and the seriousness of the risk and the fact that the wife has a choice. In *National Westminster Bank plc v Amin* [2002] 1 FLR 735 this point was confirmed. The wife should be asked whether she is content that the solicitor writes to the bank confirming that he has explained the transaction to her. The solicitor should obtain from the bank any information needed to give the advice. It is not necessary that the solicitor should act only for the wife, as this may not be practical for various reasons. However, the solicitor's legal and professional duties, assumed when accepting instructions to advise the wife, were owed to her alone. This is the situation which arose in *Banco Exterior Internacional v Mann* [1995] 1 All ER 936, where the wife was inhibited in the discussion with her solicitor who was also acting for her husband. However, where a solicitor is acting for both parties, he should consider whether there was any conflict of duty or interest and what the best interests of the wife are.

Further, in *Etridge*, the court held that the solicitor is not the bank's agent. So, the bank may assume that the advice has been given properly.

It can be seen that the decision of the House of Lords in *Etridge* has both clarified and widened the principle established in the *O'Brien* case as it has come to be applied in the intervening cases.

Further reading

Smith, R. J., *Property Law*, 5th edn, Longman, 2006, chapter 22.

15

Perpetuities and accumulations

Introduction

On undergraduate courses, the law of perpetuities and accumulations has been a topic in decline. Many courses have abandoned any separate treatment of it; yet it nevertheless provides the background for the drafting of trusts of land and of other assets. There can also be few law students who never encounter the law of perpetuities in their studies, even if it is only in passing as in trusts of imperfect obligation and gifts for members of a club (usually studied in equity and trusts). It may be that the new legislation on perpetuities and accumulations will revive this topic on undergraduate courses.

Although a new regime was introduced in the Perpetuities and Accumulations Act 2009, the Act is not (with one exception) retrospective. The first important matter to note in dealing with a problem question on perpetuities therefore is when the disposition was made. There are three periods for this:

- The period before 16 July 1964: the common law applies, with modification (age-reducing under the Law of Property Act 1925, s. 163).
- The period from 16 July 1964 until 5 April 2010: the common law is applied first, but if the disposition would then be void for perpetuity, there is 'wait and see' for the statutory lives introduced by the PAA 1964, as well as other refinements introduced by that Act.
- The period from 6 April 2010: this establishes an automatic perpetuity period of 125 years with 'wait and see' for that period.

The first of the three questions in this chapter deals with the regime under the 2009 Act; the other two questions involve the law applicable to dispositions that were made before 6 April 2010.

Because a cool head is needed in tackling a perpetuities or accumulations problem, it is probably best not to attempt such a question as your first answer.

Question 1

Consider the significance of the Perpetuities and Accumulations Act 2009.

Commentary

As the question refers to the 'significance' of the **2009 Act,** a good answer needs not merely to describe what the changes are, but also to consider why they were made, and to assess both their importance and what their impact will be.

Answer plan

- Background to the **2009 Act**—merits of a law against perpetuities.
- Generally not retrospective (only instruments created after 5 April 2010).
- Scope of changes:
  - limited to 'family-type' interests;
  - automatic 125 year perpetuity period;
  - 'wait and see' for that period if necessary;
  - exclusion of class members (as under **1964 Act**);
  - but no age-reducing, unborn widow trap, or fertility presumptions;
  - when can substitute 100-year period under previous regime;
  - no change to rule against perpetual trusts;
  - impact on accumulations of income.
- Conclusion, including continuing importance of **PAA 1964**.

Suggested answer

The Perpetuities and Accumulations Act 2009 (PAA 2009), which is largely the product of recommendations of the Law Commission made in 1998 (*The Rules against Perpetuities and Excessive Accumulations*), is designed to simplify the law on perpetuities and accumulations so as to ensure that the vast majority of dispositions that are made do not infringe the rules. There was some support for the total abolition of the rule against perpetuities (notably from Baroness Deech, during the passage of the Bill through the House of Lords), and there is no doubt that inheritance tax and capital gains tax generally discourage testators from attempting to tie up their property for very long periods. Nevertheless, it was considered that there was merit in providing a long-stop, so as to prevent an eccentric testator from trying to tie property up in trust for potentially hundreds or even thousands of years.

The PAA 2009 was brought into force on 6 April 2010, and there is no doubt that it has considerably modified this area of the law. However, the changes that the Act makes are (with one limited exception) not retrospective. The objection to retrospective legislation in this area is that it might deprive some beneficiaries of their property rights; this would be both against the tradition of English law, and also might contravene Article 1 of the First Protocol to the European Convention on Human Rights. The new Act therefore applies only to dispositions made after 5 April 2010; dispositions made before 6 April 2010 continue to be governed by the law applicable before that date. As the law of perpetuities had previously been amended (again without retrospective effect) by the Perpetuities and Accumulations Act 1964 (PAA 1964), this area of the law has become increasingly complicated.

The new regime under the PAA 2009 applies to an instrument that takes effect on or after 6 April 2010: PAA 2009, s. 6(1), and the Perpetuities and Accumulations Act 2009 (Commencement) Order 2010 (SI 2010/37). An *inter vivos* trust takes effect on the date the trust is made. There is, however, a qualification to this where a disposition is effected by will, since it was recognised that many testators might have made their wills before the Act came into force and by reference to a perpetuity period under the previous law. The Act deals with this by providing that (subject to s.12, discussed below) it does not apply to a will of a testator who dies on or after 6 April 2010 if the will was executed before that date: PAA 2009, s. 15(1).

The new law of perpetuities applies essentially only to interests arising under trusts: PAA 2009, s. 1. It no longer applies to options, rights of pre-emption or future easements. The effect is to exclude commercial interests from the scope of the rule and to limit it to the types of interest for which it was originally designed, namely family-type interests.

There is an automatic perpetuity period of 125 years, notwithstanding any other period that the trust, will or other instrument, might purport to specify. It follows from this that under the PAA 2009 (in contrast to the PAA 1964) there are no statutory lives in being. The period of 125 years was selected because it can be considered to approximate to the longest life span that might be attained in modern times (just over 100 years) plus 21 years. A period of 80 years (which a settlor could have selected under the PAA 1964) was regarded as too short.

'Wait and see' applies (as under the PAA 1964) until such time as it becomes established that the vesting must occur (if at all) after the end of the perpetuity period (i.e. 125 years): PAA 2009, s. 7(2). This is different from the PAA 1964, where 'wait and see' applies only if the interest would otherwise be void at common law. Under the PAA 2009, no reference is made to the common law because the PAA 2009 is independent of the common law.

Apart from 'wait and see', the PAA 2009 adopts only one specific gift-saving device from the PAA 1964: namely, exclusion of members of a class. If it is apparent when the instrument is made, or becomes apparent later, that the inclusion of certain members of a class would cause the estate or interest to be void for remoteness, those persons are treated as excluded from the class: PAA 2009, s. 8(1), (2).

The 2009 Act does not provide for age-reducing; age-reducing (if necessary) to 21 in order to save a gift from remoteness was appropriate with a perpetuity period of lives in being plus 21 years, but the provision of a fixed term of 125 years makes it redundant. Furthermore, whereas the PAA 1964, s. 5, makes provision for the 'unborn widow' trap, the PAA 2009 does not. The Law Commission Report of 1998 explains that the problem that section 'seeks to address does not arise in a world where the only perpetuity period is a fixed term of years': para. 8.29(4) (p. 107).

The presumptions as to fertility contained in the PAA 1964 are not in the PAA 2009; this is a recognition of the fact that with modern scientific techniques (including the freezing of sperm and embryos), a woman can give birth to a child well after the age of 55, and a person can be born many years after his or her parents' death.

The PAA 2009 contains one provision that does have retrospective effect. This is s. 12, which applies where an instrument made under the previous regime specifies a period of perpetuity by reference to lives in being and the trustees believe it is 'difficult or not reasonably practical' to ascertain whether the lives have ended (and therefore whether the perpetuity period has ended). The trustees may by deed declare this, and substitute for the specified perpetuity period a period of 100 years. It will be noted that this period is shorter than the 125 years that otherwise applies under the PAA 2009. The reason for the difference is that HM Revenue and Customs feared that enabling trustees of existing trusts to opt for a 125-year period might enable them to defer the payment of inheritance or capital gains tax, whereas a period of 100 years would, it was surmised, be overall neutral from a tax point of view.

The PAA 2009 affects only the rule of perpetuity called the rule against remoteness of vesting; it expressly makes no change to the other rule of perpetuity called the rule against perpetual trusts: PAA 2009, s. 18. Thus, as under the previous law, a trust of imperfect obligation (i.e. a non-charitable purpose trust) will be void from the start if it might endure longer than the perpetuity period of 21 years, or a life in being plus 21 years.

It is in respect of accumulations of income that the PAA 2009 is likely to have the biggest practical impact. The Law Commission concluded that the restrictions on excessive accumulations of income had no compelling policy objective, and that the rules were unnecessarily complex, and sometimes frustrated settlors' intentions and produced anomalous results: para. 10.11 (p. 127). Acting on this, PAA 2009, s. 13, abolishes restrictions on excessive accumulations of income in a private trust. In the case of a charitable trust, the new Act continues the policy of imposing restrictions on accumulation, since charities are expected to apply income to their purposes and not merely to accumulate it. The new Act restricts accumulation of income under a charitable trust to 21 years, except where the accumulation is provided by the court or by the Charity Commission: s. 14. As the Law Commission pointed out, however, charitable trusts may still be able to build up a reserve fund beyond this period if, with the approval of the Charity Commission, the trustees merely retain the income: paras 9.32 (p. 119), and 10.18 (p. 129).

A concern that was voiced during the passage of what became the PAA 2009 through Parliament was that the new legislation was being introduced before it is known how successful the PAA 1964 will be. Even the oldest trusts created under the PAA 1964 are mostly still within the period of 'wait and see'; it is hardly surprising therefore that there are currently no cases on the main provisions of that Act. Indeed, it is likely to be about the middle of this century before the PAA 1964 gives rise to much litigation. What is clear is that, as the main provisions of the PAA 2009 are not retrospective, the PAA 1964 will remain the governing statute for hundreds of thousands of trusts for many decades to come, and will remain important until well into the twenty-second century.

Question 2

(a) By her will, Tess, who died in 1963, devised Greenacre to the first child of Algy who should attain the age of 25. Algy (who was an orphaned bachelor at Tess's death) had three children: Belinda, Charles, and Damian, who were born in 1984, 1989, and 1990 respectively. Algy died on 31 December 1991. Belinda died in 2008 aged 24. Discuss who is or may become entitled to Greenacre.

(b) How, if at all, would your answer to (a) differ if Tess had died in 1978?

Commentary

This is a classic type of question on perpetuities. The alternative dates of Tess's death are important, and the student should spot this straight away. Thus, in part **(a)**, her death in 1963 means that the relevant rules are those of common law as modified by the **Law of Property Act 1925, s. 163**. In part **(b)**, by contrast, her death in 1978 means that, even if the disposition is void at common law, it may nevertheless be saved by the **Perpetuities and Accumulations Act 1964**.

The fact that the gift is contingent upon attaining 25 should make the candidate suspicious that the question might involve (as indeed it does) age-reducing. Age-reducing operates differently under the **1964 Act**, so this is a further difference between the answers to parts **(a)** and **(b)**. Under the **1964 Act**, 'wait and see' applies before age-reducing. How exactly it applies, however, remains an unsolved mystery, though legal sleuths have suggested various possibilities. The problem is designed to test your ability to spot the difficulty of applying age-reducing on these particular facts. A good answer will not flinch from tackling these issues.

Answer plan

(a) Death of T in 1963 (so subject to perpetuity rules pre-PAA 1964)

- Statement of rule against remoteness of vesting.
- Explain that void for perpetuity at common law.
- Apply age-reducing in **LPA 1925, s. 163**.

(b) Death of T in 1976 (so subject to PAA 1964)

- Since void at common law, subject to 'wait and see' (**PAA 1964, s. 3**):
  - statutory lives (**PAA 1964,. 3(5)**);
  - 'wait and see' ended with B's death in 2008.
- Apply 'age reducing' (**PAA 1964, s. 4(1)**) on B's death:
  - different ways in which **s. 4(1)** might be applied.

Suggested answer

(a) At common law, a gift is void for perpetuity unless, at the time the gift is made, it is certain that, if it is going to vest at all, it will do so within the perpetuity period. The basic perpetuity period at common law is 21 years after the death of a 'life in being', i.e. the life of a person alive or *en ventre sa mère* (i.e. conceived but not yet born) at the date the gift is made. A gift is vested for the purposes of perpetuity only when the person entitled to it is in existence and ascertained, when the size of his interest is ascertained, and when any conditions attached to the gift are satisfied. A gift by will is made at the death of the testator.

The devise by Tess is therefore void at common law because, as Algy is alive at Tess's death, there is a possibility, looking at matters from the point of Tess's death, that the first child of Algy to satisfy the condition of attaining 25 will do so more than 21 years after the death of Algy.

However, in the case of a gift (such as that made by Tess) which is made after 1925 but before 16 July 1964, special provision is made by the Law of Property Act 1925, s. 163. This states that where a gift is void for remoteness because the age specified for vesting exceeds 21 years, the age of 21 years is to be substituted. This means that, from the death of Tess, the age of 21 was substituted as the age for vesting. Thus Belinda attained a vested interest on her 21st birthday. Therefore, unless Belinda disposed of Greenacre *inter vivos*, it will, on her death, have passed under her will or intestacy.

(b) In the case of a gift made after 15 July 1964, a gift which is void for perpetuity at common law may be saved by the Perpetuities and Accumulations Act 1964. As Tess died in 1978, the Act applies to her devise. The Law of Property Act 1925, s. 163 does not apply, and is repealed in respect of post-1964 Act dispositions. Instead a gift (such as Tess's) which is void at common law is subject to the regime of 'wait and see' under s. 3, and to age-reducing under s. 4.

Section 3 is applied first. This provides that, where a disposition would apart from the provisions of that section and ss. 4 and 5, be void for remoteness of vesting, the disposition is treated, until such time as it becomes established that the vesting must occur (if at all) after the end of the perpetuity period, as if it were not subject to the rule against perpetuities. For the purposes of 'wait and see', the perpetuity period is determined by reference to the statutory lives specified in s. 3(5). Algy is a statutory life because he was an individual in being and ascertainable at the commencement of the perpetuity period (s. 3(4)(a)) who falls within s. 3(5)(c), i.e. he was a person, any of whose children, if subsequently born, would fall within para. (b)(ii). Thus, since Belinda is capable of attaining 25 within 21 years of the death of Algy, there would have been a period of waiting to see if Belinda did in fact attain 25. Since neither Charles nor Damian can attain 25 within 21 years of Algy's death, the death of Belinda at the age of 24 was the moment at which it became clear that 'wait and see' could not save the gift.

Section 4(1) is applied on the death of Belinda, because the devise of Greenacre would not have been void for perpetuity at common law had the specified age been 21 instead of 25 (s. 4(1)(b)). The reason is that, whenever Algy dies, his children must always attain 21 years by the end of a period of 21 years (plus a period *en ventre sa mère*) after his death. Section 4(1) provides, in effect, that the age should be reduced only so far as is necessary to save the gift from being void for remoteness. This is somewhat ambiguous: as discussed by Pritchard [1969] *CLJ* 284, there are several possible interpretations.

First, s. 4(1) may mean that the age of 23 is substituted at this point, since this is sufficient to save the gift for Charles. 'Wait and see' is thereupon applied again under s. 3. Thus if Charles attains 23, Greenacre vests in him. Were Charles to die under the age of 23, it becomes clear upon his death that 'wait and see' cannot save the disposition. Section 4(1) is therefore applied once more to reduce the age to 22, which is sufficient to prevent the gift from being void for remoteness in relation to Damian. If Damian attains 22, his interest vests. In the event of Damian's death under the age of 22, Greenacre falls into Tess's residuary estate, or (failing a residuary gift) passes to her next-of-kin. This construction, which leads to age-reduction by stages, might be supported by the words of s. 4(1)(a), which state only 'apart from this section', not 'apart from this section and section 3'.

Secondly, s. 4(1) may mean that the age substituted is such as is necessary to save it from remoteness in all eventualities: age-reduction is therefore once-for-all. On this basis, age-reduction is applied on one occasion only (upon the death of Belinda) to reduce the age to 22. If this is the case, then Charles acquires a vested interest upon his birthday in 2011. This construction derives support from the opening words of s. 4(1), which refer to 'a subsequent time' not to 'a subsequent time or times'.

A curious consequence of 'wait and see' in combination with either of these interpretations of age-reducing is that Belinda died without having attained a vested interest, even though she had attained an age higher than either Charles or Damian is required to reach under s. 4(1). A third possibility therefore arises, namely that when s. 4(1) reduces the age of vesting (whether to 23 or to 22), it does so retrospectively. This would mean that Belinda, who died after attaining either of those ages, is now to be treated as having died with a vested interest in Greenacre, which passes under her will or intestacy.

There are merits in each approach: but which construction is the correct one can be resolved only by the courts.

Question 3

By her will, a testatrix who died in 1986, devised Orangeacre 'to such of my grandchildren as shall be admitted as a solicitor, but if none of my grandchildren shall be so admitted then to my cousin, Ruth'.

The testatrix had two children, Alan and Beth, both of whom were living at her death. Alan (a widower) had two children then alive: Clare (then aged 4) and Darren (then aged 2). Beth was unmarried at her mother's death. In 2005, Beth gave birth to a child, Ellen.

Consider the validity and effect of the gift in the light of each of the following *alternative* sets of circumstances:

(a) In 2006, Clare was admitted as a solicitor. In 2008, Beth gave birth to a second child, Fiona.

(b) Clare died in a road accident in 2006 before being admitted as a solicitor. Alan, Beth, and Darren died in the same accident. Ellen is therefore the only surviving grandchild of the testatrix.

Commentary

This is a classic question on perpetuities under the **PAA 1964**, this time involving contingent class gifts, the class-closing rule, class-splitting, and expectant and dependent interests. Class-closing has nothing itself to do with perpetuities, but its effect (which ensures early vesting) can sometimes save a gift that would otherwise be void at common law.

Answer plan

(a)
- Contingent class gift.
- Void at common law (cannot be good in part).
- Post-**PAA 1964** gift, so apply 'wait and see' (ibid., **s. 3(1)**):
  - statutory lives (ibid., **s. 3(5)**);
  - C's interest vested in 2006:

–if class-closing rule then applies:

F is excluded from class;

C's interest vested subject to open;

–if class-closing rule ousted by contrary intention:

continue to 'wait and see';

F excluded if not qualified in time (ibid., **s. 4(4)**).

(b)
- 'Wait and see' if E attains vested interest within perpetuity period (ibid., **s. 3(1)**).
- If E does not, limitation to R void, since *might* vest too late.
- 'Wait and see' if R's interest does *in fact* vest in time:
  - statutory lives (ibid., **s. 3(5)**).
- Position if E dies not admitted during the perpetuity period.
- Position if E is still alive but not admitted at end of such period:
  - acceleration (ibid., **s. 6**) not save gift to R, since separate contingency;
  - so reverter to testatrix's estate.

Suggested answer

(a) The gift to the testatrix's grandchildren is a class gift, because the share to which each member becomes entitled depends upon the number of members who take. The gift is also contingent because it does not vest until the requirement of being admitted as a solicitor is fulfilled. At common law the gift to the testatrix's grandchildren is void for perpetuity. This is because, looking at matters from the moment of the testatrix's death, there is the possibility that more grandchildren will be born subsequently, who will not therefore rank as lives in being, and any of whom may be admitted more than 21 years after the death of any person now living. The interests of some members of the class might therefore vest outside the perpetuity period of a life or lives in being plus 21 years. The fact that the interests of some members of the class who are alive at the testatrix's death, namely Clare and Darren, must vest, if at all, within their own lives, does not save the gift; at common law a class gift cannot be good in part.

Although the testatrix's gift is void at common law, since it was made after 15 July 1964 it may be saved by the application of the principle of 'wait and see' under the Perpetuities and Accumulations Act 1964, s. 3(1). It is necessary to wait and see if any grandchildren of the testatrix are admitted as solicitors within 21 years of the dropping of the last statutory life under the Act (s. 3(4)). The statutory lives for this purpose are the lives of Clare and Darren (both within s. 3(5)(b)(i)), and Alan and Beth (both within s. 3(5)(c)).

Applying 'wait and see', Clare in 2006 satisfied the contingency attached to the gift. The size of her share was not then calculable, however. When she was admitted, Clare was one of three grandchildren; but the birth of a further grandchild (such as Fiona) who satisfies the contingency within the perpetuity period would diminish Clare's share, which would be highly inconvenient for her. This problem is avoided if the rule known as the rule in *Andrews v Partington* (1791) 3 Bro CC 401 applies. This states that, where there is a class gift, the class closes as soon as the first member of the class attains a vested interest and is entitled to demand his share. If the rule were to apply here, the class would close when Clare is admitted as a solicitor. This would mean that future born grandchildren (such as Fiona) would be excluded from the class, and therefore from the gift.

The application of the rule would make it possible to calculate the minimum size of Clare's share, i.e. one-third. Its maximum size would still remain uncertain until the other two members of the class (Darren and Ellen) are either admitted or die, or, in the case of Ellen, until it is clear that her interest, if it is to vest at all, must vest outside the perpetuity period (s. 3(1)). Thus if, for instance, Darren were to die without being admitted as a solicitor, Clare's vested share would increase from one-third to one-half. If Ellen were similarly to die during the perpetuity period without being admitted, Clare's vested interest would increase to the whole of Orangeacre. Clare's share, upon her being admitted as a solicitor in 2006, would thus be vested subject to open, i.e. vested as to one-third, with the possibility that it might become vested in respect of a further proportion at some time in the future.

Although convenient for those within the class, the class-closing rule operates harshly against those, like Fiona, whom it excludes. For this reason, the courts are, in modern times, more willing to oust the application of the rule (which is merely one of construction) by finding that the testator had a contrary intention (*Re Henderson's Trusts* [1969] 1 WLR 651). This is particularly the case in circumstances where (as in the problem) there is a likelihood of future members of the class being born. It is, therefore, necessary to construe the testatrix's gift in the context of the will as a whole to ascertain if there is a contrary intention.

If the rule is held not to apply, the class remains open, and it is necessary to continue to 'wait and see' until the end of the statutory perpetuity period if the interests of Fiona and any other future born grandchildren of the testatrix vest in time. If, at the end of such perpetuity period, Fiona has not been admitted as a solicitor, she is excluded from the class (s. 4(4)). Any other future-born grandchildren who have not been admitted by that date are similarly excluded. Under the 1964 Act, therefore, a class gift, can (in contrast to the rule at common law) be good in part.

(b) In these circumstances, it is necessary to 'wait and see' under s. 3(1) if Ellen, who is now the only person who can satisfy the contingency, attains a vested interest within the perpetuity period under the 1964 Act. Since the accident caused the dropping of all the statutory lives, this means a further period of 21 years of 'wait and see'. Ellen will be only 22 at the end of the perpetuity period and is therefore very unlikely to be admitted as a solicitor in time. 'Wait and see' applies however since it is not yet established that the vesting 'must' occur, if at all, until too remote a time: s. 3(1).

If Ellen is not admitted in time, the class gift becomes void for perpetuity. It is then necessary to consider the validity of the second limitation, which is also contingent, in favour of Ruth. This gift is also void for perpetuity at common law because, at the time of the testatrix's death, there is a possibility that the class of grandchildren could include future born grandchildren who may be admitted as solicitors more than 21 years after the death of Ruth. There is therefore the possibility that Ruth's interest may vest too late (***Proctor v Bishop of Bath and Wells*** **(1794) 2 Hy Bl 358**).

Since the gift to Ruth is void at common law, it is necessary first to 'wait and see' if Ruth's interest does in fact vest in time. For this purpose, the relevant statutory lives are Ruth herself (s. 3(5)(b)(ii)), her parents and grandparents (s. 3(5)(c)). If Ellen dies within this period without having been admitted, the gift to Ruth vests either in her or (if she is dead) in her estate. The latter outcome is possible because the contingency attached to the gift is not personal to Ruth. Her interest is therefore transmissible on her death, and will vest in her estate on the contingency being satisfied (Ryder, *Hawkins and Ryder on the Construction of Wills*, 3rd edn, 1965). In such circumstances, Orangeacre would pass under Ruth's will or intestacy.

What, however, is to happen if, at the end of the perpetuity period relevant to the limitation for Ruth, Ellen, whilst not having been admitted, is nevertheless still alive? Had the gift to Ruth been expressed merely to be 'subject to' the disposition to the grandchildren, **s. 6 of the 1964 Act** would have applied, and Ruth's interest would have been accelerated, i.e. it would have vested in her estate at the end of the perpetuity period because the prior gift is void for remoteness. As it is worded in the problem, however, the gift to Ruth cannot be saved by s. 6. That section says that the vesting of an interest shall not be prevented from being accelerated on the failure of a prior interest 'by reason only' that the failure arises because of remoteness. Since, however, the gift to Ruth is expressed to be contingent upon none of the testatrix's grandchildren being admitted, this contingency is not met where Ellen could be admitted outside the perpetuity period. Acceleration is not, therefore, possible. In these circumstances, the gift to Ruth also becomes void for remoteness, and Orangeacre reverts to the testatrix's estate.

Further reading

Maudsley, R. H., *The Modern Law of Perpetuities*, Butterworths, 1979.

Morris, J. H. C., and Wade, H. W. R., 'Perpetuities Reform at Last' (1964) 80 *LQR* 486.

Oakley, A. J., *Megarry's Manual of the Law of Real Property*, 8th edn, Sweet & Maxwell, 2002, chapter 6.

Pritchard, P., 'Two Petty Perpetuity Puzzles' [1969] *CLJ* 284.

Index

Introductory Note

References such as "178–9" indicate (not necessarily continuous) discussion of a topic across a range of pages. Wherever possible in the case of topics with many references, these have either been divided into sub-topics or only the most significant discussions of the topic are listed. Because the entire work is about 'land law', the use of this term (and certain others which occur constantly throughout the book) as an entry point has been minimized. Information will be found under the corresponding detailed topics.

A

D

G

H

I

J

R

S

U

V

W

Candidate No.

EXAM PAPER

If you're serious about exam success, it's time to *Concentrate!*

Each guide in the ***Concentrate*** series shows you what to expect in your law exam, what examiners are looking for, and how to achieve extra marks.

- Written by experts
- Developed with students
- Designed for success

For a full list of titles available and forthcoming please visit the website

If you're struggling with your course or worried about exams, don't panic, just *concentrate!*

Buy yours from your campus bookshop, online, or direct from OUP **www.oxfordtextbooks.co.uk/law/revision**

Visit **www.oxfordtextbooks.co.uk/orc/concentrate/** for a wealth of online resources including a podcast of exam and revision guidance, diagnostic tests, understanding your marks, interactive flashcard glossaries and cases, and multiple choice questions with instant feedback.